Pragmatism as a Principle and Method
of Right Thinking

Preston A. Tuttle Collection, Institute for Studies in Pragmaticism, Texas Tech University.

Pragmatism as a Principle and Method of Right Thinking

by Charles Sanders Peirce

The 1903 Harvard *Lectures on Pragmatism*

Edited and Introduced,
with a Commentary,
by Patricia Ann Turrisi

State University of New York Press

B
945
P43
P73
1997
c.2

Published by
State University of New York Press, Albany

© 1997 State University of New York

Printed in the United States of America

For information, address State University of New York Press, State University Plaza, Albany, N.Y., 12246

Production by Diane Ganeles
Marketing by Theresa Abad Swierzowski

Library of Congress Cataloging-in-Publication Data

Peirce, Charles S. (Charles Sanders), 1839–1914.
    Pragmatism as a principle and method of right thinking : the 1903 Harvard lectures on pragmatism / Charles Sanders Peirce.
        p.   cm.
    Includes index.
    ISBN 0-7914-3265-3 (alk. paper). — ISBN 0-7914-3266-1 (pbk. : alk. paper)
    1. Pragmatism.   I. Title.
    B945.P43P73   1996
    144'.3—dc20   96-14144
                                                                CIP

10 9 8 7 6 5 4 3 2 1

CONTENTS

Acknowledgments   vii

Editorial Procedures   ix

Abbreviations   xi

Introduction   1
Patricia Ann Turrisi

Commentary   21
Patricia Ann Turrisi

Lecture One   37

Lecture Two   49

Lecture Three   59

Lecture Four   65

Lecture Five   77

Lecture Six   89

Lecture Seven   99

Pragmatism as a Principle and Method of Right Thinking   107
Charles Sanders Peirce

Lecture One   109

Lecture Two   123

Lecture Three   167

Lecture Four   189

Lecture Five   205

Lecture Six   221

Lecture Seven   241

Notes   257

Index   287

ACKNOWLEDGMENTS

My deepest gratitude goes toward Dennis Fuller for his generosity of personal spirit as well as the time and attention he gave to this project and sacrificed from his own. I would also like to thank Kenneth Laine Ketner for not only a great deal of practical help, but for creating an environment at The Institute for Studies in Pragmaticism at Texas Tech University which makes Charles Sanders Peirce seem to walk among us as if he were still thinking and writing. Deborah Heathcock was a research assistant *par excellence* insofar as she brought a considerable refinement to the work by flushing out historical details of the philosophical and scientific worlds of the nineteenth century. I am grateful to the University of North Carolina at Wilmington Charles L. Cahill Awards for Faculty Research and Development Committee for granting me several awards which enabled me to visit archives at Harvard University and Texas Tech University. Thanks also to the University of North Carolina at Wilmington for supporting me with a 1993 Summer Incentives Award, which gave me extra courage at the critical opening stages of putting words to paper. I would like to dedicate this volume to my daughters, Rosa and Sophia Fuller, whose bright spirits sustained me with love and affection throughout.

EDITORIAL
PROCEDURES

This edition of *Pragmatism* is based upon manuscripts from the Peirce Papers Collection in the Houghton Library, according to the following plan: MS 301 (lecture one); MS 302–MS 306 (lecture two); MS 307 (notes on lecture three); MS 308 (lecture three); MS 309 (lecture four); MS 310 and MS 311 (notes on lecture five); MS 312 (lecture five); MS 314 and MS 316 (lecture six), and MS 315 (lecture seven).

The purpose of this volume was to provide a study edition. Accordingly, every effort has been made to produce a readable text. Since many lectures have multiple drafts, drafts most likely to have been delivered appear in the main text. Philosophically significant deletions and portions of rejected drafts appear in notes at the end of the book. Selected alternate formulations of passages or drafts likewise appear at the end of the book, organized lecture by lecture. Editorial apparatus has been kept simple, following the conventions below:

"[ ]" indicates an editorial insertion.

"< >" indicates a deletion.

"<< >>" indicates a deletion within a deletion.

Ampersands have been spelled out as "and." Peirce's compositional style and spelling have been preserved; misspellings have been invisibly corrected. Conservative corrections to punctuation have been applied in order to maintain Peirce's cadence for the modern reader.

ABBREVIATIONS

The following abbreviations are used to refer to standard editions of Peirce's works or to archival collections of writings and correspondence by or about Peirce.

CP   *Collected Papers of Charles Sanders Peirce*, edited by Charles Hartshorne, Paul Weiss (volumes 1–6) and Arthur Burks (volumes 7–8) (Cambridge, The Belknap Press of Harvard University Press, 1931–1958), followed by volume and paragraph number.

HUA   Harvard University Archives

HLWJ   Correspondence from the William James Collection *The Correspondence of the James Library*, 1959, in the Houghton Library of Harvard University.

L   Letters written by Charles Sanders Peirce in the Peirce Papers Collection in the Houghton Library of Harvard University, followed by a number catalogued in Richard R. Robin, *Annotated Catalogue of the Papers of Charles S. Peirce* (Amherst: University of Massachusetts Press, 1967) or in Richard R. Robin, "The Peirce Papers: A Supplementary Catalogue," *Transactions of the Charles S. Peirce Society*, 7 (1971):37–57.

MS   Manuscripts from the Peirce Papers Collection of the Houghton Library of Harvard University, followed by a number catalogued in Richard R. Robin, *Annotated Catalogue of the Papers of Charles S. Peirce* (Amherst: University of Massachusetts Press, 1967) or in Richard R. Robin, "The Peirce Papers: A Supplementary Catalogue," *Transactions of the Charles S. Peirce Society*, 7 (1971):37–57.

INTRODUCTION

Patricia Ann Turrisi

The story of how and why Charles Peirce came to present a series of lectures on his idea of pragmatism at Harvard University in 1903 has its start in certain unhappy events the year before. In 1902 he had hoped he would obtain the funds he needed to spend his time over the next several years at work on the preparation and publication of a number of "memoirs" that collectively would have set out his conception of "*a unitary system of logic in all its parts*" (L 75).

On 12 April 1902, Peirce wrote a letter to the president of the newly formed Carnegie Institution of Washington in answer to a "circular letter" from its executive committee that invited "any contribution . . . toward a conception of the work of the Institution" (L 75). He proposed that the institution should study "the science of the Laws of Development of Science." And this science, he continued, "must be an offshoot of logic and must rest on a sound general theory of logic." He then offered his own services in pursuit of this study and pronounced his readiness "to accept some assistance from the Carnegie Institution to do so." Indeed, he concluded, "I ask for that assistance." Three months later he formally submitted a lengthy "application for aid from the Carnegie Institution" in support of his "scientific work" on the "theory of the methods of science"—that is, on "the science of logic." He asked that the institution provide him with five hundred books of his choice and funds in an amount sufficient to support him and his wife over a period of five or six years.

Before Peirce sent out either his answer to the "circular letter" or his July application, he had asked a number of his friends and associates to send recommendations to the Carnegie Institution that it aid him in his work on logic. William James, then a professor of philosophy at Harvard University, sent a letter to the "chairman" of the institution on March 21. In it, he represented Peirce to be "a man of genius in the purest sense of the word," indeed a man "in the very front rank of American thinkers," whose "Logic when published will unquestionably (in spite of certain prob-

1

able obvious oddities) be recognized all over the world as an epoch-making work" (L 75). James claimed, ambiguously, that he, "for example," owed more to Peirce's ideas "than to those of anyone but [Josiah] Royce." It should be noted that James regularly supposed that the difference between his ideas and Peirce's had to be a result of a number of eccentricities in Peirce's turn of mind. He would then conclude that one could rightly and safely ignore these few aberrant ideas. These differences would hold a definite place in Peirce's mind in the period that followed. James recalled in his letter that "Peirce has proved unable (some malignant witch having cast a spell upon him in his cradle, no doubt) to make more than the barest living, and now, as I understand it, with this Magnus Opus on his mind, has no regularly remunerative support." Therefore, he concluded, the Carnegie Institution, "ignoring all personal questions, and regarding only the interests of originality in Science," should "consider Mr. Peirce's case as one for favorable treatment." He assured the institution that he could think of no "more appropriate case for help."

Josiah Royce, then also a professor of philosophy at Harvard, wrote a letter to the president of the Carnegie Institution on Peirce's behalf, a few days after James had written his. Royce's letter exhibits a familiarity with, and an understanding of, the project that Peirce proposed to carry out, with the aid of Carnegie funds, that is absent from the letter James had sent. Peirce's "methods of work," Royce explained, which unite the "exactness of a mathematician with the speculative ingenuity of a really great philosopher," hold the "promise [of] very great results" in the areas of the "study of the methods of science and the comparative study of the types of concepts which have been developed in the various sciences" (L 75).[1] And, he continued, what Peirce "has already done" in his work on "the Algebra of Logic, on the Logic of Relatives, and on the theory of the Categories" has resulted in "quite a revolution in the study of exact Logic." He concluded:

> From the point of view of the interests of Logic, of Philosophy in general, and of all students of general science, I am therefore sure that Mr. Peirce's researches in the mentioned fields are thoroughly worthy of whatever endowment is necessary to secure the effective revision, the final preparation, and the publication, of his still incomplete work in Logic, whether it be printed as one whole, or in separate memoirs. . . . It will be a great loss to the world if those of his researches which have not yet been put into final shape, do not receive the finishing touches, and are not published.

Royce's reference to the publication of Peirce's work in the form of a series of "memoirs" anticipated one of Peirce's own suggestions to the Carnegie Institution in his July 15 application.

Royce in his letter, like James in his, called the attention of the Carnegie Institution to Peirce's extreme "need of assistance." Peirce, he told them, "is now obliged to earn a living by various literary and other tasks that do not contribute to science." The result, he believed, is that Peirce "lives more or less from hand to mouth, and probably has no savings." And, since Peirce is "past sixty years of age," it is not to be expected that "his powers [can] indefinitely continue to respond to the calls made upon him." Royce ended his letter with the hope that Peirce would receive the aid he needed so that "his later results will not be lost to the world."

The executive committee of the Carnegie Institution decided on 26 November 1902 to "defer action" on Peirce's case "for the present." Peirce rightly understood this postponement to be effectively a denial of his application. In a letter he wrote William James on December 1, he stated that, in his interpretation, the executive committee's "wording" amounted to "a refusal of all assistance" (HLWJ). He admitted to James the violence of his reaction: "I had not thought just that possible; I see now that I had not, by the shock it gives me." He reported nonetheless that he felt considerable "relief from the painful tension" of his wait on the Carnegie committee's decision. But, he bitterly told James, he also felt himself to be "condemned" to do his work "in a world where nobody can understand" the force of his need to do the very work that "God" had evidently placed him in this life to do.

A few years before, Peirce had remarked on the presence, in "history and life," of "three classes of men" (CP 1.43). To members of the first class, whose interest is the "qualities of feelings," nature is aesthetically presented in the form of a "picture." Such men, Peirce noted, "create art." To members of the second class, whose interest is the exercise of "power," nature is practically presented in the shape of a business "opportunity." Such men create wealth. And, to members of the third class, whose interest is "nothing . . . but reason," nature is rationally presented in the form of a "cosmos, so admirable, that to penetrate to its ways seems to them the only thing that makes life worth living." Such men create science. Peirce clearly perceived that he fit only in this last class, the class of the "natural scientific men," those with a "passion to learn," and "the only men that have any real success in scientific research." What he faced with his Carnegie application then turned out to be the difficulty very often faced when a member of one class tries to persuade members of another class that what, in his experience, "makes life worth living," is worthy of the support of these others.

Despite what Peirce believed to be the defeat of his Carnegie application, he assured James, in his December 1 letter, that he would "keep right on doing the work as well as adverse circumstances will permit." These circumstances included "a dwindling wood-pile," a "furnace out of order," and a "meagre food" supply. To alleviate these conditions and to permit the work to be done, Peirce informed James that he would, in the "meantime," readily "accept any employment whatever in which [he] could give satisfaction." One such possible employment, he suggested, "would be that of a professor of logic at Columbia [University] or elsewhere." He then set out a number of conditions that any such future employment would have to meet:

> I should wish to teach what I know and can prove to be true and not what I know and can prove is not true. I cannot teach that sound reasoning depends on what the logic books are mostly full of, nor that that matter is true, nor that sound reasoning has anything to gain by being worked as an algebraical calculus. Exactitude is necessary; but it is not the exactitude of a machine. I should teach a large class about ten or a dozen practical maxims and how to use them.

But, he then declared, he would not teach most students any but a "vague idea" of the science of logic. "The methodeutic whose foundation is the scientific theory of logic is useful to everybody," he reminded James, "but there are only a few for whom it is well to examine that foundation." Only one student in a thousand, it seems, would not suffer a worse "mental health" as a result of such "fundamental inquiries."

Once he had laid out these restrictions on his possible employment, he then undiplomatically advised James, his possible intermediary in his contact with possible employers, that what James termed "pragmatism" happened to be in need of "some modification." Peirce believed that he could "satisfy" James that pragmatism "can receive no sound support from psychology," such as James had laboriously endeavored to provide, and that both "the logical basis and proof" of pragmatism and "its relation to the categories" (Firstness: quality; Secondness: reaction; Thirdness: representation) "have first to be made clear before it can be accurately applied except in very simple ways" (HLWJ). He then concluded with the statement that he could address these matters no further in this letter. But his series of lectures on pragmatism, delivered at Harvard the next year (1903), turned out to be an elaboration on these same corrections of the version of pragmatism that James had so famously set forth.

On November 29, three days after the executive committee of the Carnegie Institution had determined it would put off its ultimate verdict in the matter of Peirce's application, and one day after the secretary of the institution had sent Peirce a notice of the delay, Marcus Baker, its assistant secretary, also sent Peirce a letter. He represented the action of the committee more literally, and thereupon more positively, than Peirce did in his letter to James. The executive committee, he reported, had "met and awarded certain grants" and had "many more" applications, like Peirce's, "still pending" (L 75). He insisted that he could "only guess" what the committee would finally decide in the case of Peirce's "proposition about the Logic." He then said that he could "not guess what the decision will be" but that he hoped that his own communication with the secretary, evidently on the side of Peirce's "proposition," would "hasten a decision." It seems likely that this note helped persuade Peirce that he should have his friends contact the Carnegie Institution in one last attempt to win its aid in support of his work. Letters to the institution were then sent on Peirce's behalf by many prominent individuals: John Dewey, then director of the School of Education at the University of Chicago; G. Stanley Hall, professor of psychology and president of Clark University; George S. Fullerton, professor of philosophy at the University of Pennsylvania; James E. Creighton, professor of logic and metaphysics at Cornell University; Dickinson S. Miller, instructor of philosophy at Harvard University; Wilmon Henry Sheldon, professor of philosophy at Columbia University; John Trowbridge, professor of physics at Harvard; Edward C. Pickering, director of the Harvard Observatory; Percival Lowell, director of the Lowell Observatory in Flagstaff, Arizona; William E. Story, professor of mathematics at Clark; Henry Cabot Lodge, United States senator; Oliver Wendell Holmes, Jr., associate justice of the Supreme Court of the United States; Theodore Roosevelt, president of the United States; Peirce's brothers: James Mill Peirce, a Harvard professor of mathematics, and Herbert Henry Davis Peirce, assistant secretary in the State Department of the United States; and several others.

The executive committee of the Carnegie Institution finally put an end to the matter when it approved a resolution on 12 May 1903. It stated that the institution would not fund any work on the "preparation" of any "treatise on logic" but would instead limit its aid to those at "work in the fields of the natural sciences" (L 75). The committee evidently would not believe, or could not understand, Peirce's claim that "logic is the science which . . . is the very key stone in the arch of scientific truth" (L 75).

The end of any chance of aid from the Carnegie Institution left Peirce in a destitute condition. He had written William James, in the midst of the process of application, on 12 June 1902, what his reaction would have to be if he finally received no aid:

> If the Carnegie Institution will do nothing, my duty will be to continue to endeavor to do the work I seem to have been put into the world to do; and when the moment arrives at which there

seems to be no rational hope of making my life useful, my duty, as
I see it, will be to treat my life just as I would an aching tooth that
there was no hope of making useful. I will have it out. I am not
going to act harshly; but it looks as if it were coming to that, and
when it does, I wish my friends to know that what I do I do from
long deliberated conviction. (HLWJ)

Such sentiments echoed desperate declamations that James had uttered in
his own life and had to have had a definite effect. Several months before
the Carnegie committee finally announced its resolution not to fund any
work on logic, Peirce's included, James initiated the steps that would very
soon result in Peirce's 1903 Harvard lectures on pragmatism.

On 27 February 1903, Peirce's brother, James Mill Peirce, then a professor of mathematics at Harvard, sent a note to William James, from his
home on Kirkland Place in Cambridge:

I have a line from Charles begging to have a Lowell course arranged for him for next winter. . . . I have not mentioned Law-
rence Lowell's offer of a course to [Charles] yet. The reason I have
not is that I wished not to cause a conflict with the Carnegie
proposition. . . . I did, however, in writing to [Charles] say that Mr.
Lowell would probably offer him a course. Lowell's offer was of six
or eight lectures. He would not wish to offer more than eight, I
think. Nor do I think it would do to ask for an advance of money,
greatly as Charles needs it. That must be arranged in some other
way, and such a sum as $600 (which [Charles] speaks of to me)
would be quite out of the question from any source, I fear. It is
not surprising that [Charles] is out of patience with the eternal
postponement of action by the Carnegie Committee. I fear that
not much can be hoped for in that quarter. The evil prevails, as
usually happens. The Lowell Lectures remain. If they were only to
come on this spring, we might take breath. Do you think a collection of Charles's book notices [that is, his book reviews] could
have any sale or could find a publisher? (L 681)[2]

The next day, February 28, William James (evidently in consideration of
the idea in James Mill Peirce's note that a course of lectures in the spring
that would provide Charles Peirce with $600 would permit them a respite
from his importunities) proposed, in a letter to the president of Harvard
University, Charles William Eliot, that the Harvard Corporation should engage Peirce to come to the university and present "half a dozen lectures"
on philosophy and logic (HUA).[3] James had, he reminded Eliot, put forth

the same idea "some 5 years ago" when he had asked the corporation if it would "appoint" Peirce to deliver "a short course of lectures on Logic," on the condition that James could privately raise the needed money. The corporation had then declined, but Peirce's "lectures were given at Mrs. Bull's in Brattle Street, and were a great success, so far as arousing strong interest in advanced men went."[4] James then told Eliot what Peirce needed and what his lectures would offer:

> Peirce wants to devote the rest of his life to the writing of a logic which will undeniably (although in some points excentric [sic]) be a great book. Meanwhile, he has apparently *no* means. I am willing to help financially again, and venture (since the Corporation has partly changed its composition) to renew my old question. My class in [philosophy] 3 has this year been dosed with some of Peirce's ideas at second hand, and is (I know) full of curiosity to hear his voice. . . . He is one of our 3 or 4 first American philosophers, and it seems to me that his genius is deserving of some official recognition. Half a dozen lectures, at 100 dollars a piece, would seem to me about right.[5]

James concluded his letter with the statement that the Harvard Corporation should "change its earlier mind" and approve an engagement with Peirce to deliver this series of lectures. The corporation, in under two weeks, did approve the plan that James had proposed: Peirce would present six lectures under the auspices of the university; he would receive six hundred dollars in payment; and James would have to raise the money from private sources.[6]

On 13 March 1903, James informed Peirce in a letter that the Harvard Corporation had voted its sanction of Peirce's presentation of a lecture series. President Eliot had told James "to communicate the appointment" (HLWJ). James related the conditions: six lectures (Peirce could lecture on any topic he chose and could name the lectures with any titles he liked) and "a remuneration of 600 dollars." He assured Peirce that the fifty or so students he had had in his philosophy 3 course were "well primed with 'pragmatism' and 'tychism' and would be glad to hear of them from [Peirce] direct."[7] But if Peirce chose to lecture on "synechism," he would, James believed, "have virgin soil" with these students. James advised Peirce that he could, if he preferred, merely "repeat" his "former lectures, or certain ones of them," or he could, if he chose, "stick to logic proper." But James reminded Peirce that he, because he had such a "bad head for logic and mathematics," would definitely be "most interested" in what he believed to be Peirce's "more concrete evolutionary and metaphysical ideas." When James talked to Peirce, he admitted his own philosophical deficiencies; when he talked to others, he complained of Peirce's philosophical peculiarities. He seems not to have noticed the irony of his statement in this same letter that "whatever [Peirce] may say, on whatever subject, [he] will be sure to catch and excite the best sort of man, and to pass over the heads of others."

On March 16, Peirce received the letter that James had sent him with the word on his appointment by the university to deliver a series of lectures. He "instantly" drafted and mailed off his own letter in reply (HLWJ). He thanked James and admitted that "nothing could be so gratifying" under the circumstances. He then immediately set to work and explained what the character of the lectures would have to be. At the outset, he determined that he could not properly compact "a course on Logic" into only six lectures. Students in such a course would have to have "ample illustrations" that would "exhibit the application of the logic" in "the history of the sciences" and in each separate science. Logic, Peirce submitted, "is the matter of a liberal education." He seems likely to have intended this somewhat ironic statement, that his six lectures would not constitute an entire "course on logic," to be one that would meet the fear that James had expressed that his own "bad head for logic" would not let him duly appreciate a lecture series on the topic. What Peirce decided, then, is that he should limit the range of his lectures to a consideration of the "single subject of pragmatism." But this "pragmatism," he went on to tell James, is, in the manner that he understood it, "one of the propositions of logic," and not, in the manner of the interpretation that James had put on it, a matter of psychology. Peirce could already tell James, in his March 16 reply, what topics he would discuss in the six lectures: the "foundation, definition and limitation" of pragmatism, as well as its "application to philosophy, to the sciences, and to the conduct of life."[8]

The fact that Peirce could immediately provide James with a concise and accurate statement of the theme of the lectures he would present would seem to be evidence of his claim, in his March 16 letter, that he had "little to do to produce the lectures" other than "to abridge greatly" a manuscript that he "already" had—that is, to "compress it to about one fourth of its bulk." But no such manuscript has been found in Peirce's papers, or is likely to have been available to be compressed by him at the time. The manuscripts of his drafts of the lectures seem rather to have been the result of an extraordinary outburst of philosophical creativity that he sustained over the period of the lecture series. While he left it to James to "fix the dates" of the lectures, he told him that he would "prefer to have about an uninterrupted week of hard work for each lecture." He also indicated that he would want to have "say ten days" before he would have to present the first lecture. But he had not remembered, when he wrote this, that he had to be in Washington, D. C., from April 21 to April 24 to attend a meeting of the National Academy of Sciences, of which he was a member. He sent James a letter the next day, March 17, with this information, and stated his readiness to present the lectures two days a week, if it were considered "very desirable" (HLWJ). But "it would be better," he reminded James, if he had a week to work on each one. He specifically proposed that he present the first lecture on the very next Monday, March 23, and one each Monday after then, until April 27.

James answered Peirce's letters of March 16 and 17 with a letter he sent out on Thursday, March 19. He informed Peirce that, in conformance with the "suggestions" in Peirce's two letters, he had proceeded to have the *Harvard University Calendar* publish, the next day, a "general description of the course" that he had "copied" from Peirce's March 16 letter, and an announcement that Peirce would offer the first lecture in the series on Monday, March 23, at 8:00 P.M. in Room 11 of Sever Hall (HUA).[9] James omitted to tell Peirce, in his letter, the specific title he had conferred on the course of lectures: *Pragmatism as a Principle and Method of Right Thinking*. He said merely that he "rejoice[d]" that the topic Peirce had selected "is 'pragmatism'." Peirce had told James, in his March 16 letter, that he would "leave it" to him "to announce the subject of the lectures." The title that James formulated and announced is evidently his translation, into his own terms, of Peirce's statement that the "single subject" of his lectures would be "pragmatism" understood as "one of the propositions of logic." A proposition of logic is turned into a principle and method of right thinking. James typically obscured, in this manner, the difference between his and Peirce's interpretations of pragmatism. Peirce tried to set out this difference in precise terms; James tried to cover it over. Right thinking might include logic but it might also include James's explanation of thinking in terms of the processes of psychology and, ultimately, physiology. The title that Peirce put on these lectures, in his manuscripts, is simply *Lectures on Pragmatism*.

On March 20, Peirce, still in his home in Milford, Pennsylvania, received a telegram from James. It informed him that the day of the lectures had been switched from Mondays to Thursdays. The first lecture then would have to be delivered on March 26. Peirce arrived in Boston on a train at 6:00 P.M. on Wednesday, March 25, and went to James's house on Irving Street in Cambridge. He moved into nearby Felton Hall, when his wife, Juliette, arrived in town on Sunday, March 29. James told Peirce in his March 19 letter that he would like to introduce him to the audiences at the lectures and provide him with any other assistance he could, but would likely miss the second lecture because he suffered from a "bad state of nervous fatigue and may have to run away." He did invite a number of his students and others to a reception at his house after the first lecture to meet with Peirce.

The *Harvard Crimson* announced, in an article on Peirce's lecture series in its March 26 edition, that Peirce would, in his first lecture, offer a "definition" of pragmatism and "an explanation of its terms" (HUA). The *Crimson* piece offered its own definition of pragmatism: a "system of philosophy, first so named by Mr. Peirce, which views philosophical questions primarily from the standpoint of their practical bearing upon life." James is likely to have authored the *Crimson's* definition; if he did, it provides further evidence of his inclination to obscure the difference between his and Peirce's ideas. The definition is not one that would fit Peirce's idea that pragmatism is "one of the propositions of logic," or his interest in the application of pragmatism in philosophy and the natural sciences, as well as in the "conduct of life."

On March 31, five days after Peirce's first lecture, on pragmatism and the normative sciences, James rancorously avouched a number of derisive comments on the lecture and on Peirce's character in a letter he sent to Dickinson S. Miller, then a Harvard instructor in philosophy and psychology (and someone who had sent a letter in support of Peirce's application to the Carnegie Institution). James told Miller that he considered Peirce's lecture to have turned out to be a "great disappointment" (HLWJ). Peirce had not declared what James believed he should have declared—that is, what he would have declared—and what he might have vainly believed he could dispose Peirce to declare with his more psychologistic formulation of the title of the lecture course. Peirce, James said it seemed to him, had "rather woefully 'gone off' in the past 5 years." He gratuitously and, it seems, spitefully voiced his "doubt" that Peirce had "any very distinct idea of where" his interpretation of pragmatism happened to be "coming out." Peirce's pragmatism had "gone off" and "come out" in these Harvard lectures with an undismissible representation of the difference between his interpretation of the doctrine and James's.

But James would not tell Miller what specifically he found blameworthy in the *content* of Peirce's lecture. He instead berated the *form* of the discussion after the lecture because, he claimed, it "degenerated into an interminable dialog" between Peirce and a member of the audience on the "nature of mathematical reasoning," with "each replying to the last sentences of the other and so drifting along without a plan." James's estimate of this "dialog" is not really reliable inasmuch as it came from his admittedly "bad head" in the area of "logic and mathematics." He confessed his "fear" to Miller that the audience at Peirce's lectures would "fall off a good deal," but emphatically claimed that *he*, nevertheless, had done his "duty." James then indulged in an acrimonious assault on Peirce's character and work in a succession of insults and lies that surely must have left Miller dumbfounded:

> Damn your half-successes, your imperfect geniuses. I'm tired of making allowances for them and propping them up. As Alice [Howe Gibbens James, William James's wife] says, Peirce has never *constrained* himself in his life. Selfish, conceited, affected, a monster of desultory intellect, he has become now a seedy, almost sordid, old man, without even any intellectual residuum from his work that can be called a finished construction, only "suggestions," and begging old age.

The deeply systematic character of Peirce's 1903 Harvard lectures, like many of his other works, utterly refuted the lie that he had produced only a number of "desultory" if ingenious "suggestions" in the areas of logic and philosophy but had erected no "finished construction." The currency of this lie, then and today, is due in no small measure to James's incognizant and antipathetic reception of Peirce's ideas. James could see a number of Peirce's suggestive "trees" but he had no mind to see his systematic "forest." The truculence of his assault on Peirce's personality and philosophy in his letter to Miller is a measure of the frustration he must have felt when he heard Peirce declare an interpretation of pragmatism that he could barely understand, if only because it systematically contradicted his own. Peirce's unconstrained penchant to declare publicly what he had determined to be philosophically true, no matter whose feathers it might ruffle and no matter what interests it might contravene, had to have seemed, in James's mind, after he had put his own reputation on the line in Peirce's interest, to be a selfish conceit and affectation.

A number of James's Harvard associates, students and friends, in Peirce's audience as well as James, would likely have perceived that Peirce, the "founder of pragmatism" in James's own phrase, had presented a formulation of pragmatism that utterly opposed the interpretation that James had widely professed. But James could not rebut the philosophic content of Peirce's lecture, merely its form—that is, the fact that Peirce had publicly declared the difference between his and James's ideas, and in a form that James, and others with his turn of mind, would find abstruse. James cautioned Miller at the close of his letter not to betray what he had told him: "Only don't let on to any one all that I have said about Peirce!"

Peirce delivered the second lecture in the series on April 2. The *Harvard University Calendar* announced that the title of the lecture would be "Phenomenology; or, The Doctrine of Categories." The *Harvard Crimson*

Patricia Ann Turrisi

promised that, "in connection with the subject, . . . Mr. Peirce will discuss the elementary constituents of thought." James was not in attendance at the lecture; he had traveled to Asheville, North Carolina, where he went to recuperate from his "nervous fatigue" and a case of tonsillitis.

James mentioned Peirce's lectures in a letter he sent from Asheville on April 8 to F. C. S. Schiller, a British pragmatist and a professor of philosophy at Oxford University:

> Charles Peirce is now giving six public lectures on "pragmatism" at Harvard, which I managed to get up for his benefit, pecuniary and professional. He is a hopeless crank and failure in many ways, but a really extraordinary intellect.[10]

He assured Schiller that he knew of no other "mind," besides Peirce's, with "so many different kinds of spotty intensity or vigor."

The Harvard *Calendar* issued the information that Peirce, in his third lecture on April 9, would talk on "The Application of the Category of Pragmatism." A statement in smaller letters beneath the announcement exhibited Peirce's impatience with participants in the course who had not come to the second lecture: "Those who were unable to attend the second lecture had better procure the MS. of that lecture from Mr. Peirce, 34 Felton Hall, before attending the third lecture." The *Crimson* article on the third lecture mentioned the same title but also provided an explanation:

> The lecture will consist almost wholly of a defense of all three categories discussed in the last lecture. These categories, or largest classes into which objects of knowledge can be systematically arranged, are sensation, perception and thought. One or more of these categories are defended by the different schools of metaphysics and Mr. Peirce defends all three.

The *Crimson* concluded with a statement similar to the one in the *Calendar*: "As this third lecture depends greatly upon the second lecture, all who missed the second lecture would do well to get the manuscript of it at 34 Felton Hall before attending the lecture tonight." Peirce clearly became the source of the announcements of his lectures in these Harvard publications once he arrived in Cambridge.

Both the *Calendar* and the *Crimson* reported that the title of Peirce's fourth lecture on April 16 would be "The Seven Systems of Metaphysics." Hugo Münsterberg, the chair of the Harvard philosophy department and a professor of psychology, invited Peirce to his house on Ware Street the next day to participate in "a most informal social evening" at the monthly assembly of the "members of our Philosophical Seminary." He asked Peirce, "Will you not give us the pleasure and do us the honor to join our little company?" He assured Peirce that he should "come most informally—no evening dress" and that "we shall be delighted to have you with us." Peirce is likely to have attended. The university went into a recess in the week from April 19 to April 26. Peirce went to Washington, D. C., in the middle of the week to be at a meeting of the National Academy of Sciences.

Neither the *Calendar* nor the *Crimson* could announce a title of Peirce's fifth lecture on April 30; he had not provided them with one. But the *Crimson* did report that Peirce would enter in the lecture into an examination of the normative sciences "which are generally considered to be logic, ethics, and aesthetics." And, it continued, "from an explanation of the relation of these three, Mr. Peirce will proceed to a discussion of 'truth' and that which we imply by the 'meaning' of anything" (HUA).

On the next Wednesday, May 6, the day before Peirce would offer his sixth and last lecture in the series, James sent him a letter from his summer house on Chocorua Lake in New Hampshire where he had, in his words, "succeeded in flying away" from Cambridge the day before. He told Peirce that he had not come to see him in the last days before he left Cambridge because he had had to do a considerable amount of work on Ph.D. examinations and he did not expect to return "until the evening of the 14th when more Ph.D. business begins" (HLWJ). James stated that he was "sorry" he would not hear Peirce's last lecture and that he hoped Peirce felt "satisfied with the result" of the series. He consoled Peirce with the observation that "*big* audiences can never be expected in such subjects," but he believed that Peirce "'drew' *well*, all things considered." Peirce should, it seemed to James, find his satisfaction not in the quality of his lectures but in the quantity of his audience.

Peirce delivered his sixth lecture on May 7. The *Calendar* in its May 1 edition had no title available yet to put in its announcement, but the *Crimson* article on the day of the lecture could report that Peirce would talk on "The Nature of Meaning." Sometime in the period before this lecture, Peirce decided that he should offer a seventh lecture in the series. The *Calendar* printed an announcement in its May 8 edition that Peirce would deliver a seventh and "Concluding Lecture" on May 14. Peirce had to have submitted this information to the editor of the *Calendar* no later than 10 A.M. the day before. The *Crimson* reported that Peirce would offer another lecture in the series on pragmatism in its May 9 issue. On May 13 the *Harvard Bulletin* affirmed that Peirce had "decided to give a supplementary lecture to his recent series" (HUA). It explained that "Mr. Peirce will give the summary of his previous lectures and will put in clearer light the relation of the views maintained to the general doctrine of pragmatism." The *Bulletin* also announced in the same article that Peirce would offer yet another lecture, but this time not under the auspices of the department of philosophy:

> By invitation of the Division of Mathematics Mr. Peirce will speak in Sever 8 next Friday at 8 o'clock on "Multitude and Continuity." The lecture will deal with "Number" and "Continuous Quantity," and reference will be made to Cantor and other writers on these subjects. This lecture is specially intended for students in philosophy and mathematics, but will be open to the public.

The *Crimson* advertised the lecture on mathematics in its May 15 issue, but stated that it would be offered under the auspices of the philosophy department:

> Mr. Charles Peirce [Harvard class of] '59 will give a lecture under the auspices of the Department of Philosophy on "Conceptions of Mathematical Multitude and Continuity" this evening at 8 o'clock in Sever 8. The lecture will be open to the public but will be especially interesting to students of philosophy for whom it is primarily intended.

Both the divisions of philosophy and mathematics may have sponsored the May 15 lecture, or the *Crimson* article may have been a correction of the information in the *Bulletin*. Peirce wrote "To students of Philosophy" on the title page of his manuscript of the lecture on "Multitude and Continuity" (MS 316a). And he similarly limited his salutation in the first sentence of the lecture: "I address you as students of philosophy."

Peirce delivered one lecture on one day, his seventh and last lecture in the series on pragmatism on May 14, and another lecture on the very next day, May 15, on some mathematical ideas that, he believed, further contributed to the proof of pragmatism. He mentioned the lecture on mathematics in his seventh lecture on pragmatism. He said that, in an explanation of the relations between different doctrines of induction, he would have to "anticipate a little" the concepts that he planned to "further explain" the next day in his lecture "on multitude and continuity" (MS 315). He then entered into an analysis of the "sophism" of Achilles and the tortoise. His manuscript of the May 15 lecture comes to a halt in the middle of page 14, after he has recounted some of the recent developments in mathematics as well as his own contributions, and initiated an explanation of his system of "existential graphs." The manuscript also includes his criticism of those professors of philosophy who have exhibited no interest in mathematics:

> Mathematicians always have been the very best reasoners in the world; while metaphysicians always have been the very worst. Therein is reason enough why students of philosophy should not neglect mathematics. But during the last thirty years, there has been an extraordinary mathematical development of the general doctrine of multitude (including, of course, infinity) and of continuity. Philosophers would fall short of their well earned reputation as dunces if they paid much attention to this until it begins to ring in their ears from all quarters. But you would not have come here tonight unless you were philosophers rather in the etymological sense of the word than according to the wont of those [who] profess logic and metaphysics—unless you were philosophers of the school of Royce rather than of the school of Hamilton. (MS 316a)

He could as well have said, rather than the school of James.

James returned to Cambridge from his house in New Hampshire late in the day on May 14. He may have arrived on campus in time to hear Peirce's seventh lecture at 8:00 P.M. but he would not have expected Peirce to have scheduled it. He included no mention of the seventh lecture or the May 15 lecture on mathematics in a letter he sent out on May 15 to Mrs. Jacobi:

> On my return from a journey last night, I find your letter. I thought I had written to you that the lectures were assured. They have now been given, to a good audience, and have done C. S. P. a lot of good. Next [academic] year he has some Lowell lectures in Boston, but I fear no great result from the Carnegie direction, and after all who can wonder, he being the strange and unruly being that he is. Men who use no self-restraint, end by becoming beggars! I thank you for your share in the help.[11]

James's stay in the country had not rehabilitated his own sense of restraint or his spirit of magnanimity. On May 18, almost a week after the fact, Peirce's brother Herbert sent him the notice of the Carnegie executive committee's resolution not to fund any work on logic, his included.

Sometime after James's return to Cambridge in the middle of May, Peirce loaned him copies (most likely, his manuscripts) of two of the lectures he had not attended: the second lecture and either the sixth or the seventh. He evidently told James that he would like to have the entire lecture series published. James returned the two lectures on June 5 in the mail from New Hampshire to Peirce's home in Milford, Pennsylvania. He said in a separate letter he sent Peirce that he believed the two lectures to be "wonderful things":

> I have read the Second one twice—but so original, and your cate-
> gories are so unusual to other minds, that although I recognize
> the region of thought and the profundity and reality of the level
> on which you move, I do not yet assimilate the various theses in
> the sense of being able to make a use of them for my own pur-
> poses. I may get to it later; but at present event 1st, 2nd & 3rd-
> ness are outside my own sphere of practically applying things, and
> I am not sure even whether I apprehend them as you mean them
> to be apprehended. I get, throughout your whole business, only
> the sense of something dazzling and imminent in the way of
> truth. This is very likely partly due to my mind being so non-
> mathematical and to my slight interest in logic. (HLWJ)

James believed that most members of Peirce's audience had to have shared his "complaint" that the lectures were not sufficiently accessible to the minds of "auditors" with but little knowledge of mathematics and logic. He hoped, he said, that Peirce would not attempt to have these lectures pub- lished in the same form that he had presented them:

> They need too much mediation by more illustration, at which you
> are excellent (non-mathematical ones if possible), and by a good
> deal of interstitial expansion and comparison with other modes of
> thought.

He insisted that Peirce should revise the lectures with an "ignoramus in view as [the] auditor":

> As things stand, it is only highly skilled technicians and profes-
> sionals who will sniff the rare perfume of your thought and, *after
> you are dead*, trace things back to your genius. You ought to gain
> a bigger audience *when living*.

James advised Peirce that he could not "start with too low an idea" of the "intelligence" of his audience: "Look at me, as one!" he said.

Peirce answered James's letter on June 8. He admitted that his Har- vard audience had not been sufficiently "fit" to understand the "pure theory" he had offered them in the field of logic. The audience had really needed "logical training—lessons, not lectures" (HLWJ). But Peirce had arrived at another interpretation of James's letter and a different idea of the intelligibility of his Harvard lectures when, in October 1904, he remembered the affair in a letter to Christine Ladd-Franklin, then a lecturer in logic and psychology at Johns Hopkins University and one of his former students:

> In the spring of 1903 I was invited, by the influence of James, Royce and Munsterberg to give a course of lectures in Harvard University on Pragmatism. I had intended to print them; but James said he could not understand them himself and could not recommend their being printed. I do not myself think there is any difficulty in understanding them, but all modern psychologists are so soaked with sensationalism that they can not understand anything that does not mean that, and mistranslate into the ideas of [Wilhelm] Wundt whatever one says about logic. . . . How can I, to whom nothing seems so thoroughly real as generals, and who regard Truth and Justice as *literally* the most powerful powers in the world, expect to be understood by the thoroughgoing Wundtian?[12]

Peirce had already perceived that the difference between his and James's ideas on pragmatism would have to be confronted, before the Harvard lectures became an issue. When he heard that he would deliver a series of lectures at Harvard, he immediately decided that he would set out the difference and elaborate his doctrine that pragmatism is a "proposition of logic" and not the function of human psychology that James believed it to be. His seven lectures clearly delineate the difference between his logical realism and James's psychological nominalism. But James adopted the position that he could not understand Peirce's lectures, not really because he lacked the knowledge of logic and mathematics needed to understand them, but because the ideas that Peirce wanted to present, criticisms of James's ideas, could not, James believed in vain, be presented in an intelligible discourse. James, therefore, successfully prevented the publication of Peirce's 1903 Harvard lectures on pragmatism in his and Peirce's lifetime.

Notes

1. Peirce wrote on his copy of Royce's letter that "Royce is the Greatest Metaphysician now living and one of the half dozen best logicians."

2. Peirce delivered eight Lowell Lectures at the Lowell Institute in Boston between November 23 and December 17. He published many book reviews in *The Nation* and other journals. See *A Comprehensive Bibliography of The Published Works of Charles Sanders Peirce with a Bibliography of Secondary Studies*, 2nd ed., edited by Kenneth Laine Ketner (Bowling Green, Ohio: Philosophy Documentation Center, 1986).

3. Harvard University Archives, Charles William Eliot Collection, William James to Charles William Eliot, 2 February 1903.

4. For a published edition of the Cambridge Conferences Lectures of 1898, see Charles Sanders Peirce, *Reasoning and the Logic of Things*, edited by Kenneth Laine Ketner, with an introduction by Kenneth Laine Ketner and Hilary Putnam (Cambridge, Mass.: Harvard University Press, 1992).

5. On the very day, February 28, that William James sent his letter to Eliot, with his plea that the Harvard Corporation should approve Peirce to offer a lecture series, he disparaged Peirce in a letter to his own brother, Henry James: "I am beset by a crowd of cranks (C. S. Peirce now again), but I suppose that that is inevitable as one grows old & prosperous oneself" (HLWJ). James's unseemly profession of injury and complacency is particularly vulgar.

6. The Harvard Corporation soon received the money it needed to pay Peirce. Its receipt of the six hundred dollars is recorded in the College Records of 30 March 1903:
Gifts for Lectures on Philosophy
Voted that the gift of one hundred dollars, received from Mr. James M. Barnard, towards the payment for six lectures on Philosophy to be given by Mr. Charles S. Peirce, to be gratefully accepted.
The same motion and vote is recorded in each of these cases:
Dr. Mary Putnam Jacobi $100
Mr. John T. Morse, Jr. $150
Prof. A. Marquand $ 25
Prof. William James $175
Prof. E. C. Pickering $ 50
See College Records, 30 March 1903, in the Harvard University Archives.
James had sent this letter to Dr. Jacobi:
The Corporation of Harvard has at last done the decent thing by Chas. Peirce, and authorized a course of six University Lectures by him, at six hundred dollars, the money to be supplied by me. Remembering the extremely practical help you gave five years ago, I venture to ask whether you think you may possibly help me out again. I hate to beg you for money and stand ready to make the whole good, if need be, but I think I am sure of about 150 dollars here, without going far, and I am writing to one other person in N. Y. Queer problem, C. S. P.!
This letter is located in the Mary Putnam Jacobi Collection, Schlesinger Library, Radcliffe College.

7. Philosophy 3 was said, in the 1903 Harvard University *Bulletin of Courses*, to be an intermediate course "For Undergraduates and Graduates"; the student

would enroll in this course between courses "primary for Undergraduates" and those "Primary for Graduates." The *Bulletin* offered this summary of the course:

> *The Philosophy of Nature*, with especial reference to Man's place in Nature.—The Fundamental Conceptions of Science; the relation of Mind and Body; Evolution. Pearson's Grammar of Science; Ward's Naturalism and Agnosticism. Lectures and theses.

See the Harvard University *Bulletin of Courses*, 1903, in the Harvard University Archives.

8. Peirce clearly believed that the invitation he received to deliver a series of lectures at Harvard in the spring of 1903 had directly resulted from his troubles with his Carnegie application. He concluded, in a letter he sent to J. McKeen Cattell, one of his former students and then the chairman of the department of psychology at Columbia University, that the "inaction" of the Carnegie executive committee has secured him "friends from unexpected quarters":

> President Eliot has invited me to deliver a course of lectures in Harvard University and I have also been invited to deliver lectures at the Lowell Institute in Boston where I have already given two courses & other material help is promised, all of it due to the unwillingness of the [Carnegie] executive committee to help & I do not think the feeling has subsided.

This letter is located in The Library of Congress Manuscript Collection, Charles S. Peirce to J. McKeen Cattell, 19 December 1902.

9. The announcement in the *Harvard University Calendar*, Vol. XXII, No. 25, March 20, 1903, read, under "[MARCH] 23, MONDAY":
DIVISION OF PHILOSOPHY LECTURES:
Pragmatism as a Principle and Method of Right Thinking.
I. *Introduction.* Mr. CHARLES SANDERS PEIRCE. *Sever* 11, 8 P.M. Open to the public.
The "general description" of the lecture series, in the same number of the *Calendar*, read, under "NOTES":

> *The Division of Philosophy Lectures*
> The Division of Philosophy announces six lectures by MR. CHARLES SANDERS PEIRCE, to be given in Sever 11, at 8 o'clock, on successive Monday evenings, beginning March 23d. The subject of the course will be: Pragmatism, as a principle and method of right thinking. The lectures will successively treat of its foundation, definition, and limitation, and of its applications to philosophy, to the sciences, and to the conduct of life. The lectures will be open to the public.

Sever Hall, designed by H. H. Richardson and built in 1880, is a red-brick building that stands on one side of Harvard Yard. It housed classrooms when Peirce delivered his 1903 lectures in Room 11, and still stands there today.

10. William James, *The Letters of William James,* ed. by his son, Henry James (Boston: Atlantic Monthly Press [1920]; New York: Kraus Reprint, 1969), v. 2, p. 375.

11. Mary Putnam Jacobi Collection, Schlesinger Library, 15 May 1903, Radcliffe College.

12. Charles S. Peirce to Christine Ladd-Franklin, 20 October 1904, in Christine Ladd-Franklin, "Charles S. Peirce at the Johns Hopkins," *The Journal of Philosophy, Psychology, and Scientific Methods,* 13 (1916): 719–20.

COMMENTARY

Patricia Ann Turrisi

LECTURE ONE

Delivered on March 26, 1903, the first lecture was advertised in the *Harvard University Calendar* as the "Introduction" to the series *Pragmatism as a Principle and Method of Right Thinking*. In the March 26 edition of the *Harvard Crimson*, additional information was provided:

> "Pragmatism" is that system of philosophy, first so named by Mr. Peirce, which views philosophical questions primarily from the standpoint of their practical bearing upon life. The lecture tonight will be a definition of the system and an explanation of its terms.

While the *Harvard Crimson* advertisement seems to have been written by someone other than Peirce, the *Harvard Bulletin* announcement appears to have been written, or at least directed, by him:

> The Department of Philosophy announces a series of six lectures by Mr. Charles Sanders Peirce '59 formerly assistant in the U.S. Coast Survey and for some time lecturer at Johns Hopkins University, to be given in Sever 11 at 8 o'clock on successive Thursday evenings, beginning March 26. The lecturer will discuss the development of this philosophical system, its definition, its scope, and its application to the sciences, to philosophy, and to the conduct of life.

The schedule was changed and the number of lectures increased, but the topics of discussion remained consistent with this initial description. The difference between the *Crimson* and the *Bulletin* descriptions is perhaps an immediate reason for Peirce's initial remarks about the differences between his and other definitions of the meaning of pragmatism, and for his emphasis upon "philosophical system" as opposed to "practical bearing on life," which sounds suspiciously unlike Peirce, and more like James, the possible writer of the *Crimson* advertisement.

A proof of pragmatism is proposed in these lectures. In order to appreciate the proof, it is necessary first to define what pragmatism is, a task for which an application of the pragmatic maxim would be fitted. In order to clarify its meaning, Peirce used a method he recommended for such matters in his 1891 article, "The Architecture of Theories"—that is, "to make a systematic study of the conceptions out of which a philosophical theory may be built, in order to ascertain what place each conception may fitly occupy in such a theory and to what uses it is adapted" (CP 6.9). Peirce's systematic study of pragmatism in relation to logic began to appear around 1898, and peaked in 1903, when the definition of pragmatism and its role in logic was established in these lectures.

Pragmatism as a Logical Maxim

The first lecture of Peirce's 1903 series on *Pragmatism as a Principle and Method of Right Thinking* introduced his audience to a variety of issues, many of which would have been familiar to a student of Peirce at the time. The significance of pragmatism in Peirce's systematic philosophy of logic is one important exception. Published sources alone would not have enabled scholars to remark adequately on the logical nature of his pragmatism. But lecture notes and correspondence furnish us with an account of his motivation for embarking on a revision of pragmatism in this regard in the latter stage of his career. By 1903, Peirce had long had regrets about the directions in which his pragmatic doctrine had taken due to what he sensed to be the incompleteness of its original articulation. That year the opportunity to speak to William James's students, "well primed in pragmatism," was used to address these deficiencies in his presentation. A redefinition of pragmatism in its logical role would have to begin with a criticism of the effects of the "pragmatic maxim," as put forth in 1878: "Consider what effects that might conceivably have practical bearings we conceive the object of our conception to have: then, our conception of those effects is the whole of our conception of the object." The "object" of his inquiry in these lectures was the very concept of pragmatism itself.

While, in Peirce's opinion, other "pragmatists" were not properly concerned with the definition of pragmatism, he believed the definition of any term to be a serious matter having normative value. In his "Ethics of Terminology," written shortly after the lectures on pragmatism, he defended the notion that it becomes the duty of science to accept and preserve the name given to a conception by its inventor. He stated that:

> . . . every symbol is a living thing, in a very strict sense that is no mere figment of speech. The body of the symbol changes slowly,

but its meaning inevitably grows, incorporates new elements and throws off old ones. But the effort of all should be to keep the *essence* of every scientific term unchanged and exact; although absolute exactitude is not so much as conceivable.[1]

Peirce claimed to have invented *pragmatism* and was acknowledged as such by others. Users of the term pragmatism seemed to Peirce to have honored the term without honoring the conception.

In an effort to preserve the "essence" of pragmatism, the 1903 lectures contain an argument for Peirce's own definition and, consequently, for whatever conceivable effects are implied by it. Indeed, as a precursor of the general principles set forth in the 1903 lectures, in the 1901 Baldwin's *Dictionary of Philosophy and Psychology*, Peirce's entry on pragmatism (written circa 1899) follows James's. In it, he argued against James's assumption, in *Will to Believe* and *Philosophical Conceptions and Practical Results*, that the end of humanity is action:

If it be admitted, on the contrary, that action wants an end, and that that end must be something of a general description, then *the spirit of the maxim itself*, which is that we must look to the upshot of our concepts in order rightly to apprehend them, would direct us towards something different from practical facts, namely, to general ideas, as the true interpreters of our thought.

As I shall demonstrate, he argued for a reevaluation of pragmatism from the point of view of its logical purpose:

[I] would venture to suggest that [the pragmatic maxim] should always be put into practice with conscientious thoroughness, but that, when that has been done, and not before, a still higher grade of clearness of thought can be attained by remembering that the only ultimate good which the practical facts to which it directs attention can subserve is to further the development of concrete reasonableness; so that the meaning of the concept does not lie in any individual reactions at all, but in the manner in which those reactions contribute to that development.[2]

This statement was written specifically with James in mind, but also such pragmatists as Schiller, who Peirce claimed had "missed the point" in not understanding that pragmatistic technique is required in order to think *any* thought (HL, C. S. Peirce/W. James, 11/25/02).

Therefore, Peirce proposed an inquiry into the question, "Is pragmatism true?" He wished the appeal of pragmatism to lie not only in its psychological efficacy in easing doubt, but in its logical efficacy in promoting a greater scientific knowledge of reality—that is, a concrete reasonableness. The fact that he made this inquiry at all is highly significant inasmuch as it is not duplicated by any other "pragmatist." Demonstration of the *truth* of pragmatism was required by Peirce because he considered it to be a logical maxim and not a speculative doctrine.

However, the question of what *constitutes* a proof per se, in Peirce's view, is also problematic. What can *truth* mean here? What kind of proof is required to demonstrate its truth? While Fisch and McCarthy each note the presence of a proof, an account of this proof's specific dependence on an explanation of the role of pragmatism in the science of logic has never been explored.[3]

McCarthy accounts for this dependence somewhat, but his statement of the *proof* primarily focuses upon the dependence of logic on ethics and esthetics. He looks away from the systematic classification of sciences given by Peirce as a locus for the proof in lectures one through five. He states:

> The first lecture sets out the problem, shows that it is a problem—i.e., that there is a real question about the truth of pragmatism—and gives a plan for the subsequent inquiry. The next three lectures are taken up by the first part of the plan, the exposition of the categories—phenomenological in the second and third as well as metaphysical in the fourth. . . . *This confirms what one suspected already, viz., that the second, third and fourth lectures were intended more to familiarize the audience with Peirce's modes of thought than to contribute anything directly to the proof* [my emphasis]. In any case that is my opinion and I will have little more to say about them.[4]

But Peirce's published writings, letters and unpublished manuscripts, clearly indicate that he found the "ladder of the sciences" necessary for grounding logic as a science and thereby pragmatism as a logical maxim. Hence, McCarthy throws out the very evidence that would place pragmatism in the appropriate context for considering its logical value.

Under the inspiration of Kant, Peirce sought to build logical thought architectonically upon the whole range of the sciences. It seems unlikely that his notion of *proof* would be unaffected by his notion of the place of logic among the sciences. He wrote in 1898:

Logic requires that the more abstract sciences should be developed earlier than the more concrete ones. For the more concrete sciences require as fundamental principles the results of the more abstract sciences, while the latter only make use of the results of the former as data; and if one fact is wanting, some other will generally serve to support the same generalization. (CP 6.1)

As a result, he proposed a method of solving problems—that is, a recommendation concerning how inquiries ought to be conducted:

That systems ought to be constructed architectonically has been preached since Kant, but I do not think the full import of the maxim has by any means been apprehended. What I would recommend is that every person who wishes to form an opinion concerning fundamental problems should first of all make a complete survey of human knowledge, should take note of all the valuable ideas in each branch of science, should observe in just what respect each has been successful and where it has failed, in order that, in the light of the thorough acquaintance so attained of the available materials for a philosophical theory and of the nature and strength of each, he may proceed to the study of what the problem of philosophy consists in, and of the proper way of solving it. I must not be understood as endeavoring to state fully all that these preparatory studies should embrace; on the contrary, *I purposely slur over many points, in order to give emphasis to one special recommendation, namely, to make a systematic study of the conceptions out of which a philosophical theory may be built, in order to ascertain what place each conception may fitly occupy in such a theory, and to what uses it is adapted* [my emphasis]. (CP 6.9)

In support of this view, he gave at least three other accounts of the architectonic of scientific theories in the years 1902 to 1904 which agree with the account given in lecture one of the 1903 pragmatism series.[5]

By 1902 he was ready to give a full account of his theory of reasoning. His application for a Carnegie Institution grant in 1902, "Methods of Science," proposed three dozen "memoirs" which would "persuade of the scientific nature of logic" (L 75). He stated in Memoir No. 9 "On the Bearing of Esthetics and Ethics Upon Logic":

I show that Ethics depends essentially upon Esthetics and Logic upon Ethics. The latter dependence I had shown less fully in 1869

(Journal of Speculative Philosophy, Vol. II, pp. 207 et seq.). But the methods of reasoning by which the truths of logic are established must be mathematical, such reasoning alone being evident independently of any logical doctrine.

He proposed to expand on mathematical methods of discovering and establishing the truths of logic in Memoir No. 14. *A Prospectus on Reasoning*, circa 1904 (MS 693a) reflects a similar orientation, but adds, as in the 1903 lectures, that the normative sciences themselves depend upon phenomenology, which is dependent upon mathematics. On 25 November 1902, subsequent to his Carnegie proposal and just prior to giving the 1903 lectures on pragmatism, Peirce wrote to James:

> I think I could satisfy you that your view of pragmatism requires some modification, that it is the logical basis and proof of it (and it can receive no sound support from psychology) and its relation to the categories that have first to be made clear before it can be accurately applied except in very simple ways. (HL, C. S. Peirce/W. James, 12/01/02)

And these lectures give us his most complete account of the hierarchy of the sciences in which logic falls.

The first five lectures in *Pragmatism as a Principle and Method of Right Thinking* provide essential elements of the proof, contrary to McCarthy's claim that the proof begins late in lecture five. If the recollection of pragmatism's conceivable effects is, as Peirce suggested, an integral part of this proof, it is indeed necessary to locate pragmatism correctly within logic and logic within its place among the other sciences.

Pragmatism's Efficacy versus Pragmatism's Truth: The Need for a Proof

It was clear to Peirce as well as to an array of pragmatists what pragmatism could do in the way of guiding practical action, if applied correctly. In the first lecture on pragmatism, Peirce concurred with his earliest formulation of pragmatism by illustrating its efficacy in solving a paradox in a problem concerning probability. In the area of thought experiments and, indeed, in the application of these to practical conduct, pragmatism works. Peirce added that "pragmatism is generally practiced by successful men." Efficient men are distinguished from inefficient men through the practical advantage of being able to think pragmatically.

Pragmatism's *usefulness* on the level of directing its practitioners to specific conclusions is eminently demonstrable. But as Peirce pointed out in his Baldwin's *Dictionary* article, its general meaning is a different matter. Peirce regarded the practical skill of using pragmatic technique as valuable but not in any great need of elucidation. By contrast, readers of William James's works prior to 1903 were treated almost exclusively to descriptions of pragmatic skills and techniques implying its value for practical action. Justifications of pragmatism even later in James's works—for example, in his 1907 Lowell lectures on pragmatism—are made in terms of its usefulness, under the presumption that practical utility is its own best defense. He cites his mentors and colleagues in his dedication and preface, referring to the utilitarian, John Stuart Mill, as one "whom my fancy likes to picture as our leader."[6]

The direction of pragmatic studies typified by James's work—which was not grounded on any greater justification than efficacy—convinced Peirce that pragmatism had gone too far without its necessary *logical* justification. And a vindication of its role as a maxim of logic would serve the end of the "spirit of pragmatism," in promoting concrete reasonableness as a general concern.

Peirce distinguished use from justification in a criticism of his own early account:

> There is no doubt, then that pragmatism opens a very easy road to the solution of an immense variety of questions. But it does not follow from that that it is true. (CP 5.26)

In fact, the ease with which such a method "so resolves the most difficult of problems" (CP 5.26) is deceptive. In the history of science, immensely simple hypotheses, which originally promised to explain much, have had to be greatly modified to accommodate further reflection in order that science make progress. If pragmatism is as good as even the most successful hypotheses, it is either not as simple a hypothesis as it seems, or it is in need of modification or at least greater justification.

Peirce attempted an examination of the status of pragmatism by means of its justification. He argued:

> Which is the *proof* that the possible practical consequences of a concept constitute the sum total of the concept? The <proof> argument upon which I rested the maxim in my original paper was that *belief* consists *mainly* [my emphasis] in being deliberately prepared to adopt the formula believed in as the guide to action.

> If this be in truth the nature of belief, then undoubtedly the proposition believed in can itself be nothing but a maxim of conduct. That I believe is quite evident.
>
> But *how do we know* that belief is nothing but the deliberate preparedness to act according to the formula believed?
>
> My original article carried this back to a psychological principle. The conception of truth according to me was developed out of an original impulse to act consistently, to have a definite intention. . . . (MS 301; CP 5.27–28)

But in the first lecture, Peirce admitted he did address the issue of the justification of pragmatism in the 1877–1878 papers ("The Fixation of Belief" and "How to Make Our Ideas Clear"), albeit on *psychological* grounds, which he now recognized as inadequate in terms of a *logical* proof. Specifically, the "psychological principle" that stood behind the notion that "belief is nothing but the deliberate preparedness to act" was the principle that when the irritation of doubt is sufficient, a person rendered in two by indecision will seek to overcome doubt. The impulse to overcome doubt, Peirce claimed in 1878, is "the motive for thinking" (CP 5.397). He referred to his initial analysis in 1877, that "doubt is an uneasy and dissatisfied state from which we struggle to free ourselves and pass into the state of belief, while the latter is a calm and satisfactory state which we do not wish to avoid, or to change to a belief in anything else" (CP 5.372).

Interpretations of the meaning of the pragmatic maxim arising from Peirce's arguments for it in 1878 are based upon his apparent identification of the definition of an apprehension with a definition of a belief—that is, that belief is "nothing but the deliberate preparedness to act according to the formula believed." The specific difference between the accounts of 1878 and 1903 rests upon the question of whether belief, the "proof" or "argument" upon which the pragmatic maxim rests, is "*mainly*" a deliberate preparedness to act or is, in fact, "*nothing but*" a "preparedness to act."

If Peirce had held that the definition of belief carried no other possible meaning than the one above, his original definition of belief and, thereby, of the basis of the truth of the pragmatic maxim, would not have been logically defensible, even if psychologically so. Fortunately, the pragmatic maxim describes the *apprehension* of the meaning of a concept. Peirce then questioned whether (1) apprehension is identical to belief as he defined belief, and (2) belief should be defined as *merely* a propensity to act in accordance with a proposition. Peirce most definitely seemed to be attempting to make a very important distinction between a concept to which one is willing to assent and a concept which one may understand, without necessarily assenting to it—that is, between a definition of "concept" that emphasizes its psychological acceptability and a definition that emphasizes its logical acceptability. While it may appear obvious that one must first apprehend a concept in order to assent to it, it is by no means established that one must assent to a concept in order to apprehend it or even that apprehension of a concept must lead to a "preparedness to act." If the meaning of the apprehension of a concept is considered independently of "belief" so expressed as a propensity to act, as Peirce's plan shows it must be, it becomes possible for the first time to evaluate pragmatism as a logical doctrine. Peirce's proof of pragmatism is a demonstration that, as a scientific doctrine, it belongs to the science of logic, rather than to the less fundamental, special science of psychology.

Peirce and his readers from 1878 on were persuaded of the definition of belief by the psychological principle so justifying it in his 1877–1878 articles, "The Fixation of Belief" and "How to Make Our Ideas Clear." The uncomfortable sensation that accompanies indecision motivates action toward avoiding that sensation. But the question remained in 1903 how to explain why, in the first place, human beings are constituted so as to embody this particular psychological principle. A psychological condition is itself in need of a logical justification. In 1903 Peirce called for an explanation of the human tendency to desire and to be able to accomplish deliberate preparations for actions in the form of beliefs. Perhaps this could be done from an evolutionary perspective, but then the question of the proof per se would remain as the question of whether pragmatism could be provided with any sound *logical* basis.

The reason for Peirce's hesitation in supplying an evolutionary account of the psychological "motive for thinking" that lies behind pragmatism is complex. The dependence of psychological principles upon logical ones in his architectonic classification of the sciences is itself grounded upon the notion that general psychological propensities among humans have evolved in response to logical necessities. In other words, insofar as true beliefs have been formed, they have promoted human existence in a proportion greater than beliefs that are false and so have been retained by "natural selection." In a very general manner, psychological tendencies reflect a kind of recognition of logical truths, the investigation of the conditions for the possibility of which cannot be conducted exclusively by reference to history or evolution.

The Role of Pragmatism in Logic and the Role of Logic in the Architectonic of Science

The purpose of a proof of pragmatism is to account for the possibility that a well-known psychological condition—namely, doubt, as the motivator for thought—is grounded in a set of *logical* conditions and is not somehow independent or prior to the logical conditions affecting a thinker. These logical conditions are what concerned Peirce throughout the 1903 lectures on pragmatism and almost exclusively in the first five lectures.

It ought to be iterated that the purpose of logic was conceived by Peirce not as a formulaic rendering of conclusions from premises, but as a means of elucidating the basic elements of reasoning.[7] Peirce claimed that pragmatism supplied a tool for accomplishing that purpose. But the account of the elements of reasoning themselves does not proceed directly *from* logic. Rather, these elements are observed and recorded by logical means. In saying that "logic requires that the more abstract sciences should be developed earlier than the concrete ones," he did not mean that an abstract science *causes* a concrete one, but that the subject matter of concrete sciences is realized by the hand of abstract science. "For the more concrete sciences require as fundamental principles the results of the more abstract sciences" (CP 6.1). Furthermore, abstract sciences make use of the results of concrete sciences "as data" (CP 6.1).

Peirce delineated the relationship of logic to other sciences in terms of abstractness and concreteness in order to show where the data logic produces is used, as well as to show from whence logic receives its data. The very nature of the data received and produced by logic is that which the pragmatic maxim aids in interpreting. And so it is essential to a "proof" of pragmatism—that is, a proof of its truth as a maxim of logical conduct—to identify exactly with what logical conduct is concerned.

Then and only then is it possible to "prove" whether pragmatism is or is not a tool of logic, or of something else or of nothing at all. Thereby, Peirce followed his own recommendation:

> To make a systematic study of the conceptions out of which a philosophical theory may be built in order to ascertain what place each conception may fitly occupy in such a theory, and to what uses it is adapted.

In this case, he planned to examine logic as if it were the science of a species of conduct, viz., reasoning (CP 6.9).

To that specific end, Peirce placed his proof within an architectonic of scientific knowledge. Contrary to Jeremiah McCarthy's opinion that "the second, third and fourth lectures were intended more to familiarize the audience with Peirce's modes of thought than to contribute anything directly to the proof," these lectures speak directly to the notion of proof as proper contextualization by demonstrating the "place each conception may fitly occupy" in reference to the pragmatic maxim.[8] At any rate, the specific relatedness of Peirce's "modes of thought" to one another would have been unfamiliar to any audience since Peirce admitted he had only just understood it correctly himself. Peirce was not merely reiterating his "modes of thought," but was presenting what was for him a *new* doctrine of pragmatism's exact occupation within logic and for other "pragmatists," a renewed doctrine of the status of pragmatism within philosophy.

In contrast to "pragmatists" whose doctrines no longer bear a strong resemblance to the pragmatism developed around 1872 or so in the "Metaphysical Club,"[9] Peirce denied that pragmatism is a "sublime principle of speculative philosophy" (CP 5.18). In a deleted passage from his first lecture, he stated:

> The direst fault I find with all the people who pose as pragmatists is that they all write philosophy in more or less lively styles and are sometimes even entertaining. It is plain that to be deep one must be dull. I do not know what fault these writers find with me because they never mention me; but I suspect that if they did they would find me flippant for making pragmatism to be a mere maxim of logic instead of being what they all hold it to be, a sublime principle of theoretical philosophy. (MS 301)

A maxim of logic would have to aid the aim of logic. Its effects would have to serve logical ends. But the truth about the role of logic within the sciences—that is, the demarcation and foundation of logical ends—Peirce disclosed, had not occurred to him at the time he originated his pragmatic doctrine.

The novel idea Peirce developed and defended in these first four lectures as well as in the rest is the place of logic within the normative sciences, and theirs in reference to the science of phenomenology. In order to prove the truth of pragmatism, a maxim of a fairly abstract science, data from more concrete sciences are useful as per the general structure of architectonic set out in 1891. Thus, not only will the placement of logic within the sciences serve to elucidate the place pragmatism occupies in logic, but will outline the sources for data by which to support the generalizations of pragmatism. Peirce wrote to James in November 1902, shortly before being invited to lecture on pragmatism:

> My own view in 1877 was crude. Even when I gave my Cambridge lectures [in 1898], I had not really got to the bottom of it or seen the unity of the whole thing. It was not until after that that I obtained the proof that logic must be founded on ethics, of which it is a higher development. Even then, I was for some time so

stupid as not to see that ethics rests in the same manner on a
foundation of esthetics. (HL, C. S. Peirce/W. James, 11/25/02)

Lecture one restates and justifies this position and lectures two through
six amplify it.

Continuing in this letter, Peirce summarizes the relation of the normative sciences to the universal categories:

> These three normative sciences correspond to my three catego-
> ries, which in their psychological aspect, appear as Feeling, Reac-
> tion, Thought. . . . The true nature of pragmatism cannot be un-
> derstood without them.

The foundation of the normative sciences is further defined and justified in
his first lecture:

> But before we can attack any normative science, any science
> which proposes to separate the sheep from the goats [as each of
> the normative sciences do in matters of thought, conduct, and
> admirability], it is plain that there must be a preliminary inquiry
> which shall justify the attempt to establish such dualism. This
> must be a science that does *not* draw any distinction of good and
> bad in any sense whatever, but just contemplates phenomena as
> they are, simply opens its eyes and describes what it sees. Not
> what it sees in the real as distinguished from figment,—not re-
> garding any such dichotomy but simply describing the object as a
> phenomenon, and stating what it finds in all phenomena alike.
> (MS 301)

This science is of course the science of the categories, of phenomenology,
which Peirce discussed in the second, third, and fourth lectures.

The architectonic is not complete, however, without resting phenomenology upon *its* ground. Phenomenology, "the most primal of all the positive sciences," rests on no other "positive science," but does depend on a
"Conditional or Hypothetical Science of Pure Mathematics." A "positive
science," though an "inquiry which seeks for positive knowledge, that is
for knowledge as may conveniently be expressed in a *categorical proposition*," would seem to exclude normative sciences insofar as they ask "not
what *is* but what *ought to be*." However, these, said Peirce, "nevertheless
are positive sciences since it is by asserting positive, categorical truth that
they are able to show that what they call good really is so; and the right
reason, right effort, and right being of which they treat derive that charac-

ter from positive categorical fact." Contrasted with positive science, the aim of Pure Mathematics is "to discover not how things actually are, but how they might be supposed to be, if not in our universe, then in some other." Peirce added:

> A Phenomenology which does not reckon with pure mathematics, a science hardly come to years of discretion when Hegel wrote, will be the same pitiful clubfooted affair that Hegel produced.

This comment explains a great deal about the inclusion in the second lecture of an account of one-value, Dichotomic and Trichotomic mathematics, and other kinds of pure mathematics, in their relation to the logic of relations. James's view that its "lack of nonmathematical examples" was a deficiency of the lectures, expressed in a letter discouraging Peirce from publishing them, results from a misunderstanding of the role of "mathematical examples" in the proof. As far as the establishment of pragmatism's dependence on the "science of hypotheses"—that is, on mathematics— goes, Peirce's use of "mathematical examples" is a *proficiency* of the lectures.

Overall, the purpose for a discussion of mathematics in these lectures is to demonstrate the basis of logic in a science "independent" of logic. In lecture two, Peirce stated that the Boolean algebra of logic which, "if developed by means of arrays of letters with conventional signs to signify relations in between them" may "equally be developed by means of diagrams—composed of lines and dots, and this in various ways of which the *Eulerian diagrams* form one example while my *Existential Graphs and Entitative Graphs* are others" (MS 302). He mentioned that "no masterly presentation has ever been given" of this mathematics, but that he had attempted it several times himself (MS 302).

Ultimately, what fragments of the system Peirce has chosen to reveal in these lectures were not intended to be a rehash of his "modes of thought," but rather an upending of conventional ideas concerning logic. He claimed, "this exact logic of relatives . . . simply dynamites all our traditional notions of logic and with them Kant's Critic of the Pure Reason which was founded upon them" (MS 302). This claim deserves further exploration and not as a mere tidbit about Peircean notions of logic but as a key to the architectonically arranged sciences that depend on logic, and ultimately upon mathematics, for their principles.

And so, the "apparently aimless beating about the bush" of which Peirce spoke (CP 5.130) at the beginning of what Jeremiah McCarthy takes to be Peirce's proof of pragmatism is actually not aimless at all, but an integral part of an inquiry into the truth of pragmatism. A look at its foundation in logic, and in turn the normative sciences, phenomenology and pure mathematics, is a look at the construction of a systematic array of sciences in which pragmatism serves as a precipitator and clarifier of the data and principles of science.

It is appropriate to include Peirce's remarks to James here in defense of claiming this "background" to be *part* of a pragmatic proof for pragmatism. He wrote on 25 November 1902, comparing himself with other pragmatists, "I seem to myself to be the sole depository at present of the completely developed system which all hangs together and cannot receive any proper presentation in fragments" (HL, C. S. Peirce/W. James, 11/25/02).

A week later, in discussing the publication of his logic and pragmatism's dependence upon it, Peirce stated:

> Were all the parts of my system separately published, the mathematician would approve of the mathematical part, the physicist of the physical part, the ethicist would admit the ethical part to be a contribution of some weight, and so on, but the principal thing would remain unpublished; for this depends upon the way the parts are fitted together, which is not the most obvious thing, and would then wholly escape notice. (HL, C. S. Peirce/W. James, 12/01/02)

These statements are not at all surprising coming from a proponent of a logic of relations whose explicit task is to discover and exhibit "the way the parts are fitted together." Peirce essentially followed through in the 1903 lectures on his promising Introduction, giving not only the "proof" summarized from lecture five on, but a wider proof that makes intelligible the architectonically defined parameters of logic and thereby pragmatism. It is not the intention of this essay to justify every claim made by Peirce about his system. Rather, I have suggested, by way of constructing the outline of the system wherein the hypothesis of the pragmatic maxim falls, that the elaboration of its foundation constitutes a stage of its proof, that of defining its purpose and function, the clear apprehension of the "data" and principles of logic.

LECTURE TWO

The *Harvard Crimson* advertised Peirce's second lecture, in its Thursday, 2 April 1903, edition:

> Mr. Charles Sanders Peirce '59 will deliver the second of his series of six lectures on "Pragmatism as a Principle and Method of Right Thinking," under the auspices of the Department of Philosophy, in Sever 11 this evening at 8 o'clock. In connection with the subject for tonight, "Phenomenology or the Doctrine of Categories," Mr. Peirce will discuss the elementary constituents of thought. The lecture is open to the public.

From the notes Peirce made in the margins of two preliminary drafts, it is probable that both drafts were written after he gave the first lecture on March 26 and after one of the three drafts (MSS 304–306) in which he actually discussed his advertised subject, "Phenomenology or the Doctrine of Categories." He wrote on the notebook cover of the second draft of lecture two (MS 303) in which he discussed mathematics as a foundation for the normative sciences and *not* as a foundation for phenomenology per se: "Rejected. No time for this. And it would need two if not three lectures." He had first intended to present a sketch of mathematics and its relation to pragmatism, but had despaired of doing justice to the topic in one hour, and decided to move on down the architectonic as outlined in lecture one.

There are significant differences between the methods one might use when giving a short course of lectures to an audience of beginning students and when performing a systematic study of a subject when there are no time or length restrictions, and one's potential audience is assumed to have the skills and experience required for understanding the subject matter. However much William James felt that the students were prepared, Peirce was plagued by the limitations on the time allowed for giving the lectures. There was simply not enough time to supply his students with all they were lacking in the necessary background of knowledge in logic, philosophy, and science. His audience of 1903 heard a brief, distilled version of his thoughts. However, the multiple drafts included here reveal an evolving set of ideas that we can appreciate today as a sample of a cross section of Peirce's mind.

Moreover, Peirce expressed his suffering over having to make decisions about cutting the length of his discourses in the form of several apologia which defined his style of work. His concern over how to proceed in a restricted set of circumstances on a study that demanded his full and eloquent attention reached its peak as he prepared to deliver lecture two. The following comments are intended to illuminate the way in which Peirce sought to maintain his intellectual integrity while sticking to a strict budget of resources.

A Method of Work and its Application

There are five extant manuscript drafts for lecture two, which cover two major and distinct topics in the foundations of pragmatism. Hence, the significance of three hitherto unpublished drafts, MSS 302–304, two of which concern mathematical topics, may be self-evident. But a general justification for including Peirce's earliest drafts for lecture two, which, in all probability, he did not deliver, is necessary. In order to explain sufficiently my justification, I will append some very interesting—also previously unpublished— portions of MS 311 and MS 312. These manuscript portions not only open a window upon Peirce's techniques of thinking from his own point of view, but are texts that illuminate the pragmatic method of "consideration" of an "object of conception," by expanding on what such a consideration entails in practical fact when applied to a philosophical topic.

On the reasonable supposition that final drafts are the best expressions of the intentions of a writer, MS 302 and MS 303 were not published in *Collected Papers of Charles Sanders Peirce.* Nor was MS 304 published, a manuscript draft on which Peirce wrote "To be rewritten and compressed." However, it was presumably satisfactory enough in its basic content (phenomenology) to have prompted Peirce to submit what must have been its very description as the advertisement for lecture two in the April 2 edition of *Harvard Crimson,* as well as for him to remain committed to the topic throughout two more full-length drafts (MS 305 and MS 306), which were eventually published in part as CP 5.41–5.65.

However reasonable the editorial supposition is that final drafts are best for the work of writers, Peirce, in this endeavor, was not only a writer. He was a lecturer who was also seeking to engage his audience in a season of unusual and difficult philosophical thought. Thus, having understood the mood and perhaps abilities and level of preparation of his students at the first lecture, given these limitations, he seems to have struggled to strike the right tones, from then on. But Peirce is always Peirce, a thinker who writes to think and thinks as he writes. And so it might be wise to proceed editorially on a different supposition, that a lecturer might write what is most interesting to *him* immediately and then only in later versions of his talk, might he come around to recognizing the practical facts of the classroom, the talents and backgrounds of the actual students, and time restrictions.

In this edition, the supposition will be that it is possible that Peirce's first drafts contain a fairly uncensored, not yet refined, treatment of the subject matter of his topic *as he worked out his own ideas*, from the point of view of the subject matter rather than as he might have composed it and reduced it for a Harvard audience. And thus, first drafts would, and indeed do, in this case, contain thoughts and formulations that might not have survived the final cuts, but nevertheless more truly reflect the inferential process undergone by Peirce. There are expressions of his frustration with the abbreviated format of the lectures in almost every one of the sixteen drafts, but the most pointed expressions of it grieve at *philosophical* losses beyond his control. For example, "I can really do nothing more [here] than to state some of the chief conclusions to which I have been led, with the merest hints of the nature of the arguments by which I have been led to them, especially since I cannot assume that you have any acquaintance with the real logic of modern thought as I conceive it" (MS 312). Early drafts provide a better idea of his "arguments." For this reason and also to dispel the notion, influenced by the misrepresentation of the scope of Peirce's arguments, that his thought is fragmentary or confused, I have accorded early drafts priority in this edition whenever possible.

Insofar as Peirce's technique as a writer must be acknowledged to have been more painstaking and intensely precise, he is not, under his own terms, writing as he is accustomed, but in a considerably looser style, albeit not, in his opinion, without sacrifices. Given that only seven days elapsed between the night of lecture one and the date of lecture two, five drafts seems prodigious. However, multiple drafts were common for Peirce, throughout his entire career, and on almost any and every topic to which he directed his attention. The plurality of issues discussed in these drafts is striking. It can be explained by the relative novelty of one of the main revelations of the lectures as a whole, and by the place the discussion of this issue would have occupied in his method of inquiry. As he confessed to James, it only recently occurred to him that the normative sciences occupy a foundational role in the sciences in general and are built upon one another. Peirce attempted, in these lectures, to meet the requirements of his

self-described method of study, to draw up a fresh statement of the fruits
of a long analysis, then endeavor to enlarge it, and "especially to make it
join homogenously with other results." That Peirce viewed this final phase
as a lifelong task, if necessary, is evident in lecture one, which took up the
topic of pragmatism some thirty years after its inception, in order to relate
it to "other results." The synthetic nature of this stage would, if shared
with an audience, require enormous preparation, a theme on which Peirce
began his discussion of "liberal education" in MS 303.

In order to better understand what Peirce may have had on his mind,
his remarks about his own writing and thinking require examination. For
example, his description of the method of "how I go to work in studying
philosophy" invites comparison with such works as Descartes's *Rules for
the Direction of Mind* and Leibniz's numerous writings on method between 1669 and 1712. But only on reflection does the surprising fact
emerge that such guides for conducting philosophy are rare. A candidate
Peirce might have considered is Ockham's Razor, but this is a single rule
and not an explicit system of rules. It might be assumed that an *implicit*
method always exists within a philosophical discipline, but even if this
were true, it does not detract from the novelty of this explicit set of guide-
lines set forth by one of the great modern philosophers. Peirce protested
that the current trend in philosophy was antithetical to exact, minute, and
mathematical precision in inquiry:

> But what I particularly wanted to come to in speaking of my way
> of philosophizing was to point out to you that it is nothing if not
> *minute*. I certainly endeavor to generalize as far as I can find
> support for generalization; but I depend on the sedulous care with
> which I scrutinize every point. What is commonly called "breadth
> of treatment" of philosophical questions is my soul's abhorrence.
> My analysis is so detailed and minute, that it would be impossible
> in these lectures to give you any specimen of it. I can really do
> nothing more than to state most of the chief conclusions to which
> I have been led, with the merest hints of the nature of the argu-
> ments by which I have been led to them, especially since I cannot
> assume that you have any acquaintance with the real logic of
> modern thought as I conceive it. While I have the warmest admi-
> ration for the great metaphysicians and psychologists of the uni-
> versity who are among the world's leaders in their departments, I
> cannot but think it deeply lamentable that true, modern, exact,
> non-psychological logic, which ought to form the background of a
> liberal education, does not receive sufficient attention here to be
> at all in evidence. As time goes on the consequences of this ne-
> glect will be deeply graven. (MS 312)

However, *we* can have a specimen since we are not limited to hearing the final versions, but can see the preliminary efforts. Two versions of Peirce's rules below certainly represent his explanation of himself as a careful writer. But more interestingly, the two drafts show Peirce's frame of mind as a writer. In the first draft, he is less definite about what actual events might be expected to occur as a result of his technique. He is more defensive in the second draft about the value of his method and makes an overt attempt to persuade a reader of its utility in the case at hand. I have numbered the comparable points in the enumerations of the stages:

(1) from MS 311

Some of you may possibly remark some discordancy between what I say now on this subject and some former expressions. I had better explain that my opinions on ethics and esthetics are not so well matured as my opinions on logic. My processes of forming philosophical opinions are excessively slow. I believe I have a reputation for alertness of intellect which is not merited. How little it is so would appear plainly enough if I were to describe to you my method of discussing with myself a philosophical question. Perhaps it may be useful to you if I briefly outline this method. In the first place, I endeavor, as far as possible, to avoid attacking questions which seem possibly to depend upon questions which I have not already thoroughly considered at least once.

[1] I then set down my question in writing as accurately as I can, which is in itself, sometimes, a matter of difficulty and doubt.

[2] That done I write down in the briefest, but most complete and exact terms, every argument I have read, heard or can imagine to be maintained, first on one side and then on the other of the question.

[2a] Some of these arguments admit of brief and decisive refutations which I also set down.

[3] I then reflect upon the matter and, without entering into the merits of the case, state what the general nature of the considerations appears to me to be upon which the decision should be made to turn, with the reasons.

[3a] I add the indication, or sometimes a full statement of other ways of considering the question which I know to have been employed or which might naturally be employed, and show as clearly

as I can what degree of weight ought to be attributed to each and why.

[3b] There usually appears to me to be but one way in which the question can be decisively discussed, and I proceed to set down the points of that discussion, together with all the doubts that may arise.

[3c] If I find the question depends upon some other which I have not fully considered, I put the whole thing aside, until that other question shall have been considered. Frequently the original question will take a new and broader form, so that I amend what I have written or begin over again. Or it may be that while a broader question is suggested and noted, the discussion is completed on the original lines. Sometimes I come upon indications that there is some other way of considering the matter without my being able to formulate that other way. In that case, I shall have a mass of tentative notes which may prove useful when I shall come to understand the subject better. I ultimately amend again and again reviewing every part of the argument as critically as I can.

[4] It then very often happens that besides this preferred mode of treatment some others merit some attention, especially if it turns out that they tend to modify the conclusion. I set down whatever seems worth noting respecting each. I now go back to my two lists of arguments first set down, which will by this time probably have been augmented and briefly note, in regard to each one, what seems to dispose of it in the way of acceptance or rejection.

[5] Arrived at this point, I put away my notes and pass to something else. But in process of time I shall recur to the original question, probably in a somewhat different form and from a different point of view: and I am always disposed to be sceptical about the value of my former discussion.

[5a] Indeed, what brings me back to the question will commonly be some new light in which I see, or suspect, that there is some consideration whose importance I had not appreciated, and I find myself disposed and encourage the disposition to regard my former discussion as wooden and unintelligent.

[6] I now do the whole thing over again without consulting my former notes of which I do not retain any precise recollection. Having completed this second examination,

[7] I get out my former notes, and critically compare them. Even where they agree there will sometimes be a slight difference which upon careful consideration suggests some doubt. Now it is precisely doubts that I am at this stage endeavoring to develop. Combining the two discussions, I do the best justice I can to the problem and again lay it aside.

[8] After a time, usually a long time, the matter comes up for a third time, and I now invariably find that my ideas have, as it were, become shaken down into a more compacted, connected, and generalized mass. I go over my notes once more, work out to the end any doubts that I am able to resolve, and get a thorough grasp of my own opinions. What is not now indelibly impressed upon my mind I would rather it were disencumbered from.

[9] For now is to begin a long course of cultivation of the conceptions I have thus far gained. This process I continue to perform, for the most part, pen in hand. I draw up my statement afresh, omitting what seems to be of too little worth for preservation. I criticize it in every philosophical aspect which seems to me just.

[10] I endeavor to enlarge it and especially to make it join homogeneously with other results.

[11] In that way statements which I may print and which to readers who take them for momentary inspirations may seem decidedly brilliant are to me who remember what dozens of times they have gone through my mill, are well-known for the monuments of my stupidity that they really are.

(2) from MS 312

You may perhaps gain some useful hints if I describe to you how I go to work in studying philosophy. I shall merely sketch the outline of the proceeding without going into details. I mostly work pen in hand and although important steps are taken while I am away from my writing-table, they are recorded at once.

[1] A given question in philosophy comes up for discussion, never mind how.

[2] I begin by writing out a collation upon it. That is, I begin by setting down briefly yet sufficiently and as formally as possible all the arguments which I have used on the one side or which seem

to me likely to be used on that side; and then I do the same for the other side. Such of the arguments as admit of ready refutation,

[2a] I at once set down the refutations of.

[3] Next, without going into the merits of the case, I draw up a list of the general methods in which a solution of the problem might be sought.

[3a] If some of them appear to be quite futile, I draw up brief formal statements of the reasons of this futility.

[3b] One of the methods will appear to me to be the one which ought to be decisive, and I carefully set down the reason why keeping a good look out for special circumstances which might annul this reason. Other methods may appear to me to have a secondary utility and I further set down the reasons for this and for my estimate of just how far and where those methods are valuable. Search is made for objections to all these reasons, and any that seem considerable are formally set down and refuted.

[3c] But if, in the course of this part of the discussion or at a later stage, it appears that the question in hand depends upon another which I have never submitted to any systematic examination or concerning which, since my last examination of it, any considerable grounds of doubt have been found, I put aside the first examination until this other question shall have been at least provisionally settled in my mind.

[4] If no such interruption takes place, I take up first the principal method and afterwards the subsidiary or secondary methods and apply them with the severest critical scrutiny of which I am master, setting down always brief and formal but sufficient statements of all the steps of the argumentation, and disposing of all objections either by assent or refutation. I also dispose, in the same way, of all the arguments which have not already been disposed of. Having this brief drawn up I study it with the minutest care to detect any loop-holes, and sometimes amend it more or less radically and even giving the question itself a new and broader turn, and this is sometimes done three or four times over, before I am satisfied with the discussion.

[5] I then put the paper away and dismiss the matter from my mind. Sometimes I do so in despair of being able at the time to

obtain any clear light on the subject; for when such light is not at hand my experience is that hard thinking is of very little use. There is nothing to be done but wait until the light comes from some other source. But even when my discussion does seem satisfactory at first, yet my experience of my own stupidity is such that I always mutter to my intellect, "Very well, you have only to possess yourself in patience and the inadequacy of your present ideas will appear plainly enough in due time."

[5a] In fact, after a long time, something or other flashes a new light on the old question, and only too often I find that strenuous as was my scrutiny of the previous arguments, I have committed some horrible stupidity.

[6] At last, my ideas seem ripe for a new setting of them in order; and I make a second collation of the question without looking at the first but endeavoring to proceed quite as if the question were a new one.

[7] This second collation is drawn up just as the first one was; only, when it is complete, I get out the first and compare the two with minute criticism, both where they differ and where they agree.

[8] It may seem to me best to allow the matter to go over for a third collation; but commonly I consider that I am now well started upon the right track; or at any rate all that can be done in this way has been done. I impress the cardinal considerations on my mind, and perhaps draw up a note of anything difficult to bear in mind exactly; and I then look upon all the labor so far performed as a mere exercise of no value, except in the parts which have impressed me.

[9 & 10] It now remains to treat my conception of the problem like a seedling tree, which must have water, nutriment, sunlight, shade, and air and frequent breaking of the ground about it, in order that it may grow into something worthy of respect. These operations I also carry out, pen in hand, with intervals of digestion; and by drawing up new statements at irregular intervals according to the state of my reflections, but probably averaging a year in length, after I have made from half a dozen to a dozen of these, I begin to feel that I have carried the discussion as far as I am likely ever to do. There is no single logical point in the present lectures, for example, however small, which has not undergone at least four such digestions, and most of them a dozen or more.

[11] That, gentlemen, is my way of philosophizing in which I have learned to place much confidence. The expression "swift as thought" ought to gain for you a new meaning as applied to my thought. It becomes equivalent to "agile as a slime-mould." Anybody who knows how I think as I myself do must be impressed by my awful stupidity. But I am fortunately capable of a vast amount of drudgery, and I never lose confidence that I shall ultimately accomplish any intellectual task that I set myself provided I live long enough. In that particular I will pose as a model to young philosophers.

Finally, if Peirce's contention that pragmatism is a "tool" of logic is to be taken seriously, it is imperative that students of his pragmatism study the method by which he examined a topic. While Peirce wrote into his drafts a series of apologies for not giving his "arguments" in full, it is likewise the case that his method of going to work in studying philosophy is a case study in the pragmatic method. Further, it illustrates the orderly habits of a scientist who keeps good records, respects thoroughness and conscientious attention to detail, and organizes his thoughts rigorously and often. His method of working indicates that the same features to which he alluded generally in his first lecture would apply to pragmatism as a "maxim of logic" rather than as a "sublime principle of speculative philosophy." That is, the approximately ten stages of inquiry that he outlined are designed to yield an exact, strictly reasoned intellectual product, a set of conclusions that are as close to a full examination of a topic as is humanly possible.

Some Pedagogical Considerations

Peirce's estimation of the members of his audience was that they were less mature in their intellectual development than he *on every point*. There seems to have been little he could do to improve their knowledge in such a short period. Peirce's somewhat touchy reminder in an advertisement for lecture three—"Those who were unable to attend the second lecture had better procure the MS. of that lecture from Mr. Peirce, 34 Felton Hall, before attending the third lecture"—suggests what is certainly a perennial question in the minds of teachers and scholars: "For whom is intellectual labor performed?" The earlier drafts for each lecture more likely, then, represent Peirce's attempt to justify his own progress on each philosophical issue by recalling the evidence for his "compacting, connecting and generalizing of the mass of analysis" (MS 311) such as he did *regardless* of the audience, for the issue's sake alone. We have the opportunity here not to mistake the result for the reasoning that produced it.

A small but substantial volume of Peirce's writings on the philosophy of education could be compiled.[1] The case could be made that, over a period of years, Peirce found the educational authorities of his time to be deficient in the intellectual demands they made upon their charges as well as upon themselves. Peirce's own education, both formal and informal, at the knee of Benjamin Peirce, was utterly exceptional, then and now.[2] Peirce was certainly aware of his singularity and this qualifies him to judge the rest. The case for his lifelong interest in pedagogy can likewise be made.[3] Peirce's criticisms and suggestions for corrective programs took several forms. The years surrounding 1903 found him writing such pieces as his lectures to the Adirondack Summer School (1905), "Common Sense" (1898) and the various remarks and segments on study and education in these lectures.[4] A remarkably concise pedagogy is expressed in the prologue of MS 303 on "100 lessons in a liberal education" (included here as lecture two: Phenomenology or the Doctrine of Categories; Part A: Mathematics as a Basis of Logic, draft two). By 1905 Peirce concluded that "if I had a class in logic to conduct for a year, I should harp still, as I used to do at the Johns Hopkins, upon the maieutic character of my office,— which means that I should do all I could to make my hearers think for themselves."[5] This "maieutic" character was developed in Peirce's introductory remarks in MS 304:

Certainly, in philosophy what a man does not think out for himself he never understands at all. Nothing can be learned out of books or lectures. They have to be treated not as oracles but simply as facts to be studied like any other facts. That, at any rate, is the way in which I would have you treat my lectures. Call no man master, or at any rate not me.

The common thread in these writings, as illustrated beautifully in manuscripts 303 and 304 and, of course, in the pieces on his method of work (in which he wished to serve "as a model"), is attention to the minutiae of world and intellect as well as a respect for the systematic character of each, and their systematic relations to one another. For Peirce, prematurely reductive insights were anathema, and were one of the few phenomena which, from his earliest days on, could incite him to public pessimism.[6] His passion for the cultivation of intellectual counterparts also seems a likely reason for his producing draft after draft until the exact result he required was accomplished. So, for anyone contemplating a life or even a short stint in the lecture business, the process of thinking through the presentation of an idea to an audience, the draft sequence in MSS 302–306 supplies an excellent portrayal of a lecturer's labors.

LECTURE THREE

The April 9 edition of the *Harvard Crimson* advertised:

THIRD LECTURE BY MR. C. S. PEIRCE

Mr. Charles Sanders Peirce '59 will deliver the third of his series of six public lectures on "Pragmatism as a Principle and Method of Right Thinking" in Sever 11 this evening at 8 o'clock. The subject for tonight is "The Application of the Category to Pragmatism." The lecture will consist almost wholly of a defense of all three categories discussed in the last lecture. These categories, or largest classes into which objects of knowledge can be systematically arranged, are sensation, perception and thought. One or more of these categories are defended by the different schools of metaphysics and Mr. Peirce defends all three. As this third lecture depends greatly upon the second lecture, all who missed the second lecture would do well to get the manuscript of it at 34 Felton Hall before attending the lecture tonight.

The lecture's title appears to have been misprinted by the *Harvard Crimson* and was certainly meant to state, "The Application of the *Categories* to Pragmatism." Peirce's first draft of lecture three (MS 307) was entitled "The Categories continued," which accounts for what is undoubtedly his own insertion into the advertisement of the reminder to "get the manuscript" of the second lecture. He titled the second draft (MS 308), "The Categories Defended," an indication that, by this draft, his focus was clearly intended to be upon an account of the irreducibility of each category to the others, and to the essential character of each category in a comprehensive explanation of thought. He treated the "other systems of metaphysics" peremptorily in this draft, mentioning several which recognize only one or two of the three categories, while in the first draft he offered an extended diatribe against the corruption of logical studies in general. The topic was given its due in the fourth lecture, "The Seven

Systems of Metaphysics." The real value of lecture three resides in (1) the further definition of the categories, conducted through (a) an explanation of their "degenerate" forms, as a means of throwing light upon their genuine forms and (b) a defense of the irreducibility of each category to the others, as a means of throwing light upon the process of knowledge, and (2) the discussion of the analogy of maps to consciousness, a model that has been and should be of enormous use in the study of mind.

The text of lecture three included here is Peirce's second draft, with alternate formulations of passages from his first draft where either the second draft is obscure or the first draft offers additional information omitted from the second draft. The course of each draft is essentially similar, but the second draft includes illustrations and explanations not included in the first. Unlike the second lecture, lecture three develops only one specific topic, the categories as such. However, the audience at the lecture was expected to follow the reason for including a discussion of the categories in the first place: only if a true picture of thinking can be had can the methods and techniques for sharpening thinking, vis-à-vis pragmatism, achieve success.

A General Theory of Modeling Applied to Thought[1]

A major difficulty in accurately portraying thought is that not all thoughts that may be thought are, in fact, consciously thought. It is impossible to experience each and every thought directly, so general inferences about the nature of thought and thinking must be drawn from experiences that represent the whole but are by no means identical with it. These obstacles to the recognition of the patterns and processes of thinking are not unknown to philosophers traditionally, nor would any philosopher in the nineteenth or twentieth century have considered it unusual to discuss thought from the point of view of subjects and restrictions upon subjects. Peirce did so as well. It was extraordinary, in the context of philosophy as it was conducted in 1903, for *objects* to be discussed in the same terms as *subjects*, as he does with his categories.

Peirce designated categories as belonging neither to thought alone nor to "being" alone, but to phenomena. Phenomena are not understood in Kant's way, as distinguished from noumena. A rough definition of phenomena as understood by Peirce is "all apparent things of all apparent manner or kind." Phenomena are inclusive of things (including intangibles) that may be identified and studied. Peirce did not discuss how the characteristics of phenomena revealed by phenomenology are related to one another in this lecture, but rather in lecture five, where he gives a defense of the reality of the categories. Here, he began with the presumption that all phenomena—regardless of the manner in which they present themselves to human apprehension—are enough *alike* in categorical terms that they can be compared with one another with illuminating effect.

Recognition of a set of graduated modes of apprehension was traditional in philosophy but, in Peirce's view, somewhat neglected, as an issue of science, in his age. As a remedy, the manner *and distinctions in manner* in which appearances appear was the object of study of his phenomenology. The specific phenomena that concerned Peirce in these lectures happened not to be physical artifacts, natural or man-made, but thoughts. But in order to describe thoughts as phenomena, subjected to categorical distinctions as such, Peirce must also discuss phenomena in general, which equally include "nonthoughts," equally subjected to categorical distinctions.

In order to explain abstruse phenomena, specifically the elements and the movement of thought, Peirce resorted to a mathematician's device, the model. It would be fair to say that Peirce was one of the first to develop a theory of modeling in general. Peirce's mind ran to mathematical modeling as a result of his formal training and professional experience. For example, when he worked as a cartographer, Peirce tackled the challenges of accurate mapping as a set of mathematical modeling problems. A general theory of modeling, one that does not necessarily include calculation per se, but performs the other functions of models, by similar means, has evolved. The method of mathematical mapping as it is understood by contemporary mathematicians reveals its basic features. A contemporary mathematics text states:

> The development of a mathematical model usually takes four steps: First we observe something in the real world (a ball bearing falling from rest or the trachea contracting during a cough, for example) and construct a system of mathematical variables and relationships that imitate some of its important features. We build a mathematical metaphor for what we see. Next we apply (usually) existing mathematics to the variables and relationships in the model to draw conclusions about the system under study. Finally we check the information against observation to see if the model has predictive value. We also investigate the possibility that the model applies to other systems. The really good models are the ones that lead to conclusions that are consistent with observation, that have predictive value and broad application, and that are not too hard to use.[2]

A later chapter in this text adds that "literally thousands of things in biology, chemistry, economics, engineering, finance, geology, medicine and other fields (the list would fill pages) are modeled and calculated by exactly this process."[3] The process described as "mathematical modeling" is itself a general form of specific modeling, albeit of a limited scope, considering that other, more general, nonmathematical forms are possible.

Peirce availed himself of a further generalization in his method of studying thought by replacing specifically mathematical variables and relationships with general, logical ones. In his article on "Logic" for Baldwin's *Dictionary*, produced in the period directly preceding these lectures, Peirce sketched the role of "mathematical" reasoning in logic. Logic is roughly defined as being occupied with the issue of the classification of arguments. Peirce divided logic into *logica utens*, a reasoner's classification of arguments "antecedent to any systematic study of the subject," and *logica docens*, which "studies the constituent parts of arguments and produces a classification of arguments."[4] This part of logic, which he calls "critic," stands in need of another part:

> It is further generally recognized that another doctrine follows after critic, and which belongs to, or is closely connected with, logic. Precisely what this should contain is not agreed; but it must contain the general conditions requisite for the attainment of truth. Since it may be held to contain more, one hesitates to call it heuristic. It is often called Method; but as this word is also used in the concrete, methodic or methodeutic would be better.
>
> For deciding what is good logic and what bad, appeal is made by different writers to one or more, generally several, of these eight sources: to direct dicta of consciousness, to psychology, to the usages of language, to metaphysical philosophy, to history, to everyday observation, to mathematics, and to some process of dialectic. In the middle ages appeal was frequently made to authority.[5]

A thumbnail sketch of these appeals reappears in the discussion of Sigwart and others in lecture three. Of particular interest is Peirce's explanation of the mathematical appeal. The similarity between his account and the contemporary description of mathematical modeling above is striking:

> In mathematical reasoning there is a sort of observation. For a geometrical diagram or array of algebraical symbols is constructed according to an abstractly stated precept, and between the parts of such [a] diagram or array certain relations are ob-

served to obtain, other than those which were expressed in the precept. These being abstractly stated, and being generalized, so as to apply to every diagram constructed according to the same precept, give the conclusion. Some logicians hold that an equally satisfactory method depends upon a kind of inward observation, which is not mathematical, since it is not diagrammatic, the development of a conception and its inevitable transformation being observed and generalized somewhat as in mathematics; and those logicians base their science upon such a method, which may conveniently be termed, and is sometimes termed, a Dialectic.[6]

Peirce does not use the contemporary term, *model*. But his notion of a "representamen" and his study of diagrammatic thought display the concept of modeling in the contemporary sense. "Representation" is the manifestation of generality, which Peirce calls the category of Thirdness. In his view, not only may models (representamens) be made artificially by human thinkers for specific purposes, but models may be adopted from nature. In its most perfect form, a model expresses both the fixed elements in its source and the relations and development of these elements. In other words, a model potentially embodies both what is observable at some fixed moment by its modeler (creator) and what may be observed even if the modeler has neglected to do so.

The variety of forms available to a modeler is without limit, though the appropriateness of the form to the object being modeled would practically restrict the modeler. A diagram, graph, or picture may provide a model, as may a text. Not only is Peirce's text such a model for his thought, it *is about* the nature of modeling and gives illustrations of modeling throughout. Categorial analysis of the elements of thought is a technique of modeling, and he meant to explain his technique in the lecture. The application of the technique is in need of a further refining tool, pragmatism, described as a "whetstone" in a later lecture. But the rough rules of the technique itself are outlined here.

The Definitions and Value of Degenerate Forms of Thirdness

Peirce's text, or by his definition, any text, is a *symbol*—that is, a representamen—of the pure type.

A symbol is a representamen which fulfills its function regardless of any continuity or analogy with its object and equally regardless of any *factual* connection therewith, but solely and simply because it will be interpreted to be a representamen. Such for example is any general word, sentence, or book. (MS 308)

It is the task of interpretation to determine what precisely such a general word, sentence, or book does represent. The symbol symbolizes, at the very least, what the author of the symbol presumes the symbol represents to a listener or a reader, what the author's thoughts are. No book is an exception to this definition and we must take the author's word for it that his book represents his thought.

Peirce's explanation of the degenerate forms of the categories, especially of Thirdness, laid out the manner in which models function, either as genuine representations or as partial or reduced representations. A point that must be immediately clarified if Peirce's intention concerning the meaning of the "degeneracy" of the categories is to be respected is that he is not claiming that, in a state of degeneracy, thoughts that are representative of some object inadequately represent this object. In fact, it is the particular objects themselves, in some cases, which are incapable of being represented otherwise than by degenerate forms of representation. The objects themselves are degenerate.

Consider, for example, the play *Hamlet*. Shakespeare's text is a *symbol*—that is, a pure representamen of his thought. All parts of the play are "symbolic" in this sense, including the play within a play which Hamlet commissions in Act III. Nonetheless, this play introduces "degenerate" forms of representation, both *indexical* and *iconic*. Peirce defined an icon as a degenerate form of a representamen that "fulfills the function of a representamen by virtue of a character which it possesses in itself and would possess just the same though its object did not exist" (MS 308). His example of an icon is the statue of a centaur. Even if a centaur does not exist, the statue of one has its own shape, dimensions and esthetic value. Any statue, also one of an existing object upon which it was modeled, would be iconic insofar as it has qualities of its own. And so Peirce declared the icon "qualitatively degenerate." The play within *Hamlet* has its own virtues, its own shape and dimensions, even its own title, "The Mousetrap." And while it seems to imitate events that perhaps did happen, as an icon it shows the events that it models *as if* they had certain qualities, whether they in fact had those qualities or not. Even if an actual king had not had poison poured in his ear by his brother while sleeping, the play within the play represents this event to Hamlet and the court audience for whom "The Mousetrap" is produced.

The content of the play indicates its indexical nature. Peirce defined an index as "a representamen which fulfills the function of a representamen by virtue of a character which it could not have if its object did not exist but which it will continue to have just the same whether it be interpreted as a representamen or not" (MS 308). Peirce cited a hygrometer, as an illustration. The hygrometer provides an index of relative humidity by means of a figure that the instrument indicates representing the level of humidity in the area near the instrument, even if one can interpret this level to represent the humidity beyond the immediate vicinity of the hygrometer. A barometer or a thermometer is likewise such an index. Peirce called the index a "reactionally degenerate" form because it is the result of a test or an experiment. The reaction indexed need not be physical, but may be intellectual, emotional, or moral. In *Hamlet*, the play within the play represents the treachery of regicide and fratricide, whether or not it is interpreted to be a reference to the actual regicide and fratricide of the actual king of Denmark. The fact that it is so interpreted in *Hamlet* by members of the court audience is in addition to their recognition of (and reaction to) the treachery of such an act, in general, that the play within the play serves to index.

While Peirce gave examples of degenerate forms of Thirdness which only relate to a single object, it is also possible for a single object to have several degenerate forms at once, as well as a relatively genuine form, as in the case of the play *Hamlet*. The point of discoursing upon the degeneracy of forms is not to catalogue all possible forms, but to show that the degenerate forms of Thirdness are structures of thought which do reflect, and in fact represent, objects of thought. They are worth noting as elements of the model of reasoning upon which pragmatism may be applied. Degenerate forms of representamens are adequate models of phenomena that present degenerate forms of Thirdness. Peirce concluded that a model can be no more adequate than the object on which it is modeled.

The most powerful model Peirce built in this lecture, the map of self-consciousness, is also perhaps the most enigmatic inasmuch as it may be unclear initially what this model serves to represent. The map analogy was introduced to illustrate the notion that "the most degenerate form of Thirdness is where we conceive a mere quality of Feeling, or Firstness, to represent itself to itself as Representation." Peirce believed an example of this form would be "Pure Self-Consciousness, which might be roughly described as a mere feeling that has a dark instinct of being a germ of thought" (MS 308). Technically, the example is intended to show how the most minimal standards of Thirdness are met, as a means of defining Thirdness. The model of self-consciousness that Peirce constructed consists in a symbol, an index, and an icon, but the object upon which it is modeled does not explicitly exhibit such definite signs of either genuine or degenerate Thirdness. It is only in the modeling that this "most degenerate" form is shown to be an instance of Thirdness.

How is consciousness represented to itself? Peirce's stated objective is to demonstrate that the "pure self-consciousness" of certain "philosophers of the past" can be rendered comprehensible. So he produced his model, a representation of his thought (about thought about thought), in the form of an analogy. The map he discussed is, by analogy, a model of self-consciousness. The discussion of the map is also a model of the map, a representation of the imaginary map in the form of Peirce's text. Peirce wanted us to think about the map and what it means. But the persistence of discussions about mapping strategies in this lecture should not be overlooked. Peirce asked his listeners to imagine the map of a region that lies in that region and that represents the region point by point. Such a map would necessarily depict itself in the form of a map that would depict itself and so to infinity. In agreement with Royce, self-consciousness is portrayed as self-representative, and, also agreeing with Royce, infinite.[7] The listener should now understand what it would mean for a phenomenon to "represent itself to itself as Representation." The larger point that the *discussion* of the map makes is more obscure, perhaps, but more important: a representation may be more or less "genuine"—that is *self*-sufficient—but, by definition, it is not *all-sufficient*. In other words, there must be some distinction between an object and its representation, or else the representation is not a representation at all. This clearly is a lesson about modeling. Lest a model be not a model that instructs and elucidates, but a mere duplication of its object (if that were possible), the modeler selects distinctive aspects of the object to put in the model. What might seem to be a shortcoming of a modeler, the "inability" to model exactly, is, in fact, a virtue of modeling. If phenomena, potential objects of thought, exhibit *sets* of characteristics, the modeler of phenomena, the thinker who speaks, writes, or draws, or even simply formulates his own thoughts to himself, *must* survey the sets of characteristics one at a time or in relation to other sets. To survey all simultaneously, Peirce would claim is a job for God or some infinite mind. The very raison d'être of Peirce's categorial analysis is that it is necessary for human beings to slow down and break up experience in order to comprehend it. "Degenerate" forms have their uses after all.

By no means was Peirce rejecting the knowledge that an analysis of degeneracy provides. Because the categories are *universal*—that is, everywhere—no object is an unalloyed case of any one category, but some objects have a predominance of one or another categorial characteristic. A useful way of thinking about the purpose of the degenerate forms of the categories is that they express imperfect rationality, a character present in both objects of thought and in thought about objects of thought. Not all objects are flawlessly or genuinely instances of firsts, seconds, or thirds, and so, in order to comprehend these objects with acuity, it is necessary for thought to take "degenerate" forms as well. This kind of thought is far from being a mistake or an error, but rather is a response to the "degenerate" character of the object it apprehends. Mistakes are always possible as well, but Peirce was not interested in discussing flaws in reasoning in this lecture. Rather, he discussed legitimate *varieties* of mental action available to human thinkers.

LECTURE FOUR

An announcement for a "FOURTH LECTURE BY MR. C. S. PEIRCE" appeared on page 1 of the *Harvard Crimson* on Thursday, 16 April 1903:

Mr. Charles Sanders Peirce '59 will give the fourth of his series of six public lectures on "Pragmatism as a Principle and Method of Right Thinking" in Sever 11 this evening at 8 o'clock. His subject will be "The Seven Systems of Metaphysics."

The six systems of metaphysics that cannot account for all three categories were again given the briefest of treatments. The additional information that Peirce provided, however, is valuable. He accounted for the differences between the styles of metaphysics in terms of their positive treatments of the categories of their choice and their negative attitudes to the other categories. The seventh system, which acknowledges the reality of all three categories, includes a number of subdivisions. Peirce chose to account for one such subdivision of the seventh system, his own. His doctrine of the reality of each of the three categories is the real topic of this lecture.

Peirce considered his defense of the reality of Thirdness the most important piece of this lecture, that of the reality of Firstness the next in significance, and then that of the reality of Secondness. Approximately ninety years later, his ranking still seems to reflect what is most needed.

The Reality of Thirdness:
A Condition for the Possibility of Science

Peirce introduced the first line of his defense of the reality of Thirdness with the hypothesis that there is a principle or cause operative in nature that accounts for the regularity of natural events. As Peirce described individual events that adhere to a law of nature, the brute fact or compulsory nature of these events is ipso facto real. However, their Sec-

59

ondness—that is, their reactionary character (for example, in the reaction of an object to being let go in a gravitational field)—is melded somehow to a *rule* or general proposition that "all solid bodies fall in the absence of any upward force or pressure." The confidence that the general proposition is a proper basis for predicting events requires an account. Now either, said Peirce, regular events occur as a matter of chance alone, or there is a reason, a cause of the regularity of those events said to be lawful. Peirce dismissed the rationality of the hypothesis of chance.

But his dismissal was not summary. Just as Hegel's refutation of phrenology (consisting of a blow to the head of the phrenologist) made obvious the ludicrous character of the demand for a discursive argument against phrenology, Peirce's own appeal to the "experiment" of dropping a stone drove his point home with a joke. If the phrenologist takes his art seriously, a blow to the head is an appropriate response. And to anyone who would flirt with not taking seriously the reality of the law of nature regarding falling objects, a joke "demonstration" of the rock that is dropped is the most appropriate rejoinder.

The serious background of Peirce's proposed demonstration is his notion of science. Some of its features are recognizable by the light of contemporary standards. In putting forward the following set of hypotheses for comparison, Peirce held that the one contradicts the other; both cannot be acceptable simultaneously and, if one is true, the other is not true:

> 1st, the uniformity with which those stones have fallen has been due to mere chance and affords no ground whatever, not the slightest, for any expectation that the next stone that shall be let go will fall; or

> 2nd, the uniformity with which stones have fallen has been due to *some active general principle,* in which case it would be a strange coincidence that it should cease to act at the moment my prediction was based upon it. (MS 309)

Furthermore, Peirce insisted upon the possibility of holding an experiment that would support a prediction based upon the second hypothesis, since it is an experiment that could conceivably falsify the hypothesis. There is, in fact, no experiment that could falsify the first hypothesis. It is unfalsifiable because not only would a proponent of the first hypothesis deny that the uniformity of the behavior of falling stones is due to a principle, but that *any* uniformity can be due to any principle. So the evident regularity and likewise the possible randomness of certain events are, under the first hypothesis, attributed to "chance." Thereby no event at all is able to provide a falsifying instance to the "rule" of the first hypothesis. It is an unscientific hypothesis, which is why Peirce claimed that no reasonable person would accept it.

There is no conceivable proof of the "chance" hypothesis whereas proofs of the "law" hypothesis abound and can be conducted with relative ease in the course of the observation of natural events.

An additional point that Peirce made in an alternative draft deserves some analysis:

> The Physicist prides himself on being a Specialist. He would not have it supposed that he busies himself with a *Weltanschauung*, not even a general conception of the physical universe. He is experimenting upon a certain phenomenon and confines himself to making out the relation of that phenomenon to phenomena that are well known. The consequence of this is that when time comes to enunciate any very general principle,—such as that of the Conservation of Energy,—you find there are a dozen physicists who have been long convinced of it, but probably thought it derogatory to say so,—or their Academy or Poggendorf refused to publish their memoir,—and very likely it will turn out that the earliest discoverable enunciation of it belonged to some obscure person outside the ranks of the professional physicists. That is probably less true today than it was fifty years ago. At any rate, it certainly ought to be the duty of some class of physicists to study the general question. (MS 309)

Here a subtle point is made about the classification of the sciences: there ought to be a scientific study of the general features of the world in which scientists operate made from the point of view of science. Why should it be a *physicist* who makes a study of the "general question" of Weltanschauung? It is partially because, even though physicists do not self-consciously attempt to derive a "general conception of the physical universe," they nonetheless operate under one, a picture of the world analogous to a *logica utens*, that makes it possible for them to conduct science as a meaningful human endeavor. That is, physicists do have a conception of the universe such that, presumably, their own experiments and thoughts are not futile and empty. Primarily, especially in Peirce's view, the physicist is an experimentalist, implying that there is a point in doing experiments, that they have some bearing on whether a general hypothesis, for which an experiment is a test, is true or not. If someone were seriously to believe the first hypothesis, that "the uniformity with which those stones have fallen has been due to mere chance and affords no ground whatever, not the slightest, for any expectation that the next stone that shall be let go will fall," as well as believing the general hypothesis of which this hypothesis is an application, that any apparent uniformity is due to chance, then there would be no worthwhile inquiry possible.

The condition for the possibility of conducting science is that hypotheses like the second hypothesis be adopted, as well as the general hypothesis from which it is a derivation, virtually a physicist's Weltanschauung, that uniformities in nature may be attributed to "some active general principle."

The Reality of Firstness and Secondness:
The Universe as an Argument

Defending the reality of Firstness, Peirce offered this observation:

[The] different metaphysical conceptions of the younger physicists do not differ from that of the older physicists in respect to making Qualities to be mere illusions. But when one considers the matter from a *logical* point of view the notion that qualities are illusions and play no part in the real universe shows itself to be a peculiarly *unfounded* opinion. (MS 309)

The question one ought to consider, when deciding whether some experience is an illusion or not, seems to be whether the experience could have gone some other way, not whether the experience should not have gone on at all, a question more in line with the consideration of some experience as a *delusion*. Peirce responded both to the conception that qualities are mere illusions and that they are mere delusions.

That an experience of a quality, a percept, might have occurred some other way than it did is in no way under the control of a perceiver. There may be some control of this experience, but it would be in the hands of the source of the perception. Peirce recognized two grades of the experience of Firstness, viz., the perception and the perceptual judgment. Neither one, he believed, is controllable (that is, under the self-control of a person), and so neither one can be deemed to be "good" or "bad." Perceptions and perceptual judgments are *like* inferences insofar as they are determinations from premises. The premisses of perceptions are the Firstnesses in nature. The premisses of perceptual judgments are perceptions.

Firstness is a reality that consists in its uncontrollable *presence* and its effect upon consciousness. Firstness is a phenomenon without which other reasonings would be impossible.

Peirce presented an anthropomorphic argument that no other possibility than that Firstness must be real will satisfy human thought. He appealed to a cosmology that holds that humans are made of the same stuff as the rest of the universe, so it is to be expected that their thoughts operate on lines sympathetic to the common substances, and their rise and run in the universe. Just as human inference must have a set of premises upon which to draw, as in explicit reasonings of a deductive kind, previous inferences *whose "premisses" are existent qualities* must exist for percepts to come about. Percepts and perceptual judgments in thought are like conclusions drawn from Firstnesses (qualities) in nature.

Peirce's idea that the universe is an argument led him to suppose interpretations from both logical and religious points of view. His religious defense of the reality of Firstness is his hypothesis that the mind of God generated an orderly pattern of relations whose grounds and developments may be observed by humans. The role Firstnesses play in the "economy of the universe" is as a set of phenomena whose reality is required if the universe is to be considered meaningful.

The logical interpretation of the claim that the universe is an argument is more unusual. Peirce understood any phenomena to be "evidence" or premises, with other phenomena as conclusions, even though they are not *claims* in the form of *propositions*, formally articulated as constituents of what would conventionally be viewed as "arguments." The trouble Peirce took, in lecture three, to define a "symbol" as the relatively genuine form of a Thirdness or a representation serves a new purpose in his defense of the reality of Firstness. He determined that syllogisms are "symbols" of the arguments presented by phenomena. That is, we identify the arguments in nature as we conceive them, by means of symbols, such as propositions. The beings and relations represented are other arguments, in nature, not in fact *identical* to the symbols used to represent them. The premisses of these arguments are, in some cases, real Firstnesses.

The defense of the reality of Secondness is faced with the objection that only feelings and the law of the succession of feelings are real—that is, given that feelings are real—the succession of feeling upon feeling that occurs in human experience is determined by a law internal to the feelings themselves. Peirce's introduction of the phenomenon of surprise was designed to illustrate that feelings are not merely determined by previous feelings, but by other elements of experience. That is, a feeling may be a reaction, a Second, to a feeling, a First. His demonstration proves that it is absurd to think of a feeling of surprise as the result of an inference. If one experiences surprise, it is most decidedly not because one has already determined that the object of surprise is a unique occurrence and *therefore* surprising.

The truth about being surprised is that one expects one thing and gets another. What causes the initial shock that constitutes a feeling of surprise is that, whatever the unique occurrence happens to be, it *is not* a certain something that was expected. A surprise is recognized because of its negation of what one had expected. One determines what it is that is surprising after the fact of being surprised, not in order to be surprised. A surprise is truly reactive and indicates a Secondness, irreducible to either a Firstness or a Thirdness.

Again, the proof of the *reality* of a category is that a class of phenomena (e.g., a class of phenomena in the realm of consciousness) cannot be identified in any other manner than as an instance of that category. The illustration of the phenomenon of "surprise" is meant to be a model of an experience of Secondness; and an experience of Secondness, it should be recalled, is a model of a really existent Secondness. If *nature*'s pedagogy is practical jokes, it is clear that Secondness, too, plays a role in the "economy of the universe." Experiences teach *us* something. Specifically, "surprises" can teach us a great deal, especially about any misconceptions we might have about relations. The growth of the universe itself is also fed by surprises. Elsewhere, Peirce has remarked that the reasonableness of the universe is unfinished and that it must be undergoing a continuous growth from nonexistence to existence (CP 1.175). He was a proponent of a general evolutionary theory, which included nonbiological elements of existence as well.[1] Surprise and chance play creative roles in the production of radical novelty in the natural universe.

LECTURE FIVE

On Thursday, April 30, Peirce's *Harvard Crimson* advertisement showed what he intended to discuss:

> Normative sciences which are generally considered to be logic, ethics, and aesthetics. From an explanation of the relation of these three, Mr. Peirce will proceed to a discussion of "truth" and that which we imply by the "meaning" of anything.

This lecture fits with the plan suggested by the first lecture, to trace the definition of pragmatism by elucidating its role in logic and its place in an architecture of theories. But the problem of pragmatism is such that its solution requires a more precise conception of the endeavor of philosophy itself. Peirce had not overlooked the possibility of applying the results of his phenomenology to the problem of pragmatism—that is, using the categories as a means of examining the phenomenon of philosophy and in turn pragmatism.

The Proper Division of Philosophy

In the second of his three drafts of this lecture, Peirce elaborated on the tasks of philosophy, on the basis of an application of his three categories:

> I have explained that by Philosophy I mean that department of Positive Science, or Science of Fact, which does not yet busy itself to gather facts, but merely takes these that are already in undoubted possession of us all and learns what it can from them.

> The first task of Philosophy is to examine the universal phenomenon and make out what its elements are. This study I call Phenomenology after Hegel. I have endeavored to present to your apprehensions a series of Three such Elements forming a com-

plete list in its way and according to my experience of the study of philosophy the most important system of universal Categories or Elements of the Phenomenon. And these three were recognized, though somewhat imperfectly, by Hegel, and indeed have, in imperfect ways, been recognized since man was man, and long before.

Phenomenology may be said to be the study of the Phenomenon in its Firstness, that is, as it immediately presents itself.

The second task of Philosophy might be expected to be the study of the Phenomenon in its Secondness, that is, in so far we can act upon it and it upon us. This I take to be the task of the Normative Sciences.

The third and final task of Philosophy, which will not fall within the scope of these lectures, ought, according to the same formula, to be the study of the Phenomenon in its Thirdness, that is to say, in the process by which it is evolved; and that I understand to represent Metaphysics. (MS 311)

And thus he proposed to examine normative science according to the definition that "normative science treats of the laws of the relation of phenomena to ends, that is, it treats of Phenomena in their Secondness" (MS 312). He set out the course of his analysis in this manner:

I propose to begin this lecture with some remarks upon the nature of Normative Science in general, and then to go on to explain successively what Esthetics, Ethics, and Logic are. I shall then glance at the different divisions of Logic in order to show just where the problem of pragmatism comes in. We shall then be able to see what that problem is and to enter upon the resolution of it. (MS 311)

Beginning with a general remark, he then further defined his conception of normative science:

Normative science ought to examine all questions relating to the possible consistent ends of phenomena. Not merely what the ends are and what are the conditions of conformity to those ends, or their mere quantity of goodness and badness, but also, the diversity in the different paths by which such ends may be pursued, and the different stadia in those paths; as well as the different ways in which the ends may be missed. I will not pretend that this description is all that might be desired. On the contrary, here is one of the innumerable points at which my doctrine is not sufficiently worked out. (MS 311)

Indeed, Peirce had not forgotten that phenomenology rests upon mathematical sciences and it is likely that his motivation to give an additional lecture solely on the topic of multitude and continuity was strengthened at this point. In the first draft of lecture five, he said as much, marking the fact that he planned to put aside these particular mathematical matters for the remaining scheduled lectures:

> I will now repeat the offer I made at the last lecture. If the philosophical students can, with the assent of those who govern philosophical studies, find the time to listen to two lectures or even to one concerning the logic of multitude and continuity I should be happy to give them. (MS 310)

The Foundation of the Normative Sciences in Esthetics

It is generally admitted that Peirce devoted little of his philosophical energies to the development of an esthetic philosophy and, by his own account, this is confirmed:

> The first year of my own serious study of philosophy, in 1856, forty-seven years ago was devoted to esthetics. My good angel must have prompted me to take up first that branch of philosophy which ought immediately to follow the study of the categories, and to study it in a German book which though it was too old to be sensibly influenced by Hegel was nevertheless one of those books in which the three categories in an almost unrecognizable disguise, played a great part. It was Schiller's *Ästhetische Briefe*,—a very good book for an infant philosopher.[1]

> After that I pressed to Logic and to the analytic part of the Critic of Pure Reason, and I am sorry to confess that I have entirely neglected esthetics; so that, though I am now obliged to say a few words about it, I am constrained to preface them with the acknowledgment of my incompetence. (MS 310)[2]

However, in the years immediately preceding his efforts to complete his account of logic, he was pressed into some further reflection upon esthetics, albeit in its role as a normative science beside ethics and logic.

Shortly before his lectures on pragmatism in 1903, Peirce confessed to William James in a letter dated 25 November 1902 that, as late as 1898, he was only dimly aware of the relationship of esthetics to ethics and logic, and of the significance of esthetics for pragmatism:

> My own view in 1877 was crude. Even when I gave my Cambridge lectures I had not really got to the bottom of it or seen the unity of the whole thing.[3] It was not until after that that I obtained the proof that logic must be founded on ethics, of which it is a higher development. Even then, I was for some time so stupid as not to see that ethics rests in the same manner on a foundation of esthetics—by which, it is needless to say, I don't mean milk and water and sugar.
>
> These three normative sciences correspond to my three categories, which in their psychological aspect, appear as Feeling, Reaction, Thought. I have advanced my understanding of these categories much since Cambridge days; and can now put them in a much clearer light and more convincingly. The true nature of pragmatism cannot be understood without them. It does not, as I seem to have thought at first, take Reaction as the be-all, but it takes the end-all as the be-all, and the End is something that gives its sanction to action. It is of the third category. Only one must not take a nominalistic view of thought as if it were something that a man had in his consciousness. Consciousness may mean any one of the three categories. But if it is to mean thought it is more without us than within. It is we that are in it, rather than it in any of us. Of course I can't explain myself in a few words, but I think it would do the psychologists a great service to explain to them my conception of the nature of thought. (HL)

While we have no explicitly rendered system of esthetics from Peirce, it is nonetheless possible to discover and articulate his *esthetica utens*, analogous to a *logica utens*. It should be recalled that Peirce allowed two means for measuring the goodness or badness, and then the strength, of good arguments:

> In all reasoning . . . there is a more or less conscious reference to a general method, implying some commencement of such a clas-

sification of arguments as the logician attempts. Such a classification of arguments, antecedent to any systematic study of the subject, is called the reasoner's *logica utens*, in contradistinction to the result of the scientific study, which is called *logica docens*.[4]

It ought to be possible to divide the means by which one makes esthetic judgments likewise into informal and formal methods. Schiller's *Äs-thetische Briefe* or Kant's *Critique of Judgment* would be considered articulations of formal systems. Peirce's criteria for esthetic judgment, though faintly sketched, nonetheless also point to a system of classification.

A few brief statements delineate Peirce's notion of esthetic. First, he expressed doubt that "there is any such quality" as "esthetic badness." He took exception to the claim *de gustibus non est disputandum* as it is interpreted by most people, that "there is no valid standard of taste, and nothing per se beautiful." No one disputes that the sun is bright and hot because the reality of radiant energy is, too, indisputable. It is self-evident, and so may be the reality of beauty. Preference for one or another object in consequence of a conviction that it is beautiful or not is a matter not of esthetic judgment. Repugnance, for example, is the result of being *distracted* from a purely esthetic judgment "by consideration of the *unsuitability* of the object for some purpose." Thus, "if one abstracts from moral considerations a clever thief or a naughty woman may be a very pretty spectacle" (MS 310). The doctrine of the influence of an educated sensibility upon esthetic judgments is one Peirce probably found in Schiller. In *esthetica utens* fashion, he gave his own conclusions:

> In short I am inclined in my esthetic judgments to think as the true Kentuckian about whiskey: *possibly* some may be better than others, but all are esthetically good. (MS 310)

and, furthermore, he said:

> As a matter of opinion, I believe that Glory shines out in everything like the sun and that any esthetic odiousness is merely our Unfeelingness resulting from obscurations due to our own moral and intellectual aberration. (MS 310)

Were it not for the possibility, added to those of attraction and repugnance, of *indifference* of feeling toward an object, it might appear that Peirce was embracing an unmitigated hedonism. However his comments seem to suggest otherwise. It would be a mistake to confuse esthetic approbation with pleasure as such. Esthetic goodness lies not in the power to give enjoyment, but in the evocation of a unified experience of feeling, regardless of the particular quality of that feeling. Peirce elaborated on this:

> In the light of the doctrine of categories I should say that an object, to be esthetically good, must have a multitude of parts so related to one another as to impart a positive simple immediate quality to their totality; and whatever does this is, in so far, esthetically good, no matter what the particular quality of the total may be. If that quality be such as to nauseate us, to scare us, or otherwise to disturb us to the point of throwing us out of the mood of esthetic enjoyment, out of the mood of simply contemplating the embodiment of the quality,—just, for example, as the Alps affected the people of old times, when the state of civilization was such that an impression of great power was inseparably associated with lively apprehension and terror,—then the object remains nonetheless esthetically good, although people in our condition are incapacitated from a calm esthetic contemplation of it. (MS 312)

By Peirce's definition, it is possible to be terrified of something beautiful as well as fascinated by it. The relativity of one's response is to be expected, on the basis of the moral training of one's sensibility. Perhaps the only nonbeautiful objects possible, then, are objects that universally evoke no response of feeling whatsoever, a condition that is barely conceivable. Moreover, Peirce maintained, an alteration in the intensity with which "the quality of the whole" is conveyed, cannot alter the esthetic goodness of an object:

> If it be correct, it will follow that there is no such thing as positive esthetic badness; and since by goodness we chiefly in this discussion mean merely the absence of badness, or faultlessness, there will be no such thing as esthetic goodness. All there will be will be various esthetic qualities, that is simple qualities of totalities not capable of full embodiment in the parts, which qualities may be more decided and strong in one case than in another. But the very reduction of the intensity may be an esthetic quality; nay, it *will* be so; and I am seriously inclined to doubt there being any distinction of pure esthetic betterness and worseness. My notion would be that there are innumerable varieties of esthetic quality, but no purely esthetic grade of excellence. (MS 312)

It should be clear why Peirce claimed that esthetics is a normative science that serves as a foundation for ethics. Given the general findings of phenomenology (that is, the reality of the three categories), after the first task of philosophy, that is, the study of the phenomenon "as it immediately presents itself," the second task of philosophy is to determine the facts concerning how we act upon phenomena and how these phenomena act upon us—that is, *reaction*, the Secondness of phenomena. This office falls to normative science, whose first charge is to make out the determinations of things whose ends are defined in terms of *quality* or feeling. Part of Peirce's conception of the esthetic as foundational is that, in an architectonic division of labor, esthetic performs a role that is indispensable for the whole project of normative science. Peirce put this division in these terms:

> Supposing, however, that normative science divides into esthetics, ethics, and logic, then it is easily perceived, from any standpoint, that this division is governed by the three categories. For normative science in general being the science of the laws of conformity of things to ends, esthetics considers those things whose ends are to embody qualities of feeling, ethics those things whose ends lie in action, and logic those things whose end is to represent something. (MS 312)

Even if esthetic is related in this manner to the whole of normative science, there is still the problem of discovering why it might be claimed that the foundation of ethics lies in esthetics.

It is fairly easy to determine, at this stage, why Peirce considered logic to have its proximate foundation in ethics. "Ethics is the study of what ends of action we are deliberately prepared to adopt" (MS 312). Ethics is the study of deliberate—that is, self-controlled—that is, reasonable—actions, of which thought is a species. Thus, logic is the study of a kind of self-controlled action, specifically reasoning. "Ethics," claimed Peirce, "the genuine ethics, as contradistinguished from that branch of anthropology which in our day often passes under the name of ethics,—this genuine ethics is the normative science *par excellence* because an *end*, the essential object of normative science, is germane to a voluntary act in a primary way in which is it germane to nothing else" (MS 312). For this reason, Peirce at first doubted that esthetics could be a true normative science, and it becomes doubtful that ethics has its ground in esthetics, which is not specifically the study only of *self-controlled* feelings.

Peirce's justification of the primacy of esthetics in relation to ethics in the normative sciences is somewhat perplexing. He offered this explanation:

> On the other hand, an ultimate end of action *deliberately* adopted,—that is to say, *reasonably* adopted,—must be a state of

things that *reasonably recommends itself in itself*, aside from any ulterior consideration. It must be an *admirable ideal*, having the only kind of goodness that such an ideal *can* have, namely, esthetic goodness. From this point of view, the morally good appears as a particular species of the esthetically good. (MS 312)

A plausible explanation of his account might be the following: It is always possible to ask why some end is deliberately adopted, either in action or thought; in this case, specifically in action. In thought, Peirce argued that it is always the case that arguments find their conclusions as a result of either an implicit (*logica utens*) or explicit (*logica docens*) classification—that is, by analogy with a standard type of argument that has an analogous form. Why choose a conclusion? Because one wishes to conform to a pattern of reasoning in accordance with which one would choose some such conclusion. Likewise, in ethics, self-controlled conduct follows a similar pattern. Some plan of action must reasonably recommend itself in order for a moral choice to be considered deliberate and thereby a matter of ethics. Upon what basis are actions reasonable? They are admirable per se. But how they come to be *admirable*, certainly a term that belongs to the nomenclature of esthetic, is a matter of feeling, first and foremost.

While it would seem that the human condition is left in a precarious—if not an utterly dangerous position—by having moral decisions rest upon feeling, two justifications suggest themselves for Peirce's claims. First, according to the definition of the role of the normative sciences, it is neither reprehensible nor inappropriate to study the influence of esthetic notions of the admirable upon ethics. Peirce discussed this in his second draft:

> Another very common misconception of the normative sciences is that their sole function is to expound the distinction between bad and good, as it is deliberately accepted, *esthetics* in respect to mere appearance in itself regardless of all ulterior considerations, *ethics* in respect to the ultimate aim of action, *logic* in respect to representations, especially symbols, and still more especially in their relation to their objects. But this is too narrow a conception of the problem of normative science, which tends to give it too exclusive a relation to practice. (MS 311)

The fact is, Peirce insisted, "the Normative Sciences proper are not studies conducted with any eye to the production of practical effects." Instead, he concluded, their "ultimate end" is merely but appropriately the "right understanding of the matter to which they relate" (MS 312). Practice is not the focus of the normative sciences but of the applied arts. What normative science "ought to examine," in accordance with its philosophical function, is the problem of the "possible" not the actually existent ends of phenomena.

Also, Peirce might have admitted that the education of the sensibilities is possible, in the manner of Schiller's doctrine of esthetic education, since the relation between the esthetic, the ethical and the logical is not merely a bottom-up or a top-down affair. Specifically, feeling is not a one-sidedly mechanical reaction to the stimulus of some object, but is malleable and therefore educable.

The Role of Ethics in the Determination of Ultimate Aims

Peirce next considered the problem of ethical goodness. Once an esthetic ideal is proposed as an ultimate end of action, it remains to be determined whether that end is possible. Peirce's criticism of Kant's categorical imperative was dazzling insofar as he not only rejected it as "an eternal pronouncement," as he believed Kant would have it, but also rejected all previous attempts to criticize it. He entertained it provisionally as one of the possible modes of ultimate aims. Kant's imperative qualifies as a good aim, not because it is irrefutable and cannot be disregarded, but *because* it can be denied. Were it not possible to deny the "voice of conscience," in regard to some esthetic ideal one has proposed to adopt for oneself, then there would be no deliberateness in the adoption of the "imperative." And ethical goodness consists in the deliberate, rational, self-controlled adoption of an aim. Peirce concluded:

> An aim which cannot be adopted and consistently pursued is a bad aim. It cannot properly be called an ultimate aim at all. The only moral evil is not to have an ultimate aim. (MS 312)

The problem of ethics then is to "ascertain what end is possible."

Special sciences, including psychology, cannot offer any suggestions here. Elsewhere, Peirce denied in general terms that the special sciences can in any way provide the foundation for the normative sciences:

> The facts that men for the most part show a natural disposition to approve nearly the same arguments that logic approves, nearly the same acts that ethics approves, and nearly the same works of art that esthetics approves, may be regarded as tending to support the

conclusions of logic, ethics, and esthetics. But such support is perfectly insignificant; and when it comes to a particular case, to urge that anything is sound and good logically, morally, or esthetically, for no better reason than that men have a natural tendency to think so, I care not how strong and imperious that tendency may be, is as pernicious a fallacy as ever was. (MS 312)

Here, too, the reason is plain. The "problem of ethics," Peirce said, "is to ascertain what end is possible." He continued:

It might be thoughtlessly supposed that *special science* could aid in this ascertainment. But that would rest on a misconception of the nature of an absolute aim, which is what *would* be pursued under all possible circumstances,—that is even although the contingent facts ascertained by special sciences were entirely different from what they are. (MS 312)

The answer lies in considering what an ultimate aim, "capable of being pursued in an indefinitely prolonged course of action, can be." Appropriately for this lecture, we learn about the task of ethics. Unfortunately, Peirce only provided a few hints about how this task could be accomplished.

An ultimate aim, to be ascertained by ethics, Peirce declared, must not only "accord with a free development of the agent's own esthetic quality," but "it is requisite that it should not ultimately tend to be disturbed by the reactions upon the agent of that outward world which is supposed in the very idea of action" (MS 312). Whether it is even possible to meet these two conditions is a metaphysical, not a normative, issue. These conditions, however, provide a test of possible aims when ethics is conceived as "the study of what ends of action we are deliberately prepared to adopt." It should be obvious that any number of ends would be impossible to adopt since they would not meet these two conditions. For example, if someone proposes, as an esthetic ideal, being in the condition of extreme excitement at all times, and is willing to pursue that end by relentlessly taking risks, he should recognize that the outward world—that is, his own body or laws regarding his activities—may interfere with that pursuit. Or, should one adopt no ideal deliberately, but receive no interference at all from the outer world, it cannot then be claimed that an ethical goodness is achieved. Of course, the task of ethics is to delineate the possibilities of ends and such impossible ends are everywhere.

The Good of Logic

Peirce devoted the remainder of lecture five to the definition of logical goodness. A point that is more comprehensively made in the next lecture appears here first. Peirce noted that, in the matter of "logical goodness or *truth*," the texts in logic tend to be faulty. He proposed to correct them. These texts pronounce a distinction between "*logical truth*," which some of them rightly confine to arguments that do not promise more than they perform, and *material truth* which belongs to propositions." It is said, in these texts, that material truth, because it is what veracity aims to be, is a "higher grade of truth than mere logical truth." Peirce would not admit this last claim and offered this correction:

> In the first place, all our knowledge rests upon perceptual judgments. These are necessarily veracious. . . . Now consider any other judgment I may make. That is a conclusion of inferences ultimately based on perceptual judgments, and since these are indisputable all the truth which my judgment can have must consist in the logical correctness of those inferences. . . . To say that a proposition is certainly true means simply that it never can be found out to be false, or in other words that it is derived by logically correct arguments from veracious judgments. Consequently, the only difference between material truth and the logical correctness of argumentation is that the *latter* refers to a single line of argument and the *former* to all the arguments which could have a given proposition or its denial as their conclusion. . . . It appears, then, that logical goodness is simply the excellence of arguments. (MS 312)

The logically more "fundamental goodness" of an argument is its "soundness and weight," that is, "its really having the force that it pretends to have and that force being great." Peirce then entered into an analysis of what constitutes the "soundness" of an argument. He started with the identification of the "three radically different kinds of arguments," viz., abduction, induction and deduction. These forms of argument continued to be prime topics in the rest of the lectures.

LECTURE SIX

Peirce, in his first draft of this lecture, put his explanation and proof of pragmatism in the light of its place within the philosophical sciences:

> The question before us throughout this whole course of lectures has been what is the *meaning* of a philosophical conception in general,—what the *ultimate* meaning of it consists in. In order that we might have some assurance of not having overlooked any important element of the problem, I thought I ought to insist upon a somewhat systematic review of the different elements of all phenomena, their relations to normative science, and in particular to symbols. We at length come down to the specific question, What is the *ultimate* meaning of a symbol? (MS 313)

The title, listed in the *Harvard Crimson* for Thursday, May 7, advertised his intent:

MR. PEIRCE'S LAST LECTURE

Mr. Charles Sanders Peirce '59 will deliver the last of his series of six public lectures on "Pragmatism as a Principle and Method of Right Thinking," under the auspices of the Department of Philosophy in Sever 11, this evening at 8 o'clock. His lecture will be on "The Nature of Meaning," and will be open to the public.

The first draft (MS 313) is similar in the line of argument and basic content of sections I and II of the second draft (MS 314 and MS 316 together). The second draft compressed sections I and II of the first draft and added a third and a fourth section. Even so, Peirce wrote, on the title page of the second draft, "first 35 pages as delivered," indicating that the rest of the lecture was *not* delivered in the form it was written. Sections III and IV of the second draft deal more directly with pragmatism than any of the other lectures after lecture one. Given that the lecture on the stated topic of the series had finally arrived in full force, it might have been inevitable that yet another lecture would be needed.

Generality in Perceptual Judgments

Section I in both draft versions is concerned with one major point: perceptual judgments, like all judgments, "involve" generality. This is a complex matter, since, depending upon one's training in logic, the greater objection might be either to the claim that *all* judgments involve generality, or to the claim that perceptual judgments involve generality. Insofar as Peirce's analysis treated the generality of all predicates, the number or kind of the subjects of judgments is irrelevant. The special attribute of a *particular* proposition is that it "asserts that some thing, reacting in the universe, something said to be designatable, but not designated, has certain general characters." A *universal* proposition, on the other hand, is one that "[asserts that] any object there may be of a certain general description will have a certain character" (MS 313). As for singular propositions, Peirce did not believe that they were, in fact, general propositions, but that a general proposition could be deduced from a singular one. Even the most apparently stubborn exceptions to this rule, in the instances where the predicate appears to be singular as well as the subject, can be found to involve generality. For example, Peirce acknowledged that the proposition "Tully is Cicero" means that the one and only Tully is the one and only Cicero. To dispute such a meaning would be absurd. But the logic of relations also enables us to recognize that the *general* concept of identity is the backbone of the meaning of the proposition.

Likewise, in a perceptual judgment, much more than a single sense experience is asserted of a singular subject. If one states that "the front door on my house is white," not only is the sensible attribute of whiteness ascribed specifically to my front door, its association with a general category of objects, "white things," is also asserted. This brief explication should have been enough to support Peirce's conclusion that "Thirdness pours in upon us through every avenue of sense" (MS 314).

Nonetheless, Peirce must have sounded out his audience in previous sessions, and was concerned with meeting a possible further objection. On the side of "Bishop Berkeley or Hobbes"—and the student of the history of philosophy will certainly recognize this side to be a part of Hume's view as well—it might be argued that it is inconsistent to claim that generality is involved in propositions that refer to single reacting objects. The problem Peirce noted issues from special cases. In asserting the perceptual judgment that event A is previous to event B, a universal rule is also asserted, that A bears a certain relation, u, to B:

> To say that A is previous to B means not only that A is in the relation u to B but *also* that A is in the relation u to everything there may be to which B is in this same relation. So then to assert previousness is to assert two general rules, first, that nothing whatever is u to itself, and second, that there is nothing whatever to which B is u but to which A is not u. (MS 313)

Thus it is not inconsistent for "reacting single events" to involve generality. Indeed, Peirce smartly remarked that in order even to make use of language, one needs to be aware of some general conceptions of logic, and the use of language implies the apprehension of these general conceptions.

And though mere previousness does not involve continuity or infinity, the perceptual judgment of the appearance of an uninterrupted flow of time is unavoidable. The mere claim that the assertion of previousness asserts two general rules in regard to events A and B in their relation, u, is unobjectionable compared to the claim that perception of many "previousnesses" leads to the perceptual judgment of an uninterrupted flow of time. Ultimately, Peirce concluded that there is no advantage in asserting that time consists of a series of fixed states that have no intrinsic relation to one another. For such an assertion leaves the ineradicable impression that such events are ultimately inexplicable. When Peirce wrote to James that he found the problem of Achilles and the tortoise to be, at heart, not a problem at all, but wished to give a talk on the topic, no doubt he meant to develop his ideas further on this section, which he ultimately dropped from lecture six.

Logical Goodness and Logical Soundness

Section II returns to the issue, outlined in lecture five, of the definition of logical goodness. Logical "soundness" is a term Peirce used to denote logical goodness, which he demonstrated in lecture five to be an attribute of argumentation or inference. "Soundness" should not be taken here in its narrower, contemporary definition: the condition of a valid deductive argument having true, not false, premises.

Soundness is goodness in a number of forms, depending upon the class of argument. The goodness, in the sense of the correctness of an argumentation, of a deducton differs from that of an induction and likewise from that of an abduction. For Peirce, soundness encompassed formal correctness as well as truth. But the "truth" of a fact, determined by an argument and stated in its conclusion, for example, is not judged, or able to be judged, by a "dictum of direct consciousness"—that is, by any psychological inclination. As he did in "The Fixation of Belief," Peirce emphasized that facts can be experienced by individuals, but individuals are not the final arbiters of what is or is not a fact. There is considerable historical evidence in favor of this point. Any number of assertions of fact, held absolutely, have been overturned, in fields as different as medicine and physics.

Reflecting upon the history of the proposal of Columbus that the earth is spherical, or upon the germ theory of disease, the same pattern of the development of the verification of a fact can be traced as in Peirce's example, which was meant to demonstrate that psychological tendencies have no ultimate place in the determination of soundness:

> In my definition of soundness, I have said not one word of the tendency of the human mind to perceive certain consequences. That will operate to make an argument more or less *clear*; but according to me if a certain conjunction of the planets renders the death of a certain monarch a result the like of which would happen in every analogous case in this universe or in any universe, that renders the argument that he will die because of that conjuncture of the planets, a sound argument, no matter how utterly nonsensical it may appear to every intelligent man. (MS 313)

Of course, this applies equally to bad arguments, even many that no intelligent person would find nonsensical. If there is no likelihood that a "result the like of which would happen in every analogous case in this universe or in any universe" could occur, an argument proposing that it will is still patently bad, regardless of its having universal approval. Such are the arguments which predict a flat earth or the consequences of an overabundance of black bile. In general, arguments that meet Peirce's standards of "soundness" represent a reality that is "independent of how *I* represent it to be or how *you* do or how any generations of men may represent it to be" (MS 313).

The End of Thought

Since "any kind of goodness consists in the adaptation of its subject to its *end*," Peirce considered the end of thought. A brief criticism of utilitarianism ensued, whereupon Peirce revealed that the essential flaw of utilitarians, but not necessarily of utilitarianism, is the evasion of questions about *ultimate* ends. Utilitarianism, insofar as it does consider the ends of either action or desires, is pragmatistic. But the vulgar utilitarians of Peirce's acquaintance consulted their "present desires" only and did not reckon the purpose of these desires or their suitability to an ultimate end. The practical "pragmatist" of the twentieth century evolved from the "vulgar utilitarian" of Peirce's description and is familiar in several forms—for example, in the classroom, as the antagonist of ideal values, or in business as the individual loyal to the corporation who refuses to reflect upon the long-term consequences of its practices. This is a mistake that Peirce wished to avoid in logic. So he did ask "What is the use of thinking?" Since "it is the argument alone that is the subject of logical goodness and badness," as established in the previous lecture, "we have therefore to ask what the end of argumentation is," to what does it ultimately lead.

The object of argumentation is not, as "the Germans" maintained, "simply to satisfy one's logical feeling." The "goodness of reasoning" does not consist "in that esthetic satisfaction alone."[1] While it may be surprising that Peirce denied that the goodness of reasoning consists in "esthetic satisfaction," it is perhaps the choice of words only that implies that logic would not have an end in esthetic experience. The problem with "the Germans" is not so much that they make an appeal to esthetic feeling in determining the good of logic, but that their definition of the esthetic is flawed. Peirce criticized the "feeling" of logical correctness claimed by Sigwart and his followers in the previous lectures, but nowhere is his criticism so pointed as in his Baldwin's *Dictionary* article on logic:

> The appeal to direct consciousness consists in pronouncing certain reasoning to be good or bad because it is felt to be so. This is a very common method. Sigwart, for example, bases all logic upon our invincible mental repulsion against contradiction, or, as he calls it, "the immediate feeling of necessity" (*Logic*, § 3, 2). Those who think it worth while to make any defense at all of this proceeding urge [that], in effect, however far the logician may push his criticisms of reasoning, still in doing so, he must reason, and so must ultimately rely upon his instinctive recognition of good and bad reasoning. Whence it follows that, in Sigwart's words, "every system of logic must rest upon this principle." It is, however, to be noted that among the dicta of direct consciousness, many pronounce certain reasonings to be bad. If, therefore, such dicta are to be relied upon, man not only usually has a tendency to reason right, but also sometimes has a tendency to reason

wrong; and if that be so, the validity of reasoning cannot *consist* in a man's having a tendency to reason in that way. Some say that the validity of reasoning consists in the "definitive dictum" of consciousness; but it has been replied that certain propositions in Euclid were studied for two thousand years by countless keen minds, all of whom had an immediate feeling of evidence concerning their proofs, until at last flaws were detected in those proofs, and are now admitted by all competent persons; and it is claimed that this illustrates how far from possible it is to make direct appeal to a definitive pronouncement.[2]

Hence, his remark in this lecture, that "This might do if we were gods and not subject to the force of experience," both dismissed the possibility of a flawless "instinct" for reasoning resting on the criterion of "esthetic satisfaction" and introduced the criterion of logical tests. But if the "force of experience" is acknowledged to be a factor in the sculpting of sound argumentation, "experience" requires careful definition. If experience offered only "blind compulsion," then there would be no point in reasoning nor any possibility of reasoning, such as it is, having anything to do with experience.

The remaining possibility is that experience, like nature, is a teacher, and that the goodness of reasoning is the prediction of facts: "an argument is sound if it necessarily must predict facts in the measure in which it promises to do so" (MS 313). It should be noted that Peirce's criterion of soundness in reasoning presupposed that facts (but possibly not all facts) occur with enough regularity to warrant the analysis of this regularity, a presumption he defended in lecture four, when discussing the reality of the categories.

Arguments perform the task of "predicting facts" in three forms. A "necessary" or deductive argument "is valid if and only if the state of things represented in its conclusion would be realized in every supposable constitution of the universe in which the premises should be true" (MS 313). The facts determined by the conclusion are contingent upon the hypotheses given in the premises. *Should* the hypothetical situation posed by its premises come to pass, a valid deductive argument presents a state of affairs that would also come to pass.

Peirce states that facts exposited in the conclusion of necessary arguments are not the results of experimentation, whereas inductive arguments "put a theory to the test." Insofar as the power and meaning of deductions do not rely upon a concordance of the premises with actual states of affairs in existence in the world, "experiment"—that is, observation of *whether* or *how much* the provisional states of affairs described in the premisses and the conclusion actually occurs—is irrelevant to the end of deduction. Insofar as the technique of determining the conclusions of deductive arguments is concerned, observation of a certain kind does take place. But observation in mathematical reasoning, for example, is an *inspection* of the premisses. This is a kind of "experiment" quite distinct from looking from premisses to experience for confirmation that the premisses describe actual states of affairs. What is inspected are the circumstances and character of the affairs being described, regardless of whether they correspond to those of existent affairs.

The "experimentalism" involved is that of trial and error, to see if the premisses can be correctly transformed, according to legitimate rules of deductive inference, into other propositions suitable to be called conclusive. Students of symbolic logic find a similar kind of inspection useful for solving proofs in natural deduction. Given general rules, the premisses can be transformed into new sets of premisses that eventually yield a final inference, a "conclusion," the goal or intended interpretant of the proof.

Peirce returned to mathematical modeling as a means of showing how inferences are made in his second draft. Lectures five and six refined his reasons for thinking about modeling in the first place. Modeling is a means of discovering "meaning," which he set out to define in a precise and technical sense. It is unfortunate that he did not himself undertake the "grand life-study" described in lecture six:

> In deduction, or necessary reasoning, we set out from a hypothetical state of things which we define in certain abstracted respects. Among the characters to which we pay no attention in this mode of argument is whether or not the hypothesis of our premisses conforms more or less to the state of things in the outward world. We consider this hypothetical state of things and are led to conclude that, however it may be with the universe in other respects, wherever and whenever the hypothesis may be realized, something else not explicitly supposed in that hypothesis will be true invariably. Our inference is valid if and only if there really is such a relation between the state of things supposed in the premisses and the state of things stated in the conclusion. Whether this really be so or not is a question of reality, and has nothing at all to do with how we may be inclined to think. If a given person is unable to see the connection, the argument is none the less valid, provided that relation of real facts really subsists. If the entire human race were unable to see the connection, the argument

would be none the less sound, although it would not be humanly clear. Let us see precisely how we assure ourselves of the reality of the connection. Here, as everywhere throughout logic, the study of relatives has been of the greatest service. The simple syllogisms which are alone considered by the old inexact logicians are such very rudimentary forms that it is practically impossible to discern in them the essential features of deductive inference until our attention has been called to these features in higher forms of deduction. All necessary reasoning without exception is diagrammatic. That is, we construct an icon of our hypothetical state of things and proceed to observe it. This observation leads us to suspect that something is true, which we may or may not be able to formulate with precision, and we proceed to inquire whether it is true or not. For this purpose it is necessary to form a plan of investigation and this is the most difficult part of the whole operation. We not only have to select the features of the diagram which it will be pertinent to pay attention to, but it is also of great importance to return again and again to certain features. Otherwise, although our conclusions may be correct they will not be the particular conclusions at which we are aiming. But the greatest point of art consists in the introduction of suitable *abstractions*. By this I mean such a transformation of our diagrams that characters of one diagram may appear in another as things. A familiar example is where in analysis we treat operations as themselves the subject of operations. Let me say that it would make *a grand life-study* [my emphasis] to give an account of this operation of planning a mathematical demonstration. Sundry sporadic maxims are afloat among mathematicians, and several meritorious books have been written upon the subject but nothing broad and masterly. With the modern reformed mathematics and with my own and other logical results as a basis such a theory of the plan of demonstration is no longer a superhuman task. Having thus determined the plan of the reasoning, we proceed to the reasoning itself, and this I have ascertained can be reduced to three kinds of steps. The first consists in copulating separate propositions into one compound proposition. The second consists in omitting something from a proposition without possibility of introducing error. The third consists in inserting something into a proposition without introducing error. (MS 314)

Anyone who has labored through proofs for the integrals of trigonometric functions or for finding approximations of roots by Newton's method in calculus, for example, or of DeMorgan's rules in logic, recognizes these steps as well as perhaps admires the acuity of observation required by the original founders of these proofs. Meaning is discovered from the premisses, and although anyone, if careful, can follow the reasoning after the fact, it is certainly the case that not everyone is in a position to originate the proofs. Thus Peirce may have been too overstated in his view of deduction as nonexperiential, although the kind of experience involved looks inward at the thinker's thoughts rather than outward, at the meeting of thoughts and objects not exclusively in thought.

The end of inductive arguments is to determine to what extent a given theory represents the facts—that is, the ratio of experiences expected to take place according to the "theory" represented by the induction and the actual experiences of the kind that do take place. Observation of this ratio yields a quantity; the closer the quantity is to one, the more sound the argument. Abductive arguments are sound insofar as they offer a theory to explain facts that are surprising or contrary to expectations. Abductions present promising suggestions but no warrant or test within abduction can fortify these suggestions. Abductions perform the labor of providing "theories" for further argumentations, both deductive and inductive.

The "meaning" of an argument, then, is its conclusion, which is the interpretation of its end. Peirce tried two formulations for explaining meaning in this lecture. They are both worthy of serious study:

> The end of argumentation is, of course, the drawing of its conclusion. This conclusion is the intended interpretant of the argument considered as a symbol. When we ask a person what he *means* by something he has said, we ask him to declare the intended interpretation of what he has said. . . .

> The word *meaning* has not, hitherto, been used as a technical term of logic. It is currently employed in three main ways. First, it is used, but quite improperly, to refer to the sensuous image a word calls up, with its emotional coloring, and all those unanalyzed associations that belong to a familiar expression. One might say "I did not venture, in something I had to say in French, to use the word *cabaret*, because I was not sure of its precise shade of *meaning*." But even in this use of the word it refers to the interpretation that would be attached to the word by a person familiar with the language. Secondly, it is sometimes used, also improperly, to [indicate] the individual subject intended to be referred to. A person lets slip a *boutade* and then reflecting that the

one he is addressing might interpret it as a personal reflection, adds "Oh, I don't *mean* you." But here again there is a reference to an interpretation. I think there is no doubt that popular usage fully justifies me in adopting the word *meaning* as a technical term of logic to refer to the *total intended interpretant* of a symbol. (MS 313)

An alternate formulation in his next draft states:

What we call the *meaning* of a proposition embraces every obvious necessary deduction from it. Considered as the beginning of an analysis of what the meaning of the word "meaning" is, it is a valuable remark. (MS 314)

Thus meaning has to do with the totality of the context of a proposition, such context being expressed in the form of premises.

The Problem of Ultimate Meaning

The final problem of lecture six is derived from a recognition that multiple conclusions are possible in any inquiry into meaning. How is the determination of an "ultimate" meaning to be made? Peirce attempted in each draft to solve the problem. In the first draft, the issue is posed:

We must, therefore, ask, is there no *ultimate* meaning? Cannot the process of drawing conclusion after conclusion be carried so far as finally to result in something in which no nonsense or ambiguity *can* lurk? Here is a difficult question which must engage our serious attention. (MS 313)

And in the second draft, the statement of the issue, as a problem not yet solved, marks the end of the third section of the lecture:

On the whole, then, if by the *meaning* of a term, proposition, or argument,[3] we understand the entire general intended interpretant, then the meaning of an argument is explicit. It is its conclusion, while the meaning of a proposition or term is all that that proposition or term could contribute to the conclusion of a demonstrative argument. But while this analysis will be found useful, it is by no means sufficient to cut off all nonsense or to enable us to judge of the maxim of pragmatism. What we need is an account

of the *ultimate* meaning of a term. To this problem we have to
address ourselves. (MS 314)

Peirce avowed that the study of the logic of relations brought about his
realization that "all conceptions, however abstracted and lofty, were capable of being defined with perfect formal precision in terms of the conceptions of everyday life" (MS 313). Even so, the question remaining in the
mind of the audience must have been the same as one suggested in
Peirce's mind by Kant:

> Kant and the logicians with whose writings he was alone ac-
> quainted,—he was far from being a thorough student of logic,
> notwithstanding his great natural power as a logician,—consis-
> tently neglected the logic of relations; and the consequence was
> that the only account they were in condition to give of the mean-
> ing of a term, its "signification" as they called it, was that it was
> composed of all the terms which could be essentially predicated of
> that term. Consequently, either the analysis of the signification
> must be capable of [being] pushed on further and further, without
> limit,—an opinion which Kant expresses in a well-known passage
> but which he did not develop,—or, what was more usual, one
> ultimately reached certain absolutely simple conceptions such as
> Being, Quality, Relation, Agency, Freedom, etc., which were re-
> garded as absolutely incapable of definition and of being in the
> highest degree luminous and clear. It is marvelous what a follow-
> ing this opinion that those excessively abstracted conceptions
> were in themselves in the highest degree simple and facile ob-
> tained, notwithstanding its repugnancy to good sense. One of the
> many important services which the logic of relations has rendered
> has been that of showing that these so-called simple conceptions,
> notwithstanding their being unaffected by the particular kind of
> combination recognized in non-relative logic, are nevertheless ca-
> pable of analysis in consequence of their implying various modes
> of relationship. For example, no conceptions are simpler than
> those of Firstness, Secondness, and Thirdness; but this has not
> prevented my defining them and that in a most effective manner
> since all the assertions I have made concerning them have been
> deduced from those definitions. (MS 314)

The criticism of Kant is that he presented a false dilemma: either the
undefinability of terms due to the endless results of inquiry into their
signification or the undefinability of terms due to the termination of the

inquiry in undefinable conceptions. Peirce presented an alternative method of the definition of terms by means of a logic of relatives. It must also be noted that not all terms are of interest to an inquirer. And since "the ideal of *meaning* is such as to involve some reference to a *purpose*," given that the word *meaning* is defined to be "the intended interpretant of a symbol," it is possible to refine the meaning of a representamen presented in an argument to a specific and finite result. This Peirce promised for the next lecture.

LECTURE SEVEN

Sometime before Peirce delivered his sixth lecture, it was decided that he would offer a seventh in the series. No record of any arrangement to pay him an additional amount has survived. The *Harvard Bulletin* announced the lecture on May 13 as well as yet another lecture to be presented the day after the seventh on certain concepts of mathematics:

MORE LECTURES BY MR. PEIRCE

Mr. Charles S. Peirce '59 has decided to give a supplementary lecture to his recent series under the auspices of the Department of Philosophy on "Pragmatism as a Principle and Method of Right Thinking." The lecture will take place next Thursday in Sever 11 at 8 o'clock and will be open to the public. Mr. Peirce will give the summary of his previous lectures and will put in clearer light the relation of the views maintained to the general doctrine of pragmatism.

By invitation of the Division of Mathematics Mr. Peirce will speak in Sever 8 next Friday at 8 o'clock on "Multitude and Continuity." The lecture will deal with "Number" and "Continuous Quantity," and reference will be made to Cantor and other writers on these subjects. This lecture is specially intended for students in philosophy and mathematics, but will also be open to the public. (HUA)

A manuscript notebook, intended as the beginning of a draft on "Multitude and Continuity," with the notation "A Lecture to students of Philosophy to be delivered in Harvard University, 1903 May 15" on its title page, is an incomplete set of prefatory remarks. Whatever relation "multitude and continuity" may have to "Pragmatism as a Principle and Method of Right Thinking" is left unstated by its author. And so, unfortunately, the last lecture for our purposes must be lecture seven.

Psychological versus Logical Determinations
of the Ultimate End of Reasoning

Peirce's conclusions on the general topic of these lectures could not have been better prepared. Having proceeded through phenomenology, as the foundation of the normative sciences, and having witnessed a demonstration of the end (or ends) of logic in the three classes of arguments, his audience was prepared to have the question answered, "What can be the *ultimate* end of reasoning?"

Peirce's answer in 1877, when he first embarked in print on an account of thinking, was "psychological," a criticism he made in lecture one. After he had then stated, in "The Fixation of Belief," that "the object of reasoning is to find out, from the consideration of what we already know, something else which we do not know," he restricted the objects of thought to beliefs. He said then:

> The irritation of doubt causes a struggle to attain a state of belief. I shall term this struggle *Inquiry* though it must be admitted that this is sometimes not a very apt designation. (CP 5.374)

Though it would have been legitimate in 1903 to note that doubt creates a sensation that an inquirer wishes to terminate, it would still have been a point about human *psychology*. The termination of doubt could only result *psychologically* in yet another psychological sensation—relief. But in 1877, the link (and, by implication, the difference) between the feeling of doubt, or relief from doubt, and the logical character, good or bad, of the sources of doubt, was not yet Peirce's concern. Numerous statements in the set of lectures before us, however, present his criticism of conflating psychological with logical activity. In examining reactions to beliefs, which could only take the form of conclusions—that is, propositions—he determined that while psychological and logical activity might be *concurrent*, it is nonetheless the case that a psychological response is dependent on logic and not vice versa. A doubter who does not *logically* criticize the belief he doubts, is nonetheless logical in the sense that he utilizes a *logica utens*. If one experiences doubt, it might be as an accidental coincidence with the *logical* unsoundness of the belief. It might just as well happen as a matter of accident that doubt of a logically sound belief might occur. Or it might be that one's ideas were in fact unsound and that one felt doubt, after the fact of a logical criticism, as a psychological consequence.

In 1877 Peirce understood the activity of inquiry to be framed by the question, "what, of my several choices of beliefs, is the one with which I am most satisfied?" Thus, it is not surprising that the ultimate end of inquiry would be a cessation of belief in one opinion and the adoption of another. As he stated it:

> The sole object of inquiry is the settlement of opinion. We may fancy that this is not enough for us, and that we seek, not merely an opinion, but a true opinion. But put this fancy to the test, and it proves groundless; for as soon as a firm belief is reached we are entirely satisfied, whether the belief is true or false. (CP 5.375)

In other words, he had sounded the inclinations of inquirers and had found that their satisfaction lay in seizing whatever belief settled doubt. "Settlement" or "fixation" implied that the problem Peirce was concerned with several decades before the revision of pragmatism in these lectures was how to choose between known members of a set of possible beliefs. Methods of fixing belief constituted means of applying one or another criterion in the choice of beliefs. These methods were not so much in the service of a *logica utens* as a *psychologica utens*. The overall urgency of an inquiry was thought to arise from a need, to relieve the pain of doubt. The logical questions remained untouched.

But the *"ultimate* end of reasoning," as Peirce was conceiving it in 1903, was problematic for exactly the reason above. Kant's conclusion, as Peirce interpreted it, was that opinions could be replaced by other opinions (about the "significations" of a term), presumably ad infinitum. What, if any, opinion would be paramount to the rest? How could one then even propose to pursue an *ultimate* end of reasoning? The endpoint of reasoning, if conceived as a series of "opinions," is of dubious value. And if one starts with opinions of no provenance, it can be no other way. So, the origin of beliefs at the beginning of reasoning was Peirce's primary concern. The vitally necessary issue to be addressed in lecture seven was the beginning of reasoning, the beginning of deliberate logical inquiry.

It was evident from the first three methods of the "fixation of belief" that Peirce described in 1877, that (nonscientific) inquirers do not seek much in the way of hypotheses beyond what is immediately at hand. A glaring fault of the methods of tenacity, authority, and a priorism (among other faults) is that the belief one fixes upon can only be as good as the best among those ready to hand. The inquirer is not possessed of any particular method for *arriving* at hypotheses for his consideration. In fact, the essential character of the first three methods, including a priorism, the most "deliberate" kind of thinking of these three, is the accidental nature of their inquiries. Thinkers who believe themselves to be original are merely the dupes of the cultures in which they live. Thus, the problem with the initial set of beliefs from which one has to choose is that none of them are subject to a critical scrutiny as to their worthiness of being considered. The tenacious thinker simply surveys the landscape of ideas and fixes upon the first one he sees. The subject of the method of authority just happens to be a citizen of some state or institution. Such a thinker is like the individual described by Alexis de Tocqueville in *Democracy in America*: having no love of critical method and no inkling of the history of the clash of ideas, each thinks exactly as the others (under the press of the same material conditions) while imagining that he is a sovereign among thinkers.[1] The scientific reasoner has no relevant advantage over the rest insofar as he, too, lacks any comprehension of the logic of the initial conditions of an inquiry. His only apparent advantage is *psychological*. Scientific inquirers are willing to endure more pain, more doubt, or their tolerance for doubt is higher. While they fix opinions "in the long run," after giving due weight to experience and reality, which is defined as independent of what you or I believe it to be, they have no real grasp of the logical principle or method by which inquiry begins. Peirce was simply much more aware in 1903 that in order to properly comprehend inquiry, and *perform* inquiry with proper care, the means by which cognition takes place, in the first place, must be acknowledged.

The Cotary Propositions of Pragmatism

If pragmatism is to be understood correctly as a maxim of logic, which is a normative science, then it has to describe a deliberate and considered activity, or one that is mainly so:

> Consider what effects that might conceivably have practical bearings we conceive the object of our conception to have. Then, our conception of these effects is the whole of our conception of the object. (MS 301)

The first sentence of the maxim was explained in the previous lectures. Briefly, it advises us to think about the ends of the object of our conception. What does this object do? What are its effects, in terms of Firstness, Secondness, and Thirdness? There are all sorts of objects of conceptions that have all sorts of conceivable effects and "practical bearings" or ends. How can these be best characterized? Peirce's cotary propositions concern the second sentence of the maxim and treat the manner in which "our conception of these effects" is possible. How does the object of our conception come to be an object of our conception such that we *can* consider its effects? The answer to this is provided by an anatomy of cognition. Sec-

tions I and II of the seventh lecture define and defend the cotary propositions. Sections III, IV and V reflect upon the proposal that pragmatism is
the logic of abduction.

The cotary propositions are (1) *Nihil est in intellectu quin prius
fuerat in sensu.* (Nothing is in the intellect without first having been in
the senses), (2) "perceptual judgments contain general elements, so that
universal propositions are deducible from them," and (3) "abductive inference shades into perceptual judgment without any sharp line of demarcation between them; or in other words our first premisses, the perceptual
judgments, are to be regarded as an extreme case of abductive inferences,
from which they differ in being absolutely beyond criticism" (MS 315).

In further explanation of the second cotary proposition, which was
treated also in lecture six, Peirce drew a diagram typical of a number of
drawings that illustrate visual illusions. The drawing of a stone wall is
attributed to Benjamin Peirce, whom Peirce supposed must have been
using it to make the same point. The drawing also resembles the wall
surrounding Peirce's study at Arisbe, his house in Milford, Pennsylvania.
The single serpentine line may be conceived in two different ways, either
as a meaningless figure or as a stone wall. He claimed, about this and
other visual illusions:

> The most striking thing is that a certain theory of interpretation
> of the figure has all the appearance of being given in perception.
> The first time it is shown to us, it seems as completely beyond the
> control of rational criticism as any percept is; but after many rep-
> etitions of the familiar experiment, the illusion wears off, becom-
> ing first less decided, and ultimately ceasing completely. (MS 315)

Deliberately contrived visual illusions are like other perceptions. There appear to be almost rigidly contained principles that give us perceptions in
the form in which we experience them. The drawing can be either a line or
a wall, but no stretch of the imagination allows us to interpret it as a
drawing of a cat or a seascape. The fact that the trick of visual illusion
"wears out" is not a disanalogous element in the comparison of illusions to
other perceptions. Even though we know illusions have several interpretations, we are certain of no such thing about other perceptions. We nonetheless undergo a process of aligning our interpretations of perceptions
with specific general elements, beyond which we cannot go in our judgments. The particular experience of any of these perceptions is a perception of one of these general aspects, because "the very decided preference
of our perception for one mode of classing the percept shows that this
classification is contained in the perceptual judgment" (MS 315). Peirce's

illustrations demonstrate that (1) there *are* classifications under which we experience perceptions and we would not even be able to experience these perceptions without them, and (2) the classifications are (in a qualified sense) beyond our control and thereby are contained within the perception itself.

What qualifications pertain to our inability to control perceptual judgments? In an obvious manner, it is possible to be trained to recognize, and thus to refine, one's sense of the general character of perceptions. The amateur chili taster may only give one or two interpretations to his perceptions, perhaps "hot" and "not as hot," whereas it is not only possible to distinguish many more degrees of heat, but also to decide upon other interpretations, such as relative smokiness, savoriness, and sweetness. However, all this really means is that a perception may be rich in general elements, containing several simultaneously, and that practice leads to familiarity with these elements. A less obvious qualification upon our lack of control of perceptions is that this does not entail that the experience is not controlled in some other way. The nature of the source of the perception is determinative of the perception. This is what is meant by claiming that "the perceptual judgment is the result of a process" as well as that perceptual judgments are the first premises of thought. They are premises whose subjects are the sources of the perceptions, the causes of perceptions, the "real thing" that "controls," in a manner of speaking, that which is perceived.

In defense of the first cotary proposition, the third must be explained. Perceptions and abductions are siblings; the nature of both is to be inferential. The psychological sensations accompanying abduction, with few exceptions, have been the dominant focus of scholarship.[2] Likewise, focus on the psychological character of perception and perceptual judgments has been dominant in the history of philosophy, and now in psychology. Peirce's unique focus is nonetheless indispensable. If perceptions are the result of a process, and the process is *like* that of abductive inference, the similarity lies in their both proceeding from the unknown to the known, or the unapprehended to the apprehended. Also, each has a set of premisses. In abduction, it is clear that the premisses consist of (1) the observation of a given fact and (2) a general notion as to the nature of the association of that fact with others. These are the elements of a hypothesis that explains the fact. The conclusion of an abduction is the hypothesis that the fact is explicable by that notion. The "idea of putting together what we had never before dreamed of putting together" is responsible for the inference. In the case of a perception, the premiss is real generality insofar as it is available by means of the senses.

But could any new element come into thought from anywhere but perceptual judgments? All three cotary propositions ought to be considered together, for the first holds that nothing enters the intellect *except* through perception, and the third says that perception, from which general elements are deduced (so says the second), is of the same species as abduction. The discussion of abduction was initiated because, while it may be agreed that perception does introduce new concepts into the intellect, it may not be the only source of such concepts. It is then reasonable to suppose that the sort of inference that does initiate hypotheses for consideration—that is, abductive inference—is a candidate for introducing new concepts as well. Peirce argued that nothing new arises in the conclusion of an abduction that was not first in its premises. The conclusion of an abduction merely puts forward the suggestion that a plausible condition of a fact that would explain the fact is, indeed, an explanation of the fact.

This may appear to beg the question, for it may be asked now: How do the elements of the explanation in the conclusion get into *the premises?* Peirce's answer lies in recalling the likeness of abductions to perceptions. He claimed that "the only symptom by which the two can be distinguished is that we cannot form the least conception of what it would be to deny the perceptual judgment" while "an abductive suggestion, however, is something whose truth *can* be questioned or even denied" (MS 315). The general elements, acknowledged to be deducible from perceptual judgment in a separate proof, in an abduction, are, likewise, implicit in the perceptual judgments. In other words, the premises for the premises of an abductive inference are real generalities or Thirdnesses. So there is no other possible source of new conceptions.

Proof as Enumeration

Sections III, IV, and V of lecture seven, are, in terms of philosophical style and accomplishment, one of the best illustrations of following one's own method in one's own work that we can hope to find in Western thought. The promise of a proof, made in the first lecture, has been carried out, and in the manner of philosophy, has dealt with facts that are before us and with nothing that is arcane or esoteric. The proof is a philosophical one, but one that justifies the principles and methods already inherent in all sound reasoning.

Here, finally, the styling of the proof Peirce first introduced in lecture one is completely apparent. We wished to know at first, and he wished to be able to tell us, what pragmatism is, when taken in the sense of a logical maxim. At last it is apparent that, in all these lectures when Peirce told us that he could not succeed in making his case in a short space of time, he was not merely making excuses, but was elaborating on the nature of his method, indeed on *pragmatism* as a "principle and method of right thinking." The final parts of the seventh lecture not only sketch the details that make the drawing of pragmatism identifiable, but pragmatistically accomplish the *performance* of the end of the inquiry into the proof of pragmatism. This double function of the final lecture can be understood better if its resonance with its latent sources is revealed. Peirce's style of proof bears a resemblance to both a style of philosophical proof and a style of mathematical proof.[3]

Descartes's method is similar to the method that is followed in the mathematical calculus, although the techniques of the calculus are "exact." His works on method precede the first papers on the calculus by several decades, but the methods of work are strikingly similar. In finding the areas and volumes of irregular but continuous figures, for example, the calculus breaks the figures down into portions that can be measured exactly, with the presumption that, usually, the greater the number of portions, the less allowance for over- or underestimates. Then a sum of the measurements of the portions is calculated. This sum is an approximation of the precise measure of area or volume the figure occupies. Or, in taking the roots of a continuous line, Newton's method begins with a guess at the number of the root. Then, by using his equation a number of times, each use yielding a closer approximation, a "best" approximation is reached when the same number results at least twice. More precise determinations of some roots can also be taken if one is willing to allow an increased number of decimal places in the calculation when estimating a result. In general, the calculus is a method for approximating measurements by breaking down the object to be measured into pieces that can be measured exactly, and then reuniting the pieces for a sum of their measurements. These sums are enumerations, analogous to the *enumerations* of Descartes's "Discourse on the Method of Rightly Conducting the Reason."

It is important to note that mathematicians who invented and use the calculus, unlike philosophers who deal with reasoning, have been *forced* to deal with the fact of continuity. *Continuous* functions are the focus of the calculus. And in continuous lines, for example, it is apparent that multitudes of points are involved, the fact of individual points in multitudes being nothing but a *discontinuous* element of the lines. Thus, mathematicians must deal, in the calculus, with both continuity and discontinuity. It is beyond doubt that the merit of the calculus is its ability to overcome the disparity between continuity and discontinuity. The terms used for the results of calculus are "sums," "integrals," "estimates," "approximations." No mathematician believes that, in approximating the measure of some object, the object has in fact no particular measure. The term approximation implies that, in comparison to the thing approximated, it is not identical. An approximation or an enumeration is like a model or an interpretant of the thing modeled. However, the reality of the precise measure of the thing modeled is no less a fact because it is articulated and understood in approximate terms.

We can only guess what Peirce wished to say about "Multitude and Continuity" on the evening following lecture seven. He was interested throughout the latter lectures on pragmatism in the philosophical problem of reconciling *continuity*, such as the kind found in perceptual judgments—discussed in lecture six and briefly mentioned again in lecture seven—with *discontinuity*, or as he termed it, multitudes. In lecture seven, section IV, the final element of the explanation of the pragmatic maxim is that it prescribes as a "principle and method of right thinking," an enumeration of the conceivable effects of an object of conception. Peirce himself followed the method of enumeration in this lecture series. Lecture seven is an enumerative conclusion of the findings of the analysis of the logic of discovery with the end of defining pragmatism as a maxim of logic. The meaning of the term "end," which Peirce used so frequently throughout these lectures, certainly should be taken as "purpose" as he so often states. But an end is also a sum of all the parts that can have their measures taken as in the calculus. Thus he follows his own maxim in thinking of the end in the sense of a sum. His references to Achilles and the tortoise and to other paradoxes and problems concerning continuity and discontinuity in philosophy can be understood in the light of this concern. He is both defending the nature of continuity as real and writing in the stance of a thinker who is describing what he believes to be a matter of continuity, reasoning in accordance with the maxim of pragmatism.

The final enumeration of the meaning of the pragmatic maxim requires that one more element be disclosed, the "question of the logic of abduction." After all, this is a simple matter. When considering the practical issue of how we, as a matter of fact, follow out an inquiry according to the pragmatic maxim, it is necessary to ascribe to thought a means of generating suggestions as to what conceivable effects an object of inquiry may have.

A deduction, to return to an idea in the previous lecture, performs the function of making a *prediction* as to what would occur if the notion concluded by an abduction were to turn out to be the case. Recall that the "prediction of facts" is said to be the end of reasoning. "Turning out to be the case" requires that a hypothesis be processed by deduction first, logically, if not chronologically. The deductive process works out what sorts of conclusions are necessary. The inductive process finds the ratio of the frequency by which these logically necessary results determined by deduction do in fact occur. Should the abduction hit its target, and the deductive analysis be performed soundly, the inductive results will demonstrate a high frequency. That is, the concept initially posed in the abduction will turn out to have been a fairly accurate approximation of experience, an explanation of experience.

Notes

Lecture One

1. "Ethics of Terminology," *Syllabus of Certain Topics of Logic* (Boston: Mudge, 1903); in P1035 of the microfiche edition published by Bowling Green: Philosophy Documentation Center, as catalogued in *A Comprehensive Bibliography of the Published Works of Charles Sanders Peirce*, 2nd rev. ed., by K. L. Ketner.

2. James Mark Baldwin, ed., *Dictionary of Philosophy and Psychology* (Gloucester, Mass.: P. Smith, 1960, c. 1901), pp. 321–22.

3. Max H. Fisch, "The 'Proof' of Pragmatism," *Pragmatism and Purpose: Essays Presented to Thomas A. Goudge*, ed. L. W. Sumner, John G. Slater, and Fred Wilson (Toronto: University of Toronto Press, 1981), pp. 28–40. Fisch notes that the "best accounts of the 'proof' so far published are those by Manley Thompson [in 1953, *The Pragmatic Philosophy of C. S. Peirce*, University of Chicago Press] and John J. Fitzgerald [in 1966, *Peirce's Theory of Signs as Foundation for Pragmatism*, The Hague: Mouton]." Fisch observes that neither made use of unpublished manuscripts, which would have led them to assign pragmatism "neither to speculative grammar nor to critic, but to methodeutic." A similar omission informs Jeremiah McCarthy in "Peirce's Proof of Pragmatism," *Transactions of the Charles S. Peirce Society* 26 (1990): 63–113.

4. McCarthy, "Peirce's Proof," p. 67.

5. See Memoir No. 1, "On the Classification of the Theoretic Sciences of Research" in L 75 (1902). Peirce outlines a "catalogue of the sciences to exhibit the most important of the relations of logical dependence among them" in order to "give, from a general survey of science, an idea of the place of logic among the sciences." See also "Syllabus of Certain Topics" (1903) in CP 1.180–202, originally published by Alfred Mudge & Son, Boston, as an accompaniment to *Lectures on Logic* delivered at the Lowell Institute. See also "Reason's Conscience: A Practical Treatise on the Theory of Discovery; Wherein Logic is conceived as Semiotic," MS 693a (circa 1904). Peirce was concerned with the relation of the sciences to one another in general at least as early as 1891 in "The Architecture of Theories," CP 6.7–34.

6. James dedicated the published edition of *Pragmatism, A New Name for Some Old Ways of Thinking* to "the memory of John Stuart Mill, from whom I first learned the pragmatic openness of mind and whom my fancy likes to picture as our

leader were he alive today" in *Pragmatism*, edited by Bruce Kuklick (Indianapolis: Hackett Publishing Company, 1981), p. 2. The preface to James's *Pragmatism* gives references to works by John Dewey, F. C. S. Schiller, J. Milhaud, Le Roy, Blondel, De Sailly, and a "book on Pragmatism, in the French language, to be published very soon" by Papini (in Kuklick, *Pragmatism*, p. 3). Peirce was not mentioned by name, but James claimed that "the founder of pragmatism himself recently gave a course of lectures at the Lowell Institute with that very word in its title,—flashes of brilliant light relieved against Cimmerian darkness. None of us, I fancy, understood *all* that he said—yet here I stand, making a very similar venture" (in Kuklick, *Pragmatism*, pp. 7–8).

7. See Robert W. Burch, *A Peircean Reduction Thesis* (Lubbock: Texas Tech University Press, 1991). Burch gives an account of Peirce's algebraic logic which supports the thesis that logic's purpose is to analyze and display logical relations rather than calculate arguments.

8. McCarthy, "Peirce's Proof," p. 67 and note 19, p. 111. Peirce's first four lectures reflect a complete lack of confidence in the Harvard student's grounding in logic or science, both requirements for the proof's effectiveness. See Item 698 of *The Correspondence of the James Library* in which Peirce states, in reference to the difficulties of teaching "pure theory":

> I don't think even my Harvard audience was quite fit for that. What they need is logical training,—lessons, not lectures.

For a discussion of lessons in logic, see lecture two, MS 302. There, Peirce stated that thirty-six out of one hundred lessons in a liberal education would:

> suffice really to teach the leading principles of logic, and logic, the ability to think well, constitutes about three-eighths of a truly liberal education. . . . A liberal education ought to be a living organism and logic may truly be said to be the heart of it. But I do not say that six lectures on a fragment of logic will have the same proportionate value. It will be like cutting out five-sixths of a man's heart and leaving him with the remainder. Or rather it would be that if lectures were lessons which they certainly are far from being.

9. Edward C. Moore et al. eds., *Writings of Charles S. Peirce, A Chronological Edition*, vol. 2 (Bloomington: Indiana University Press, 1984), p. xxxvi. The editors date the founding of the Metaphysical Club at Cambridge, "in which pragmatism was born," to 1872. Indeed, in a 1909 treatise on "Meaning" (MS 619), which recounts his philosophical development, Peirce attributed the origin of the doctrine of pragmatism to a club consisting of "some dozen philosophical friends" which formed "a year or two" after a series of nine of his papers on logic were published in the years 1867–9. See David Gruender's "Pragmatism, Science, and Metaphysics," in *The Relevance of Charles Peirce*, LaSalle, Illinois: The Hegeler Institute, 1983,

pp. 275–76, for a demonstration supporting the fact that the earliest passage in which "something like the pragmatic principle occurs" is in Peirce's 1868 article, "Some Consequences of Four Incapacities." Peirce's paper was one of four published that year by *The Journal of Speculative Philosophy*.

Lecture Two

1. See the excerpts in the chapter, "Science and Education" in *Charles S. Peirce: Selected Writings*, edited with an introduction and notes by Philip P. Wiener (New York: Dover Publications, 1966) originally published as *Values in a Universe of Chance* (New York: Doubleday & Company, 1958). See especially section "20. Definition and Function of a University," which includes a definition written for the *Century Dictionary*, 1889, a review of *Clark University, 1889–1899: Decennial Celebration*, written in 1900, and an excerpt from a Fourth of July address in Paris, 1880. Also compare Peirce's opening remarks in MS 303 with "21. Logic and Liberal Education," from the Johns Hopkins University circulars of November 1882, as excerpted by Max H. Fisch and Jackson I. Cope, "Peirce at the Johns Hopkins University," in *Studies in the Philosophy of C. S. Peirce*, ed. Philip P. Wiener and Frederic H. Young.

2. A complete treatment of Peirce's life and intellectual development as influenced by his family and especially with reference to his father Benjamin Peirce, and his circle of contemporaries, has not yet been produced. However, Peirce's childhood and youthful manuscripts published in *Writings of Charles S. Peirce, A Chronological Edition*, vol. 1, edited by Edward C. Moore et al. (Bloomington: Indiana University Press, 1984) contribute to this portrait as does Michael L. Raposa's chapter on "Scientific Theism" in *Peirce's Philosophy of Religion* (Peirce Studies Number 5; Bloomington, Indiana: Indiana University Press, 1989). Raposa remarks (p. 8):

> Some of the seeds of Charles Peirce's mature, full-blown objective idealism [for example] can already be detected . . . in his father's lectures on the philosophy of science. Similarly, other themes and perspectives that would emerge and take shape in the former's life-long speculations can be traced back to certain elements in Benjamin's thought. *This is not to suggest that all of these notions originated with the elder Peirce; they were ingredients of the intellectual environment that nurtured both father and son* [my emphasis]. Clearly, however, the relationship between the two was an especially powerful one, and it was rooted in and sustained by an ongoing intellectual conversation that had a profound impact on Charles as a boy and young man, regardless of the extent to which he was later to develop and transform, or altogether abandon, his father's arguments and ideas.

For an account of the scientific and academic background in the period 1846–1861 and preceding, see Robert V. Bruce, *The Launching of Modern American Science*

(New York: Alfred A. Knopf, 1987), especially his discussion of the rise and fall of the Lazzaroni, Benjamin's intellectual "club."

3. Peirce wrote an occasional review of educational textbooks, e.g., of "Educational Textbooks" for *The Nation*, vol. 14 (April 11, 1871), pp. 244–46, which can be found in the microfiche edition, *Charles Sanders Peirce: Complete Published Works, including Selected Secondary Materials*, Johnson Associates, 1977, as catalogued in *Peirce, A Comprehensive Bibliography*, second edition, revised, edited by Kenneth Laine Ketner (Philosophy Documentation Center, Bowling Green State University, Bowling Green, Ohio, 1986) P00066 Fiche 8; of *The Teaching of Elementary Mathematics*, by David Eugene Smith, for *The Nation*, vol. 70 (March 22, 1900), p. 230, found on microfiche P00727: Fiche 119 and an occasional article on the same, e.g., "The Logic of Mathematics in Relation to Education" for *Educational Review*, vol. 15 (March 1898), pp. 209–16, on microfiche P00653: Fiche 115. However, a better sample of his works designed for educational purposes can be found in Manuscripts 164–98, the "Mathematical Textbooks" series as documented by Richard S. Robin, *Annotated Catalogue of the Papers of Charles S. Peirce* (University of Massachusetts Press, 1967), pp. 18–21. Carolyn Eisele writes, in her "Introductions to the New Elements of Mathematics" in *Studies in the Scientific and Mathematical Philosophy of Charles S. Peirce* (The Hague: Mouton Publishers, 1979):

> The editor [Eisele] believes that Peirce had in mind [circa 1895] a Primary Arithmetic consisting of the Elementary Arithmetic as given in MS. 189 (Lydia Peirce's Primary Arithmetic) and MS. 181 (Primary Arithmetic—MS. 182 is a draft of 181 with Suggestions to Teachers); a Vulgar Arithmetic, as developed in MS. 178 (C. S. Peirce's Vulgar Arithmetic: Its Chief Features) for teachers; a Practical Arithmetic, as given in MSS. 167 and 168. In an Advanced Arithmetic he probably intended to encompass number theory as given, for example, in Familiar Letters about the Art of Reasoning (MS. 186) and in Amazing Mazes; and Secundals, the binary system so popular today.

Peirce had truly made an exhaustive study of arithmetic textbooks. There is still extant a sheaf of pages entitled *Copy and notes for arithmetic* (MS 1545) in which he registered his reactions to some of the textbooks he had examined. For example, the Wentworth and Hill book is deemed "No doubt the best advanced arithmetic. Most intelligent and bright. Printing tolerably good." And Ray's *New Higher Mathematics* brings forth: "This has been immensely popular. It contains many tables and everything a little fuller than most arithmetics. Easy to surpass it in all its strong points. Contains a great deal of information. Little useless stuff. Its logic is beneath contempt."

4. See the "Prologue" from MS 1334, lecture one to the Adirondack Summer School, 1905, in the "Charles Sanders Peirce" chapter, with an introduction by Kenneth Laine Ketner, in *Classical American Philosophy, Essential Readings and*

Interpretive Essays, edited by John J. Stuhr (New York: Oxford University Press, 1987), p. 38. Peirce wrote that "If I had a class in logic to conduct for a year, I should harp still, as I used to do at the Johns Hopkins, upon the maieutic character of my office,—which means that I should do all I could to make my hearers think for themselves." "Common Sense" is from MS 435, lecture one, "On Detached Ideas in General, and on Vitally Important Topics as such," 1898. There Peirce claimed that "good instruction in reasoning is exceedingly rare." One of the reasons noted was that teachers of logic cannot respond to the questions of students who are puzzled by what is actually a logical flaw in a passage. The teacher "probably never really saw the true logic of the passage," but "thinks he does because, owing to long familiarity, he has lost the sense of coming up against an invisible barrier that the boy feels" (p. 40). He recommends that teachers both avoid autocratic rule over students and "prevent the scholars getting puffed up with their logical acquirements." He warns that "[the teacher] will wish to impregnate [students] with the right way of looking at reasoning before they shall be aware that they have learned anything; and he will not mind giving considerable time to that, for it is worth a great deal" (p. 40).

5. Stuhr, *Classical American Philosophy*, p. 38.

6. See CP 1.135–75, "The First Rule of Reason," which is "Do Not Block the Way of Inquiry." Specifically, four barriers to good reasoning are responsible for setbacks and lack of progress in science: (1) overconfident assertion of "self-evident truth," which is "quite as easy to doubt as to believe," (2) declaring some object "absolutely unknowable," when in fact historically, just such objects are frequently comprehensible within a short time of the expression of such skepticism, (3) maintaining that "this, that, or the other element of science is basic, ultimate, independent of aught else, and utterly inexplicable—not so much from any defect in our knowing [as opposed to the second barrier] as because there is nothing beneath it to know," and (4) "holding that this or that law or truth has found its last and perfect formulation—and especially that the ordinary and usual course of nature never can be broken through." The doctrine of fallibilism is posited as the antidote to the above. An example of reduction which combines (1) and (4) above is observed by Peirce in "Evolutionary Love" (CP 6.287–317) in the form of the "greed-philosophy," an ill-conceived application of the doctrine of political economy. He predicts dire consequence for this case of reductionist belief: "The Reign of Terror was very bad; but now the Gradgrind banner [a reference to the character in Charles Dickens's *Hard Times* who embodies the "greed-philosophy"] has been this century long flaunting in the face of heaven, with an insolence to provoke the very skies to scowl and rumble. Soon a flash and quick peal will shake economists out of their complacency, too late. The twentieth century, in its latter half, shall surely see the deluge-tempest burst upon the social order—to clear upon a world as deep in ruin as that greed-philosophy has long plunged it into guilt" (CP 6.292).

Lecture Three

1. Interpreters of Peirce's diagrammatic thought, who develop the argument that it is the keystone to Peirce's thought, include Robert W. Burch, in *A Peircean*

Reduction Thesis (Lubbock: Texas Tech University Press, 1991); Beverley E. Kent in *Charles S. Peirce: Logic and the Classification of the Sciences* (Kingston: McGill-Queen's University Press, 1987); Kenneth Laine Ketner, in "Peirce on Diagrammatic Thought: Some Consequences for Contemporary Semiotic Science," in *Zeichen und Realität*, ed. K. Oehler (Tübingen: Stauffenburg Verlag, 1984); "The early history of computer design: Charles Sanders Peirce and Marquand's logical machines," *The Princeton Library Chronicle*, 45 (1984): 186–224; "How Hintikka misunderstood Peirce's account of theorematic reasoning," *Transactions of the Charles S. Peirce Society* (1985): 407–18; "Peirce's 'most lucid and interesting' paper: An Introduction to Cenopythagoreanism," *International Philosophical Quarterly* 26 (1986): 375–92; "Peirce and Turing: Comparisons and Conjectures," *Semiotica* 68 (1988): 33–61: "Hartshorne and the Basis of Peirce's Categories," in *Hartshorne, Process Philosophy, and Theology* (Albany: State University of New York Press, 1989); *Elements of Logic: An Introduction to Peirce's Existential Graphs* (Lubbock: Arisbe Associates, 1990) [includes software for learning Peirce's diagrammatic logic]; "Novel Science, or How Contemporary Social Science is Not Well, and Why Literature and Semeiotic Provide a Cure," *Semiotica* 93 (1993): 33–59; and Patrick Samway, S. J., *A Thief of Peirce: The Letters of Kenneth Laine Ketner and Walker Percy* (Jackson: University Press of Mississippi, 1995).

2. George B. Thomas and Ross L. Finney, *Calculus and Analytic Geometry*, 8th ed. (New York: Addison Wesley Publishing Company, 1992), pp. 250–51.

3. Ibid., p. 384.

4. Charles Sanders Peirce, "Logic," *Dictionary of Philosophy and Psychology*, vol. II , edited by James Mark Baldwin (Gloucester, Mass.: Peter Smith, 1960; copyright, 1901 by the Macmillan Company), p. 21.

5. Ibid.

6. Ibid., p. 23.

7. Royce's map imagery in his "Supplementary Essay" to *The World and the Individual*, first published in 1899, was used by Peirce to illustrate a self-representative system as part of a proof that self-representative systems can be comprehensible and infinite—that is, can be understood as in a one-to-one correspondence with a proper subset of itself. Royce did demonstrate that the self-representative system of a map of a region which also includes a map of this map of a region but whose map would also include the map of the map of the region, is infinite in the mathematical definition. As in Peirce's use of the mapping system, Royce's discussion claimed the maps are analogous to human self-consciousness. Peirce had no objection to Royce's proof and Royce acknowledged, in "Supplementary Essay," his obligation to Peirce for his concept of the quantitative infinite "not only for the stimulus gained from his various published comments and discussions bearing upon the concept of the Infinite, but for the guidance and the suggestions due to some unpublished lectures of his which I had the good fortune to hear" (Josiah Royce, *The World and the Individual*, New York: Dover Publications, 1959, p. xix).

In his manuscript, Peirce denied credit both to himself and to Royce for the origin of the metaphor, but claims to have used it himself some thirty years earlier.

Lecture Four

1. For an analysis of the development of Peirce's evolutionary philosophy, including bibliography, see Patricia Ann Turrisi, "Charles S. Peirce's Evolutionary Metaphysics: The Growth of Reasonableness in Nature, Mind and Science" (Ph.D. dissertation, Dept. of Philosophy, The Pennsylvania State University, 1986).

2. "Notes on Scientific Philosophy" (CP 1.126–75, esp. 1.174–75) and "Evolutionary Love" (CP 6.287–317) consider the role of "leaps" in the progress of science and culture.

Lecture Five

1. Reference is to Friedrich Schiller, *Briefe über die ästhetische Erziehung des Menschen* 1794–1795.

2. Peirce recounts his first acquaintance with philosophical ideas in similar fashion in several autobiographical sketches. For the earliest such narrative, see Edward C. Moore et al., eds., *Writings of Charles S. Peirce, A Chronological Edition*, vol. 1 (Bloomington: Indiana University Press, 1982), pp. 2, 10–12.

3. "Cambridge lectures" refers to the Cambridge Conferences Lectures of 1898; in the published edition: Charles S. Peirce, *Reasoning and the Logic of Things*, edited by Kenneth Laine Ketner, with an introduction by Kenneth Laine Ketner and Hilary Putnam (Cambridge, Mass.: Harvard University Press, 1992).

4. Charles Sanders Peirce, "Logic," *Dictionary of Philosophy and Psychology*, vol. II, edited by James Mark Baldwin (Gloucester, Mass.: Peter Smith, 1960; copyright, 1901 by the Macmillan Company), p. 21.

Lecture Six

1. For an overview of "eight sources" by which writers decide "what is good logic and what bad," see Charles Sanders Peirce, "Logic," *Dictionary of Philosophy and Psychology*, vol. II, edited by James Mark Baldwin (Gloucester, Mass.: Peter Smith, 1960; copyright, 1901 by the Macmillan Company), pp. 21–22.

2. Ibid., pp. 20–21.

3. It may seem initially puzzling that "term," "proposition," and "argument" are grouped together as if their meaning could be equivalently defined. When considered from the point of view of their ends, however, their diversity becomes a distinction without a difference. Peirce must have been concerned to make this clear because section IV begins with its explanation:

> Let us ask then what the *end* of a term is. It is plain that no use can be made of it until it is introduced into a proposition; and when it is intro-

duced into the proposition it must form the predicate or some predicative constituent of the predicate. For the subjects of a proposition merely fulfil the function of indices and involve no general conception whatever, while a term is essentially general, although it may involve indexical constituents.

A further explanation of "term" is also provided; by "term" he meant "rhema" which is a term (a common noun) which "contains a verb within itself." "Butcher" is a term; "is a butcher" is a rhema. By calling rhemata by the name terms, he acknowledged that English and a handful of other languages are peculiar in that common nouns are distinct from verbs whereas in primitive languages (e.g., Old Egyptian and Arabic) "there is strictly no such thing as a common noun." Nor are there distinct words equivalent to the English copula in these languages, which should be considered the norm. Peirce dated the naming of the copula to no earlier than the time of Abelard. Aristotle's usual usage is not to use a (copulative) verb as a separate part of the proposition, though he does so occasionally in accord with another mode of expression in the Greek language. Thus, a term, for Peirce, is a rhema which is necessarily predicative.

Lecture Seven

1. For an illustration of a form of fixing belief that could stand as a textbook example of a priori reasoning, see the First Book, "Influence of Democracy on the Progress of Opinion in the United States," especially chapter 1, "Philosophical method among the Americans" and chapter 2, "Of the principal source of belief among democratic nations" in Alexis de Tocqueville, the Henry Reeve text as revised by Francis Bowen, now further corrected and edited with introduction, editorial notes, and bibliographies by Phillips Bradley, *Democracy in America*, vol. 2 (New York: Knopf, circa 1945).

2. For a comprehensive survey and criticism of the scholarship on abduction, see Patricia A. Turrisi, "Peirce's Logic of Discovery: Abduction and the Universal Categories" in *Transactions of the Charles S. Peirce Society* 26 (1990): 465–97.

3. Recall that in lecture two, he attempted two drafts concerning "[his] method of work." It is atypical of Peirce not to acknowledge his sources and indeed his method differs from Descartes's on several points, notably in his criticism of Descartes's notion of "clear and distinct ideas," as outlined in "How to Make Our Ideas Clear" in 1898. These very lectures comprehensively explain the elements of which an inquiry is constituted, elements that are unlike Descartes's. The likeness of Peirce's and Descartes's methods does not arise from the similarity of the elements of objects of inquiry that are analyzed, but from the technique of taking the elements together in an abstractive or intellectual intuition as the last stage of inquiry. See excerpts from manuscripts 311 and 312 in this introduction, lecture two.

Lectures on Pragmatism
Lecture I.

A certain maxim of Logic which I have
called Pragmatism has recommended itself
to me for divers reasons and on sundry considera
tions. Having taken it as my guide in most of
my thought, I find (as the years of my knowledge
of it lengthen, my sense of the importance of it
presses upon me
more and more. If it is only true, it is
certainly a wonderfully efficient instrument It
is not to philosophy only that it is applicable.
I have found it of signal service in every branch
of science that I have studied. My want of skill
in practical affairs does not prevent me from
perceiving the advantage of being well imbued
with pragmatism in the conduct of life.

PRAGMATISM AS A PRINCIPLE
AND METHOD OF RIGHT THINKING

LECTURE ONE: INTRODUCTION

A certain maxim of Logic which I have called Pragmatism has recommended itself to me for diverse reasons and on sundry considerations. Having taken it as my guide in most of my thought, I find that as the years of my knowledge of it lengthen, my sense of the importance of it presses upon me more and more. If it is only true, it is certainly a wonderfully efficient instrument. It is not to philosophy only that it is applicable. I have found it of signal service in every branch of science that I have studied. My want of skill in practical affairs does not prevent me from perceiving the advantage of being well imbued with pragmatism in the conduct of life.

Yet I am free to confess that objections to this way of thinking have forced themselves upon me and have been found more formidable the further my plummet has been dropped into the abyss of philosophy, and the closer my questioning at each new attempt to fathom its depths.

I propose, then, to submit to your judgment in half a dozen lectures an examination of the *pros* and *cons* of pragmatism by means of which I hope to show you the result of allowing to both *pros* and *cons* their full legitimate values. With more time I would gladly follow up the guiding thread so caught up and go on to ascertain what are the veritable conclusions, or at least the genera of veritable conclusions, to which a carefully rectified pragmatism will truly lead. If you find what I say acceptable you will have learned something worth your while. If you can refute me, the gain will be chiefly on my side; but even in that <event> I anticipate your acknowledging, when I take my leave of you, that the discussion has not been without profit; and in future years I am confident that you will recur to these thoughts and find that you have more to thank me for than you could understand at first.

I suppose I may take it for granted that you all know what *pragmatism* is. I have met with a number of definitions of it lately, against none of which I am much disposed to raise any violent protest. Yet to say exactly what pragmatism is describes pretty well what you and I have to puzzle out together.

We must start with some rough approximation of it, and I am inclined to think that the shape in which I first stated [it] will be the most useful one to adopt as matter to work upon, chiefly because it is the form most personal to your lecturer, and which for that reason he can discourse most intelligently. Besides pragmatism and personality are more or less of the same kidney.

I sent forth my statement in January 1878; and for about twenty years never heard from it again. I let fly my dove; and that dove has never come back to me to this very day. But of late quite a brood of young ones have been fluttering about, from the feathers of which I might fancy that mine had found a brood. To speak plainly, a considerable number of philosophers have lately written as they might have written in case they had been reading either what I wrote but were ashamed to confess it, or had been reading something that some reader of mine had read. For they seem quite disposed to adopt my term *pragmatism*.

<If they are ashamed of me, I am not at all so of them, for they are as bright and witty a company as one could desire to be among, quite distinguished for their terse and buoyant style. The most ridiculous avowal a man could well stumble over would be that he had learned anything of a logician. Surely every man dabbles in philosophy <<more or less>> early or late, and if you can find any philosopher who doesn't deem himself to have penetrated a little deeper into philosophy than any other that ever lived, you will have found something curious. <<You may be sure that he is not the one whose dabbling has been the shallowest.>> Now in order to be a really deep philosopher it is necessary to deny that anybody else knows the ABC of metaphysics and especially to find fault with those who hold substantially the same opinions as you do yourself. The direst fault I find with all the people who pose as pragmatists is that they all write philosophy in more or less lively styles and are sometimes even entertaining. It is plain that to be deep one must be dull. I do not know what fault these writers find with me because they never mention me; but I suspect that if they did they would find me flippant for making pragmatism to be a mere maxim of logic instead of being what they all hold it to be, a sublime principle of theoretical philosophy.>[1]

In order to be admitted to better philosophical standing <among them> I have endeavored to put pragmatism as I understand it into the same form of a philosophical theorem. I have not succeeded any better than this:

Pragmatism is the principle that every theoretical judgment expressible in a sentence in the indicative mood is a confused form of thought whose only meaning, if it has any, lies in its tendency to enforce a corresponding practical maxim expressible as a conditional sentence with its apodosis in the imperative mood.[2]

But the Maxim of Pragmatism, as I originally stated it, *Revue philoso-phique* VII 47, 48 and *Pop. Sci. Monthly* XII p. 293, is as follows:

Consider what effects that might conceivably have practical bearings we conceive the object of our conception to have: then, our conception of those effects is the whole of our conception of the object.

Considérer quels sont les effets pratiques que nous pensons pouvoir être produits par l'objet de notre conception. La conception de tous ces effets est la conception complète de l'objet.

Pour développer le sens d'une pensée, il faut donc simplement déter-miner quelles habitudes elle produit, car le sens d'une chose consiste sim-plement dans les habitudes qu'elle implique. La caractère d'une habitude dépend de la façon dont elle peut nous faire agir non pas seulement dans telle circonstance probable, mais dans toute circonstance possible, si im-probable qu'elle puisse être. Ce qu'est une habitude dépend de ces deux points: quand et comment elle fait agir. Pour le premier point: quand? tout stimulant à l'action dérive d'une perception; pour le second point: comment? le but de toute action est d'amener au résultat sensible. Nous atteignons ainsi le tangible et le pratique comme base de toute différence de pensée, si subtile qu'elle puisse être.

The utility of the maxim provided it is only true appears in a sufficient light in the original article. I will here add a few examples which were not given in that paper.

There are many problems connected with probabilities which are sub-ject to doubt. One of them, for example, is this: Suppose an infinitely large company of infinitely rich men sit down to play against an infinitely rich bank at a game of chance, at which neither side has any advantage, each one betting a franc against a franc at each bet. Suppose that each player continues to play until he has netted a gain of one franc and then retires, surrendering his place to a new player.

The chance that a player will ultimately net a gain of a franc may be calculated as follows:

Let X_ℓ be a player's chance if he were to continue playing indefinitely of ever netting a gain of ℓ francs.

But after he has netted a gain of 1 franc, his chance of doing which is X_1, he is no richer than before, since he is infinitely rich. Consequently his chance of winning the second franc, after he has won the first, is the same as his chance of winning the first franc. That is, it is X_1 and his chance of winning both is $X_2 = (X_1)^2$. And so in general $X_\ell = (X_1)^\ell$.

Now his chance of netting a gain of 1 franc, X_1, is the sum of the chances of the two ways in which it may come about; namely by first winning the first bet of which the chance is 1/2, and by first losing the first bet and then netting a gain of 2 francs of which the chance is $1/2\,X_1^2$.

Therefore $X_1 = 1/2 + 1/2\,X_1^2$

or $X_1^2 - 2X_1 + 1 = 0$

or $(X_1 - 1)^2 = 0$

But if the square of a number is zero, the number itself is zero. Therefore

$X_1 - 1 = 0$

or $X_1 = 1$

Consequently, the books would say it was dead certain that any player will ultimately net his winning of a franc and retire. If so it must be certain that *every* player would win his franc and would retire.

Consequently there would be a continual outflow of money from the bank. And yet, since the game is an even one, the banker would not net any loss. How is this paradox to be explained?

The theory of probabilities is full of paradoxes and puzzles. Let us, then, apply the maxim of pragmatism to the solution of them.

In order to do this, we must ask *What is meant by saying that the probability of an event has a certain value, p?* According to the maxim of pragmatism, then, we must ask what practical difference it can make whether the value is *p* or something else. Then we must ask how are probabilities applied to practical affairs. The answer is that the great business of insurance depends upon it. Probability is used in insurance to determine how much must be paid on a certain risk to make it safe to pay a certain sum if the event insured against should occur. Then, we must ask how can it be safe to engage to pay a large sum if an uncertain event occurs. The answer is that the insurance company does a very large business and is able to ascertain pretty closely out of a thousand risks of a given description how many in any one year will be losses. The business problem is this. The number of policies of a certain description that can be sold in a year will depend on the price set up on them. Let *p* be that price, and let *n* be the number that can be sold at that price, so that the larger *p* is, the smaller *n* will be. Now *n* being a large number a certain proportion *q* of these policies, *qn* in all, will be losses during the year; and if ℓ be the loss on each, $qn\,\ell$ will be the total loss. Then what the insurance company has to do is to set *p* at such a figure that $pn - q\ell n$ or $(p - q\ell)n$ shall reach its maximum possible value.

The solution of this equation is

$$p = q\ell + \delta p/\delta n \; n$$

where $\delta p/\delta n$ is the amount by which the price would have to be lowered in order to sell one policy more. Of course if the price were raised instead of lowered just one policy fewer would be sold. For then by so lowering the profit from being

$$(p - q\ell)\, n$$

would be changed to

$$(p - q\ell - \delta p/\delta n)\, (n + 1)$$

that is, to

$$(p - q\ell)\, n + p - q\ell - \delta p/\delta n\, (n + 1)$$

and this being less than before

$$q\ell + \delta p/\delta n\, (n + 1) > p$$

and by raising it, the change would be to

$$(p - q\ell + \delta p/\delta n)\, (n - 1)$$

that is, to

$$(p - q\ell)\, n - p + q\ell + \delta p/\delta n\, (n - 1)$$

—and this being less than before

$$p > q\ell + \delta p/\delta n\, (n - 1).$$

So since p is intermediate between

$$q\ell + \delta p/\delta n\, n + \delta p/\delta n$$

and $\qquad q\ell + \delta p/\delta n\, n - \delta p/\delta n$

and $\delta p/\delta n$ is very small, it must be very close to the truth to write

$$p = q\ell + \delta p/\delta n\, n.$$

This is the problem of insurance. Now in order that probability may have any bearing on this problem, it is obvious that it must be of the nature of a *real fact* and not a mere *state of mind*. For facts only enter into the solution of the problem of insurance. And this fact must evidently be a fact of statistics.

Without now going into certain reasons of detail that I should enter into if I were lecturing on probabilities, it must be that probability is a *statistical ratio* and further in order to satisfy still more special conditions, it is convenient, for the class of problems to which insurance belongs, to make it the statistical ratio of the number of experiential occurrences of a specific kind to the number of experiential occurrences of a generic kind, in the long run.

In order, then, that probability should mean anything, it will be requisite to specify to what *species* of event it refers and to what *genus* of event it refers. It also refers to a *long run*, that is, to an indefinitely long series of occurrences taken together in the order of their occurrence in possible experience.

In this view of the matter, we note, to begin with that a given species of event considered as belonging to a given genus of events does not necessarily have any definite probability. Because the probability is the ratio of one infinite multitude to another. Now infinity divided by infinity is altogether indeterminate, except in special cases.

It is very easy to give examples of events that have no definite probability. If a person agrees toss up a cent again and again forever and beginning as soon as the first head turns up whenever two heads are separated by any odd number of tails in the succession of throws [that person agrees] to pay 2 to that power in cents provided that whenever the two successive heads are separated by any even number of throws he receives 2 to that power in cents, it is impossible to say what the probability will be that he comes out a winner.

In half of the cases after the first head the next throw will be a head and he will receive $(-2)^0 = 1$ cent. Which since it happens half the time will be in the long run a winning of 1/2 a cent per head thrown.

But in half of the other half the cases, that is in 1/4 of all the cases, one tail will intervene and he will have to receive $(-2)^1 = -2$ cents, i.e., he will have to pay 2 cents, which happening 1/4 of the time will make an average loss of 1/2 a cent per head thrown.

But in half the remaining quarter of the cases, i.e., 1/8 of all the cases, two tails will intervene and he will receive $(-2)^2 = 4$ cents which happening once every eight times will be worth 1/2 a cent per head thrown and so on; so that his account in the long run will be

$$1/2 - 1/2 + 1/2 - 1/2 + 1/2 - 1/2 + 1/2 - 1/2 \text{ } ad \text{ } infinitum,$$

the sum of which may be 1/2 or may be *zero*. Or rather it is quite indeterminate.

If instead of being paid $(-2)^n$ when n is the number of intervening tails, he were paid $(-2)^{n^2}$ the result would be he would probably either win or lose enormously without there being any definite probability that it would be winning rather than losing.

I think I may recommend this game with confidence to gamblers as being the most frightful ruin yet invented; and a little cheating would do everything in it.

Now let us revert to our original problem and consider the state of things after every other bet. After the second

G/G   1/4 of the players will have gained, gone out, and been replaced by players who have gained and gone out so that a number of

francs equal to half the number of seats will have been paid out
by the bank

G/L   1/4 of the players will have gained and gone out and been replaced by players who have lost, making the bank even

L/G   1/4 of the players will have lost and then gained making the
bank and them even

L/L   1/4 of the players will have lost twice making a gain to the
bank of half as many francs as there are seats at the table.

The bank then will be where it was. Players to the number of three quarters of the seats will have netted their franc each; but players to the number of a quarter of the seats will have lost two francs each and another
equal number one franc each, just paying for the gains of those who have
retired.

That is the way it will happen every time. Just before the fifth bet of
the players at the table, 3/8 will have lost nothing, 1/4 will have lost 1
franc, 1/4 two francs, 1/16 three francs and 1/16 four francs. Thus some
will always have lost a good deal. Those who sit at the table will among
them always have paid just what those who have gone out have carried
away.

But it will be asked How then can it happen that *all* gain? I reply that
I never said that all would gain, I only said the probability was 1 that any
one would ultimately gain his franc. But does not probability 1 mean certainty? Not at all, it only means that the ratio of the number of those who
ultimately gain to the total number is 1. Since the number of seats at the
table is infinite the ratio of the number of those who never gain to the
number of seats may be zero and yet they may be infinitely numerous. So
that probabilities 1 and 0 are very far from corresponding to certainty *pro*
and *con*.

If I were to go into practical matters, the advantage of pragmatism, of
looking at the substantial practical issue, would be still more apparent. But
here pragmatism is generally practiced by successful men. In fact, the genus of efficient men [is] mainly distinguished from the inefficient precisely
by this.

There is, no doubt, then that pragmatism opens a very easy road to
the solution of an immense variety of questions. But it does not at all
follow from that that it is true. On the contrary, one may very properly
entertain a suspicion of any method which so resolves the most difficult
questions into easy problems. No doubt Ockham's razor is logically sound.
A hypothesis should be stripped of every feature which is in no wise called
for to furnish an explanation of observed facts. *Entia non sunt multiplicanda praeter necessitatem*; only we may very well doubt whether a very
simple hypothesis can contain every factor that is necessary. Certain it is

that most hypotheses which at first seemed to unite great simplicity with entire sufficiency have had to be greatly complicated in the further progress of science.

What is the *proof* that the possible practical consequences of a concept constitute the sum total of the concept? The argument upon which I rested the maxim in my original paper was that *belief* consists mainly in being deliberately prepared to adopt the formula believed in as the guide to action. If this be in truth the nature of belief, then undoubtedly the proposition believed in can itself be nothing but a maxim of conduct. That I believe is quite evident.

But *how do we know* that belief is nothing but the deliberate preparedness to act according to the formula believed?

My original article carried this back to a psychological principle. The conception of truth according to me was developed out of an original impulse to act consistently, to have a definite intention. But in the first place, this was not very clearly made out, and in the second place, I do not think it satisfactory to reduce such fundamental things to facts of psychology. For man could alter his nature, or his environment would alter it if he did not voluntarily do so, if the impulse were not what was advantageous or fitting. Why has evolution made man's mind to be so constructed? That is the question we must nowadays ask, and all attempts to ground the fundamentals of logic on psychology are seen to be essentially shallow.

The question of the nature of belief, or in other words the question of what the true logical analysis of the act of judgment is, is the question upon which logicians of late years have chiefly concentrated their energies. Is the pragmatistic answer satisfactory?

Do we not all perceive that *judgment* is something closely allied to *assertion*? That is the view that ordinary speech entertains. A man or woman will be heard to use the phrase "I says to myself." That is *judgment* is held to be either no more than an *assertion to oneself* or at any rate something very like that.

Now it is a fairly easy problem to analyze the nature of *assertion*. To find an easily dissected example, we shall naturally take a case where the assertive element is magnified,—a very formal assertion, such as an affidavit. Here a man goes before a notary or magistrate and takes such action that if what he says is not true, evil consequences will be visited upon him, and this he does with a view to thus causing other men to be affected just as they would if the proposition sworn to had presented itself to them as a perceptual fact.

We thus see that the act of assertion is an act of a totally different nature from the act of apprehending the meaning of the proposition and we cannot expect that any analysis of what assertion is or any analysis of what *judgment* or *belief* is, if that act is at all allied to assertion, should throw any light at all on the widely different question of what the apprehension of the meaning of a proposition is.

What is the difference between making an *assertion* and *laying a wager*? Both are acts whereby the agent deliberately subjects himself to evil consequences if a certain proposition is not true. Only when he offers to bet he hopes the other man will make himself responsible in the same way for the truth of the contrary proposition; while when he makes an *assertion* he always (or almost always) wishes the man to whom he makes it to be led to do what he does. Accordingly in our vernacular "I will bet" so and so, is the phrase expressive of a private opinion which one does not expect others to share while "You bet" _____ is a form of assertion intended to cause another to follow suit.

Such then seems at least in a preliminary glance at the matter to be a satisfactory account of assertion. Now let us pass to judgment and belief. There can, of course, be no question that a man will act in accordance with his belief so far as his belief has any practical consequences. The only doubt is whether this is *all* that belief is, whether belief is a mere nullity so far as it does not influence conduct. What possible effect upon conduct can it have, for example, to believe that the diagonal of a square is incommensurable with the side? Name a discrepancy E no matter how small, and the diagonal differs from a rational quantity by much less than that. Prof. Newcomb in his calculus and all mathematicians of his rather antiquated fashion think that they have proved two quantities to be equal when they have proved that they differ by less than any assignable quantity. I once tried hard to make Newcomb say whether the diagonal of the square differed from a rational fraction of the side or not; but he saw what I was driving at and would not answer. The proposition that the diagonal is incommensurable has stood in the textbooks from time immemorial without ever being assailed and I am sure that the most modern type of mathematician holds to it most decidedly. Yet it seems quite absurd to say that there is any objective practical difference between commensurable and incommensurable.

Of course you can say if you like that the act of expressing a quantity as a rational fraction is a piece of conduct and that it is in itself a *practical* difference that one kind of quantity can be so expressed and the other not. But a thinker must be shallow indeed if he does not see that to admit a species of practicality that consists in one's conduct about words and modes of expression is at once to break down all the bars against the nonsense that pragmatism is designed to exclude.

What the pragmatist has his pragmatism for is to be able to say here is a definition and it does not differ at all from your confusedly apprehended conception because there is no *practical* difference. But what is to prevent his opponent from replying that there is a practical difference which consists in his recognizing one as his conception and not the other. That is, one is expressible in a way in which the other is not expressible.

Pragmatism is completely volatilized if you admit that sort of practicality.

It must be understood that all I am now attempting to show is that Pragmatism is apparently a matter of such great probable concern, and at the same time so much doubt hangs over its legitimacy, that it will be well worth our while to make a methodical, scientific, and thorough examination of the whole question, so as to make sure of our ground, and obtain some secure method for such a preliminary filtration of questions as pragmatism professes to furnish.

Let us, then, enter upon this inquiry. But before doing so let us mark out the proposed course of it. That should always be done in such cases, even if circumstances subsequently require the plan to be modified, as they usually will.

Although our inquiry is to be an inquiry into truth, whatever the truth may turn out to be, and therefore of course is not to be influenced by any liking for pragmatism or any pride in it as an American doctrine, yet still we do not come to this inquiry any more than anybody comes to any inquiry in that blank state that the lawyers pretend to insist upon as desirable, though I give them credit for enough common sense to know better.

We have some reason already to think there is some truth in pragmatism although we also have some reason to think that there is something wrong with it. For unless both branches of this statement were true we should do wrong to waste time and energy upon the inquiry we are undertaking.

I will, therefore, presume that there is enough truth in it to render a preliminary glance at ethics desirable. For if, as pragmatism teaches us, what we think is to be interpreted in terms of what we are prepared to do, then surely *logic*, or the doctrine of what we ought to think, must be an application of the doctrine of what we deliberately choose to do, which is Ethics.

But we cannot get any clue to the secret of Ethics,—a most entrancing field of thought but sown broadcast with pitfalls,—until we have first made up our formula for what it is that we are prepared to admire. I do not care what doctrine of ethics be embraced, it will always be so. Suppose, for example, our maxim of ethics to be Pearson's that all our action ought to be directed toward the perpetuation of the biological stock to which we belong. Then the question will arise, On what principle should it be deemed such a fine thing for this stock to survive,—or a fine thing at all?

Is there nothing in the world or *in posse* that would be admirable *per se* except copulation and swarming? Is swarming a fine thing at all apart from any results that it may lead to? The course of thought will follow a parallel line if we consider Marshall's ethical maxim: Act to restrain the impulses which demand immediate reaction, in order that the impulse-order determined by the existence of impulses of less strength, but of wider significance, may have full weight in the guidance of your life. Although I have not as clear an apprehension as I could wish of the philosophy of this very close, but too technical, thinker, yet I presume that he would not be among those who would object to making Ethics dependent upon Esthetics. Certainly, this maxim which I have just read to you from his latest book supposes that it is a fine thing for an impulse to have its way, but yet not an equally fine thing for one impulse to have its way and for another impulse to have its way. There is a preference which depends upon the *significance* of impulses, whatever that may mean. It supposes that there is some ideal state of things which, regardless of how it should be brought about and independently of any ulterior reason whatsoever, is held to be good or fine. In short, ethics must rest upon a doctrine which without at all considering what our conduct is to be, divides ideally possible states of things into two classes, those that would be admirable and those that would [be] unadmirable, and undertakes to define precisely what it is that constitutes the admirableness of an ideal. Its problem is to determine by analysis what it is that one ought deliberately to admire *per se* in itself regardless of what it may lead to and regardless of its bearings upon human conduct. I call that inquiry *Esthetics*, because it is generally said that the three normative sciences are logic, ethics, and esthetics, being the three doctrines that distinguish good and the bad, *Logic* in regard to representations of truth, *Ethics* in regard to efforts of will, and *Esthetics* in objects considered simply in their presentation. Now that third normative science can be no other than that which I have described. It is evidently the basic normative science upon which as a foundation the doctrine of ethics must be reared to be surmounted in its turn by the doctrine of logic.

But before we can attack any normative science, any science which proposes to separate the sheep from the goats, it is plain that there must be a preliminary inquiry which shall justify the attempt to establish such dualism. This must be a science that does *not* draw any distinction of good and bad in any sense whatever, but just contemplates phenomena as they are, simply opens its eyes and describes what it sees. Not what it sees in the real as distinguished from figment,—not regarding any such dichotomy but simply describing the object, as a phenomenon, and stating what it finds in all phenomena alike. This is the science which Hegel made his starting-point, under the name of the *Phänomenologie des Geistes,*—although he considered it in a fatally narrow spirit, since he restricted himself to what *actually* forces itself on the mind and so colored his whole philosophy with the ignoration of the distinction of essence and existence and so gave it the nominalistic and I might say in a certain sense the *pragmatoidal* character in which the worst [of] the Hegelian errors have their origin. I will so far follow Hegel as to call this science *Phenomenology* although I will not restrict it to the observation and analysis of *experience* but extend it to describing all the features that are common to whatever is *experienced* or might conceivably be experienced or become an object of study in any way direct or indirect.

Hegel was quite right in holding that it was the business of this science to bring out and make clear the *Categories* or fundamental modes. He was also right in holding that these *categories* are of two kinds, the Universal categories all of which apply to everything and the series of categories consisting of phases of evolution.

As to these latter, I am satisfied that Hegel has not approximated to any correct catalogue of them. It may be that here and there, in the long wanderings of his Encyclopedia, he has been a little warmed by the truth. But in all its main features his catalogue is utterly wrong, according to me. I have made long and arduous studies of this matter, but I have not been able to draw up any catalogue that satisfies me. My studies, if they are ever published, will I believe be found helpful to future students of this most difficult problem, but in these lectures I shall have little to say on that subject. The case is quite different with the three Universal Categories, which Hegel, by the way, does not look upon as Categories at all, or at least he does not call them so, but as three stages of thinking. In regard to these, it appears to me that Hegel is so nearly right that my own doctrine might very will be taken for a variety of Hegelianism, although in point of fact it was determined in my mind by considerations entirely foreign to Hegel, at a time when my attitude toward Hegelianism was one of contempt. There was no influence upon me from Hegel unless it was of so occult a kind as to entirely escape my ken; and if there was such an occult influence, it strikes me as about as good an argument for the essential truth of the doctrine, as is the coincidence that Hegel and I arrived in quite independent ways substantially to the same result.

This science of phenomenology, then, must be taken as the basis upon which normative science is to be erected, and accordingly must claim our first attention.

This science of Phenomenology is in my view the most primal of all the positive sciences. That is, it is not based, as to its principles, upon any other *positive science.* By a *positive* science I mean an inquiry which seeks for positive knowledge, that is for such knowledge as may conveniently be expressed in a *categorical proposition*. Logic and the other normative sciences, although they ask not what *is* but what *ought to be*, nevertheless are positive sciences since it is by asserting positive, categorical truth that they are able to show that what they call good really is so; and the right reason, right effort, and right being of which they treat derive that character from positive categorical fact.

Perhaps you will ask me whether it is possible to conceive of a science which should not aim to declare that something is positively or categorically true. I reply that it is not only possible to conceive of such a science, but that such science exists and flourishes, and Phenomenology which does not depend upon any other *positive science* nevertheless must, if it is to be properly grounded, be made to depend upon the Conditional or Hypothetical Science of *Pure Mathematics*, whose only aim is to discover not how things actually are, but how they might be supposed to be, if not in our universe, then in some other. A Phenomenology which does not reckon with pure mathematics, a science hardly come to years of discretion when Hegel wrote, will be the same pitiful clubfooted affair that Hegel produced.

LECTURE TWO: PHENOMENOLOGY OR THE DOCTRINE OF CATEGORIES
PART A: MATHEMATICS AS A BASIS OF LOGIC
(DRAFT ONE)

If I were asked to give a young gentleman a liberal education in 100 lessons, I should devote 50 lessons to teaching some small branch, no matter which, thoroughly,—say perhaps to boiling an egg,—or at any rate so nearly thoroughly so that the young man should begin to know what thoroughness really means,—and should never thereafter be guilty of the ridiculous conceit of fancying that he knew English, for example. The other fifty I would distribute as follows: three lessons should teach the science of mathematics, one esthetics, two ethics, one metaphysics, one psychology, one the living and dead languages, one history, geography, and statistics ancient and modern, one dynamics and physics, one chemistry, one biology, one astronomy, geology, and physical geography, one law, divinity, medicine and the other applied sciences, and the remaining 36 should be devoted to logic. Thereupon I would give him a certificate to the effect that he was a more truly educated man than two-thirds of the doctors of philosophy the world over, and this certificate would have the singularity of being strictly true.

For thirty-six lessons into which the teacher should throw his whole soul would suffice really to teach the leading principles of logic, and logic, the ability to think well, constitutes about three-eighths of a truly liberal education. But it is a mighty important three-eighths. A liberal education ought to be a living organism and logic may truly be said to be the heart of it. But I do not say that six lectures on a fragment of logic will have the same proportionate value. It will be like cutting out five-sixths of a man's heart and leaving him the remainder. Or rather it would be that if lectures were *lessons*, which they certainly are far from being.

Now, gentlemen, every minute counts. There remain about fifty in which to present to you glimpses of those conceptions of mathematics which have any relation to our problem.

123

Pure Mathematics is the study of pure hypotheses regardless of any analogies they may have in our universe. The simplest possible hypothesis would be that there is a single element

A

and nothing more. The mathematics of this consists in a single proposition, as follows: There is nothing that can be said of A.

The next branch of mathematics we come to supposes two elements, or, as analogy suggests that we should call them, two *values*. We might denote them by B and M, the initials of *bonum* and *malum*. They are different. In regard to anything, *X*, we may inquire whether under any assumption it is B or M. We know that it cannot be both. We also know that it is one or the other; for that is our hypothesis.

The resulting mathematics if developed by means of arrays of letters with conventional signs to signify relations between them will constitute the Boolean algebra of logic.[1] It may equally be developed by means of diagrams composed of lines and dots, and this in various ways of which the *Eulerian diagrams* form one example while my *Existential Graphs* and *Entitative Graphs* are others.[2]

Of this mathematics under its original limitations confining its applicability [to] non-relative logic no masterly presentation has ever been given. The nearest approach to such a thing in print is contained in the first two chapters of my paper in Vol. III of the *Am. Jour. Math.*; and I may mention that Schröder's criticism of my definitions of aggregation and composition there given, although at first I assented to it, is all wrong and that the demonstration which Schröder professes to demonstrate cannot exist does exist and is perfect. But the whole thing is bad; first, because it does not treat the subject from the point of view of pure mathematics, as it should have done; and second, because the fundamental propositions are not made out. I follow too much in the footsteps of ordinary numerical algebra. And the sketch of the algebra of the copula is very insufficient.[3]

I devoted some months last year to attempting a strict presentation and found it an extremely difficult job. I have the thing all type written but I am far from being satisfied with it. I shall try again one of these days, if I can find where with all to keep body and soul together while I am doing the work.

This kind of mathematics is rather poverty-stricken as to valuable ideas as might naturally be expected. Nevertheless, there is one. The relation expressed by the copula of inclusion the fundamental importance of which I was the first to discover and to demonstrate in 1870 is a matter on which I regret not having time to discourse at large. It is the relation which B has to itself, which M has to itself, and which M has to B but which B has not to M.

This is the first germination in mathematics of that wonderful conception of greater and less and of all systems however complicated having dimensions, each in itself linear.

I call this kind of mathematics which rests on the hypothesis of two objects, elements, or values, *Dichotomic Mathematics*.

In 1870 I made a contribution to this subject which nobody who masters the subject can deny was the most important excepting Boole's original work that ever has been made.

I think it was in 1883 that I printed at my own expense a brochure presenting the pure mathematical aspect of this,—not by any means as well as I could now do but still tolerably. When it was done and I was correcting the last proof, it suddenly occurred to me that it was after all nothing but Cayley's theory of matrices, which appeared when I was a little boy.[4] However, I took a copy of it to the great algebraist Sylvester.[5] He read it and said very disdainfully—Why it is nothing but my *umbral notation*. I felt squelched and never sent out the copies. But I was a little comforted later by finding that what Sylvester called *"my* umbral notation" had first been published in 1693 by another man of some talent, named Godfry William Leibniz. He himself speaks of it as *"une ouverture assez extraordinaire."* You will see it in its original French in Muir's admirable *Theory of Determinants in the Historical Order of its Development.*[6] Sylvester's name *umbra*, which is the only distinctive name the thing has ever received, must, I fear, be retained, although *ion* or *radicle* would be far better. For who ever heard of two shadows combining together to form a substance!

They are things that do not exist. That is to say they do not belong to the universe of the fundamental hypothesis, being neither B nor M, in the dichotomic mathematics. In other mathematics, they have no existence in the universe of quantity. But joined together in sets, they do. They are just like chemical radicles, each having a certain number of unsatisfied wants. When each of these is satisfied by union with another, the completely saturated whole has an existence in the universe of quantity. Surely the word *umbra* utterly fails to suggest all that; while the word *radicle* gives the idea exactly.

The mathematics which results from following out this idea of Leibniz which I rediscovered for myself and applied to dichotomic mathematics is, in mathematics taken generally, now most usually called the theory of matrices.

But I do not think that the icon of a matrix exhibits the idea quite so well as the idea of a chemical radicle does.

The application of this idea to logic gives the *exact logic of relatives*. DeMorgan had before me developed to some extent the logic of relatives.[7]

Schröder thought I greatly exaggerated the importance of DeMorgan's work. But Schröder greatly exaggerated the merits of that particular algebra of mine to the study of which his third volume is mainly devoted.

This exact logic of relatives, and even in some degree DeMorgan's development, simply dynamites all our traditional notions of logic and with them Kant's Critic of the Pure Reason which was founded upon them.

But I must tell you that all that you can find in print of my work on logic are simply scattered outcroppings here and there of a rich vein which remains unpublished. Most of it I suppose has been written down; but no human being could ever put together the fragments. I could not myself do so. All I could do would be to make an entirely new presentation and this I could only do in five or six years of hard work devoted to that alone. Since I am now 63 years old and since all this is matter calculated to make a difference in man's future intellectual development, I can only say that if the *genus homo* is so foolish as not to set me at the task, I shall lean back in my chair and take my ease. I have done a great work wholly without any kind of aid, and now I am willing to undergo the last great effort which must finish me up in order to give men the benefit of what I have done. But if I am not in a situation to do so but have to earn my living, why that will be infinitely the more comfortable way of completing the number of my days; and if anybody supposes that I shall regret missing the fame that might attach to the name of C. S. Peirce,—a name that won't be mine much longer,—I shall only say that he can indulge that fancy without my taking the trouble to contradict him. I have reached the age when I think of my home as being on the other side rather than on this uninteresting planet.

Taking leave of dichotomic mathematics, I may mention that trichotomic mathematics which starts from the fundamental hypothesis of three elements • • has never received any development at all, to speak of, although it would certainly be extremely interesting and a field in which there would be soil for the growth of great and wonderful works of genius.

Let me call your attention to the circumstance that there is only one way in which 3 things can be arranged. ABC and CBA are different provided you recognize the difference of shape of B and C toward their right and their left sides. But if you do that, you are dealing with more than 3 objects. You are dealing with A, B viewed from the left, B viewed from the right, C viewed from the left, C viewed from the right.

If ABC are mere designations of dots on a line ⟋•⟍ the arrangement CBA is merely the arrangement ABC viewed from the other side. That is, you introduce a fourth and fifth object which is the pair of objects implied in the idea of passing through one way or the other. We may represent this idea of passing through the series one way or the other by two additional dots, which we may call I and J. Then indeed

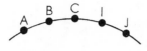

and

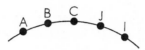

are different.

But it may be asked whether ABC and BCA (that is, ACB) are not different arrangements. I reply No. They are so when you conceive that in ABC from A you can pass to B and from B to C but cannot in the same way pass from C to A. But this is substantially to suppose a fourth object that puts a stop to the passage. For if I have ABC as dots on a line 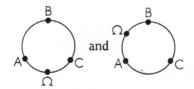 nothing prevents my completing the oval and then I can as well begin at B as at A and describe the arrangement as one in which if I pass from B to C I may go on beyond C to A. This I can do unless a stop, say Ω, is inserted.
Then of course

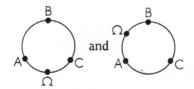

are different.

But it may be asked whether three objects ABC may not be conceived to be so related that AB have a particular connection with one another while C stands apart from them. To that I reply that that particular mode of connection is either described and made definite or it is not. In the latter case, if it be merely that there is *some* respect in which AB are connected together while C stands unconnected, then this not merely *may be* the case, but it *must be* the case. Namely A and B are any way specially connected in that they are members of the special pair AB while C stands apart in that respect. So this will not be the ground of any distinction between one arrangement of three things and another.

But if you describe that respect in which A and B agree, then that constitutes a fourth object which you introduce, a sort of hyphen between A and B.

So the theorem stands that there is but one possible arrangement of 3 objects. How about 4 objects? Could they be arranged in more than one way? You will tell me perhaps that I have just shown that there are three arrangements.

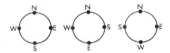

But if anybody [believed] there were three arrangements of 4 objects, it must have been you. I certainly did not.

Four objects *on one line* are *in reference to that line* in one or other of three orders. But any four objects can have three different lines drawn through them so as [to] be at once in all three arrangements.

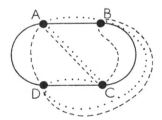
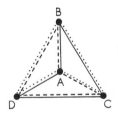

This shows that unless the particular mode of drawing the line is specified, in which case there are *at least* five objects, four objects can only be arranged in one way.

Following out this idea, we soon see that no number of objects can be *in themselves* arranged at all. Indeed, when this has once been proved, it seems to be self-evident. But there is another self-evident truth. Let those who are taking notes, note this; because axioms are a highly distinctive class of truths, as everybody will admit. I proceed then to enunciate this:

It is self-evident that every truth of pure mathematics is self-evident if you regard it from a suitable point of view.

And conversely, nothing that has not been expressly enunciated in your original hypothesis can be self-evident unless you regard it from a suitable point of view.

That will be worth thinking over when you get home because it is an *aperçu* into the nature of pure mathematics.

As to arrangements, we see that an arrangement is neither an ordinary object nor is it equivalent to any finite number of ordinary objects.

An arrangement is a relation.

A relation is an object; but it is not an ordinary object.

Let us return to the chemical idea. I call an object with one unsatisfied valency a *monad*, with two a *dyad*, with three a *triad*, etc., with more than two a *polyad*. With none at all a *medad*.

In our very simplest hypothesis of but one object, that one is plainly a *medad*. As there is nothing whatever that can be said of it, it is just the same as blank nothingness. So much truth there is in the proposition that *pure being* is *blank nothingness*.[8]

But in dichotomic mathematics we distinguish between the two objects, M and B. Then we *ipso facto* suppose not merely these two objects but also sixteen different relations between them. Or if we exclude the idea of a thing being related to itself there are four. These relations are *dyads*. And the two objects since they can enter into these relations are *monads*. If they had been *medads* they would be perfectly indistinguishable and would have been merely one.

The different relations of the two to one another have themselves a system of relations between them. How many? To write down the number of them would require seventy-eight figures.

These again have their relations and I could not tell you even how many figures would be required to write the number. The number of figures required merely to write down the number of figures would be too great.

The infinite series now begins to get its second wind.

These however are merely the dyadic relations which we have been considering. There are also triadic, tetradic, etc., relations which are vastly more numerous.

Part A: Mathematics as a Basis of Logic
(Draft Two)[1]

I feel that I must not waste time; and yet an investigation, in order to be really solid, must not confine itself too closely to a question set beforehand. Let us not set our thoughts on pragmatism but survey the whole ground and let the evidences for or against pragmatism or in favor of a modification of it come when they will without being teased.

Pure mathematics is the study of pure hypotheses regardless of any analogies that they may present to the state of our own universe. It would be wild to deny that there is such a science, as actively flourishing and progressive a science as any in the whole circle, if sciences can properly be said to form a circle. It certainly never would do to embrace pragmatism in any sense in which it should conflict with this great fact.

Mathematics, as everybody knows, is the most ancient of the sciences; that is, it was the first to attain a scientific condition. It shows today many traces of its ancient lineage, some of which are excellences while others are unfortunate inheritances. The Greeks were very fine reasoners. Throughout the XVIIIth century, the opinion prevailed among mathematicians that the strictness of Greek reasoning was unnecessary and stood in the way of advances in mathematics. But about the middle of the XIXth century it was found that in important respects the Greek understanding of geometry had been truer than that of the moderns. Gradually, beginning we may say with Cauchy early in the XIXth century a vast reform has been effected in the logic of mathematics which even yet is not completed.[2] This has quite revolutionized our conception of what mathematics is, and of many of the objects with which it deals, as well as of the logical relations between the different branches and the logical procedure. We are now far above the Greeks; but pure mathematics as it exists today is a decidedly youthful science in such an immature state that any student of logical power may very likely be in possession of important *aperçus* that have not yet become common property.

That mathematical reasoning is by no means confined to quantity is now generally perceived, so that it now becomes an extremely interesting logical question why quantity should play so great a part in it. It is recognized that the main business, if not the only business, of mathematics is the study of pure hypotheses and their consequences, or, as some say, the study of the consequences of pure hypotheses only. The Greeks approached this conception without attaining to it.

In the procedure of *all* mathematics whatsoever, the observation of diagrams plays a great part. That this is true in geometry was shown, though rather vaguely, by Stuart Mill in his logic.[3] It is not so obvious that algebra makes use of the observation of visual images; but I do not think there ought to be any doubt of it. Arrays of letters are observed, although these are mixed with conventional signs with which we associate certain so-called "rules," which are really permissions to make certain transformations. There is still some question how far the observation of imaginary, or artificial constructions, with experimentation upon them is logically essential to the procedure of mathematics, as to some extent it certainly is, even in the strictest Weierstrassian method, and how far it is merely a psychological convenience. I have sometimes been tempted to think that mathematics differed from an ordinary inductive science hardly at all except for the circumstance that experimentation which in the positive sciences is so costly in money, time, and energy, is in mathematics performed with such facility that the highest inductive certainty is attained almost in the twinkling of an eye. But it is rash to go so far as this. The mathematician, unless he greatly deludes himself, the possibility of which must be considered, reaches conclusions which are at once enormously and very definitely general and yet, but for the possibility of mere blunders, are absolutely infallible. Anybody who fancies that inductive reasoning can achieve anything like this has not made a sufficient study of inductive reasoning.

Induction is no doubt generalization and mathematicians,—especially mathematicians of power,—are so vastly superior to all other men in their power of generalization, that this may be taken as their distinctive characteristic. When we are dealing with the real world cold water gets dashed upon any generalizing passion that is not well held in check. There are very few rules in natural science, if there are any at all, that will bear being extended to the most *extreme cases*. Even that invaluable rule that the sum of the angles of a plane triangle is equal to two right angles shows signs of breaking down when by the aid of photometric considerations and that of the numbers of stars of different brightness, we compare statistically that component of stellar proper motions that is due wholly to the real motions of the stars with that component that is partly due to the motion of the solar system. But when we come to pure mathematics we not only do not avoid the extension of principles to extreme cases, but on the contrary that is one of the most valuable of mathematical methods. In regard to any ordinary function for example, if we only know for what values of the variable it becomes zero and for what values it becomes infinite, we only need to know a single finite value to know all there is to be known about it.

No minute analysis of any piece of characteristically mathematical reasoning has ever appeared in print. There are numbers of attempts which profess to be successful. There have even been professed representations of the reasoning of whole books of Euclid in the forms of traditional syllogistic. But when you come to examine them, you find that the whole gist of the reasoning, every step in the progress of the thought which amounts to anything, instead of being analyzed logically is simply stated in the form of a premiss. The only attempts that are in any important degree exceptions to this are Mill's analysis of the *pons asinorum* which has its value, but which relates to too slight a bit of reasoning to teach much and

Dedekind's little book on the foundation of arithmetic with Schröder's re-statement of it.[4] This is certainly very instructive work. Yet it is open to both the same criticisms. In the first place, the mathematics illustrated is, most of it, of too low an order to bring out in strong colors the real peculiarities of mathematical thought; and in addition to that, the real mathematical thinking is, after all, only stated in pretty much the old fashion of all mathematical writers, that of abridged hints. It is not really analyzed into its logical steps. Every now and then the intelligent reader will say, "I wonder how he got the idea of proceeding so and so." But it is just at these points that the fine mathematical thinking comes in. It is left undissected.

When I first got the general algebra of logic into smooth running order, by a method that has lain nearly twenty years in manuscript and which I have lately concluded that it is so impossible to get it printed that it had better be burned, when I first found myself in possession of this machinery I promised myself that I should see the whole working of the mathematical reason unveiled directly. But when I came to try it, I found it was the same old story, except that more steps were now analyzed. About the same amount as in Dedekind's and Schröder's subsequent attempts. Between these steps there were unanalyzed parts which appeared more clearly in my representation than in theirs for the reason that I attempted to analyze a higher kind of mathematics. I was thus forced to the recognition in mathematics of a frequent recurrence of a peculiar kind of logical step, which when it is once explained is so very obvious that it seems wonderful that it should have escaped recognition so long. I could not make any exact statement of it without being led into technical developments that I desire to avoid and which are besides precluded by my being obliged to compress what I have to say into six lectures. But I can give you a general idea of what the step is so that you will be able by subsequently studying over any piece of mathematics to gain a tolerable notion of how it emerges in mathematics.

Let me at this point recall to your minds that the correlatives *abstract* and *concrete* are used in two very little connected senses in philosophy. In one sense, they differ little from *general* and *special* or *particular*, and are for that reason hardly indispensable terms; though that is the usual meaning in German, which is so to say pushed to an extreme in Hegel's use of the words. The other sense in which for example *hard* is concrete and *hardness* is abstract, is more usual in English than in other languages for the reason that English is more influenced by medieval terminology than other languages. This use of the words is fully as well authorized as the other if not more so; and this is the sense in which I shall exclusively employ the words. Hard is concrete; hardness abstract.

You remember the old satire which represents one of the old school of medical men,—one of that breed to whom medicine and logic seemed to be closely allied sciences,—who, asked why opium puts people to sleep, answers very sapiently "because it has a dormitive virtue." Instead of an explanation he simply transforms the premiss by the introduction of an *abstraction*, an abstract noun in place of a concrete predicate. It is a poignant satire, because everybody is supposed to know well enough that this transformation from a *concrete predicate* to an abstract noun in an oblique case, is a mere transformation of language that leaves the thought absolutely untouched. I knew this as well as everybody else until I had arrived at that point in my analysis of the reasoning of mathematics where I found that this despised juggle of abstraction is an essential part of almost every really helpful step in mathematics; and since then what I used to know so very clearly does not appear to be at all so. There are useful abstractions and there are comparatively idle ones; and that one about *dormitive virtue*, which was invented with a view to being as silly as one could, of course does not rank high among abstractions. Nevertheless, when one closely scrutinizes it and puts it under a magnifying glass,—one can detect something in it that is not pure nonsense. The statement that opium puts people to sleep may, I think, be understood as an induction from many cases in which we have tried the experiment of exhibiting this drug, and have found that, if the patient is not subjected to any cerebral excitement, a moderate dose is generally followed by drowsiness, and a heavy dose by a dangerous stupor. That is simply a generalization of experience and nothing more. But surely there must be some explanation of this fact. There must be something, say to fix our ideas, perhaps some relation between a part of the molecule of morphine or other constituent of opium which is so related to some part of the molecule of nerve-protoplasm as to make a compound not so subject to metabole [μεταβολή] as natural protoplasm. But then perhaps the explanation is something different from this. Something or other, however, there must be in opium, some peculiarity of it which if it were understood would explain our invariably observing that the exhibition of this drug is followed by sleep. That much we may assert with confidence; and it seems to me to be precisely this which is asserted in saying that opium has a dormitive virtue which explains its putting people to sleep. It is not an explanation; but it is good sound doctrine, namely that *some*thing in opium must explain the facts observed.

Thus you see that even in this example which was invented with a view to showing abstraction at its very idlest, the abstraction is not after all entirely senseless. It really does represent a step in sound reasoning.

Before going on to consider mathematical abstractions, let us ask ourselves how an *abstraction*, meaning that which an abstract noun denotes, is to be defined. It would be no proper definition of it to say that it is that which an abstract noun denotes. That would not be an analysis but a device for eluding analysis, quite similar to the old teacher's offering *dormitive virtue* as an explanation of opium's putting people asleep. An abstraction is something denoted by a noun substantive, something having a name; and therefore, whether it be a reality or whether it be a figment, it belongs to the category of *substance*, and is in proper philosophical terminology to be called a *substance,* or thing. Now then let us ask whether it be a real substance or a fictitious and false substance. Of course, it may chance to be false. There is no magic in the operation of abstraction which should cause it to produce only truth whether its premiss is true or not. That, then, is not in question. But the question is whether an abstraction *can* be real. For the moment, I will abstain from giving a positive answer to this question; but will content myself with pointing out that upon pragmatistic principles an abstraction may be, and normally will be, *real*. For according to the pragmatistic maxim this must depend upon whether all the practical consequences of it are true. Now the only practical consequences there are or can be are embodied in the statement that what is said about it is *true*. On pragmatistic principles *reality* can mean nothing except the *truth* of statements in which the real thing is asserted. To say that opium has a dormitive virtue means nothing and can have no practical consequences except what are involved in the statement that there is some circumstance connected with opium that explains its putting people to sleep. If there truly be such a circumstance, that is all that it can possibly mean,—according to the pragmatist maxim,—to say that opium really has a dormitive virtue. Indeed, nobody but a metaphysician would dream of denying that opium *really* has a dormitive virtue. Now it certainly cannot *really* have that which is pure figment. Without, then, coming to a positive decision as yet, since the truth of pragmatism is in question, we shall if we incline to believe there is something in pragmatism also incline to believe that an abstraction may be a real substance. At the same time nobody for many centuries,—unless it was some crank,—could possibly believe that an abstraction was an ordinary primary substance. You couldn't load a pistol with dormitive virtue and shoot it into a breakfast roll. Though it is in opium, it is wholly and completely in every piece of opium in Smyrna, as well as in every piece in every joint in the Chinatown of San Francisco. It has not that kind of existence which makes things *hic et nunc*. What kind of being has it? What does its reality consist in? Why it consists in something being true of something else that has a more primary mode of substantiality. Here we have, I believe, the materials for a good definition of an abstraction.

An abstraction is a substance whose being consists in the truth of some proposition concerning a more primary substance.

By a primary substance I mean a substance whose being is independent of what may be true of anything else. Whether there is any primary substance in this sense or not we may leave the metaphysicians to wrangle about.

By a *more* primary substance I mean one whose being does not depend upon all that the being of the less primary substance [does] but only upon a part thereof.

Now, then, armed with this definition I will take a shot at the abstractions of geometry [and] endeavor to bring down one or two of them.

We may define or describe a point as a place that has no parts. It is a familiar conception to mathematicians that space may be regarded as consisting of points. We shall find that it is not true; but it will do for a rough statement.

We may define a *particle* as a portion of matter which can be, and at every instant of time is, situated in a point.

According to a very familiar conception of matter,—whether it be true or not does not concern us,—every particle is supposed to exist in such a sense that all other matter might be annihilated without this particle ceasing to exist. Supposing that to be the case the particle is, so far at least as matter is concerned, a primary substance.

Now let us imagine that a particle moves. That is, at one instant it is in one point, at another in another. That may pass as a concrete description of what happens but it is very inadequate. For according to this, the particle might be now here now there without continuity of motion.

But the geometer says, the place which a moving particle occupies on the whole in the course of time is a *line*. That may be taken as the definition of a line. And a portion of matter which at any one instant is situated in a line may be called a *filament*.

But somebody here objects. Hold, he says. This will not do. It was agreed that all matter is particles. What then is this filament? Suppose the objector is told that the filament is composed of particles. But the objector is not satisfied. What do you mean by *being composed*? Is the filament a particle? No. Well then it is not matter, for matter is particles. But my dear sir the filament is particles. Then it is not one but many and this single filament you speak of is a fiction. All there is is particles. But my dear sir, do you not understand that although all there is is particles yet there really is a filament because to say that the filament exists is simply to say that particles exist. Its mode of being is such that it consists in there being a particle in every point that a moving particle might occupy.

Thus you see that if the particles be conceived as primary substances the filaments are abstractions, that is, they are substances the being of any one of which consists in something being true of some more primary substance or substances none of them identical with this filament.

A *film* or that portion of matter that in any one instant occupies a surface will be still more abstract. For a film will be related to a filament just as a filament is related to a particle.

And a solid body will be a still more extreme case of abstraction.

Atoms are supposed to have existences independent of one another. But in that case according to our definition of an *abstraction*, a collection of atoms, such as are all the things we see and handle, are *abstractions*.

They are just as much abstractions as that celebrated jack-knife that got a new blade and then a new handle and was finally confronted with a resurrected incarnation of its former self.

There is no denying this I believe, and therefore I do not think that we need have any further scruple in admitting that abstractions may be real,—indeed, a good deal less open to suspicion of fiction than are the primary substances. So the pragmatistic decision turned out correct in this instance, though it seemed a little risky at first.

That a *collection* is a species of abstraction becomes evident as soon as one defines the term *collection*. A *collection* is a substance whose existence consists in the existence of certain other things called its *members*.

An abstraction being a substance whose existence consists in something being true of something else, when this truth is a mere truth of existence the abstraction becomes a collection.

When we reflect upon the enormous role enacted in mathematics by the conception of *collection* in all its varieties, we can guess that were there no other kinds of abstractions in the science (instead of the hosts of them that there are), still the logical operation of abstraction would be a matter of prime importance in the analysis of the logic of mathematics.

I have so much more to say than I have of time to say it in that all my statements have to be left in the rough and I know I must produce an impression of vagueness and haziness of thought that would disappear upon close examination. I shall be obliged to presume that after leaving the lecture room you will do some close thinking on your own accounts.

I have no time to speak further of the interesting and important subject of the reasoning of mathematics. Nor can I discuss Dedekind's suggestion that pure mathematics is a branch of logic. It would I think be nearer the truth (although not strictly true) to say that necessary reasoning is not one of the topics of logical discussion. I am satisfied that all necessary reasoning is of the nature of mathematical reasoning. It is always diagrammatic in a broad sense although the wordy and loose deductions of the philosophers may make use rather of auditory diagrams, if I may be allowed the expression, than with visual ones.[5] All necessary reasoning is reasoning from pure hypothesis, in this sense, that if the premiss has any truth for the real world that is an accident totally irrelevant to the relation of the conclusion to the premiss; while in the kinds of reasoning that are more peculiarly topics of logical discussion it has all the relevancy in the world.

But I must hurry on to the consideration of the different kinds of mathematics, a subject of which the slightest sketch keeping close to what is wanted for the study of pragmatism ought in itself to occupy three good lectures at least, and would be much more interesting so.

The different branches of mathematics are distinguished by the different kinds of fundamental hypotheses of which they are the developments.

The simplest conceivable hypothesis is that of a universe in which there is but one thing, say A, and nothing else whatever of any kind. The corresponding mathematics consists of a single self-evident proposition (that is, it becomes evident by logical analysis simply) as follows: Nothing whatever can be predicated of A and it is absolutely indistinguishable from *blank nothingness*.

For if anything were true of A, A would have some character or quality which character or quality would be something in the universe over and above A.

The next simplest mathematics seems to be that which I entitle *dichotomic mathematics*. The hypothesis is that there are two things distinguished from one another. We might call them B and M, these being the initials of *bonum* and *malum*. Then the problem of this mathematics will be to determine in regard to anything unrecognized, say *x*, whether it is identical with B or identical with M. It would be a mere difference of phraseology to say that there are countless things in the universe, *x*, *y*, *z*, etc., each of which has one or other of the two values B and M. The first form of statement is preferable for reasons I cannot stop to explain.

The Boolean algebra of logic is a mere application of this kind of pure mathematics. It is a form of mathematics rather poverty-stricken as to ideas. Nevertheless, it has some features which we shall find have a certain bearing upon the foundations of pragmatism.

In the first place, although the universe consists of only two primary substances, yet there will *ipso facto* be quite a wealth of abstractions. For in the first place there will be the universe of which M and B are the two parts. Then there will be three prominent *relations*. Namely, first, the relation that M has to B and that M has to nothing else, and that nothing but M has to anything. Second, there will be the converse relation that B has to M and to nothing else and that nothing but B has to anything, and, third, the relation that B has to M and to nothing else and the M has to B and to nothing else. Without counting the absurd relation that nothing has to anything. That third relation is the self-converse relation of *otherness*.

Those four relations are *dyadic relations*. That is, considered as abstractions their existence consists in something being true of two primary substances. Thus to say that M is in the relation of otherness to B is to say the M is other than B which is a fact about the two primary substances M and B.

But there are also *triadic relations*. It is true that owing to there being but two primary substances, there is no triadic relation between three different primary substances. But there can be a relation between three different dyadic relations. There are dyadic relations between dyadic relations. Thus the relation of M to B is the *converse* of the relation of B to M and this relation of *converseness* is a dyadic relation between relations.

As an example of a triadic relation between relations take the relation between the first, second, and third relations between M and B. That is the relation between first the relation of M only to B only, of B only to M only, and of otherness of M to B and of B to M. This triadic relation is a case of the general triadic relation of *aggregation*. To say that Z stands in the relation of aggregation to X and Y is to say that Z is true wherever X is true and wherever Y is true and that either X or Y is true wherever Z is true.

Another important kind of triadic relation between dyadic relations is where R is in the relation of relative product of P into Q where P, Q, R are dyadic relations. This means that if anything A is in the relation R to anything C there is something B such that A is in the relation P to B while B is in the relation Q to C and conversely if A is not in the relation R to C then, taking anything whatever B, either A is not P to B or else B is not Q to C.

Applying this idea of a relative product we get the conception of *identity* or the relation which M has to M and to nothing else and that B has to B and to nothing else.

I have only noticed a few of the most interesting of these abstractions.

But I have not mentioned the most interesting of all the dyadic relations, that of *inclusion*, the great importance of which, now generally recognized, was first pointed out and demonstrated by me in 1870.

It is the relation that M has to M and to B and that B has to B but that B does not have to M. It is the connecting link between the general idea of logical dependence and the idea of the sequence of quantity.

All these ideas may be said to have virtually existed in the form of the Boolean algebra originally given by Boole. But in 1870 I greatly enlarged and I may say revolutionized the subject by the virtual introduction of an entire new kind of *abstractions*.[6]

Part B: On Phenomenology
(Draft One)[1]

I regret that I found it impracticable to begin by a lecture on mathematics, because what I should have had to say would have been not only interesting and of great service to the student of metaphysics, but it would also have served to make the present lecture considerably more convincing: and I am not so rich in arguments that any can be spared. I feel that. But two lectures would have been absolutely indispensable if I had discussed the ideas [of] mathematics at all, and there would have been undue compression without three; and after all the gain to the understanding of the question of pragmatism would have been too indirect to justify such a waste of time. So those considerations are among the things that I must do without.

The task before me [in] the present lecture is to describe what is before the mind when anything is before the mind and to convince you, if I can, that my description is correct. Merely to make my description clear, so that you may understand what I mean to say, will be difficult, almost if not quite to the point of impossibility. For these are ideas which I have been constantly struggling to gain a clear apprehension of for forty years of arduous and active reflexion; and how can I possibly expect that you will be able to seize them in a single hour? I trust that if you can see what my description is meant to convey, you will not find it so hard to see that it is just. And yet I should be really sorry if you were so easily satisfied about a matter of extreme importance. Time is needed to digest these ideas and to form a definitive judgment of their truth,—*much* time. I have often been struck in reflecting upon the discourse of Him who is called the Great Teacher, with how little he cared for the matter of what he said so long as it only had germinative virtue. It must not be too lofty a truth, but something on the vulgar level of his hearer's mind. Something, however, that followed out would soon lead upward. Certainly, in philosophy what a man does not think out for himself he never understands at all. Nothing can be learned out of books or lectures. They have to be treated not as oracles but simply as facts to be studied like any other facts. That, at any rate, is the way in which I would have you treat my lectures. Call no man master, or at any rate not me. Only bear in mind that I have been a good many years trying in singleness of heart to find out how these things really are, and always disposed to doubt and criticize my own results.

When anything is present to the mind, what is the very first character to be noted in it, in every case, no matter how little elevated the object may be? Certainly, [it] is *presentness* in a certain sense. So far Hegel is quite right. Immediacy he calls it. But to say that presentness, presentness as it is present, present presentness is *abstract*, is Pure Being! is a falsity so glaring that it is a wonder to me that any mind,—let alone Hegel,— could ever be deceived by it. That the Hegelians find it all right does not surprise me, because they let Hegel do their thinking for them. How shall I show you anything so manifest? I wish we were out of doors. Philosophizing ought to be done under the light of heaven. Hegel himself in the opening of the *Phänomenologie* supposes that he and the reader are out of doors. But somehow his theory that the abstract is more primitive than the concrete blinded his eyes to what stood before them. It was more dazzling than sun-light to him. Let us try to get into an unsophisticated state so that we can perceive what is present to us. Let me read you a bit of poetry just to rinse out your thoughts.

X X X X X

This poetic mood approaches the state in which what is present appears as it is present. Do you find it so abstract and colorless? What an extraordinary idea to say that immediate consciousness is colorless! The present that shines so bright when it is most present colorless and abstract!! Father Tom's lie of the turkey gobbler lying on the flat of his back and picking the stars out of the sky,—was wanting in inventiveness compared to this, which without any elaborate machinery of a turkey gobbler and the wattles hanging over his eyes, in three words stands out a lie, sublime and classical!

Must I reason about such a matter? Very well, the *present* is just what it is, regardless of past and future, utterly ignoring anything else. All that the *present* is it just is itself regardless of aught else. It is therefore not abstracted for the abstracted is what the concrete which gives it such being as it has makes it to be. The present is that which is such as it is regardless of anything else. Utterly ignoring everything else, it is positively such as it is. Imagine a consciousness in which there is no comparison, no relation, no recognized multiplicity, no change, no imagination of *any* modification, and no reflexion, just positive character. It might be just an odour, a smell of attar. It might be just one infinite ache. It might be a piercing endless whistle. It might be anything perfectly simple except a blank. That it could not be because then it would be nothingness; and the only being that nothingness has is such being as consists in not being any one of the myriads of things that exist. Nothingness therefore is the widest contrary of that which is such as it is regardless of aught else.

The immediate, then, I declare to be that which is such as it is positively all of itself; and that I declare to be just any absolutely simple quality of feeling. It must be simple itself although it may be a perfect match for a feeling which we can discern to be highly complex. But as it is in its positiveness and absence of all relation, it must be absolutely simple. Qualities of feeling are remarkable for their myriad-million-milliard-milliasse-fold variety. But this variety is not in them as they are in their presentness, but only as they are taken into comparison and so ceasing to be mere qualities. As it *is*, in its being as quality, each quality is its own universe. There is nothing else.

This then is the first element which I perceive in whatever is before my mind. I call this element Quality.

This term is not unobjectionable because *quality* being an abstract noun, it might be thought that what I call Quality is an abstraction. Certainly it is not; for an abstraction is a substance whose being consists in something being true of a different substance. Still, it is far better to call it Quality than to call it a *quale*, for a *quale* is something which in addition to having some mode of being has a quality. A *quale* is thus a complex, while my Quality is simple. Nor could I call my Quality a Feeling, since the simplest feeling is more complex. My quality is an element of feeling. Every feeling has a greater or less degree of vividness; but vividness results from a comparison of feelings. It is the contrast between one's general state of feeling before a given sensation and during that sensation. This [is] the sense of commotion. Now every feeling appears to be accompanied by this sense of commotion which is reckoned a part of it. For we understand the vividness of a feeling to be a part of the feeling. Now my Quality is not so complex. Besides, there is a much greater objection to calling my Quality a feeling. Namely by a Feeling we mean something that arises in a mind. It is essentially something which exists only as a state of something else, namely, a mind. But my Quality is what ever it is of itself. And it would occasion frightful misconception to call it a Feeling.

I repeat then: My first category, the first element I perceive in whatever is before my mind, is Quality, meaning that which is such as it is positively and of itself regardless of aught else.

The second category that I find, the next simplest feature common to all that comes before the mind, is the element of Struggle.

This is present even in such [a] rudimentary fragment of experience as a simple feeling. For such a feeling always has a degree of vividness, high or low; and this vividness is a sense of commotion, an action and reaction, between our soul and the stimulus. If in the endeavor to find some idea which does not involve the element of struggle, we imagine a universe that consists of a single Quality that never changes, still there must be some degree of steadiness in this imagination or else we could not think about and ask whether there was an object having any positive suchness. Now this steadiness of the hypothesis that enables us to think about it,—and to mentally manipulate it,—which is a perfectly correct expression, because our thinking about the hypothesis really consists in making experiments upon it,—this steadiness, I say, consists in this, that if our mental manipulation is delicate enough, the hypothesis will resist being changed. Now there can be no resistance where there is nothing of the nature of Struggle or forceful action. By Struggle I must explain that I mean mutual action between two things regardless of any sort of Third or Medium, and in particular regardless of any Law of Action.

I should not wonder if somebody were to suggest that perhaps the idea of a law is essential to the idea of one thing acting upon another. But surely that would be the most untenable suggestion in the world considering that there is no one of us who after life-long discipline in looking at things from the necessitarian point of view has ever been able to train himself to dismiss the idea that he can perform any specifiable act of the will. It is one of the most singular instances of how a preconceived theory will blind a man to facts that many necessitarians seem to think that no-body really believes in the Freedom of the Will, the fact being that he himself believes in it when he is not theorizing. However, I do not think it worthwhile to quarrel about that. Have your necessitarianism if you ap-prove of it; but still I think you must admit that no law of nature makes a stone fall, or a Leyden jar to discharge, or a steam engine to work. A law of nature left to itself would be exactly like a court without any sheriff. A court in that predicament would probably soon be able to induce some citizen to act as a sheriff; but as long as it was without a sheriff its law would be what is very incongruously called *brutum fulmen*. It would be splendid law, the perfection of human reason; but it would remain without effect. So if a law of nature stands alone, a mere regularity, a mere unifor-mity, what in the world is it that makes solid things,—which are not mere *formulae* but *substances*,—conform to it? Why should one stone whose existence, properties, and behaviour, have no real connection with those of any other stone,—for a mere uniformity is a formula and not a real con-nection,—act like another stone? Why should a stone always behave in the same way when there is no real connection between what it does one time and what it does another time? If you want to be a nominalist and say that laws are mere generals, that is, mere formulae, than it would seem that ordinary good sense ought to make you acknowledge that there are real connections between individual things regardless of mere formulae. Now any real connection between two things involves an action of one thing on the other. If, on the other hand, you repudiate nominalism and think that laws of nature are something more than mere formulae, that there [are] real laws behind these formulae, there is room for you to take a position in opposition to this category more difficult to refute. For you may say that the being of these laws is a sort of *esse in futuro*. That is, their reality consists in the fact that events *will* happen according to the formulation of these laws, either invariably or perhaps not quite invariably, either with infinite precision or with a limited precision; and thereupon you may urge that it is impossible to say what it means or could mean to say that one thing acts upon another thing upon a single occasion regardless of any general rule. If I object that when I make a great effort to lift a heavy weight, and perhaps am unable to stir it from the ground, there is really a struggle on this occasion regardless of what happens on other occasions, your answer may be that undoubtedly I have a Quality of feeling which I call a feeling of effort, but that there would be no reason for calling it so if it were not for a more or less regular connection between this feeling and the occurrence of certain motions of matter. This is an interesting position. It is a sort of pragmatism very much like Berkeley's inasmuch as it involves the recognition of the first and third categories (as will appear when I come to describe the third) which are more or less illusive and difficult to recognize with certainty while it denies the second which is by all odds the most obvious. Of course in saying this I am merely saying how it appears to me. It remains to be seen whether the comment is just or not. Before I make my regular argumentative attack upon this quasi-Berkeleyan position, there is another comment that I should like to make upon it; and although I cannot expect that a person holding that position should clearly see the justice of this comment, it does seem to me that he might, if he tries, get enough inkling of the justice of it, some what to shake his confidence in that position. The comment is this. Your argument against this category of struggle is that a struggle regardless of law is not *intelligible*. But you have just admitted that my so-called sense of effort involves a peculiar quality of feeling; and yet a quality of feeling is not intelligible either. One can *feel* it, but it is impossible to comprehend it or express it in a general formula. It appears, then, that unintelligibility does not absolutely refute a category. It rather tends to show that intelligibility is itself a category, and that consequently to show that anything *was* intelligible would prove that it was not a category distinct from that of intelligibility. You may reply that the unintelligibility of a quality of feeling is merely a sort of negative unintelligibility very different from the positive anti-intelligibility of the action of one thing on another regardless of law; but my rejoinder is that if intelligibility is a category, it is not surprising that other categories if there are more than one other should be differently related to it. But without beating longer about the bush, I will at once show that this element of Struggle aside from law, or as I am accustomed to call it of Reaction, is so obvious and undeniable a thing that it is even the chief characteristic of experience.

I confess I cannot repress a feeling that I am almost insulting your intelligence in offering you a proof of a proposition so evident. But we can never make too sure of things, especially of principles that great philosophers have denied. The world has come to the conclusion that Hegel did deny this practically, if not theoretically; and this conclusion I think is in the main just. Some degree of injustice that I think there is in it has been due to the extreme servility of Hegel's following, which he never did anything to cure. No philosophy in all history has so suffered from this evil as his.

Experience is certainly our great and only teacher. In saying this I do not mean to enunciate any doctrine of a *tabula rasa*. Far from that, I should be willing to admit and ready to maintain that there has manifestly not been one single principle of science, from the greatest to the most minute, which has had any other origin than the power of the human mind to *originate* ideas that are true. This power, notwithstanding all it has accomplished, is so feeble that as ideas flow from the human mind the true ideas are almost drowned in the flood of false notions; and that which experience does is gradually and by a sort of fractionation, to precipitate and filter off the false ideas, and eliminate them, letting the truth flow on. But precisely how does this action of experience take place? It takes place by a series of surprises. We are expecting some result. We have that notion in our minds already. We anticipate a result and we figure to ourselves with more or less confidence what the character of that result is to be. The result comes. Sometimes it is as we expected, and we have learned nothing. We are only confirmed in our former opinion. But very often,—perhaps I should say *always* when we are sufficiently wide awake,—the result comes, when we expected it to come, but it is not such as we expected it to be: it is quite a surprise. No doubt a certain number of discoveries have come when our expectation was of a negative and colorless description, to which no particular attention is paid. A ship is sailing along in a smooth sea, the navigator having no other expectation than that of the usual monotony of a voyage, when suddenly she strikes upon a rock. Such a case is no exception to what I have been saying. It is merely a case in which there is nothing in the expectation to put attention on the strain. The majority of discoveries, however, have been the result of experimentation. Now no man makes an experiment without being more or less inclined to think that a definite interesting result will occur. For experiments are far too costly to be undertaken altogether at random and aimlessly. An experimenter does not feel sure that the result will be such as he expects, but still there is a character which he inclines to think, and in most cases strongly inclines to think, that the result will have. The truly instructive experiments are those in which the expected character does not make its appearance, and in these cases, or in the majority of them, not only does the expected character not appear but another character which was not so much as dreamed of does appear. Perhaps it may be supposed that when discoveries result from measurements, this surprise does not appear. But, in fact, such discoveries are not exceptional in that respect. It does occasionally happen that the surprise is not of a very positive character. Even those cases are not exceptions to what I am saying; and they are not common. The theory of the Moon is one of the branches of inquiry in which discovery has been almost wholly the result of measurements; and although I have never studied the subject, except in the slightest manner, I have since boyhood been interested in following the course of discovery, owing to my father's having been a student of it; so that I know exactly how the discoveries of the last fifty years have come about in that field; and I can testify that there are surprises and that they are sometimes even sudden. Naturally those that are sudden cannot present any character entirely unforeseen.

Surprise, then, is the grand characteristic of experience. Now surprise brings a strong emphasis upon the mode of consciousness which exists in all perception, namely a double consciousness at once of an *ego* and a *non-ego*, directly acting upon one another. Mind you, that my appeal is to observation, and this observation you must make for yourself. The question is what the *phenomenon* is. We are not pretending to go beneath phenomena. That is where so many readers have misunderstood Kant's refutation of Idealism. The question is, what is the content of the *Percept*? Look at it for yourself. Look at it in the particularly striking case where the phenomenon is a surprise. Does not the perception represent an Ego and a Non-ego linked, or if you please does it not present something with two terminals one within where the expectation has been displaced and the other without whence the surprise comes?

Kant, Reid and others talk of the *immediate* perception of externality. As a matter of words, merely, I think it is better to speak of it as a *direct* consciousness of the duplicity. For I would restrict the word *immediate* to that mode of consciousness in which the content of consciousness has whatever character it has regardless of anything else; while here we have a mode of consciousness in which there are two objects of consciousness and their characters are a fact that involves them both.

The question is *not* whether or not *ego* and *non-ego* are manifestations of some incomprehensible substratum which in some incomprehensible sense is the one substance of them both. The whole question is what the *perceptual facts* are.

For you may have your theory of what are the mental operations by which direct perceptual judgments are formed; and I have no objections to urge against those theories. I only say that those operations are utterly beyond our control. Whether you like them or not makes no difference in their performance. Now it is perfectly idle to criticize what you can in no measure or sense control. If you criticize a reasoning wisely, the reasoner on repeating his reasoning in the light of your criticism will perform it differently. Therefore there was good sense in your criticism. But to call an operation of the mind that nobody can alter by one iota a *good* or a *bad* operation is to use words with no meaning. Once you have carried the criticism of thought back to direct perceptual judgments, by which I mean direct interpretations in the form of judgment of what it is that is perceived in the form of an image, there rational criticism must stop, for there all power of control ends and the words *good* and *bad* cease to have any meaning.

If therefore the careful direct interpretation of perception and especially of perception that contains something surprising is that it represents two objects reacting upon one another, there is nothing to be said but that so it is.

Every idealist of any stripe, any philosopher who denies the direct perception of externality, cuts off thereby all possibility of cognizing a *relation*; and he will gain nothing by declaring that all relations are illusive appearances because it is not merely the true cognition of them that he has cut off but every mode of cognizing relations.

When a man is surprised, he knows that he is surprised. Does he know it by direct perception or by inference?[2]

Try, first, the hypothesis that it is by inference. Then the theory would have to be that, having already acquired self-consciousness, as in most cases of course he will have done, and now becoming conscious of the peculiar quality of feeling that unquestionably is an element of surprise, he attributes this feeling to himself. But the difficulty with this theory is that we do not, in the first instance, attribute a quality of feeling to ourselves. As soon as we attribute it to anything we attribute it to an object, a *non-ego*, and we only come to attribute it to ourselves when we find a particular circumstance forces us to do so. The angry man is not, at first, conscious that he is angry. He thinks only that the object of his anger is bad. Sir Anthony Absolute says: "Don't fly into such a passion, sir! Why don't you keep cool, as I do?" It is only when he comes to see things in a somewhat different light that he discovers that he had been looking at the object through the spectacles of passion. Consequently in the case of surprise, if the inferential theory is to be maintained, we must suppose that the man first pronounces the thing to be *wonderful* and does not realize that it is he who has been surprised until the *wonder*,—or the first flush of it,—has passed away. But this theory is at war with the phenomena. The facts, on the contrary, are that the man is more or less placidly expecting one result, and suddenly finds something that contrasts with [it] that forces itself upon his recognition. A duality is forced upon him. [1] His expectation, which he had been attributing to nature, but which he is now compelled to attribute to a mere inward world, and [2] a strong new phenomenon which shoves that expectation into the background and occupies its place. A sudden rupture of consciousness occurs. A single peaceful object, the thing expected, breaks, and two objects are struggling for an instant, the expectation and the new object, and the feeling of marvel, instead of preceding this experience of duality, as the inferential theory would have it, only becomes felt as a quality of the duality, and only after the duality is experienced.

We are thus driven to the other alternative that the man knows he is surprised in a direct perceptual judgment. This perception, however, certainly does not represent that it is he himself who has played a little trick upon himself. The fact that this sounds utterly absurd suffices to show that it is not the perceptual judgment. Then the perceptual judgment can only be that that object,—the Universe,—or the Truth,—or if you prefer so to call it, Nature,—something over against him, acting on him, bearing him down,—has surprised him. But if that is so, this direct perception presents an *ego* to which the smashed expectation belonged, and the *non-ego*, the sadder and wiser man, to which the new phenomenon belongs.

Now as I said before, it is idle and indeed impossible to criticize perceptual facts and find fault with them. You can only criticize *interpretations* of them. So long as you admit that perception really does represent two objects to us, an *ego* and a *non-ego*,—[1] a past self that turns out to be nothing but a self and [2] a self that is to be faithful to the Truth in future,—as long as you admit that this is represented in the very perceptual fact, that is final. It must be accepted as experience.

This reaction is a thing no more to be comprehended than blue or the perfume of a tea rose is to be comprehended. As the latter are immediate objects that are such as they are regardless of anything else, so the former, the reaction, involves two objects each of which is such as it is in virtue of the struggle with the other.

This category of Reaction, or Struggle, we are directly assured of in the case of struggle between the *ego* and the *non-ego*. Among struggles of this sort we recognize two types. Those in which the *non-ego* triumphs so completely over the *ego* that it is difficult to discern that the *ego* really offers any resistance, and those cases where we come to class the *non-ego* under the head of objects of fancy, or imagination, because they yield so readily to the *ego* that it is difficult to discern that they offer any resistance. Intermediate between these extremes of Perception and Imagination is the large class of cases where the struggle is severe and where *effort* and *resistance* are very prominent, as they are in Volition, which is really the type which exhibits the entire phenomenon with the category of reaction obtrusive and obvious.

Having by such experiences acquired this category of an object that is such as it is relatively to an opposite object, we go on to make use of it in our interpretations of phenomena, in our explanatory hypotheses concerning them. We cut a wire and instantly an armature falls off from a magnet. We join the ends again and it flies up. The Hypothesis at once suggests itself that when the wire is intact the magnet *acts* on its armature; and if all the experiential consequences that we see our way to deducing from that hypothesis are borne out by experiment, we begin to think that it is true or very like the truth.

This category is no sooner acknowledged than without admixture of any other, it applies itself to itself in such a manner as to split into two varieties, which may be called the *genuine* and the *degenerate*. They have also other appropriate titles as we shall see. I borrow the designations *genuine* and *degenerate* from the geometry of plane curves. A curve is said to be of the second order if every ray cuts it in two points, real, coincident, or imaginary. Accordingly, the ellipse, parabola, and hyperbola, which only differ metrically,—that is to say, in respect to a matter of detail,—are curves of the second order, conics. But a pair [of] rays in the plane is cut in two points by every ray. ⤡ It is therefore a curve of the second order; but we call it a *degenerate* curve of the second order, because it is really nothing more than two curves of the first order; while a *conic*, which cannot be so resolved, ⬭ is termed a *genuine curve of the second order*.

In like manner the present category of reaction essentially supposes two objects each of which is such as it is only by virtue of how the other is. If the *twoness* is merely a way of regarding the fact and in truth there is nothing of the sort,—as when we say that everything is identical with itself,—that is this category in a *degenerate* state. All dyadic relations of individual to individual belong to one or other of two types; that of A:A and that of A:B. The former is the degenerate type, the latter the genuine type. Take for example the relation of "lover of." To say that "*a woman is lover of a human being*" is to say that somewhere in the universe there are two individuals, X a woman and Y a human being, such that if we take X first and Y second, they constitute an ordered pair, or *dyad*, as I term it, of a certain collection of dyads including each lover and the objects of that lover's love and including nothing else; and each of these dyads is of the genuine type A:B; for, after all, it is only a figure of speech to say that anybody loves himself. But now suppose that in the sentence "a woman is lover of a human being" we replace "lover of" by an adjective, say *blonde* and say "a woman is a blonde human being." That is to say that there is in the universe a woman X and a human being Y such that the dyad X:Y belongs to a certain class of dyads. But these dyads all belong to the degenerate type A:A, and what is expressed is not a genuine relation at all. After we have recognized the distinction of the genuine and the degenerate forms of this category, if we define them with the slightest care we find that the genuine form,—that is the form which is not *merely* a way of looking at things,—again splits into a *relatively* degenerate and a more genuine, and in fact there is a whole chain of such distinctions. It would waste time to enter into the matter minutely. But I may mention that such distinctions as objective and subjective, outward and inward, true and false, good and bad are found upon analysis to be distinctions between genuine and degenerate duality. When I call this category, the category of *struggle*, I name it from its most extremely genuine form; but when I term it the category of *twoness*, I name it so as evidently to include the most degenerate forms.

I now come to the third category. This is that element of the phenomenon, or object of thought, which is such as it is by virtue of bringing a second and a third into connection with one another. Of course, we are familiar with such things. A sign brings the thought to which it is a sign into relation with the thing signified. It requires but small reflection to see that [relation in] any state of mind whatever. For in any state of mind in which any grown person actually is,—I do not speak of babes in arms,—there is some element of thought however simple, or something involving the relations of person to person. Indeed Professor Baldwin, who made such a careful study of two children, thinks that babies get the notion of persons extremely early. But further observations are needed before we can feel sure that this is so. But let us confine ourselves to thought. It is said we also think in words. That is not quite true; but we always think by means of some kind of signs and among the signs that we use on any occasion there are *general signs*. We open our eyes and look at something. Now if we are not in a sleepwalking state we immediately form a *judgment* as to what sort of a thing it is that we are looking at; and that judgment predicates some general quality of the object of perception. Such a predication requires the use of some general sign corresponding to an adjective or common substantive. As I am looking out the window in writing these words my eye lights on something and before I know what I am about, I have told myself that it is a *chimney*, a *perfectly square prismatic chimney*, a *chimney of red brick*, with a *drab* piece at the top. I could not think all that without thinking of something in my mind equivalent to those words. Something is thought as *general signs*. Now the idea of a sign brings in this third category.

The second category has a degenerate form. The third category has two degenerate forms. The genuine third category is where there are three objects ⌄ₐ each having a character which essentially supposes the other two. The first degenerate form is where B has a real relation to A regardless of C, and at the same time a real relation to C regardless of A, and thereby A and C are brought into a real relation which B serves to bring about, but of which, when it is brought about, B forms no essential part. A still more degenerate form is where there is not even genuine duality; as when *Consciousness* is said to be the representation of itself to itself. Consciousness is what immediate feeling becomes when what it is, as it is, a positive feeling, is ignored, and it is looked upon as a sign.[3]

Part B: On Phenomenology
(Draft Two)[1]

The last lecture was devoted to an introductory glance at Pragmatism, considered as the maxim that the entire meaning and significance of any conception lies in its *conceivably* practical bearings,—not certainly altogether in consequences that would influence our conduct so far as we can foresee our future circumstances but which in *conceivable* circumstances would go to determine how we should deliberately act, and how we should act in a practical way and not merely how we should act as affirming or denying the conception to be cleared up.

It was shown that this maxim would be so supremely important an aid to thought, provided only it be true, that it is well worth a good deal of earnest inquiry to ascertain whether or not it can be maintained in the sense in which I originally proposed it, or if not whether it is capable of rectification, so as still to leave it a maxim that can be worked. At the same time objections apparently so redoubtable presented themselves against admitting the truth of it, that it certainly ought not to be accepted until it has passed through the fire of a drastic analysis.

For example, mathematicians never would confess that it means nothing to say that the diagonal of a square is incommensurable with its side, and yet how could the distinction of commensurable and incommensurable ever become practical, in view of the fact that the diagonal of a square differs from some rational fraction of the side by less than any previously assigned quantity? Nor would this difficulty be diminished by one iota if instead of *practical* consequences we were to modify the maxim so as to make it relate to *experiential* consequences. That is quite evident.

I invite you, then, this evening to begin with me a searching examination of the nature of what we call the *meaning* or *significance* of any phrase or conception.

An examination of mathematical conceptions, such as *commensurability*, *continuity*, *infinity*, and the like, might be expected to throw some light upon our problem. But the whole subject of mathematics is only one of a number of highly pertinent topics that I shall be forced to pass over in silence owing to my being restricted to six lectures of an hour each.

Pure mathematics differs from the positive sciences in not making any categorical assertions, but only saying what would be true in case certain hypotheses were true, and not undertaking to be in the least responsible for there being anything in nature corresponding to its hypotheses, whether exactly or approximately. The positive sciences do undertake to assert what the characters of the experiential facts are. But among these positive sciences, Philosophy, as I shall use this word, and use it without any serious rupture with general usage, is distinguished from all the special theoretical sciences, whether they belong to the great Physical wing or to the great Psychical wing of special science, that is whether they be inquiries into dynamics, physics, chemistry, physiology, anatomy, astronomy, geology, etc., or whether they be inquiries into psychology, anthropology, linguistics, history, etc. Philosophy I say is distinguished from all of these by the circumstance that it does not undertake to make any special observations or to obtain any perceptions of a novel description. Microscopes and telescopes, voyages and exhumations, clairvoyants and witnesses of exceptional experience are substantially superfluous for the purposes of philosophy. It contents itself with a more attentive scrutiny and comparison of the facts of everyday life, such as present themselves to every adult and sane person, and for the most part in every day and hour of his waking life. The reason why a natural classification so draws the line between Philosophy, as *cenoscopy*, κοινοσκοπία, and Special Science, or *Idioscopy*, ἰδιοσκοπία,—to follow Jeremy Bentham's terminology,—is that very widely different bent of genius is required for the analytical work of philosophy and for the observational work of special science.

More than six lectures would be required merely to set forth in the tersest manner the reasons which have convinced me that Philosophy ought to be regarded as having three principal divisions. Its principal utility, although by no means its only utility, is to furnish a *Weltanschauung*, or conception of the universe, as a basis for the special sciences. Metaphysics is the final branch of philosophical inquiry whose business it is to work this out. But metaphysics must rest upon normative science. That was the judgment of two at least of the most influential of all philosophers, Aristotle and Kant; and Descartes, though he had studied the question less deeply, was of the same opinion. What is meant by a normative science I cannot now stop to explain. It is a theoretical not a practical science, although it is closely connected with practice. It is a positive science and not a mathematical science although its reasoning is mostly mathematical. We may say roughly that a normative science is the research into the theory of the distinction between what is good and what is bad; in the realm of cognition, in the realm of action, and in the realm of feeling, this theory being founded upon certain matters of fact that are open to the daily and hourly observation of every man and woman. Normative science is the central great department of philosophy. The initial great department of philosophy is phenomenology whose task it is to make out what are the elements of appearance that present themselves to us every hour and every minute whether we are pursuing earnest investigations or are undergoing the strangest vicissitudes of experience, or are dreamily listening to the tales of Scheherazade.

My purpose this evening is to call your attention to certain questions of phenomenology upon the answers to which, whatever they may be, our final conclusion concerning pragmatism must mainly repose at last.

Be it understood, then, that what we have to do, as students of phenomenology, is simply to open our mental eyes and look well at the phenomenon and say what are the characteristics that are never wanting in it, whether that phenomenon be something that outward experience forces upon our attention, or whether it be the wildest of dreams, or whether it be the most abstract and general of the conclusions of science. The faculties which we must endeavor to gather for this work are three. The first and foremost is that rare faculty, the faculty of seeing what stares one in the face, just as it presents itself, unreplaced by any interpretation, unsophisticated by any allowance for this or for that supposed modifying circumstance. This is the faculty of the artist who sees for example the apparent colors of nature as they appear. When the ground is covered by snow on which the sun shines brightly except where shadows fall, if you ask any ordinary man what its color appears to be, he will tell you white, pure white, whiter in the sunlight, a little greyish in the shadow. But that is not what is before his eyes that he is describing; it is his theory of what *ought* to be seen. The artist will tell him that the shadows are not grey but a dull blue and that the snow in the sunshine is of a rich yellow. That artist's observational power is what is most wanted in the study of phenomenology. The second faculty we must strive to arm ourselves with is a resolute discrimination which fastens itself like a bulldog upon the particular feature that we are studying, follows it wherever it may lurk, and detects it beneath all its disguises. The third faculty we shall need is the generalizing power of the mathematician who produces the abstract formula that comprehends the very essence of the feature under examination purified from all admixture of extraneous and irrelevant accompaniments.

A very moderate exercise of this third faculty suffices to show us that the word *Category* bears substantially the same meaning with all philosophers. For Aristotle, for Kant, and for Hegel, a category is an element of phenomena of the first rank of generality. It naturally follows that the categories are few in number, just as the chemical elements are. The business of phenomenology is to draw up a catalogue of categories and prove its sufficiency and freedom from redundancies, to make out the characteristics of each category, and to show the relations of each to the others. I find that there are at least two distinct orders of categories, which I call the particular and the universal. The particular categories form a series, or set of series, only one of each series being present, or at least predominant, in any one phenomenon. The universal categories, on the other hand, belong to every phenomenon, one being perhaps more prominent in one aspect of that phenomenon than another but all of them belonging to every phenomenon. I am not very well satisfied with this description of the two orders of categories, but I am pretty well satisfied that there are two orders. I do not recognize them in Aristotle, unless the predicaments and the predicables are the two orders. But in Kant we have Unity, Plurality, and Totality not all present at once; Reality, Negation, and Limitation not all present at once; Inherence, Causation, and Reaction not all present at once; Possibility, Necessity, and Actuality not all present at once. On the other hand, Kant's four greater categories, Quantity, Quality, Relation and Modality form what I should recognize as Kant's Universal Categories. In Hegel his long list which gives the divisions of his Encyclopedia are his Particular Categories. His three stages of thought, although he does not apply the word *category* to them, are what I should call Hegel's Universal Categories. My intention this evening is to limit myself to the Universal, or Short List of Categories, and I may say, at once, that I consider Hegel's three stages as being, roughly speaking, the correct list of Universal Categories. I regard the fact that I reached the same result as he did by a process as unlike his as possible, at a time when my attitude toward him was rather one of contempt than of awe, and without being influenced by him in any discernible way however slightly, as being a not inconsiderable argument in favor of the correctness of the list. For if I am mistaken in thinking that my thought was uninfluenced by his, it would seem to follow that that thought was of a quality which gave it a secret power, that would in itself argue pretty strongly for its truth.

Although I am going to confine myself to these three categories, yet you will understand that in an hour's lecture, what remains of the hour, it will be quite beyond my power either to treat them at all exhaustively, or to make my points as convincingly as I could do if I were less hurried by my desire to get back to my proper subject of pragmatism, or even to give you a perfectly clear notion of what I conceive these three categories to be.

What I should like to do would be to take up each category in turn and, firstly, point it out to you clearly in the phenomenon, secondly, to show what different shapes and aspects it takes and make their characteristics clear, thirdly, to put it before you in the most naked and rational form and show how this describes it in all its protean changes, fourthly, to prove to you that it is an element of the phenomenon that must by no means be ignored, and fifthly, to make it positively certain that the category is irreducible to any other or mixture of others. These five points being made with reference to each of the three categories I would drop the keystone into my arch by demonstrating that no fourth category could possibly be added to the list, and then I could go on to the moral of the whole story by showing how the chief conflicts between the different warring marshals of metaphysics arise entirely from the endeavor of each to omit from his account of the universe some one or even some two of the three Universal Categories, so that there are, as a historical fact, just seven systems, the true one giving due regard to all three categories ABC; three others that recognize two each, and three that recognize but one each.

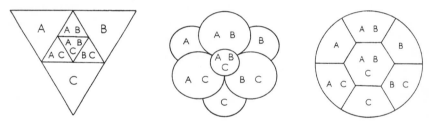

We should thus begin to get a glimmer of light upon the question of pragmatism. But you can readily see, even without knowing how intricate some of these sixteen points would necessarily be, that I could not possibly touch upon so many in one lecture and that it would be equally impossible to give more than one lecture to this extremely general question in a discussion of so special a matter as that of the merits of pragmatism. I can only touch lightly on a few of the points and leave the rest for your own meditations.

When anything is present to the mind, what is the very first and simplest character to be noted in it, in every case, no matter how little elevated the object may be? Certainly, it is its *presentness*. So far Hegel is quite right. Immediacy is his word. To say, however, that presentness, presentness as it is present, present presentness is *abstract*, is Pure Being, is a falsity so glaring, that one can only say that Hegel's theory that the abstract is more primitive than the concrete blinded his eyes to what stood before them. Go out under the blue dome of heaven and look at what is present as it appears to the artist's eye. The poetic mood approaches the state in which the present appears as it is present. Is poetry so abstract and colorless? The present is just what it is regardless of the absent, regardless of past and future. It is such as it is, utterly ignoring anything else. Consequently, it cannot be *abstracted* (which is what Hegel means by the abstract) for the abstracted is what the concrete, which gives it whatever being it has, makes it to be. The present, being such as it is while utterly ignoring everything else, is *positively* such as it is. Imagine, if you please, a consciousness in which there is no comparison, no relation, no recognized multiplicity (since parts would be other than the whole), no change, no imagination of any modification of what is positively there, no reflexion,—nothing but a simple positive character. Such a consciousness might be just an odour, say a smell of attar; or it might be one infinite dead ache; it might be the hearing of [a] piercing eternal whistle. In short, any simple and positive quality of feeling would be something which our description fits that it is such as it is quite regardless of anything else. The quality of feeling is the true psychical representative of the first category of the immediate as it is in its immediacy, of the present in its direct positive presentness. Qualities of feeling show myriad-fold variety, far beyond what the psychologists admit. This variety however is in them only insofar as they are compared and gathered into collections. But as they are in their presentness, each is sole and unique; and all the others are absolute nothingness to it,—or rather much less than nothingness, for not even a recognition as absent things or as fictions is accorded to them. The first category, then, is Quality of Feeling or whatever is such as it is positively and regardless of aught else.

The next simplest feature that is common to all that comes before the mind, and consequently, the second category, is the element of *Struggle*. It is convenient enough, although by no means necessary, to study this, at first, in a psychological instance. Imagine yourself making a strong muscular effort, say that of pressing with all your might against a half-open door. Obviously, there is a sense of resistance. There could not be effort without an equal resistance any more than there could be a resistance without an equal effort that it resists. Action and reaction are equal. If you find that the door is pushed open in spite of you, you will say that it was the person on the other side that acted and you that resisted, while if you succeed in pushing the door to, you will say that it was you who acted and the other person that resisted. In general, we call the one that succeeds by means of his effort the *agent* and the one that fails the *patient*. But as far as the element of Struggle is concerned, there is no difference between being an agent and being a patient. It is the result that decides; but what it is that is deemed to be the result for the purpose of this distinction is a detail into which we need not enter. If while you are walking quietly along the sidewalk a man carrying a ladder suddenly pokes you violently with it in the back of the head and walks on without noticing what he has done, your impression probably will be that he struck you with great violence and that you made not the slightest resistance; although in fact you must have resisted with a force equal to that of the blow. Of course, it will be understood that I am not using force in the modern sense of a moving force but in the sense of Newton's *actio*; but I must warn you that I have not time to notice such trifles. In like manner, if in pitch darkness a tremendous flash of lightening suddenly comes, you are ready [to] admit having received a shock and being acted upon, but that you reacted you may be inclined to deny. You certainly did so, however, and are conscious of having done so. The sense of shock is as much a sense of resisting as of being acted upon. So it is when anything strikes the senses. The outward excitation succeeds in producing its effect on you, while you in turn produce no discernible effect on it; and therefore you call it the agent, and overlook your own part in the reaction. On the other hand, in reading a geometrical demonstration if you draw the figure in your imagination instead of on paper, it is so easy to add to your image whatever subsidiary line is wanted, that it seems to you that you have acted on the image without the image having offered any resistance. That it is not so, however, is easily shown. For unless that image had a certain power of persisting such as it is and resisting metamorphosis, and if you were not sensible of its strength of persistence, you never could be sure that the construction you are dealing with at one stage of the demonstration was the same that you had before your mind at an earlier stage. The main distinction between the Inner and the Outer Worlds is that inner objects promptly take any modifications we wish, while outer objects are hard facts that no man can make to be other than they are. Yet tremendous as this distinction is, it is after all only relative. Inner objects do offer a certain degree of resistance and outer objects are susceptible of being modified in some measure by sufficient exertion intelligently directed.

Two very serious doubts arise concerning this category of struggle which I should be able completely to set to rest, I think, with only a little more time. But as it is, I can only suggest lines of reflexion which if you perseveringly follow out ought to bring you to the same result to which they have brought me.

The first of these doubts is whether this element of struggle is anything more than a very special kind of phenomenon, and withal an anthropomorphic conception and therefore not scientifically true.

The other doubt is whether the idea of Struggle is a simple and irresolvable element of the phenomenon, and in opposition to its being so, two

contrary parties will enter into a sort of (_____)² without remarking
how deeply they are at variance with one another. One of these parties will
be composed of those philosophers who understand themselves as wishing
to reduce everything in the phenomenon to qualities of feeling. They will
appear in the arena of psychology and will declare that there is absolutely
no such thing as a specific sense of effort. There is nothing, they will say,
but feelings excited upon muscular contraction, feelings which they may
or may not be disposed to say have their immediate excitations within the
muscles. The other party will be composed of those philosophers who say
that there can be only one absolute and only one irreducible element, and
since *Nous* is such an element, *Nous* is really the only thoroughly clear
idea there is. These philosophers will take a sort of pragmatistic stand.
They will maintain that to say that one thing acts upon another, absolutely
the only thing that can be meant is that there is a *law* according to which
under all circumstances of a certain general description certain phenomena will result; and therefore to speak of one thing as acting upon another
hic et nunc regardless of uniformity, regardless of what will happen on all
occasions, is simple nonsense.

I shall have to content myself with giving some hints as to how I
would meet this second double-headed objection, leaving the first to your
own reflexions.³ In the course of considering the second objection, the
universality of the element of struggle will get brought to light without
any special arguments to that end. But as to its being unscientific because
anthropomorphic, that is an objection of a very shallow kind, that arises
from prejudices based upon much too narrow considerations. "Anthropomorphic" is what pretty much all conceptions are at bottom; otherwise
other roots for the words in which to express them than the old Aryan
roots would have to be found. And in regard to any preference for one kind
of theory over another, it is well to remember that every single truth of
science is due to the affinity of the human soul to the soul of the universe,
imperfect as that affinity no doubt is. To say, therefore, that a conception is
one natural to man, which comes to just about the same thing as to say
that it is anthropomorphic, is as high a recommendation as one could give
to it in the eyes of an Exact Logician.⁴

I would not have anybody accept any doctrine of logic simply because
minute and thorough criticism has resulted in making me perfectly confident of its truth. But I will not allow this scruple to prevent my saying that
for my part,—who am characterized in some of the books as a Sceptic in
philosophy and have even been called a modern Hume,—I have after long
years of the severest examination became fully satisfied that, other things
being equal, an anthropomorphic conception, whether it makes the best
nucleus for a scientific working hypothesis or not, is far more likely to be

approximately true than one that is not anthropomorphic. Suppose, for example, it is a question between accepting *Telepathy* or *Spiritualism*. The former I dare say is the preferable working hypothesis because it can be more readily subjected to experimental investigation. But as long as there is no reason for believing it except phenomena that Spiritualism is equally competent to explain, I think Spiritualism is much the more likely to be approximately true, as being the more anthropomorphic and natural idea; and in like manner, as between an old-fashioned God and a modern patent Absolute, recommend me to the anthropomorphic conception if it is a question of which is the more likely to be about the truth.

As for the double-headed objection, I will first glance at that branch of it that rests upon the idea that the conception of action involves the notion of law or uniformity so that to talk of a reaction regardless of anything but the two individual reacting objects is nonsense. As to that I should say that a law of nature left to itself would be quite analogous to a court without a sheriff. A court in that predicament might probably be able to induce some citizen to act as sheriff; but until it has so provided itself with an officer who, unlike itself, could not discourse authoritatively but who could put forth the strong arm, its law might be the perfection of human reason but would remain mere fireworks, *brutum fulmen*. Just so, let a law of nature,—say the law of gravitation,—remain a mere uniformity,—a mere formula establishing a relation between terms,—and what in the world should induce a stone, which is not a term nor a concept but just a plain thing, to act in conformity to that uniformity? All other stones may have done so, and this stone too on former occasions, and it would break the uniformity for it not to do so now. But what of that? There is no use talking reason to a stone. It is deaf and it has no reason. I should ask the objector whether he was a nominalist or a scholastic realist. If he is a nominalist he holds that laws are mere generals, that is, formulae relating to mere terms; and ordinary good sense ought to force him to acknowledge that there are real connections between individual things regardless of mere formulae. Now any real connection whatsoever between individual things involves a reaction between them in the sense of this category. The objector may, however, take somewhat stronger ground by confessing himself to be a scholastic realist, holding that generals may be real. A law of nature, then, will be regarded by him as having a sort of *esse in futuro*. That is to say they will have a present reality which consists in the fact that events *will* happen according to the formulation of those laws. It would seem futile for me to attempt to reply that when, for example, I make a great effort to lift a heavy weight and perhaps am unable to stir it from the ground, there really is a struggle on this occasion regardless of what happens on other occasions; because the objector would simply admit that on such an occasion I have a quality of feeling which I call a feeling of effort, but he would urge that the only thing which makes this designation appropriate to the feeling is the regularity of connection between this feeling and certain motions of matter.

This is a position well enough taken to merit a very respectful reply. But before going into that reply, there is an observation which I should like to lay before the candid objector. Your argument against this category of Struggle is that a struggle regardless of law is not *intelligible*. Yet you have just admitted that my so-called sense of effort involves a peculiar quality of feeling. Now a quality of feeling is not intelligible, either. Nothing can be less so. One can *feel* it, but to comprehend it or express it in a general formula is out of the question. So it appears that unintelligibility does not suffice to destroy or refute a Category. Indeed, if you are to accept scholastic realism, you would seem to be almost bound to admit that *Nous*, or intelligibility, is itself a category; and in that case far from non-intelligibility's refuting a category, intelligibility would do so,—that is would prove that a conception could not be a category distinct from the category of *Nous*, or intelligibility. If it be objected that the unintelligibility of a Quality of Feeling is of a merely privative kind quite different from the aggressive and brutal anti-intelligibility of action regardless of law, the rejoinder will be that if intelligibility be a category, it is not surprising but rather inevitable that other categories should be in different relations to this one.

But without beating longer round the bush, let us come to close quarters. Experience is our only teacher. Far be it from me to enunciate any doctrine of a *tabula rasa*. For as I said a few minutes ago, there manifestly is not one drop of principle in the whole vast reservoir of established scientific theory that has sprung from any other source than the power of the human mind to *originate* ideas that are true. But this power, for all it has accomplished, is so feeble that as ideas flow from their springs in the soul, the truths are almost drowned in a flood of false notions; and that which experience does is gradually, and by a sort of fractionation, to precipitate and filter off the false ideas, eliminating them and letting the truth pour on in its mighty current.

But precisely how does this action of experience take place? It takes place by a series of surprises. There is no need of going into details. At one time a ship is sailing along in the trades over a smooth sea, the navigator having no more positive expectation than that of the usual monotony of such a voyage, when suddenly she strikes upon a rock. The majority of discoveries, however, have been the result of experimentation. Now no man makes an experiment without being more or less inclined to think that an interesting result will ensue; for experiments are much too costly of physical and psychical energy to be undertaken at random and aimlessly. And naturally nothing can possibly be learned from an experiment that turns out just as was anticipated. It is by surprises that experience teaches all she deigns to teach us.

In all the works on pedagogy that ever I read,—and they have been many, big, and heavy,—I don't remember that any one has advocated a system of teaching by practical jokes, mostly cruel. That however, describes the method of our great teacher, Experience. She says,

> Open your mouth and shut your eyes
> And I'll give you something to make you wise;

and thereupon she keeps her promise, and seems to take her pay in the fun of tormenting us.

The phenomenon of surprise in itself is highly instructive in reference to this category because of the emphasis it puts upon a mode of consciousness which can be detected in all perception, namely, a double consciousness at once of an *ego* and a *non-ego*, directly acting upon each other. Understand me well. My appeal is to observation,—observation that each of you must make for himself.

The question is what the *phenomenon* is. We make no vain pretense of going beneath phenomena. We merely ask, What is the content of the *Percept*? Everybody should be competent to answer that of himself. Examine the Percept in the particularly marked case in which it comes as a surprise. Your mind was filled [with] an imaginary object that was expected. At the moment when it was expected the vividness of the representation is exalted, and suddenly when it should come something quite different comes instead. I ask you whether at that instant of surprise there is not a double consciousness, on the one hand of an Ego, which is simply the expected idea suddenly broken off, on the other hand of the Non-Ego, which is the Strange intruder, in his abrupt entrance.

The whole question is what the *perceptual facts* are, as given in direct perceptual judgments. By a perceptual judgment, I mean a judgment asserting in propositional form what a character of a percept directly present to the mind is. The percept of course is not itself a judgment, nor can a judgment in any degree resemble a percept. It is as unlike it as are the printed letters in a book where a Madonna of Murillo is described are unlike the picture itself. You may adopt any theory that seems to you acceptable as to the psychological operations by which perceptual judgments are formed. For our present purpose it makes no difference what that theory is. All that I insist upon is that those operations, whatever they may be, are utterly beyond our control and will go on whether we are pleased with them or not. Now I say that taking the word "criticize" in the sense it bears in philosophy, that of apportioning praise and blame, it is perfectly idle to criticize anything over which you can exercise no sort of control. You may wisely criticize a reasoning, because the reasoner, in the light of your criticism, will certainly go over his reasoning again and correct it if your blame of it was just. But to pronounce an involuntary operation of the mind *good* or *bad*, has no more sense than to pronounce the proportion of weights in which hydrogen and chlorine combine, that of 1 to 35.11 to be *good* or *bad*. I said it was idle; but in point of fact "nonsensical" would have been an apter word.

If therefore our careful direct interpretation of perception, and more emphatically of such perception as involves surprise, is that the perception represents two objects reacting upon one another, that is not only a decision from which there is no appeal, but it is downright nonsense to dispute the fact that in perception two objects really do so react upon one another.

That, of course, is the doctrine of Immediate Perception which is upheld by Reid, Kant, and all dualists who understand the true nature of dualism, and the denial of which led Cartesians to the utterly absurd theory of divine assistance upon which the preestablished harmony of Leibniz is but a slight improvement. Every philosopher who denies the doctrine of Immediate Perception,—including idealists of every stripe,—by that denial cuts off all possibility of ever cognizing a *relation*. Nor will he better his position by declaring that all relations are illusive appearances, since it is not merely true knowledge of them that he has cut off but every mode of cognitive representation of them.

Part B: On Phenomenology, or the Categories
(Draft Three)

III[1]

Thus far, gentlemen, I have been insisting very strenuously upon what the most vulgar common sense has every disposition to assent to and only ingenious philosophers have been able to deceive themselves about. But now I come to a category which only a more refined form of common sense is prepared willingly to allow, the category which of the three is the chief burden of Hegel's song, a category toward which the studies of the new logico-mathematicians, Georg Cantor, and the like are steadily pointing, but to which no modern writer of any stripe, unless it be some obscure student like myself, has ever done anything approaching to justice. I wish most earnestly that instead of a few minutes I could give six lectures in opening up to you some of the most striking paths of thought to which this conception will lead any man who pursues it in a spirit of exact criticism.

There never was a sounder logical maxim of scientific procedure than Ockham's razor: *Entia non sunt multiplicanda praeter necessitatem*. That is to say; Before you try a complicated hypothesis, you should make quite sure that no simplification of it will explain the facts equally well. No matter if it takes fifty generations of arduous experimentation to explode the simpler hypothesis, and no matter how incredible it may seem that that simpler hypothesis should suffice, still, fifty generations are nothing in the life of science, which has all time before it, and in the long run, say in some thousands of generations, time will be economized by proceeding in an orderly manner, and by making it an invariable rule to try the simpler hypothesis first. Indeed, one can never be sure that the simpler hypothesis is not the true one, after all, until its cause has been fought out to the bitter end. But you will mark the limitation of my approval of Ockham's razor. It is a sound maxim of *scientific procedure*. If the question be what one ought to believe, the logic of the situation must take other factors into account. Speaking strictly, Belief is out of place in pure theoretical science, which has nothing nearer to it than the establishment of doctrines, and only the provisional establishment of them, at that. Compared with living Belief, it is nothing but a ghost. If the captain [of] a vessel on a lea [leeward] shore in a terrific storm finds himself in a critical position in which he must instantly either put his wheel to port acting on one hypothesis, or put his wheel to starboard acting on the contrary hypothesis, and his vessel will infallibly be dashed to pieces if he decides the question wrongly, Ockham's razor is not worth the stout belief of any common seaman. For stout belief *may* happen to save the ship, while *Entia non sunt multiplicanda praeter necessitatem* would be only a stupid way of spelling Shipwreck. Now in matters of real practical concern we are all in something like the situation of that sea-captain.

Philosophy, as I understand the word, is a positive theoretical science, and a science in an early stage of development. As such it has no more to do with belief than any other science. Indeed, I am bound to confess that it is at present in so unsettled a condition, that if the ordinary theorems of molecular physics and of archeology are but the ghosts of beliefs, then to my mind the doctrines of the philosophers are little better than the ghosts of ghosts. I know this is an extremely heretical opinion. The followers of Haeckel are completely in accord with the followers of Hegel in holding that what they call philosophy is a practical science and the best of guides in the formation of what they take to be Religious Beliefs. I simply note the divergence, and pass on to an unquestionable fact; namely, the fact that all modern philosophy is built upon Ockhamism; by which I mean that it is all nominalistic and that it adopts nominalism because of Ockham's razor. And there is no form of modern philosophy of which this is more essentially true than the philosophy of Hegel.

But it is not modern philosophers only who are nominalists. The nominalist *Weltanschauung* has become incorporated into what I will venture to call the very flesh and blood of the average modern mind.

The third category of which I come now to speak is precisely that whose reality is denied by nominalism. For although nominalism is not credited with any extraordinarily lofty appreciation of the powers of the human soul, yet it attributes to it a power of originating a kind of ideas the like of which Omnipotence has failed to create as real objects, and those general conceptions which men will never cease to consider the glory of the human intellect must, according to any consistent nominalism, be entirely wanting in the mind of Deity. Leibniz, the modern nominalist *par excellence*, will not admit that God has the faculty of Reason; and it seems impossible to avoid that conclusion upon nominalistic principles.

But it is not in Nominalism alone that modern thought has attributed to the human mind the miraculous power of originating a category of thought that has no counterpart at all in Heaven or Earth. Already in that strangely influential hodge-podge, the salad of Cartesianism, the doctrine stands out very emphatically that the only Force is the force of impact, which clearly belongs to the category of Reaction; and ever since Newton's *Principia* began to affect the general thought of Europe through the sympathetic spirit of Voltaire, there has been a disposition to deny any kind of action except purely mechanical action. The Corpuscular Philosophy of Boyle,—although the pious Boyle did not himself recognize its character,—was bound to come to that in the last resort; and the idea constantly gained strength throughout the eighteenth century and the nineteenth until the doctrine of the Conservation of Energy, generalized rather loosely by philosophers led to the theory of psychophysical parallelism against which there has only of recent years been any very sensible and widespread revolt. Psychophysical parallelism is merely the doctrine that mechanical action explains all the real facts, except that these facts have an internal aspect which is a little obscure and a little shadowy.

To my way of regarding philosophy, all this movement was perfectly good scientific procedure. For the simpler hypothesis which excluded the influence of ideas upon matter had to be tried and persevered in until it was thoroughly exploded. But I believe that now at last, at any time for the last thirty years, it has been apparent to every man who sufficiently considered the subject that there is a mode of influence upon external facts which cannot be resolved into mere mechanical action, so that hence forward it will be a grave error of scientific philosophy to overlook the universal presence in the phenomenon of this third category. Indeed, from the moment that the Idea of Evolution took possession of the minds of men the pure Corpuscular philosophy together with nominalism had had their doom pronounced. I grew up in Cambridge and was about twenty-one when *The Origin of Species* appeared. There was then living here a thinker who left no remains from which one could now gather what an educative influence his was upon the minds of all of us who enjoyed his intimacy,— Mr. Chauncey Wright. He had at first been a Hamiltonian but had early passed over into the warmest advocacy of the nominalism of John Stuart Mill; and being a mathematician at a time when dynamics was regarded as the loftiest branch of mathematics, he was also inclined to regard nature from a strictly mechanical point of view. But his interests were wide and he was also a student of Gray. I was away surveying in the wilds of Louisiana when Darwin's great work appeared, and though I learned by letters of the immense sensation it had created, I did not return until early in the following summer when I found Wright all enthusiasm for Darwin whose doctrines appeared to him as a sort of supplement to those of Mill. I remember well that I then made a remark to him which although he did not assent to it, evidently impressed him enough to perplex him. The remark was that these ideas of development had more vitality by far than any of his other favorite conceptions and that though they might at that moment be in his mind like a little vine clinging to the tree of Associationalism, yet after a time that vine would inevitably kill the tree. He asked me why I said that and I replied that the reason was that Mill's doctrine was nothing but a metaphysical point of view to which Darwin's, which was nourished by positive observation, must be deadly. Ten or fifteen years later, when Agnosticism was all the go, I prognosticated a short life for it, as philosophies run, for a similar reason. What the true definition of Pragmatism may be, I find it very hard to say; but in my nature it is a sort of instinctive attraction for living facts.

All nature abounds in proofs of other influences than merely mechanical action even in the physical world. They crowd in upon us at the rate of several every minute. And my observation of men has led me to this little generalization. Speaking only of men who really think for themselves and not of mere reporters, I have not found that it is the men whose lives are mostly passed within the four walls of a physical laboratory who are most inclined to be satisfied with a purely mechanical metaphysics. On the contrary, the more clearly they understand how physical forces work the more incredible it seems to them that such action should explain what happens out of doors. A larger proportion of materialists and agnostics is to be found among the thinking physiologists and other naturalists, and the largest proportion of all among those who derive their ideas of physical

science from reading popular books. These last, the Spencers, the You-
mans, and the like, seem to be possessed with the idea that science has got
the universe pretty well ciphered down to a fine point; while the Faradays
and Newtons seem to themselves like children who have picked up a few
pretty pebbles upon the ocean beach. But most of us seem to find it difficult to recognize the greatness and wonder of things familiar to us. As the
prophet is not without honor, save [in his own country,] so it is also with
phenomena.² Point out to the ordinary man evidence however conclusive
of other influence than physical action in things he sees every day, and he
will say "Well, *I* don't see as that frogs has got any pints about him that's
any different from any other frog." For that reason we welcome instances
perhaps of less real cogency but which have the merit of being rare and
strange. Such, for example, are the right-handed and left-handed screw-
structures of the molecules of those bodies which are said to be "optically
active." Of every such substance there are two varieties, or as the chemists
call them, two modifications, one of which twists a ray of light that passes
through it to the right and the other by an exactly equal amount to the
left. All the ordinary physical properties of the right-handed and left-
handed modifications are identical. Only certain faces of their crystals, often very minute, are differently placed. No chemical process can ever
transmute the one modification into the other. And their ordinary chemical behaviour is absolutely the same, so that no strictly chemical process
can separate them if they are once mixed.

Only the chemical action of one optically active substance upon another is different if they both twist the ray the same way from what it is if
they twist the ray different ways. There are certain living organisms which
feed on one modification and destroy it while leaving the other one untouched. This is presumably due to such organisms containing in their
substance, possibly in very minute proportion, some optically active body.
Now I maintain that the original segregation of levo-molecules or molecules with a left-handed twist from dextro-molecules, or molecules with a
right-handed twist is absolutely incapable of mechanical explanation. Of
course you may suppose that in the original nebula at the very composition of the world right-handed quartz was collected into one place while
left-handed quartz was collected into another place. But to suppose that is
ipso facto to suppose that that segregation was a phenomenon without any
mechanical explanation. The three laws of motion draw no dynamical distinction between right-handed and left-handed screws, and a mechanical
explanation is an explanation founded on the three laws of motion. There,
then, is a physical phenomenon absolutely inexplicable by mechanical action. This single instance suffices to overthrow the corpuscular philosophy.

LECTURE THREE:
THE CATEGORIES DEFENDED

I.

Ladies and Gentlemen:

Category the First is the Idea of that which is such as it is regardless of anything else. That is to say, it is a *Quality* of Feeling.

Category the Second is the Idea of that which is such as it is as being Second to some First, regardless of anything else and in particular regardless of any *law*, although it may conform to a law. That is to say, it is *Reaction* as an element of the Phenomenon.

Category the Third is the Idea of that which is such as it is as being a Third, or Medium, between a Second and its First. That it to say, it is *Representation* as an element of the Phenomenon.

A mere complication of Category the Third, involving no idea essentially different, will give the idea of something which is such as it is by virtue of its relations to any multitude, numeral, denumeral, or abnumerable or even to any supermultitude of correlates; so that this Category suffices of itself to give the conception of True Continuity, than which no conception yet discovered is higher.

Category the First owing to its Extremely Rudimentary character is not susceptible of any degenerate or weakened modification.

Category the Second has a *Degenerate* Form, in which there is Secondness indeed, but a weak or Secondary Secondness that is not in the pair in its own quality, but belongs to it only in a certain respect. Moreover, this degeneracy need not be absolute but may be only approximative. Thus a genus characterized by Reaction will by the determination of its essential character split into two species, one a species where the Secondness is strong, the other a species where the Secondness is weak, and the strong species will subdivide into two that will be similarly related, without any corresponding subdivision of the weak species. For example, Psychological Reaction splits into Willing, where the Secondness is strong, and Sensation, where it is weak; and Willing again subdivides into Active Willing and Inhibitive Willing, to which last dichotomy nothing in Sensation corresponds. But it must be confessed that subdivision, as such, involves something more than the second category.[1]

Category the Third exhibits two different ways of Degeneracy, where the irreducible idea of Plurality, as distinguished from Duality, is present indeed but in maimed conditions. The First degree of Degeneracy is found in an Irrational Plurality which, as it exists, in contradistinction from the form of its representation, is a mere complication of duality. We have just had an example of this in the idea of Subdivision.[2] In pure Secondness, the reacting correlates are, as I showed in the last lecture, *Singulars*, and as such are *Individuals*, not capable of further division. Consequently, the conception of Subdivision, say by repeated dichotomy, certainly involves a sort of Thirdness, but it is a Thirdness that is conceived to consist in a second Secondness.

The most degenerate Thirdness is where we conceive a mere Quality of Feeling, or Firstness, to represent itself to itself as Representation. Such, for example, would be Pure Self-Consciousness, which might be roughly described as a mere feeling that has a dark instinct of being a germ of thought.[3] This sounds nonsensical, I grant. Yet, something can be done toward rendering it comprehensible.

I remember a lady's averring that her father had heard a minister, of what complexion she did not say, open a prayer as follows: "O Thou, All-Sufficient, Self-Sufficient, Insufficient God." Now pure Self-Consciousness is Self-Sufficient, and if it is also regarded as All-Sufficient, it would seem to follow that it must be Insufficient. I ought to apologize for introducing such buffoonery into serious lectures. I do so because I seriously believe that a bit of fun helps thought and tends to keep it pragmatical.

Imagine that upon the soil of a country that has a single boundary line thus ⬤ and not ◍ or ◉, there lies a map of that same country. This map may distort the different provinces of the country to any extent. But I shall suppose that it represents every part of the country that has a single boundary by a part of the map that has a single boundary; that every part is represented as bounded by such parts as it really is bounded by, that every point of the country is represented by a single point of the map, and that every point of the map represents a single point in the country. Let us further suppose that this map is infinitely minute in its representation so that there is no speck on any grain of sand in the country that could not be seen represented upon the map if we were to examine it under a sufficiently high magnifying power. Since, then, everything on the soil of the country is shown on the map, and since the map lies on the soil of the country, the map itself will be portrayed in the map, and in this map of the map everything on the soil of the country can be discerned, including the map itself with the map of the map within its boundary. Thus there will be within the map a map of the map, and within that a map of the map of the map and so on *ad infinitum*. These maps being each within the preceding ones of the series, there will be a point contained in all of them, and this will be the map of itself. Each map which directly or indirectly represents the country is itself mapped in the next, that is, in the next is represented to be a map of the country. In other words each map is *interpreted* as such in the next. We may therefore say that each is a representation of the country *to* the next map; and that point that is in all the maps is in itself the representation of nothing but itself and to nothing but it itself. It is therefore the precise analogue of pure self-consciousness. As such it is *self-sufficient*. It is saved from being insufficient, that is, as no representation at all, by the circumstance that it is not *all-sufficient*, that is, is not a complete representation but is only a point upon a continuous map.[4]

I dare say you may have heard something like this before from Prof. Royce; but if so, you will remark an important divergency.[5] The idea itself belongs neither to him nor to me, and was used by me in this connection thirty years ago.

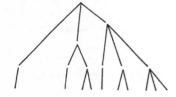
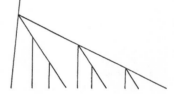

The relatively degenerate forms of the Third category do not fall into a catena, like those of the Second. What we find is this. Taking any class in whose essential idea the predominant element is Thirdness, or Representation, the self-development of that essential idea,—which development, let me say, is not to be compassed by any amount of mere "hard thinking," but only by an elaborate process founded upon experience and reason combined,—results in a *trichotomy* giving rise to three subclasses, or genera, involving respectively a relatively genuine Thirdness, a relatively reactional Thirdness or Thirdness of the lesser degree of degeneracy and a relatively qualitative Thirdness or Thirdness of the last degeneracy. This last may subdivide, and its species may even be governed by the three categories, but it will not subdivide in the manner which we are considering by the essential determinations of its conception. The genus corresponding to the lesser degree of degeneracy, the reactionally degenerate genus, will subdivide after the manner of the Second category forming a catena, while the genus of relatively genuine Thirdness will subdivide by Trichotomy just like that from which it resulted. Only as the division proceeds, the subdivisions become harder and harder to discern. The representamen, for example, divides by trichotomy into the general sign, or *symbol*, the *index*, and the *icon*. An *icon* is a representamen which fulfills the function of a representamen by virtue of a character which it possesses in itself, and would possess just the same though its object did not exist. Thus, the statue of a centaur is not, it is true, a representamen if there be no such thing as a centaur. Still, if it represents a centaur, it is by virtue of its shape; and this shape it will have, just as much whether there be a centaur or not. An *index* is a representamen which fulfills the function of a representamen by virtue of a character which it could not have if its object did not exist but which it will continue to have just the same whether it be interpreted as a representamen or not. For instance, an old-fashioned hygrometer is an *index*. For it is so contrived as to have a physical reaction with dryness and moisture in the air, so that the little man will come out if it is wet, and this would happen just the same if the use of the instrument should be entirely forgotten, so that it ceased actually to convey any information. A *symbol* is a representamen which fulfills its function regardless of any continuity or analogy with its object and equally regardless of any *factual* connection therewith, but solely and simply because it will be interpreted to be a representamen. Such for example is any general word, sentence, or book.

Of these three genera of representamens the *Icon* is the Qualitatively Degenerate, the *Index* the Reactionally Degenerate, while the *Symbol* is the relatively genuine genus.

Now the *Icon* may undoubtedly be divided according to the categories but the mere completeness of the notion of the *icon* does not imperatively call for any such division. For a pure icon does not draw any distinction between itself and its object. It represents whatever it may represent, and whatever it is like, it in so far is. It is an affair of suchness only.

It is quite otherwise with the *Index*. Here is a reactional sign, which is such by virtue of a real connection with its object. Then the question arises is this dual character in the Index so that it has two elements, by virtue of the one serving as a substitute for the particular object it does, while the other is an involved *icon* that represents the representamen itself regarded as a quality of the object,—or is there really no such dual character in the index, so that it merely denotes whatever object it happens to be really connected with just as the icon represents whatever object it happens really to resemble? Of the former, the relatively genuine form of Index, the hygrometer is an example. The connection with the weather is dualistic, so that by an involved *icon*, it actually conveys information. On the other hand any mere landmark by which a particular thing may be recognized because it is as a matter of fact associated with that thing, a proper name without signification, a pointing finger, is a degenerate index. Horatio Greenough, who designed Bunker Hill Monument, tells us in his book that he meant it to say simply "Here!" It just stands on that ground and plainly is not movable. So if we are looking for the battlefield, it will tell us whither to direct our steps.

The *Symbol* or relatively genuine form of Representamen, divides by Trichotomy into the Term, the Proposition, and the Argument. The Term corresponds to the Icon and to the degenerate Index. It does excite an icon in the imagination. The proposition conveys definite information like the genuine index, by having two parts of which the function of the one is to indicate the object meant while that of the other is to represent the representamen by exciting an icon of its quality. The argument is a representamen which does not leave the interpretant to be determined as it may by the person to whom the symbol is addressed; but separately represents what is the interpreting representation that it is intended to determine. This interpreting representation is, of course, the conclusion. It would be interesting to push these illustrations further; but I can linger nowhere. As soon as a subject begins to be interesting I am obliged to pass on to another.

II.

The three categories furnish an artificial classification of all possible systems of metaphysics which is certainly not without its utility. The scheme is shown [in the figure below]. It depends upon what ones of the three categories each system admits as important metaphysico-cosmical elements.

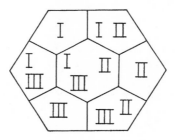

One very naturally and properly endeavors to give an account of the universe with the fewest and simplest possible categories: *Praedicamenta non sunt multiplicanda praeter necessitatem.*

We ought therefore to admire and extol the efforts of Condillac and the Associationalists to explain everything by means of qualities of feeling.

If, however, this turns out to be a failure, the next most admirable hypothesis is that of the corpuscularians, Helmholtz and the like, who would like to explain everything by means of mechanical force, which they do not distinguish from individual reaction. That again failing, the doctrine of Hegel is to be commended who regards Category the Third as the only true one. For in the Hegelian system the other two are only introduced in order to be *aufgehoben*. All the categories of Hegel's list from Pure Being up appear to me very manifestly to involve Thirdness, although he does not happen to recognize it, so immersed is he in this category. All three of these simplest systems having worked themselves out into absurdity, it is natural next in accordance with the maxim of Parsimony to try explanations of the Universe based on the recognition of two only of the Categories. The more moderate nominalists who nevertheless apply the epithet *mere* to thought and to representamens may be said to admit Categories First and Second and to deny the Third. The Berkeleyans for whom there are but two kinds of entities, souls, or centres of determinable thought, and ideas in the souls, these ideas being regarded as pure statical entities, little or nothing else than Qualities of Feeling, seem to admit Categories First and Third and to deny Secondness, which they wish to replace by Divine Creative Influence, which certainly has all the flavor of Thirdness. So far as one can make out any intelligible aim in that singular hodge-podge, the Cartesian metaphysics, it seems to have been to admit Categories Second and Third as fundamental and to deny the First. Otherwise, I do not know to whom we can attribute this opinion which certainly does not seem to be less acceptable and attractive than several others. But there are other philosophies which seem to do full justice to Categories Second and Third and to minimize the First, and among these perhaps Spinoza and Kant are to be included.

III.

I desire in the first place to defend the three Categories as the three irreducible and only constituents of thought, leaving aside for the present the question of the parts they play in the economy of the Universe.

In regard to the First, however, I trust I said enough in the last lecture. I will not return to that.

As to Category the Second, if I were asked to say of what indisputable advantage to philosophy the exact study of the logic of relations had been, and if in answering the question I considered only the manner in which it presents itself to my own mind, I should unhesitatingly mention, as its first and most unquestionable service, that it had put, in the minds of every student of it, the Category of Reaction entirely beyond all doubt as an irreducible element of thought.[6]

And yet the lamented Schröder, in the introduction to his first volume, written, it is true, as is evident enough throughout that and the second volume, before he had very thoroughly studied the logic of relations, appears to me, although probably without fully perceiving the bearing of his doctrine, to take ground quite inconsistent with such recognition of Category the Second. I shall seize this opportunity to enter my protest against the position to which I allude, that position being in my opinion fatal to any sound pragmatistic conceptions. In that Introduction Schröder proclaims himself a follower of Sigwart in regard to the fundamentals of logic; and expressly says that he dissents from my opinions because of the reasons that Sigwart has given.[7] I entertain a relatively high respect for Sigwart, such respect as I entertain for Rollin as a historian, Buffon as a naturalist, Priestley as a chemist, and Biot as a physicist. I would go so far as to pronounce him one of the most critical and exact of the inexact logicians.[8] The particular point now in question is this. I had said that the question of whether a reasoning is sound or not is purely a question of *fact*; namely the fact whether or not such premisses as those of whatever argument might be under criticism could be true while the conclusion was false, in case it was proposed as a necessary reasoning,—and in case of probable reasoning was some analogous question of *fact* corresponding to the pretensions of the argument. I thus, you will perceive, referred the matter to the Category of Reaction, to which the conceptions of existence and fact chiefly belong. But Schröder dissents from this because Sigwart has said that the question whether a given inference is logical or not must in the last resort come down to a question of how we feel,—a question of logical *Gefühl*, to use his own expression, which is to refer truth to the category of Quality of Feeling. This he undertakes to demonstrate. For, he says, if any other criterion be employed, the correctness of this criterion has to be established by reasoning; and in this reasoning that is thus antecedent to the establishment of any rational criterion there is nothing else upon which we can rely but *Gefühl*, so that *Gefühl* is that to which any other criterion must make its ultimate appeal as its ground. Good, say I. This is the sort of reasoning that advances philosophy,—a good square, explicit, and tangible fallacy, that can be squarely met and definitively refuted. What makes it the more valuable is that it is a form of argument of wide applicability in philosophy. It is on a quite similar principle that the hedonist says that the question of what is good morals and what bad must in the last resort come down to a question of feeling pleasure or pain. For, he urges, whatever we desire we take satisfaction in; and if we did not take satisfaction in it, we should not desire it. Thus the only thing we ever can desire is gratification, or pleasure; and all deliberate action must be performed with a view to enjoyment. So too every idealist sets out with an analogous argument, although he may probably shift his ground insensibly as he proceeds further. But at first he will say: When I perceive anything I am conscious; and when I am conscious of anything I am immediately conscious of something, and it is through that immediate consciousness that I become conscious of whatever is in my consciousness. Consequently, all that I learn from perception is that I have a feeling, together with whatever I infer from that as a premiss.

A single answer will suffice for all such argumentation. What they all assume to be necessary is, on the contrary, impossible. No desire can possibly desire its own gratification; no judgment can judge itself to be true; no reasoning can conclude itself to be sound. For the contrary positions stand on one ground and must stand or fall together, so that to refute one is to refute all. Take, then, the question of whether a judgment judges itself to be true. Unquestionably if one judgment does so, every judgment does so. I myself formerly gave something like the following argument to prove that every judgment does so. Consider the proposition

This proposition is not true.

This is certainly a proposition. Hence by the definition of a proposition it is either true or not. But suppose it involves no falsity. Then it will follow that it is not true and does involve falsity thus reducing that hypothesis to absurdity. The proposition is therefore not only false but absurd and self-contradictory. But all that it explicitly asserts is that it is not true. There is certainly no contradiction in saying that it is not true; it is the very conclusion we have come to. Consequently, the only way in which it can involve contradiction is by expressing at the same time the assertion that it is true. We must therefore conclude that every proposition, in the very propositional form itself, expresses the assertion of its own truth.

That may sound forcible, but it is a huge *petitio principii*. Now hear an argument on the other side of the question. If a proposition asserts its own truth it asserts something about itself; and indeed, manifestly the whole question is whether or not a proposition does assert anything about itself. If it asserts anything about itself and about its assertion it certainly asserts that it asserts what it does not assert. But if that be the case, these two propositions

It rains.
I assert that it rains.

are one and the same proposition, or if not the second forms a part of what the first asserts. But now consider the precise denials of the two. They are

It does not rain.

I do not assert that it rains.

Manifestly the second denial asserts much less than the other. Consequently the proposition which it denies asserts much more than the other. It appears, therefore, that the proposition "It rains" does not itself assert that I assert it rains; but when I utter the proposition "It rains" I afford you the evidence of your senses that I assert it rains. This appears to me unanswerable, and it was this argument which called my attention to the fallacy of my former reasoning.

Suppose two witnesses A and B to have been examined but by the law of evidence almost their whole testimony has been struck out except only this:

A testifies that B's testimony is true.
B testifies that A's testimony is false.

Common sense would certainly declare that nothing whatever was testified to. But I cannot admit that judgments of common sense should have the slightest weight in scientific logic, whose duty it is to criticize common sense and correct it.

But I have another argument of a pragmatistic kind. Although Aristotle defines a proposition as a symbol that is either true or false, that is not properly the definition of it. However, waiving the question of propriety, I have a right to use the term *proposition* for the nonce in the sense of a symbol which separately indicates its object. Then the principle that every proposition is either true or false becomes either an *axiom* or a *theorem*. But we cannot admit axioms in these days. Why then should the principle be accepted? To say that every proposition is either true or false is to say that whatever the predicate X of a proposition may be, its subject S is either X or not X. But this is the principle of Excluded Middle and the principle of excluded middle, as we saw in the last lecture, merely defines individuality. That is to say that the principle of excluded middle applies to S is no more than to say that S, the subject of the proposition, is an individual. But how can that be? We know very well that universal propositions have general subjects of which the principle of Excluded Middle is true. That is it is not true that "all men are either tall or not tall." The logic of relatives furnishes the solution, by showing that propositions usually have several subjects, that one of these subjects is the so-called Universe of Discourse, that as a general rule a proposition refers to several Universes of Discourse, the chief of which are Singulars, and that all propositions whatsoever refer to one common universe,—the Universal Universe or aggregate of all Singulars, which in ordinary language we denominate the Truth. The analysis of the Logic of Relations shows that such is the fact, and by the aid of the Categories we can easily see why it should be so. A proposition is a symbol which separately *indicates* its object, and the representation in the proposition of that object is called the subject of the proposition. Now to *indicate* is to represent in the manner in which an index represents. But an index is a representamen which is such by virtue of standing in a genuine reaction with its object, while a singular is nothing but a genuine reacting object. It does not follow that the subject of a proposition must literally be an index, although it *indicates* the object of the representamen in a manner like the mode of representation of an index. It may be a precept by following which a singular could be found. Take for example the proposition

Some woman is adored by every Catholic.

This means that a well-disposed person with sufficient means could find an index whose object should be a woman such that allowing an ill-disposed person to select an index whose object should be a Catholic, that Catholic would adore that woman.

Thus the subject of a proposition if not an index is a precept prescribing the conditions under which an index is to be had.

Consequently, though the subject need not be individual, the object to which the subject of a proposition applies must be the object of a possible index and as such it must be such as it is independently of any representamen or other Third. That is to say it must be *real*.

Consequently it is impossible that a proposition should relate to itself as its object, since as long as it has not yet been enunciated it possesses characters which are not independent of how they may be represented to be.

It is, therefore, quite impossible that a proposition should assert its own truth, or what comes to the same thing, that a desire should desire its own gratification, or that an argument should conclude its own cogency, excepting only in that sense in which a point may map itself to itself, namely, as a special case under a general representation.

Consequently, when Sigwart tells me that in reasoning about a logical criterion I have to *rely* upon a feeling of logicality, he puts the cart before the horse in an utterly impossible way. He supposes that I first *feel* that a certain inference *would* gratify my sense of logicality and then proceed to draw it. But I beg to tell him that in no case whatever is it possible to *feel* what *would* happen. We *reason* about what *would* happen and we feel what *has* happened. We first draw the inference and having drawn it, if we turn our attention to our feeling we become cognizant of a sense of satisfaction. But when we have drawn the inference we have already believed in it and are satisfied, and if we become aware that the inference gives us pleasure that is a subsequent experience upon contemplating what has happened, and it does not so much as furnish a good reason for renewed confidence in the inference, except so far as the feeling may be a sign that we should draw the same inference every time, and that it is not a mere aberration of mind.

Logic is the criticism of conscious thought, altogether analogous to moral self-control; and just as self-control never can be absolute but always must leave something uncontrolled and unchecked to act by primary impulse, so logical criticism never can be absolute but always must leave something uncriticized and unchecked. But to argue from this that logical criticism is mere feeling, would be like arguing in the other case that the only ground of morality is mere impulse.

Besides if Sigwart's reasoning is good for anything at all it goes to prove what he in fact deduces from it and founds his logic upon, namely that sound logic *consists* in the gratification of a feeling, which not only amounts to denying the distinction of truth and falsehood but would necessitate the admission that because my refutation of his position is entirely satisfactory to me and titillates my logical *Gefühl* in the most agreeable manner, therefore this refutation is, *ipso facto*, sound logic.

Were the Holy Father in Rome to take it into his head to use his Infallibility to command the Faithful, under pain of excommunication, to believe everything that any protestant ever had said or ever should say, he would put himself into a position very much like that Sigwart assumes in reducing logicality to a Quality of Feeling.

IV.

The irreducibility of the idea of Thirdness appears to me to be evidently proved in the Logic of Relations. Yet Mr. A. B. Kempe, formerly president of the London Mathematical Society, who has made an important contribution to a part of the Logic of Relations in his Memoir on Mathematical Form in the *Philosophical Transactions* for 1880, plainly does not share my opinion and without directly mentioning me calls attention to certain phenomena whose interest to his mind evidently is that he regards them as refuting the irreducibility of Thirdness.[9] This objection springing, as it does, from exact analysis, should command my most serious consideration.

In order to expound Mr. Kempe's opinion I must define a few technical terms. In ordinary logical analysis such as is required in the algebraical or other purely formal treatment, it is sufficient to consider Category the Second as a two-sided element in the phenomenon, a *Reaction*, involving two objects which are differently related to one another, but having no general distinctive characters. In like manner Category the Third in the same analysis is regarded as a triadic element of the phenomenon without there being any reason for putting one of the triad of singulars which may be concerned in it as the First, rather than either of the others, nor any one as specially Second or Third. There are other purposes, however, for which it is necessary to <distinguish> in a reaction the first object from the second by a general character common to all *firsts*, all *seconds* having their general character, and similarly in all triadic facts distinctive general characters are to be attributed to the First, the Second, and the Third of the three objects concerned. If two singulars A and B react upon one another, the action of A upon B and the action of B upon A are absolutely the same element of the phenomenon. Nevertheless, ordinary language makes the distinction of *agent* and *patient*, which, indeed, in the languages that are familiar to us is given great prominence; and this is the case with the majority of the languages of all families, as well as the Procrustean bed imposed by the grammarians allows us to make out their real character. But in all families languages are found in which little or nothing is made of the distinction. In Gaelic, for example, the usual form of expression places what we should call the subject in an oblique case,—the genitive, in that language, but in some languages it is rather an ablative or an instrumental case. This distinction of agent and patient is sometimes useful even in philosophy. That is, a formal distinction is drawn between the action of A on B and the action of B on A although they are really the same fact. In the action of A on B, the patient B is conceived to be affected by A while the agent A is unaffected by B. A is modified in the action so far as to be in an active state; but this is conceived to be a certain Quality that the agent takes on during the action in which Quality the patient in no way participates, while the patient, on the other hand, takes on a relative character which can neither exist nor be conceived to exist except as correlative to an agent. That is the distinction of agent and patient. So in a triadic fact, say, for example

A gives B to C

we make no distinction in the ordinary logic of relations between the *subject nominative*, the *direct object*, and the *indirect object*. We say that the proposition has three *logical subjects*. We regard it as a mere affair of English grammar that there are six ways of expressing this:

A gives B to C	A benefits C with B
B enriches C at expense of A	C receives B from A
C thanks A for B	B leaves A for C

These six sentences express one and the same indivisible phenomenon. Nevertheless, just as conceiving of two reacting objects we may introduce the metaphysical distinction of *agent* and *patient*, so we may meta-physically distinguish the functions of the three objects denoted by the *subject nominative*, the *direct object*, and the *indirect object*. The subject nominative denotes that one of the three objects which in the triadic fact merely assumes a nonrelative character of activity. The *direct object* is that object which in the triadic fact receives a character relative to that agent, being the *patient* of its action, while the indirect object receives a character which can neither exist nor be conceived to exist without the cooperation of the other two. When I call Category the Third the Category of Representation in which there is a Represented Object, a Representamen, and an Interpretant, I recognize that distinction. This mode of distinction is, indeed, *germane* to Thirdness, while it is *alien* to Secondness. That is to say, *agent* and *patient* as they are by themselves in their Duality are not distinguished as Agent and Patient, the distinction lies in the mode of representing them in my mind, which is a Third. Thus there is an inherent Thirdness in this mode of distinction. But a *triadic* fact is in all cases an intellectual fact. Take *giving* for example. The mere transfer of an object which A sets down and C takes up does not constitute giving. There must be a transfer of *ownership* and ownership is a matter of Law, an intellectual fact. You now begin to see how the conception of Representation is so peculiarly fit to typify the Category of Thirdness. The Object represented is supposed not to be affected by the representation. That is essential to the idea of representation. The Representamen is affected by [the] Object but is not otherwise modified in the operation of representation. It is either Qualitatively the Double of the object in the Icon, or it is a Patient on which the object really Acts, in the Index; or it is intellectually linked to the Object in such a way as to be mentally excited by that Object, in the Symbol.

It is desirable that you should understand clearly the distinction between the genuine and the degenerate Index. The Genuine Index represents the duality between the Representamen and its Object. As a whole it stands for the Object; but it has a part or element of it <which it> represents as being the Representamen, by being an *Icon* or analogue of the Object in some way; and by virtue of that duality, it conveys information about the Object. The simplest example of a genuine Index would be, say, a telescopic image of a double star. This is not an *Icon* simply, because an *Icon* is a representamen which represents its object solely be virtue of its similarity to it, as a drawing of a triangle represents a mathematical triangle. But the mere appearance of the telescopic image of a double star does not proclaim itself to be similar to the star itself. It is because we have set the circles of the equatorial so that the field must by physical compulsion contain the image of that star that it represents that star and by that means we know that the image must be an icon of the star, and information is conveyed. Such is the genuine or informational index.

A degenerate Index is a representamen which represents a single object because it is *factually* connected with it, but which conveys no information whatever. Such, for example, are the letters attached to a geometrical or other diagram. A *proper name* is substantially the same thing; for although in this case the connection of the sign with its object happens to be a purely mental association, yet that circumstance is of no importance in the functioning of the representamen. The use of letters as indices is not confined to mathematics. Lawyers particularly often discuss cases in which A contracts with B to do something. These letters are convenient substitutes for relative pronouns. A relative, demonstrative, or personal pronoun comes very near to being a mere Index, if it be not accurately so. It is far more correct so to define it than to say that a pronoun is a word placed instead of a noun. It would be nearer right to say that a common noun when subject nominative is a word put in place of a pronoun. A degenerate index may be called a *Monstrative* Index, in contradistinction to an *Informational* or Genuine Index.

A *proposition* is a symbol which like the Informational Index has a special part to represent the representamen while the whole or another special part represents the Object. The part which represents the *representamen* and which excites an *icon* in the imagination, is the Predicate. The part which indicates the object or set of objects of the representamen is called the Subject or Subjects, in grammar the subject nominative, and the objects, each of which can be replaced by a Proper Name or other *Monstrative Index* without the proposition's ceasing thereby to be a proposition. How much shall be embraced in the Predicate and how many Subjects shall be recognized depends, for the ordinary analyses of logic, upon what mode of analysis will answer the purpose in hand. If from a proposition we strike out a part and leave its place blank, this part being such that a monstrative index being put in its place, the symbol will again become a proposition, the part which remains after such erasure will be a predicate of the kind which I call a *monad*. Here are examples:

_____gives B to C
A gives_____to C
A gives B to_____

If two blanks remain, I call the predicate a *dyad*. Such are

_____ gives_____to C
_____ gives B to_____
A gives_____to_____

If there are more than two blanks, I call the predicate a *polyad*. The entire proposition may be regarded as a predicate, the circumstances under which it is uttered, the person who utters it, and all the surroundings constituting a monstrative index which will be the subject. I term an entire proposition without a blank when it is considered as a predicate a *medad*, from μηδέν. Every proposition whatever has the *Universe of Discourse* for one of its subjects and all propositions have one subject in common which we call the *Truth*. It is the aggregate of all realities, what the Hegelians call the *Absolute*.

Thus, to include more in the predicate than need be included is merely not to carry logical analysis as far as it might be carried: it does not affect its accuracy. But to include anything in a subject which might be separated from it and left in the predicate is a positive fault of analysis. To say for example that 'All men' is the subject of the proposition "All men are mortal" is incorrect. The true analysis is that "Anything" is the subject and "_____ is mortal or else not a man," is the predicate. So in "Some cat is blue-eyed" the subject is not "some cat" but "something," the predicate being "_____ is a blue-eyed cat." "Something" means that sufficient knowledge would enable us to replace the 'something' by a monstrative index and still keep the proposition true. "Anything" means that the interpreter of the proposition is free to replace the "anything" by such monstrative index as he will, and still the proposition will be true. Logicians confine themselves, apart [from] monstrative indices themselves, to 'Anything' and 'Something', two descriptions of what monstrative index may replace the subject, the one description *vague*, the other *general*. No others are required since such subjects, "All but one," "All but two," "Almost all," "Two thirds of the occasions that present themselves in experience," and the like are capable of logical analysis.

Everybody who has studied logic is aware that the only *formal* fallacies which ordinary logic detects are confusions between "Anything" and "Something." The same thing remains true in the logic of relatives except that we now meet with fallacies owing to confusions about the order of succession of "Anything" and "Something" as if one should carelessly substitute for the proposition "Every man is born of some woman" the proposition "There is some woman of whom every man is born."

Now in mathematics as it has been developed all such confusions are next to impossible for the reason that mathematicians confine their studies almost exclusively to hypotheses which present only systems of relationship that are perfectly regular or as nearly so as the nature of things allows. I could give you some amusing instances of confusions between some and all in actual mathematical treatises; but they are rare. Practically, the mathematician confines himself to the study of relations among sets of hypothetical singulars.

Now Mr. Kempe considers only mathematical relationships in that sense, that is considers only relations between single objects. Moreover, he further limits himself to relationships among enumerable sets of singulars, although mathematicians are incessantly considering denumeral or endless sets, and very often sets still more multitudinous. So confining his studies, Mr. Kempe finds that all the relationships he meets with can be represented by graphs composed of dots of various colors connected by lines. For example, the relations between ten rays of the ten-ray theorem of Optical Geometry, which von Standt demonstrated so beautifully, and which are shown in this figure:

are represented by Kempe in a graph substantially like this:

Now Mr. Kempe seems to think that because his graphs are composed of but two kinds of elements, the spots of various colors and the lines, therefore a third category is not called for. To mathematical minds this will probably seem a formidable objection. It seemed so to me when I read it, I confess. But I will give three answers to it each sufficient to completely reverse its force.

The first reply is that it is not true that Mr. Kempe's graphs only contain two kinds of elements. It no doubt seems at first glance that the dots of various colors represent Qualities, and the lines Reactions; and one then looks in vain for anything corresponding to Thirdness. The lines which are all drawn between pairs of points no doubt do in truth embody the Category of Duality. And in confirmation of this, it is to be remarked that the lines really dichotomize into two kinds, although Kempe draws but one kind. For *non-connection* is itself a species of connection. Thus in the Graph to which I have called your attention, the pairs of lines between which there are no dots are the pairs which intersect at the ten significant points of the theorem. But the spots each of which ties together any number of lines and always many either of the written kind or of the unwritten, far from representing the Category of Unity, plainly embody the Category of Plurality—the Third Category—and it is the Surface upon which the Graph is written as *one* whole which in its Unity represents the Category of Unity. So that it appears that three kinds of elements are needed for his Graphs, which therefore vindicate the third category instead of refuting it as they were supposed to do.

My second answer to Kempe is that his objection is founded upon the idea that his graphs adequately represent the systems of mathematical relationships. Now that is not true. For example, the relationships of rays of the nine-point theorem—which is that if, of two sets of three rays, each are such that two triplets of intersections of rays of different sets are collinear, this will be true also of the third set—are represented on Kempe's system by the graph [below]. Now how utterly absurd it is to say that that figure represents the relations of those rays! The relations of the rays are all triple relations. They consist in the fact that the nine rays intersect in threes in nine points. This is not shown at all. These triple relations obviously cannot be represented by any complexus of dual relations. In order to represent them therefore he would have had to introduce a third kind of element into his diagrams. This diagram expresses it with apparently only two kinds of signs, but in reality the lines have two distinct meanings.

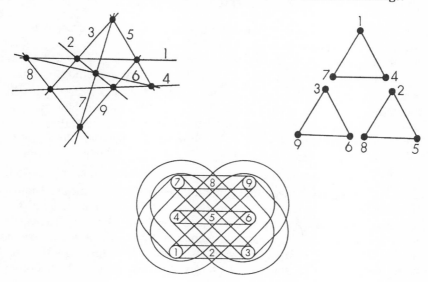

My third answer to Mr. Kempe's objection is that he has not considered all relationships. In the first place, he has not considered any that are of a general nature and generality is the home and special domain of Category the Third. In the second place even among sets of singulars he has not considered the chief relationships with which mathematics deals, namely, those which concern infinite collections of individuals; and it is among those especially, among singular relationships, that Thirdness should be expected to appear. For that reason, no conclusion adverse to Thirdness can logically be drawn from Mr. Kempe's graphs until his system has received the modifications that are necessary to enable it to express all kinds of relations. Now these modifications I have developed in the simplest and most analytic method possible,—a method so thoroughly analytic that it dissects a simple syllogism into eight or nine distinct inferential steps, so that it is by long odds the most thoroughly analytic system of logical representation yet developed, and if this system is unable to resolve Thirdness into anything else, it is safe to say that no other system can come near to doing so. It would require a long course of lectures to present this system in anything like its fullness, but I will outline some of its main features. It has the equivalents of Kempe's lines and colored dots. Only the dots have definite valencies like the atoms in chemical graphs, and instead of coloring the dots, I imitate the chemists by abbreviating the words which express them. These dots are, in fact, predicates.

Writing capital N for Napoleon Bonaparte and b for blue-eyed

$$\mathrm{N} \longrightarrow b$$

will mean that Napoleon Bonaparte was blue-eyed, because every point of the heavy line represents a singular and the continuity of this line signifies the identity of all the singulars represented by its points. ——b will mean that something blue-eyed exists. $\overline{}{}^c_b$ will mean that something is blue-eyed and something is a cat. If we join the two lines and write C^c_b it will mean that something is a cat and the same identical thing is blue-eyed, or some cat is blue-eyed. Writing ℓ for loves ——ℓ—— will mean that something loves something. N——ℓ——c will mean that Napoleon loves a cat. c——ℓ——c will mean that a cat loves a cat. $^c \smile {}^\ell \frown {}^c$ will mean that a cat loves a cat identical with itself; and this could be more simply written $^c \smile {}^\ell \supset$. So $C^\ell \!\! J$ will mean that something loves itself. If r means it rains, then simply writing r will *assert* that it rains. For that reason I call the sheet on which we write the "sheet of assertion." This sheet represents the universal Universe of Truth, and to connect a graph with this universe by writing the graph upon the sheet of assertion which represents the universe is equivalent to uniting with that universe by a heavy line. Consequently in this system the sheet on which the graphs are written is virtually a special kind of spot, and the writing of a graph on this sheet is virtually equivalent to drawing a heavy line from the spot representing the Universe to the Spot. In these respects this system differs from Kempe's. We cannot here claim either the sheet or the writing of a graph on the sheet as representing a special category as they do in Kempe's system. To enclose a graph or any portion of a graph in a lightly drawn oval shall be understood as assertively separating it from the universe of truth, that is as denying it. Thus, Ⓡ will assert that it does not rain and ⊂—ℓ—⊃ will deny that something loves something, that is, will assert that nothing loves anything. On the other hand —(ℓ)— will assert that there is something but will deny that it is true of it that it loves something. That is, it will assert that there is something that does not love anything. So —(ℓ)— will assert that there is something, say X, and something, say Y, which may or may not be identical with X, and X does not love Y; or in short there is something that does not love everything. If we deny this by writing ⊂(ℓ)⊃ we shall assert that everything loves everything. But if we write ⊂(ℓ)⊃ we shall assert that there is something that loves everything. To write (ℓ)— will assert that there is something that is not loved by anything. If we deny this we have ⊂(ℓ)⊃ or everything is loved by something.

If we write g for gives and write $\overset{A-g-B}{\underset{C}{|}}$ for A gives B to C then Ⓟ will mean "Somebody gives everybody something." Here is the entire system, and I regard it as certain that no simpler system of expressing all possible relations can be devised.

My other two answers to Kempe which would be works of supererogation must be left unperformed. I will just mention their nature. Answer number two would have consisted in the remark that Kempe does not represent in his graphs any entire system of real mathematical relationships. For example, his graph of the ten-ray theorem fails to show what triplets of rays are copunctual. This is still more strikingly the case with the nine-ray theorem of which here is the geometrical figure and here the graph drawn as Kempe has drawn them of the ten-ray theorem. In short, he has simply omitted from consideration all triadic relations and then points triumphantly to the fact that he has nothing to represent Thirdness as if that proved there was no such irreducible conception. But if his graphs were modified so as to exhibit the copunctual rays and collinear points, the triadic character of his spots would come out very clearly.

Answer number three is that Kempe not only fails altogether to represent general relations, but simply gives an icon. His graphs never express *propositions,* far less *necessary consequences.* Now I invented and developed a good many years ago such a modification of Kempe's method of representation as was required to make it really express everything in mathematics. I inserted a slight sketch of it into Baldwin's *Dictionary*. It has never been published otherwise. In consequence of my great interest in the working of that system my studies of it had always followed that line and until I came to write this lecture it had never occurred to me to examine it in respect to its relation to the categories. In doing so, I found the three Categories copiously illustrated in the system. But what was still more interesting, a certain fault in the system, by no means of a fatal kind but still a vexatious inelegance which I had often remarked but could see no way of remedying, now, when looked upon from the point of view of the categories, appeared in a new and stronger light than ever before, showing me not only how to remedy the defect that I had seen, but opening my eyes to new possibilities of perfectionment that I had never dreamed of. I wish I could present all this to you, for it is very beautiful and interesting as well [as] very instructive; but it would require several lectures and lead me quite away from Pragmatism.

It is certainly hard to believe, until one is forced to the belief, that a conception so obtrusively complex as Thirdness is should be an irreducible unanalyzable conception. What, one naturally exclaims, does this man think to convince us that a conception is complex and simple, at the same time! I might answer this by drawing a distinction. It is complex in the sense that different features may be discriminated in it, but the peculiar idea of *complexity* that it contains, although it has complexity as its object, is an unanalyzable idea. Of what is the conception of *complexity* built up? Produce it by construction without using any idea which involves it if you can.

The best way of satisfying oneself whether Thirdness is elementary or not,—at least, it would be the best way for me, who had in the first place a natural aptitude for logical analysis which has been in constant training all my life long,—and I rather think it would be the best way for anybody provided he ruminates over his analysis, returns to it again and again, and criticizes it severely and sincerely, until he reaches a complete insight into the analysis,—the best way, I say, is to take the idea of representation, say the idea of the fact that the object, A, is represented in the representation, B, so as to determine the interpretation, C,—to take this idea and endeavor to state what it consists in without introducing the idea of Thirdness at all if possible, or if you find that impossible to see what is the minimum or most degenerate form of Thirdness which will answer the purpose.

Then, having exercised yourself on that problem, take another idea in which, according to any views, Thirdness takes a more degenerate form. Try your hand at a logical analysis of the fact that A gives B to C.

Then pass to a case in which Thirdness takes a still more degenerate form, as for example the idea of "A and B." What is at once A and B involves the idea of three variables. Putting it mathematically, it is $Z = XY$ which is the equation of the simpler of the two hyperboloids, the two sheeted one as it is called.

Whoever wishes to train his logical powers will find those problems furnish capital exercise; and whoever wishes to get a just conception of the universe will find that the solutions of those problems have a more intimate connection with that conception than he could suspect in advance.

V.

I have thus far been intent on repelling attacks upon the categories which should consist in maintaining that the idea of Reaction can be reduced to that of Quality of Feeling and the idea of Representation to those of Reaction and Quality of Feeling taken together. But meantime may not the enemy have stolen upon my rear, and shall I not suddenly find myself exposed to an attack which shall run as follows:

We fully admit that you have proved, until we begin to doubt it, that Secondness is not involved in Firstness nor Thirdness in Secondness and Firstness. But you have entirely failed to prove that Firstness, Secondness, and Thirdness are independent ideas for the obvious reason that it is as plain as the nose on your face that the idea of a triplet involves the idea of pairs, and the idea of a pair the idea of units. Consequently, Thirdness is the one and sole category. This is substantially the idea of Hegel; and unquestionably it contains a truth.

Not only does Thirdness suppose and involve the ideas of Secondness and Firstness, but never will it be possible to find any Secondness or Firstness in the phenomenon that is not accompanied by Thirdness.

If the Hegelians confined themselves to that position they would find a hearty friend in my doctrine.

But they do not. Hegel is possessed with the idea that the Absolute is One. Three absolutes he would regard as a ludicrous contradiction *in adjecto*. Consequently, he wishes to make out that the three categories have not their several independent and irrefutable standings in thought. *Firstness* and *Secondness* must somehow be *aufgehoben*. But it is not true. They are in no way refuted nor refutable. Thirdness it is true involves Secondness and Firstness, in a sense. That is to say, if you have the idea of Thirdness you must have had the ideas of Secondness and Firstness to build upon. But what is required for the idea of a genuine Thirdness is an independent solid Secondness and not a Secondness that is a mere corollary of an unfounded and inconceivable Thirdness; and a similar remark may be made in reference to Firstness.

Let the Universe be an evolution of Pure Reason if you will. Yet if while you are walking in the street reflecting upon how everything is the pure distillate of Reason a man carrying a heavy pole suddenly pokes you in the small of the back, you may think there is something in the Universe that Pure Reason fails to account for; and when you look at the color *red* and ask yourself how Pure Reason could make *red* to have that utterly inexpressible and irrational positive quality it has, you will be perhaps disposed to think that Quality and Reaction have their independent standings in the Universe.

VI.

So far I have only considered whether or not the Categories must be admitted as so many independent constituents of thought. In my next lecture I shall have to examine whether they all three have their place among the realities of nature and constitute all there is in nature.

I confess I wonder how any philosopher can say "Oh *Thirdness* merely exists in thought. There is no such thing in reality." You do know I am enough of a sceptic to be unwilling to believe in the miraculous power he attributes to the mind of originating a category the like of which God could not put into the realities, and which the Divine Mind would seem not to have been able to conceive. Still, those philosophers will reply that this may be fine talk but it certainly is not argument; and I must confess that it is not. So in the next lecture the categories must be defended as realities.

LECTURE FOUR:
THE SEVEN SYSTEMS OF METAPHYSICS

I.

Pragmatism is a maxim of logic; and logic can gain not the slightest support from metaphysics. Nevertheless, I am going this evening, to break the strict development of the subject by lecturing to you on metaphysics. My reason for doing so is that I desire to familiarize you with the three categories before proceeding further in my main argument.

To treat the three categories simply as three units, regardless of their distinctiveness and of their essential correlations, will be a crude procedure from which no useful approximation to the truth of Nature were to be expected.

But when it is *not* the truth of nature that we aim to represent, but all the aberrations of the philosophers in their illogical and helter-skelter rummagings after a just conception of the world, nothing perhaps could be better than to suppose every conceivable combination of the categories, rational or irrational, to have emerged during the history of metaphysics.

Grant me that the three categories of Firstness, Secondness, and Thirdness, or Quality, Reaction, and Representation, have in truth the enormous importance for thought that I attribute to them, and it would seem that no division of theories of metaphysics could surpass in importance a division based upon the consideration of what ones of the three categories each of the different metaphysical systems have fully admitted as real constituents of nature.

It is, at any rate, a hypothesis easy to try; and the exact logic of hypothesis allots great weight to that consideration. There will be then these seven possible classes:[1]

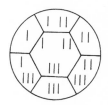

I. Nihilism, so-called; and Idealistic Sensualism.[2]
II. Strict individualism. The doctrine [of] Lutaslawski and his unpronounceable master.
III. Hegelianism of all shades.
II III. Cartesianism of all kinds, Leibnizianism, Spinozism and the metaphysics of the Physicists of today.
I III. Berkeleyanism.
I II. Ordinary Nominalism.
I II III. The metaphysics that recognizes all the categories would need at once to be subdivided. But I shall not stop to consider its subdivision. It embraces Kantism—Reid's Philosophy and the Platonic philosophy of which Aristotelianism is a special development. A great variety of thinkers call themselves Aristotelians, even the Hegelians, on the strength of special agreements. No modern philosophy or very little has any real right to the title. I should call myself an Aristotelian of the scholastic wing, approaching Scotism, but going much further in the direction of scholastic realism.

The doctrine of Aristotle is distinguished from substantially all modern philosophy <except perhaps Schelling's or mine> by its recognition of at least two grades of being. That is, besides *actual, reactive existence*, Aristotle recognizes a germinal being, an *esse in potentia* or as I like to call it an *esse in futuro*. In places Aristotle has glimpses of a distinction between ἐνέργεια and ἐντελέχεια.

Hegel's whole doctrine of *Wesen*, the most labored and the most unsuccessful part of his work, is an attempt to work out something similar. But the truth is that Hegel agrees with all other modern philosophers in recognizing no other mode of being than being *in actu*.

If I had eternity at my disposal in place of an hour, I would take up successively all the six kinds of metaphysics which fail to recognize the *reality* of all the categories and would point out the fatal defect of each. Within my hour I cannot even promise to sketch some one of the arguments for the reality of each of the three categories. I will take them up in the order of their importance for what is to follow, in view of the opinions to which I imagine you mostly incline. I will say something, first, in favor of the Reality of Thirdness; and then put in a few words a defense of real Firstness. After that, if a few minutes remain to me, I shall have something of considerable interest to add in favor of Secondness. But if not, I shall have to let that go undefended.

II.

I proceed to argue that *Thirdness* is operative in Nature.

Suppose we attack the question experimentally. Here is a stone. Now I place that stone where there will be no obstacle between it and the floor, and I will predict with confidence that as soon as I let go my hold upon the stone it will fall to the floor. I will prove that I can make a correct prediction by actual trial if you like. But I see by your faces that you all think it will be a very silly experiment. Why so? Because you all know very well that I *can* predict what will happen, and that the fact will verify my prediction.

But *how can* I know what is going to happen? You certainly do not think that it is by clairvoyance, as if the future event by its existential reactiveness could affect me directly, as in an *experience* of it, as an event scarcely past might affect me. You know very well that there is nothing of the sort in this case. Still, it remains true that I *do know* that that stone will drop, as a *fact*, as soon as I let go my hold. If I *truly know* anything, that which I know must be *real*. It would be quite absurd to say that I could be enabled to know how events are going to be determined over which I can exercise no more control than I shall be able to exercise over this stone after it shall have left my hand, that I can so peer in the future merely on the strength of any acquaintance with any pure fiction.

I know that this stone will fall if it [is] let go, because experience has convinced me that objects of this kind always do fall; and if anyone present has any doubt on the subject, I should be happy to try the experiment, and I will bet him a hundred to one on the result.

But the general proposition that all solid bodies fall in the absence of any upward force or pressure, this formula I say, is of the nature of a representation. Our nominalistic friends would be the last to dispute that. They will go so far as to say that it is a *mere* representation,—the word *mere* meaning that to be represented and really to be are two very different things; and that this formula has no being except a being represented. It certainly is of the nature of a representation. That is undeniable, I grant. And it is equally undeniable that that which is of the nature of a representation is not *ipso facto* real. In that respect there is a great contrast between an object of reaction and an object of representation. Whatever reacts is *ipso facto* real. But an object of representation is not *ipso facto* real. If I were to predict that on my letting go of the stone it would fly up in the air, that would be mere fiction; and the proof that it was so would be obtained by simply trying the experiment. That is clear. On the other hand, and by the same token, the fact that I *know* that this stone will fall to the floor when I let it go, as you all must confess, if you are not blinded by theory, that I *do* know,—and you none of you care to take up my bet, I notice,—is the proof that the formula, or uniformity, as furnishing a safe basis for prediction, is, or if you like it better, *corresponds to*, a reality.

Possibly at this point somebody may raise an objection, and say: You admit that [it] is one thing really to be and another to be represented; and you further admit that it is of the nature of the law of nature to be represented. Then it follows that it has not the mode of being of a reality. My answer to this would be that it rests upon an ambiguity. When I say that the general proposition as to what will happen whenever a certain condition may be fulfilled is of the nature of a representation I mean that it refers to experiences *in futuro* which I do not know are all of them experienced and never can know have been all experienced. But when I say that really to be is different from being represented, I mean that what really is ultimately consists in what shall be forced upon us in experience, that there is an element of brute compulsion in fact and that fact is not a mere question of reasonableness. Thus, if I say, "I shall wind up my watch every day as long as I live," I never can have a positive experience which *certainly* covers all that is here promised, because I never shall know for certain that my last day has come. But what the real fact will be does not depend upon what I represent, but upon what the experiential reactions shall be. My assertion that I shall wind up my watch every day of my life may turn out to accord with facts even though I be the most irregular of persons, by my dying before nightfall.

If we call that being true by chance, here is a case of a *general proposition* being entirely true in all its generality by chance.

Every general proposition is limited to a finite number of occasions in which it might conceivably be falsified, supposing that it is an assertion confined to what human beings may experience; and consequently it is conceivable that, although it should be true without exception, it should still only be by chance that it turns out true.

But if I see a man who is very regular in his habits and am led to offer to wager that that man will not miss winding his watch for the next month, you have your choice between two alternative hypotheses only.

1st, you may suppose that *some principle* or *cause* is *really* operative to *make* him wind his watch daily, which *active principle* may have more or less strength; or

2nd, you may suppose that it is mere chance that his actions have hitherto been regular; and in that case, that regularity in the past affords you not the slightest reason for expecting its continuance in the future, any more than if he had thrown sixes three times running *that* event would render it either more or less likely that his next throw would show sixes.

It is the same with the operations of nature. With overwhelming uniformity, in our past experience, direct and indirect, stones left free to fall have fallen. Thereupon two hypotheses only are open to us. Either

1st, the uniformity with which those stones have fallen has been due to mere chance and affords no ground whatever, not the slightest, for any expectation that the next stone that shall be let go will fall; or

2nd, the uniformity with which stones have fallen has been due to *some active general principle*, in which case it would be a strange coincidence that it should cease to act at the moment my prediction was based upon it.

That position, gentlemen, will sustain criticism. It is irrefragable.

Of course, every sane man will adopt the latter hypothesis. If he could doubt it in the case of the stone,—which he can't—and I may as well drop the stone once for all,—I told you so!—if anybody doubts this still, a thousand other such inductive predictions are getting verified every day, and he will have to suppose every one of them to be merely fortuitous in order reasonably to escape the conclusion that

General Principles are really operative in nature. That is the doctrine of scholastic realism.

III.

You may, perhaps, ask me how I connect generality with Thirdness. Various different replies, each fully satisfactory, may be made to that inquiry. The old definition of a general is *Generāle est quod nātum aptum est dici de multis*. This recognizes that the general is essentially *predicative* and therefore of the nature of a representamen. And by following out that path of suggestion we should obtain a good reply to the inquiry.

In another respect, however, the definition represents a very degenerate sort of generality. None of the scholastic logics fails to explain that *sōl* is a general term; because although there happens to be but one sun yet the term *sōl aptum nātum est dici de multis*. But that is most inadequately expressed. If *sōl* is apt to be predicated of *many*, it is apt to be predicated of any multitude however great, and since there is no maximum multitude, those objects of which it is fit to be predicated form an aggregate that exceeds all multitude. Take any two possible objects that might be called *suns* and, however much alike they may be, any multitude whatsoever of intermediate suns are alternatively possible and therefore as before these intermediate possible suns transcend all multitude. In short the idea of a general involves the idea of possible variations which no multitude of existent things could exhaust but would leave between any two not merely *many* possibilities, but possibilities absolutely beyond all multitude.

Now Thirdness is nothing but the character of an object which embodies Betweenness or Mediation in its simplest and most rudimentary form; and I use it as the name of that element of the phenomenon which is predominant wherever Mediation is predominant, and which reaches its fullness in Representation.

Thirdness as I use the term is only a synonym for Representation, to which I prefer the less colored term because its suggestions are not so narrow and special as those of the word Representation. Now it is proper to say that a general principle that is operative in the real world is of the essential nature of a Representation and of a symbol because its *modus operandi* is the same as that by which *words* produce physical effects. Nobody can deny that words do produce such effects. Take, for example, that sentence of Patrick Henry which, at the time of our revolution, was repeated by every man to his neighbor,

> Three millions of people, armed in the holy cause of Liberty, and in such a country as we possess, are invincible against any force that the enemy can bring against us.

Those words present this character of the general law of nature, they might have produced effects indefinitely transcending any that circumstances allowed them to produce. It might, for example, have happened that some American schoolboy, sailing as a passenger in the Pacific Ocean, should have idly written down those words on a slip of paper. The paper might have been tossed overboard and might have been picked up by some Tagala on a beach of the island of Luzon; and if he had had them translated to him they might easily have passed from mouth to mouth there as they did in this country, and with similar effect.

Words then do produce physical effects. It is madness to deny it. The very denial of it involves a belief in it; and nobody can consistently fail to acknowledge it until he sinks to a complete mental paresis.

But *how* do they produce their effect? They certainly do not, in their character as symbols, *directly* react upon matter. Such action as they have is merely logical. It is not even psychological. It is merely that one symbol would justify another. However, suppose that first difficulty to have been surmounted, and that they do act upon actual thoughts. That thoughts act on the physical world and *conversely*, is one of the most familiar of facts. Those who deny it are persons with whom theories are stronger than facts. But how thoughts act on things it is impossible for us, in the present state of our knowledge, so much as to make any very promising guess; although, as I will show you presently, a guess can be made which suffices to show that the problem is not beyond all hope of ultimate solution.

All this is equally true of the manner in which the laws of nature influence matter. A law is in itself nothing but a general formula or Symbol. An existing thing is simply a blind reacting thing, to which not merely all generality, but even all representation, is utterly foreign. The general formula may logically determine another, less broadly general. But it will be of its essential nature general, and its being narrower does not in the least constitute any participation in the reacting character of the thing. Here we have that great problem of the *principle of individuation* which the scholastic doctors after a century of the closest possible analysis were obliged to confess was quite incomprehensible to them. Analogy suggests that the laws of nature are ideas or resolutions in the mind of some vast consciousness, who, whether Supreme or subordinate, is a Deity relatively to us. I do not approve of mixing up Religion and Philosophy; but as a purely philosophical hypothesis, that has the advantage of being supported by analogy. Yet I cannot clearly see that beyond that support to the imagination it is of any particular scientific service.[3]

Let us now consider

The Reality of Firstness.

The popular metaphysics of today, at least among those who are influenced by physical conceptions, no doubt is that Qualities do not act in nature, and have no being except in consciousness.

My judgment, as a logician, is that the hypothesis of the older physicists is scientifically the preferable one still. It is presumably not sufficient; but the indications are that it is by the comparison of that hypothesis with the facts that we are likely the soonest to find out what hypothesis deserves to be tried next, and those who have endeavored to correct it have modified it in too many particulars at once, thereby violating the Maxim of Parsimony.

That hypothesis is that atomicules all alike, act mechanically upon one another according to one fixed law of force. This recognizes Thirdness as real not only in recognizing the reality of Law but also in recognizing the reality of Space and Time. For all these physicists, although they may hold with Leibniz that Space and Time are mere relations, not Substance as Newton thought, and *that*, whether they are supposed with Kant to be forms of intuition or not, nevertheless agree in making Space and Time to be phenomenally Real. I ought to add that they further make highly degenerate Thirdness to be real in supposing the atomicules to be immensely multitudinous. They hold Secondness, too, in the form of Reaction to be real. But as for Qualities, they are supposed to be in consciousness merely, with nothing in the real thing to correspond to them except mere degrees of more or less. Now all Quantity they will say (perhaps not always thinking quite clearly) involves just three elements: Number, Standard Unit, and an Origin. Number they may very well admit to be an affair of Thirdness. At any rate, it involves no real Quality. The Standard Unit is an affair of Reaction. If it be a standard of length, the metre used has to be transported,—that very reacting object has to be transported,—to the *Pavillon de Breteuil* and put into reaction with an object kept there. So it is with the standard of mass. And the standard of time has to be put into reaction with the heavens as a reacting object. As for the Origin that would be the affair of each person's individual consciousness, apart from the Thirdness and Secondness that it may involve. A punctual origin refers to his simpler consciousness; a *plane* origin refers to the median of his body as he stands facing *Polaris*, or to the feeling of the difference between his right and his left hand, which would be an affair of *Thirdness*.[4]

These different metaphysical conceptions of the younger physicists do not differ from that of the older physicists in respect to making Qualities to be mere illusions. But when one considers the matter from a *logical* point of view the notion that qualities are illusions and play no part in the real universe shows itself to be a peculiarly *unfounded* opinion.

Reasoning cannot possibly be divorced from *logic*; because whenever a man reasons he thinks that he is drawing a conclusion such as would be justified in every analogous case. He therefore cannot really *infer* without having a notion of a class of possible inferences, all of which are logically *good*. That distinction of *good* and *bad* he always has in mind when he infers. Logic proper is the *critics* of arguments, the pronouncing them to be good or bad. There are, as I am prepared to maintain, operations of the mind which are logically exactly analogous to inferences excepting only that they are unconscious and therefore uncontrollable and therefore not subject to criticism. But that makes all the difference in the world; for *inference* is essentially deliberate, and self-controlled. Any operation which cannot be controlled, any conclusion which is not abandoned, not merely as soon as *criticism* has pronounced against it, but in the very act of pronouncing that decree, is not of the nature of rational inference,—is not reasoning. Reasoning as deliberate is essentially critical, and it is idle to criticize as good or bad that which cannot be controlled. Reasoning essentially involves *self-control*; so that the *logica utens* is a particular species of morality. Logical goodness and badness, which we shall find is simply the distinction of *Truth* and *Falsity* in general, amounts, in the last analysis, to nothing but a particular application of the real general distinction of Moral Goodness and Badness, or Righteousness and Wickedness.[5]

To criticize as logically sound or unsound an operation of thought that cannot be controlled is not less ridiculous than it would be to pronounce the growth of your hair to be morally good or bad. The ridiculousness in both cases consists in the fact that such a critical judgment may be *pretended* but cannot really be performed, in clear thought, for on analysis it will be found absurd.

I am quite aware that this position is open to two serious objections which I have not time to discuss, but which I have carefully considered and refuted. The first is that this is making logic a question of psychology. But this I deny. Logic does rest on certain facts of experience among which are facts about men, but not upon any theory about the human mind or any theory to explain facts. The other objection is that if the distinction Good and Bad Logic is a special case of Good and Bad Morals, by the same token the distinction of Good and Bad morals is a special case of the distinction esthetic Goodness and Badness. Now to admit this is not only to admit hedonism, which no man in his senses and not blinded by theory or something worse can admit, but also having to do with the essentially Dualistic distinction of Good and Bad,—which is manifestly an affair of Category the Second,—it seeks the origin of this distinction in Esthetic Feeling which belongs to Category the First.

This last objection deceived me for many years. The reply to it involves a very important point which I shall have to postpone to the next lecture. When it first presented itself to me, all I knew of ethics was derived from the study of Jouffroy under Dr. Walker, of Kant, and of a wooden treatise by Whewell; and I was led by the objection to a line of thought which brought me to regard ethics as a mere art, or applied science, and not a pure normative science at all. But when beginning in 1883 I came to read the works of the great moralists, whose great fertility of thought [I] found in wonderful contrast to the sterility of the logicians, I was forced to recognize the dependence of Logic upon Ethics; and then took refuge in the idea that there was no science of esthetics, that because *de gustibus non est disputandum*, therefore there is no esthetic *truth* and *falsity* or generally valid goodness and badness. But I did not remain of this opinion long. I soon came to see that this whole objection rests upon a fundamental misconception. To say that morality, in the last resort, comes to an esthetic judgment is *not* hedonism,—but is directly opposed to hedonism. In the next place every pronouncement between Good and Bad certainly comes under Category the Second; and for that reason such pronouncement comes out in the voice of conscience with an absoluteness of duality which we do not find even in logic; and although I am still a perfect ignoramus in esthetics, I venture to think that the esthetic state of mind is purest when perfectly naive without any critical pronouncement, and that the esthetic critic founds his judgments upon the result of throwing himself back into such a pure naive state,—and the best critic is the man who has trained himself to do this the most perfectly.

It is a great mistake to suppose that the phenomena of pleasure and pain are mainly phenomena of feeling. Examine *pain*, which would seem to be a good deal more positive than *pleasure*. I am unable to recognize with confidence any quality of feeling common to all *pains*; and if I cannot I am sure it cannot be an easy thing for anybody. For I have gone through a systematic course of training in recognizing my feelings. I have worked with intensity for so many hours a day every day for long years to train myself to this; and it is a training which I would recommend to all of you. The artist has such a training; but most of his effort goes to reproducing in one form or another what he sees or hears, which is in every art a very complicated trade; while I have striven simply to see what it is that I see. That this limitation of the task is a great advantage is proved to me by finding that the great majority of artists are extremely narrow. Their esthetic appreciations are narrow; and this comes from their only having the power of recognizing the qualities of their percepts in certain directions.

But the majority of those who opine that pain is a quality of feeling are not even artists; and even among those who are artists there are extremely few who are *artists in pain*. But the truth is that there are certain states of mind, especially among states of mind in which Feeling has a large share, which <we> have an impulse to get rid of. That is the obvious phenomenon; and the ordinary theory is that this impulse is excited by a quality of feeling common to all those states,—a theory which is supported by the fact that this impulse is particularly energetic in regard to states in which Feeling is the predominant element. Now whether this be true or false, it is a *theory*. It is not the fact that any such common quality in all pains is readily to be recognized.

At any rate, while the whole phenomenon of pain and the whole phenomenon of pleasure are phenomena that arise within the universe of states of mind and attain no great prominence except when they concern states of mind in which Feeling is predominant, yet these phenomena themselves do not mainly consist in any common Feeling-quality of Pleasure and any common Feeling-quality of Pain, even if there are such Qualities of Feeling; but they mainly consist [in] Pain in a Struggle to give a state of mind its *quietus*, and [in] Pleasure in a peculiar mode of consciousness allied to the consciousness of *making a generalization*, in which not Feeling, but rather Cognition, is the principal constituent. This may be hard to make out as regards the lower pleasures, but they do not concern the argument we are considering. It is esthetic enjoyment which concerns us; and ignorant as I am of Art, I have a fair share of capacity for esthetic enjoyment, and it seems to me that while in esthetic enjoyment we attend to the totality of Feeling, and especially to the total resultant Quality of Feeling presented in the work of art we are contemplating, yet it is a sort of intellectual sympathy, a sense that here is a feeling that one can comprehend, a reasonable feeling. I do not succeed in saying exactly *what* it is, but it is a consciousness belonging to the category of Representation though representing something in the Category of Quality of Feeling.

In that view of the matter, the objection to the doctrine that the distinction Moral approval and disapproval is ultimately only a species [of] the distinction of Esthetic Approval and Disapproval seems to be answered.

It appears, then, that *logica utens* consisting in self-control, the distinction of logical goodness and badness must begin where control of the processes of cognition begins; and any object that antecedes the distinction, if it has to be named either good or bad, must be named *good*. For since no fault can be found with it, it must be taken at its own valuation. Goodness is a colorless quality, a mere absence of badness. Before our first parents had eaten of the fruit of the tree of knowledge of good and evil, of course, they were innocent.

Where then in the process of cognition does the possibility of controlling it begin? Certainly not before the *percept* is formed.

Even after the percept is formed there is an operation which seems to me to be quite uncontrollable. It is that of judging what it is that the person perceives. A judgment is an act of formation of a mental proposition combined with an adoption of it or act of assent to it. A percept on the other hand is an image or moving picture or other exhibition. The *perceptual judgment*, that is, the first judgment of a person as to what is before his senses, bears no more resemblance to the percept than the figure I am going to draw is like a man:

I do not see that it is possible to exercise any control over that operation or to subject it to criticism. If we can criticize it at all, as far as I can see, that criticism would be limited to performing it again and seeing whether with closer attention we get the same result. But when we so perform it again, paying now closer attention, the percept is presumably not such as it was before. I do not see what other means we have of knowing whether it is the same as it was before or not, except by comparing the former perceptual judgment and the later one. I should utterly distrust any other method of ascertaining what the character of the percept was. Consequently, until I am better advised, I shall consider the *perceptual judgment* to be utterly beyond control. Should I be wrong in this, the *Percept*, at all events, would seem to be so. It follows, then, that our perceptual judgments are the first premisses of all our reasonings and that they cannot be called in question. All our other judgments are so many theories whose only justification is that they have been and will be borne out by perceptual judgments. But the perceptual judgments declare one thing to be blue, another yellow,—one sound to be that of A, another that of U, another that of I. These are the Qualities of Feeling which the physicists say are mere illusions because there is no room for them in their theories. If the facts won't agree with the theory, so much the worse for them. They are *bad facts*. This sounds to me childish, I confess. It is like an infant that beats an inanimate object that hurts it. Indeed, this is true of all fault-finding with others than oneself and those for whose conduct one is responsible. Reprobation is a silly, thorough idleness.

But peradventure I shall be asked whether I do not admit that there is any such thing as an illusion or hallucination.[6] Oh, yes; among artists, I have known more than one case of downright hallucinatory imaginations at the beck and call of these ποιῆτας. Of course, the man knows that such obedient spectres are not real experiences, because experience is that which forces itself upon him, will-he nill-he.

Hallucinations proper,—obsessional hallucinations,—will *not* down at one's bidding, and people who are subject to them are, I know from acquaintance, accustomed to sound the people who are with them in order to ascertain whether the object before them has a being independent of their disease or not. There are also social hallucinations.[7] In such a case, a photographic camera or other instrument might be of service.

Of course, everybody admits and must admit that these apparitions are entities,—*entia*; the question is whether these *entia* belong to the class of realities or not, that is, whether they are such as they are independently of any collection of singular representations that they are so, or whether their mode of being depends upon abnormal conditions. But as for the entire universe of Qualities which the physicist would pronounce illusory, there is not the smallest shadow of just suspicion resting upon their normality. On the contrary, there is considerable evidence that colors, for example, and sounds have the same character for all mankind. Philosophers, who very properly call all things into question, have asked whether we have any reason to suppose that red looks to one eye as it does to another. Well I will skip this. Suffice it to say that there is no reason for suspecting the veracity of the senses; and the presumption is that the physics of the future will find out that they are more real than the present state of scientific theory admits of their being represented as being.[8]

Therefore, if you ask me what part Qualities can play in the economy of the universe, I shall reply that the universe is a vast representamen, a great symbol of God's purpose, working out its conclusions in living realities. Now every symbol, must have organically attached to it, its Indices of Reactions and its Icons of Qualities; and such part as these reactions and these qualities play in an argument, that they of course play in the universe, that universe being precisely an argument. In the little bit that you or I can make out this huge demonstration, our perceptual judgments are the premisses *for us* and these perceptual judgments have icons as their predicates, in which *icons* Qualities are immediately presented. But what is first for us is not first in nature. The premisses of Nature's own process are all the independent uncaused elements of fact that go to make up for the variety of nature which the necessitarian supposes to have been all in existence from the foundation of the world, but which the Tychist supposes are continually receiving new accretions. These premisses of nature, however, though they are not the *perceptual facts* that are premisses to us, nevertheless must resemble them in being premisses. We can only imagine what they are by comparing them with the premisses for us. As premisses they must involve Qualities.

Now as to their function in the economy of the Universe,—the Universe as an argument is necessarily a great work of art, a great poem,—for every fine argument is a poem and a symphony,—just as every true poem is a sound argument. But let us compare it rather with a painting,—with an impressionist seashore piece,—then every Quality in a premiss is one of the elementary colored particles of the painting; they are all meant to go together to make up the intended Quality that belongs to the whole as whole. That total effect is beyond our ken; but we can appreciate in some measure the resultant Quality of parts of the whole,—which Qualities result from the combinations of elementary Qualities that belong to the premisses.

But I shall endeavor to make this clearer in the next lecture.

The Reality of Secondness

Now I have only time to indicate in the slightest manner what I should reply to the argument against the reality of Secondness which I mentioned in the second lecture.

The only form in which this objection is really formidable is one in which Firstness and Thirdness are admitted to be real—that is *Feelings* and *Laws* of the succession of feelings; but it is maintained that to say that one thing acts upon another is merely to say that there is a certain law of succession of Feelings.

Of the various answers that might be made to this objection, the easiest that occurs to me, though by no means the most instructive, runs as follows:

We all admit that Experience is our great Teacher; and Dame Experience practices a pedagogic method which springs from her own affable and complacent nature. Her favorite way of teaching is by means of practical jokes,—the more cruel the better. To describe it more exactly Experience invariably teaches by means of *surprises*. This statement could be defended in all its length and breadth; but for the purposes of the argument it is sufficient that you should admit that it is largely true.

Now when a man is surprised he knows that he is surprised. Now comes a dilemma. Does he know he is surprised by direct perception or by inference? First try the hypothesis that it is by inference. This theory would be that a person (who must be supposed old enough to have acquired self-consciousness) on becoming conscious of that peculiar quality of feeling which unquestionably belongs to all surprise, is induced by some reason to attribute this feeling to himself. It is, however, a patent fact that we never, *in the first instance*, attribute a Quality of Feeling to ourselves. We first attribute it to a *non-ego* and only come to attribute it to ourselves when irrefragable reasons compel us to do so. Therefore, the theory would have to be that the man first pronounces the surprising object a *wonder*, and upon reflection convinces himself that it is only a wonder in the sense that he is *surprised*. That would have to be the theory. But it is in conflict with the facts which are that a man is more or less placidly *expecting* one result, and suddenly finds something in contrast to that forcing itself upon his recognition. A duality is thus forced upon him: on the one hand, his expectation which he had been attributing to Nature, but which he is now compelled to attribute to some mere inner world, and on the other hand, a strong new phenomenon which shoves that expectation into the background and occupies its place. The old expectation, which is what he was familiar with, is his inner world, or *ego*. The new phenomenon, the stranger, is from the exterior world or *non-ego*. He does not conclude that he *must* be surprised because the object is so *marvelous*. But on the contrary, it is because of the duality presenting itself as such that he [is] led by generalization to a conception of a quality of marvelousness.

Try, then, the other alternative that it is by direct perception, that is, in a direct perceptual judgment, that a man knows that he is surprised. The perceptual judgment, however, certainly does not represent that it is he himself who has played a little trick upon himself. A man cannot startle himself by jumping up with an exclamation of *Boo!* Nor could the perceptual judgment have represented anything so out of nature. The perceptual judgment, then, can only be that it is the *non-ego*, something over against the *ego* and bearing it down, is what has surprised him. But if that be so, this direct perception presents an *ego* to which the smashed expectation belonged, and the *non-ego*, the sadder and wiser man, to which the new phenomenon belongs.

Now, as I said before, it is idle and indeed really impossible, to criticize perceptual facts as *false*. You can only criticize interpretations of them. So long as you admit that perception really does represent two objects to us, an *ego* and a *non-ego*,—a past self that turns out to be a *mere* self and a self that is to be faithful to the truth in the future,—as long as you admit that this is represented in the very perceptual fact, that is final. Nothing remains but to accept it as experience. Such acceptance I ought to point out involves an acceptance of that doctrine of Immediate Perception which was advocated by Reid, Kant, etc.

LECTURE FIVE:
THE NORMATIVE SCIENCES[1]

I.[2]

Ladies and Gentlemen:

You may perhaps gain some useful hints if I describe to you how I go to work in studying philosophy. I shall merely sketch the outline of the proceeding without going into details. I mostly work pen in hand and although important steps are taken while I am away from my writing-table, they are recorded at once. A given question in philosophy comes up for discussion, never mind how. I begin by writing out a collation upon it. That is, I begin by setting down briefly yet sufficiently and as formally as possible all the arguments which I have seen used on the one side or which seem to me likely to be used on that side; and then I do the same for the other side. Such of the arguments as admit of ready refutation, I at once set down the refutations of. Next, without going into the merits of the case, I draw up a list of the general methods in which a solution of the problem might be sought. If some of them appear to be quite futile, I draw up brief formal statements of the reasons of this futility. One of the methods will appear to me to be the one which ought to be decisive, and I carefully set down the reason why, keeping a good look out for special circumstances which might annul this reason. Other methods may appear to me to have a secondary utility and I further set down the reasons for this and for my estimate of just how far and where those methods are valuable. Search is made for objections to all these reasons, and any that seem considerable are formally set down and refuted. But if, in this course of this part of the discussion or at a later stage, it appears that the question in hand depends upon another which I have never submitted to any systematic examination or concerning which, since my last examination of it, any considerable grounds of doubt have been found, I put aside the first examination until this other question shall have been at least provisionally settled in my mind. If no such interruption takes place, I take up first the principal method and afterwards the subsidiary or secondary methods and apply them with the severest critical scrutiny of which I am master, setting down always brief and formal but sufficient statements of all the steps of the argumentation, and disposing of all objections either by assent or refutation. I also dispose, in the same way, of all the arguments which have not already been disposed of. Having this brief drawn up I study it with the minutest care to detect any loop-holes, and sometimes amend it more or less radically, even giving the question itself a new and broader turn, and this is sometimes done three or four times over, before I am satisfied with the discussion. I then put the paper away and dismiss the matter from my mind. Sometimes I do so in despair of being able at the time to obtain any clear light on the subject; for when such light is not at hand my experience is that hard thinking is of very little use. There is nothing to be done but wait until the light comes from some other source. But even when my discussion does seem satisfactory at first, yet my experience of my own stupidity is such, that I always mutter to my intellect, "Very well, you have only to possess yourself in patience and the inadequacy of your present ideas will appear plainly enough in due time." In fact, after a long time, something or other flashes a new light on the old question, and only too often I find that strenuous as was my scrutiny of the previous arguments, I have committed some horrible stupidity. At last, my ideas seem ripe for a new setting of them in order; and I make a second collation of the question without looking at the first but endeavoring to proceed quite as if the question were a new one. This second collation is drawn up just as the first one was; only, when it is complete, I get out the first and compare the two with minute criticism, both where they differ and where they agree. It may seem to me best to allow the matter to go over for a third collation, but commonly I consider that I am now well started upon the right track; or at any rate all that can be done in this way has been done. I impress the cardinal considerations on my mind, and perhaps draw up a note of anything difficult to bear in mind exactly; and I then look upon all the labor so far performed as a mere exercise of no value, except in the parts which have impressed me. It now remains to treat my conception of the problem like a seedling tree, which must have water, nutriment, sunlight, shade, and air and frequent breaking of the ground about it, in order that it may grow up into something worthy of respect. These operations I also carry out, pen in hand, with intervals of digestion; and by drawing up new statements at irregular intervals according to the state of my reflections, but probably averaging a year in length, after I have made from half a dozen to a dozen of these, I begin to feel that I have carried the discussion as far as I am likely ever to do. There is no single logical point in the present lectures, for example, however small, which has not undergone at least four such digestions, and most of them a dozen or more.

That, gentlemen, is my way of philosophizing in which I have learned to place much confidence. The expression "swift as thought" ought to gain for you a new meaning as applied to my thought. It becomes equivalent to "agile as a slime-mould." Anybody who knows how I think, as I myself do, must be impressed by my awful stupidity. But I am fortunately capable of a vast amount of drudgery, and I never lose confidence that I shall ultimately accomplish any intellectual task that I set myself provided I live long enough. In that particular I will pose as a model to young philosophers.

But what I particularly wanted to come to in speaking of my way of philosophizing was to point out to you that it is nothing if not *minute*. I certainly endeavor to generalize as far as I can find support for generalization; but I depend on the sedulous care with which I scrutinize every point. What is commonly called "breadth of treatment" of philosophical questions is my soul's abhorrence. My analysis is so detailed and minute, that it would be impossible in these lectures to give you any specimen of it. I can really do nothing more than to state some of the chief conclusions to which I have been led, with the merest hints of the nature of the arguments by which I have been led to them, especially since I cannot assume that you have any acquaintance with the real logic of modern thought as I conceive it. While I have the warmest admiration for the great metaphysicians and psychologists of this university who are among the world's leaders in their departments, I cannot but think it deeply lamentable that true, modern, exact, non-psychological logic, which ought to form the background of a liberal education, does not receive sufficient attention here to be at all in evidence. As time goes on the consequences of this neglect will be deeply graven.

To return to my necessarily superficial treatment of my subject in this course of lectures, you will not, I am sure, so utterly misunderstand me as to suppose that I would have you accept any proposition in logic because I say so. Indeed, that would be impossible; for one does not know what the proposition in logic means until one fully comprehends the arguments for it. But my object in describing my way of philosophizing has been chiefly to show you that if I seem to be treating these questions in what is called a "broad way," that is merely the effect of the extreme compression which is necessary, and to warn you that the propositions to which I am able to bring little support, if they be not as true as I hold them, at least are matters worthy of careful study, and are not to be assumed to be so superficially adopted as they must seem to be from the manner in which I am here forced to treat them.

II.

I have already explained that by Philosophy I mean that department of Positive Science, or Science of Fact, which does not busy itself with gathering facts, but merely with learning what can be learned from that experience which presses in upon every one of us daily and hourly. It does not gather new facts, because it does not need them, and also because new general facts cannot be firmly established without the assumption of a metaphysical doctrine; and this, in turn, requires the cooperation of every department of philosophy; so that such new facts, however striking they may be, afford weaker support to philosophy by far than that *common experience* which nobody doubts or can doubt and which nobody ever even *pretended* to doubt except as a consequence of a belief in that experience so entire and perfect that it failed to be conscious of itself, just as an American who has never been abroad fails to perceive the characteristics of Americans; just as a writer is unaware of the peculiarities of his own style, just as none of us can see himself as others see him.

Now I am going to make a series of assertions which will sound wild; for I cannot stop to argue them, although I cannot omit them if I am to set the supports of pragmatism in their true light.

Philosophy has three grand divisions. The first is Phenomenology, which simply contemplates the Universal Phenomenon, and discerns its ubiquitous elements, Firstness, Secondness, and Thirdness, together perhaps with other series of categories. The second grand division is Normative Science, which investigates the universal and necessary laws of the relation of Phenomena to *Ends*, that is, perhaps, to Truth, Right, and Beauty. The third grand division is Metaphysics, which endeavors to comprehend the Reality of Phenomena. Now Reality is an affair of Thirdness as Thirdness, that is, in its mediation between Secondness and Firstness. Most, if not all [of] you, are, I doubt not, Nominalists; and I beg you will not take offense at a truth which is just as plain and undeniable to me as is the truth that children do not understand human life. To be a nominalist consists in the undeveloped state in one's mind of the apprehension of Thirdness as Thirdness. The remedy for it consists in allowing ideas of human life to play a greater part in one's philosophy. Metaphysics is the science of Reality. Reality consists in regularity. Real regularity is active law. Active law is efficient reasonableness, or in other words is truly reasonable reasonableness. Reasonable reasonableness is Thirdness as Thirdness.

So then the division of Philosophy into these three grand departments, whose distinctness can be established without stopping to consider the contents of Phenomenology, that is, without asking what the true categories may be, turns out to be a division according to Firstness, Secondness, and Thirdness, and is thus one of the very numerous phenomena I have met with which confirm this list of categories.

For Phenomenology treats of the universal Qualities of Phenomena in their immediate phenomenal character, in themselves as phenomena. It, thus, treats of Phenomena in their Firstness.

Normative science treats of the laws of the relation of phenomena to ends, that is, it treats of Phenomena in their Secondness.

Metaphysics, as I have just remarked, treats of Phenomena in their Thirdness.

If, then, normative science does not seem to be sufficiently described by saying that it treats of phenomena in their Secondness, this is an indication that our conception of Normative Science is too narrow; and I had come to the conclusion that this is true of even the best modes of conceiving Normative Science which have achieved any renown many years before I recognized the proper division of philosophy.

I wish I could talk for an hour to you concerning the true conception of normative science. But I shall only be able to make a few negative assertions which, even if they were proved, would not go far toward developing that conception. Normative science is not a skill, nor is it an investigation conducted with a view to the production of skill. Coriolis wrote a book on the Analytic Mechanics of the Game of Billiards. If that book does not help people in the least degree to play billiards, that is nothing against it. The book is only intended to be pure theory. In like manner, if Normative Science does not in the least tend to the development of skill, its value as Normative Science remains the same. It is purely theoretical. Of course there *are* practical sciences of reasoning and investigation, of the conduct of life, and of the production of works of art. They correspond to the Normative Sciences, and may be probably expected to receive aid from them. But they are not integrant parts of these sciences; and the reason that they are not so, mark you, is no mere formalism, but is thus, that it will be in general quite different men and two knots of men not apt to consort the one with the other who will conduct the two kinds of inquiry. Nor again is Normative Science a *special* science, that is, one of those sciences that discover new phenomena. It is not even aided in any appreciable degree by any such science, and let me say that it is no more by psychology than by any other special science. If we were to place six lots each of seven coffee beans in one pan of an equal armed balance, and forty-two coffee beans in the other pan, and were to find on trial that the two loads nearly balanced one another, this observation might be regarded as adding in some excessively slight measure to the certainty of the proposition that six times seven make forty-two; because it is conceivable that this proposition should be a mistake due to some peculiar insanity affecting the whole human race; and the experiment may possibly evade the effects of insanity, supposing that we are affected with it. In like manner, *and in just about the same degree*, the facts that men for the most part show a natural disposition to approve nearly the same arguments that logic approves, nearly the same acts that ethics approves, and nearly the same works of art that esthetics approves, may be regarded as tending to support the conclusions of logic, ethics, and esthetics. But such support is perfectly insignificant; and when it comes to a particular case, to urge that anything is sound and good logically, morally, or esthetically, for no better reason than that men have a natural tendency to think so, I care not how strong and imperious that tendency may be, is as pernicious a fallacy as ever was. Of course it is quite a different thing for a man to acknowledge that he cannot perceive that he doubts what he does not appreciably doubt.

In one of the ways I have indicated, especially the last, normative science is by the majority of writers of the present day ranked too low in the scale of the sciences. On the other hand, some students of exact logic rank *that* normative science, at least, *too high*, by virtually treating it as on a par with pure mathematics. There are three excellent reasons any one of which ought to rescue them from the error of this opinion. In the first place, the hypotheses from which the deductions of normative science proceed are *intended to conform* to positive truth of fact and those deductions derive their interest from that circumstance almost exclusively; while the hypotheses of pure mathematics are purely ideal in intention, and their interest is purely intellectual. But in the second place, the procedure of the normative sciences is *not purely deductive*, as that of mathematics is, nor even principally so. Their peculiar analyses of familiar phenomena, analyses which ought to be guided by the facts of phenomenology in a manner in which mathematics is not at all guided, separate normative science from mathematics quite radically. In the third place, there is a most intimate and essential element of normative science which is still *more* proper to it, and that is its *peculiar appreciations*, to which nothing at all in the phenomena, in themselves, correspond. These appreciations relate to the conformity of phenomena *to ends* which are not immanent within these phenomena.

There are sundry other widely spread misconceptions of the nature of normative science. One of these is that the chief, if not the only problem of normative science, is to say what is *good* and what *bad* logically, ethically, and esthetically; or what degree of goodness a given description of a phenomenon attains.

Were this the case, normative science would be, in a certain sense, *mathematical*, since it would deal entirely with a question of *quantity*. But I am strongly inclined to think that this view will not sustain critical examination. Logic classifies arguments, and in doing so recognizes different *kinds* of truth. In ethics, too, *qualities* of good are admitted by the great majority of moralists. As for esthetics, in that field qualitative differences appear to be so prominent that, abstracted from them, it is impossible to say that there is any appearance which is not esthetically good. Vulgarity and pretension, themselves, may appear quite delicious in their perfection, if we can once conquer our squeamishness about them, a squeamishness which results from a contemplation of them as possible qualities of our own handiwork. But that is a *moral* and not an *esthetic* way of considering them.

I hardly need remind you that goodness, whether esthetic, moral, or logical, may either be *negative*,—consisting in freedom from fault,—or *quantitative* consisting in the degree to which it attains. But in an inquiry such as we are now engaged upon, negative goodness is the important thing.

A subtle and almost ineradicable narrowness in the conception of normative science runs through almost all modern philosophy in making it relate exclusively to the human mind. The beautiful is conceived to be relative to human taste, right and wrong concern human conduct alone, logic deals with human reasoning. Now in the truest sense these sciences certainly are indeed sciences of mind. Only, modern philosophy has never been able quite to shake off the Cartesian idea of the mind, as something that "resides,"—such is the term,—in the pineal gland. Everybody laughs at this nowadays, and yet everybody continues to think of mind in this same general way, as something within this person or that, belonging to him and correlative to the real world. A whole course of lectures would be required to expose this error. I can only hint that if you reflect upon it without being dominated by preconceived ideas, you will soon begin to perceive that it is a very narrow view of mind. I should think it must appear so to anybody who was sufficiently soaked in the *Critic of the Pure Reason*.

I cannot linger more upon the general conception of normative science. I must come down to the particular normative sciences. These are now commonly said to be logic, ethics, and esthetics. Formerly only logic and ethics were reckoned as such. A few logicians refuse to recognize any other normative science than their own. My own opinions of ethics and esthetics are far less matured than my logical opinions. It is only since 1883 that I have numbered ethics among any special studies; and until about four years ago, I was not prepared to affirm that ethics was a normative science. As for esthetics, although the first year of my study of philosophy was devoted to this branch exclusively, yet I have since then so completely neglected it that I do not feel entitled to have any confident opinions about it. I am inclined to think that there is such a normative science; but I feel by no means sure even of that.

Supposing, however, that normative science divides into esthetics, ethics, and logic, then it is easily perceived, from any standpoint, that this division is governed by the three categories. For normative science in general being the science of the laws of conformity of things to ends, esthetics considers those things whose ends are to embody qualities of feeling, ethics those things whose ends lie in action, and logic those things whose end is to represent something.

Just at this point we begin to get upon the trail of the secret of pragmatism, after a long and apparently aimless beating about the bush. Let us glance at the relations of these three sciences to one another. Whatever opinion be entertained in regard to the scope of logic, it will be generally agreed that the heart of it lies in the classification and critics of arguments. Now it is peculiar to the nature of argument that no argument can exist without being referred to some special class of arguments. The act of inference consists in the thought that the inferred conclusion is true because *in any analogous case* an analogous conclusion *would be* true. Thus, logic is coeval with reasoning. Whoever reasons *ipso facto* virtually holds a logical doctrine, his *logica utens*. This classification is not a mere qualification of the argument. It essentially involves *an approval* of it,—a *qualitative approval*. Now such self-approval supposes *self-control*. Not that we regard our approval as *itself* a voluntary act, but that we hold the act of inference which we approve to be voluntary. That is, if we did not approve, we should not infer. There are mental operations which are as completely beyond our control as the growth of our hair. To approve or disapprove of *them* would be idle. But when we institute an experiment to test a theory, or when we imagine an extra line to be inserted in a geometrical diagram in order to determine a question in geometry, these are *voluntary acts* which our logic, whether it be of the natural or the scientific sort, *approves*. Now *the approval of a voluntary act* is a *moral* approval. *Ethics is the study of what ends of action we are deliberately prepared to adopt.* That is right action which is in conformity to ends which we are prepared deliberately to adopt. That is all there *can be* in the notion of righteousness, as it seems to me. The righteous man is the man who controls his passions, and makes them conform to such ends as he is prepared deliberately to adopt as *ultimate*. If it were in the nature of a man to be perfectly satisfied to make his personal comfort his ultimate aim, no more blame would attach to him for doing so than attaches to a hog for behaving in the same way. A logical reasoner is a reasoner who exercises great self-control in his intellectual operations; and therefore the logically good is simply a particular species of the morally good. Ethics,—the genuine normative science of ethics, as contradistinguished from that branch of anthropology which in our day often passes under the name of ethics,—this genuine ethics is the normative science *par excellence* because an *end*,—

the essential object of normative science,—is germane to a voluntary act in a primary way in which it is germane to nothing else. For that reason I have some lingering doubt as to there being any true normative science of the beautiful. On the other hand, an ultimate end of action *deliberately* adopted,—that is to say, *reasonably* adopted,—must be a state of things that *reasonably recommends itself in itself*, aside from any ulterior consideration. It must be an *admirable ideal*, having the only kind of goodness that such an ideal *can* have, namely, esthetic goodness. From this point of view, the morally good appears as a particular species of the esthetically good.

If this line of thought be sound, the morally good will be the esthetically good specially determined by a peculiar superadded element; and the logically good will be the morally good specially determined by a special superadded element. Now it will be admitted to be, at least, very likely that in order to correct or to vindicate the maxim of pragmatism, we must find out precisely what the logically good consists in; and it would appear from what has been said that in order to analyze the nature of the logically good we must first gain clear apprehensions of the nature of the esthetically good and especially that of the morally good.

So, then, incompetent as I am to it, I find the task imposed upon me of defining the esthetically good,—a work which so many philosophical artists have made as many attempts at performing. In the light of the doctrine of categories I should say that an object, to be esthetically good, must have a multitude of parts so related to one another as to impart a positive simple immediate quality to their totality; and whatever does this is, in so far, esthetically good, no matter what the particular quality of the total may be. If that quality be such as to nauseate us, to scare us, or otherwise to disturb us to the point of throwing us out of the mood of esthetic enjoyment, out of the mood of simply contemplating the embodiment of the quality,—just, for example, as the Alps affected the people of old times, when the state of civilization was such that an impression of great power was inseparably associated with lively apprehension and terror,—then the object remains nonetheless esthetically good, although people in our condition are incapacitated from a calm esthetic contemplation of it.

This suggestion must go for what it may be worth, which I dare say may be very little. If it be correct, it will follow that there is no such thing as positive esthetic badness; and since by goodness we chiefly in this discussion mean merely the absence of badness, or faultlessness, there will be no such thing as esthetic goodness. All there will be will be various esthetic qualities, that is simple qualities of totalities not capable of full embodiment in the parts, which qualities may be more decided and strong in one case than in another. But the very reduction of the intensity may be an esthetic quality; nay, it *will* be so; and I am seriously inclined to doubt there being any distinction of pure esthetic betterness and worseness. My notion would be that there are innumerable varieties of esthetic quality, but no purely esthetic grade of excellence.

But the instant that an esthetic ideal is proposed as an ultimate end of action, at that instant a categorical imperative pronounces for or against it. Kant, as you know, proposes to allow that categorical imperative to stand unchallenged as an eternal pronouncement. His position is in extreme disfavor now, and not without reason. Yet I cannot think very highly of the logic of the ordinary attempts at refuting it. The whole question is whether or not this categorical imperative be beyond control. If this voice of conscience is unsupported by ulterior reasons, is it not simply an insistent irrational howl, the hooting of an owl, which we may disregard if we can? *Why should* we pay any more attention to it than we would to the barking of a cur? If we *cannot* disregard conscience, all homilies and moral maxims are perfectly idle. But if it can be disregarded, it is, in one sense, not beyond control. It leaves us free to control ourselves. So then, it appears to me that any aim whatever which can be consistently pursued becomes, as soon as it is unfalteringly adopted, beyond all possible criticism, except the quite impertinent criticism of outsiders. An aim which *cannot* be adopted and consistently pursued is a bad aim. It cannot properly be called an ultimate aim at all. The only moral evil is not to have an ultimate aim.

Accordingly the problem of ethics is to ascertain what end is possible. It might be thoughtlessly supposed that *special science* could aid in this ascertainment. But that would rest on a misconception of the nature of an absolute aim, which is what *would* be pursued under all possible circumstances,—that is even although the contingent facts ascertained by special sciences were entirely different from what they are. Nor, on the other hand, must the definition of such [an] aim be reduced to a mere formalism.

The importance of the matter for pragmatism is obvious. For if the meaning of a symbol consists in *how* it might cause us to act, it is plain that this "how" cannot refer to the description of mechanical motions that it might cause, but must intend to refer to a description of the action as having this or that *aim*. In order to understand pragmatism, therefore, well enough to subject it to intelligent criticism, it is incumbent upon us to inquire what an ultimate aim, capable of being pursued in an indefinitely prolonged course of action, can be.

The deduction of this is somewhat intricate, on account of the number of points which have to be taken into account; and of course I cannot

go into details. In order that the aim should be immutable under all circumstances, without which it will not be an ultimate aim, it is requisite
that it should accord with a free development of the agent's own esthetic
quality. At the same time it is requisite that it should not ultimately tend
to be disturbed by the reactions upon the agent of that outward world
which is supposed in the very idea of action. It is plain that these two
conditions can be fulfilled at once only if it happens that the esthetic quality toward which the agent's free development tends and that of the ultimate action of experience upon him are parts of one esthetic total.
Whether or not this is really so, is a metaphysical question which it does
not fall within the scope of normative science to answer. If it is *not* so, the
aim is essentially *unattainable*. But just as in playing a hand of whist,
when only three tricks remain to be played, the rule is to assume that the
cards are so distributed that the odd trick can be made, so the rule of
ethics will be to adhere to the only possible absolute aim, and to hope that
it will prove attainable. Meantime, it is comforting to know that all experience is favorable to that assumption.

The ground is now cleared for the analysis of logical goodness, or the
goodness of representation. There is a special variety of esthetic goodness
that may belong to a representamen, namely, *expressiveness*. There is also
a special moral goodness of representations, namely, *veracity*. But besides
this there is a peculiar mode [of] goodness which is logical. What this
consists in we have to inquire.

The mode of being of a representamen is such that it is capable of
repetition. Take, for example, any proverb. "Evil communications corrupt
good manners." Every time this is written or spoken in English, Greek, or
any other language, and every time it is thought of it is one and the same
representamen. It is the same with a diagram or picture. It is the same
with a physical sign or symptom. If two weathercocks are different signs, it
is only in so far as they refer to different parts of the air. A representamen
which should have a unique embodiment, incapable of repetition, would
not be a representamen, but a part of the very fact represented. This repe-
titory character of the representamen involves as a consequence that it is
essential to a representamen that it should contribute to the determination of another representamen distinct from itself. For in what sense
would it be true that a representamen was repeated if it were not capable
of determining some different representamen? "Evil communications corrupt good manners" and φθείρουσιν ἤθη χρησθ' ὀμιλίαι κακαί are one
and the same representamen. They are so, however, only so far as they are
represented as being so; and it is one thing to say that "Evil communications corrupt good manners" and quite a different thing to say that Evil
communications corrupt good manners and φθείρουσιν ἤθη χρησθ'

ὁμιλίαι κακαί are two expressions of the same proverb. Thus every representamen must be capable of contributing to the determination of a representamen different from itself. Every conclusion from premisses is an instance in point; and what would be a representamen that was not capable of contributing to any ulterior conclusion? I call a representamen which is determined by another representamen an *interpretant* of the latter. Every representamen is related or is capable of being related to a reacting thing, its object, and every representamen embodies, in some sense, some quality, which may be called its *signification*, what in the case of a common name J. S. Mill calls its *connotation*, a particularly objectionable expression.

A representamen is either a *rhema*, a *proposition*, or an *argument*. An *argument* is a representamen which separately shows what interpretant it is intended to determine. A *proposition* is a representamen which is not an argument, but which separately indicates what object it is intended to represent. A *rhema* is a simple representation without such separate parts.

Esthetic goodness, or *expressiveness*, may be possessed, and in some degree must be possessed, by any kind of representamen: rhema, proposition, or argument.

Moral goodness, or *veracity*, may be possessed by a proposition or by an argument, but cannot he possessed by a rhema. A mental judgment or inference must possess some degree of veracity.

As to logical goodness, or *truth*, the statements in the books are faulty; and it is highly important for our inquiry that they should be corrected. The books distinguish between *logical truth*, which some of them rightly confine to arguments that do not promise more than they perform, and *material truth* which belongs to propositions, being that which veracity aims to be; and this is conceived to be a higher grade of truth than mere logical truth. I would correct this conception as follows. In the first place, all our knowledge rests upon perceptual judgments. These are necessarily veracious, in greater or less degree according to the effort made, but there is no meaning in saying that they have any other truth than veracity, since a perceptual judgment can never be repeated. At most we can say of a perceptual judgment that its relation to other perceptual judgments is such as to permit a simple theory of the facts. Thus I may judge that I see a clean white surface. But a moment later I may question whether the surface really was clean, and may look again more sharply. If this second more veracious judgment still asserts that I see a clean surface, the theory of the facts will be simpler than if, at my second look, I discern that the surface is soiled. Still, even in this last case, I have no right to say that my first *percept* was that of a soiled surface. I absolutely have no testimony concerning it, except my perceptual judgment, and although that was careless and had no high degree of veracity still I have to accept the only evidence in my possession. Now consider any other judgment I may make. That is a conclusion of inferences ultimately based on perceptual judgments, and since these are indisputable, all the truth which my judgment can have must consist in the logical correctness of those inferences. Or I may argue the matter in another way. To say that a proposition is false is not veracious unless the speaker has found out that it is false. Confining ourselves, therefore, to veracious propositions, to say that a proposition is false and that it has been *found* to be false are equivalent, in the sense of being necessarily either both true or both false. Consequently, to say that a proposition is *perhaps* false is the same as to say that it will *perhaps* be found out to be false. Hence to deny one of these is to deny the other. To say that a proposition is certainly true means simply that it never can be found out to be false, or in other words that it is derived by logically correct arguments from veracious perceptual judgments. Consequently, the only difference between material truth and the logical correctness of argumentation is that the *latter* refers to a single line of argument and the *former* to all the arguments which could have a given proposition or its denial as their conclusion.

Let me say to you that this reasoning needs to be scrutinized with the severest and minutest logical criticism, because pragmatism largely depends upon it.

It appears, then, that logical goodness is simply the excellence of argument;—its negative, and more fundamental, goodness being its soundness and weight, its really having the force that it pretends to have and that force being great, while its quantitative goodness consists in the degree in which it advances our knowledge. In what then does the soundness of argument consist?

In order to answer that question it is necessary to recognize three radically different kinds of arguments which I signalized in 1867 and which had been recognized by the logicians of the eighteenth century, although [those] logicians quite pardonably failed to recognize the inferential character of one of them. Indeed, I suppose that the three were given by Aristotle in the *Prior Analytics*, although the unfortunate illegibility of a single word in his manuscript and its replacement by a wrong word by his first editor, the stupid [blank], has completely altered the sense of the chapter on Abduction. At any rate, even if my conjecture is wrong, and the text must stand as it is, still Aristotle, in that chapter on Abduction, was even in that case evidently groping for that mode of inference which I call by the otherwise quite useless name of Abduction,—a word which is only employed in logic to translate the [blank] of that chapter.

These three kinds of reasoning are Abduction, Induction, and Deduction. Deduction is the only necessary reasoning. It is the reasoning of mathematics. It starts from a hypothesis, the truth or falsity of which has nothing to do with the reasoning; and of course its conclusions are equally ideal. The ordinary use of the doctrine of chances is necessary reasoning, although it is reasoning concerning probabilities. Induction is the experimental testing of a theory. The justification of it is that, although the conclusion at any stage of the investigation may be more or less erroneous, yet the further application of the same method must correct the error. The only thing that induction accomplishes is to determine the value of a quantity. It sets out with a theory and it measures the degree of concordance of that theory with fact. It never can originate any idea whatever. No more can deduction. All the ideas of science come to it by the way of Abduction. Abduction consists in studying facts and devising a theory to explain them. Its only justification is that if we are ever to understand things at all, it must be in that way.

Concerning the relations of these three modes of inference to the categories and concerning certain other details, my opinions, I confess, have wavered.[3] These points are of such a nature that only the closest students of what I have written would remark the discrepancies. Such a student might infer that I have been given to expressing myself without due consideration; but in fact I have never, in any philosophical writing,— barring anonymous contributions to newspapers,—made any statement which was not based on at least half a dozen attempts in writing to subject the whole question to a very far more minute and critical examination than could be attempted in print, these attempts being made quite independently of one another, at intervals of many months, but subsequently compared together with the most careful criticism, and being themselves based upon at least two briefs of the state of the question, covering its whole literature, as far as known to me, and carrying the criticism in the strictest logical form to its extreme beginnings, without leaving any loopholes that I was able to discern with my utmost pains, these two briefs being made at an interval of a year or more and as independently as possible, although, they were subsequently minutely compared, amended, and reduced to one. My waverings, therefore, have never been due to haste. They may argue stupidity. But I can at least claim that they prove one quality in my favor. That is that so far from my being wedded to opinions as being my own I have shown rather decided distrust of any opinion of which I have been an advocate. This perhaps ought to give a slight additional weight to those opinions in which I have never wavered,—although I need not say that the notion of any weight of authority being attached to opinions in philosophy or in science is utterly illogical and unscientific. Among those opinions which I have constantly maintained is this, that while Abductive and Inductive reasoning are utterly irreducible, either to the other or to Deduction, or Deduction to either of them, yet the only *rationale* of these methods is essentially Deductive or Necessary. If then we can state wherein the validity of Deductive reasoning lies, we shall have defined the foundation of logical goodness of whatever kind.

Now all necessary reasoning, whether it be good or bad, is of the nature of mathematical reasoning. The philosophers are fond of boasting of the pure conceptual character of their reasoning. The more conceptual it is, the nearer it approaches to verbiage. I am not speaking from surmise. My analyses of reasonings surpass in thoroughness all that has ever been done in print, whether in words or in symbols,—all that DeMorgan, Dedekind, Schröder, Peano, Russell, and others have ever done,—to such a degree as to remind one of the difference between a pencil sketch of a scene and a photograph of it. To say that I analyze the passage from the premisses to the conclusion of a syllogism in Barbara into seven or eight distinct inferential steps gives but a very inadequate idea of the thoroughness of my analysis. Let any responsible person pledge himself to go through the matter and dig it out, point by point, and he shall receive the manuscript. It is on the basis of such analysis that I declare that all necessary reasoning, be it the merest verbiage of the theologians, so far as there is any semblance of necessity in it, is mathematical reasoning. Now mathematical reasoning is diagrammatic. This is as true of algebra as of geometry. But in order to discern the features of diagrammatic reasoning, it is requisite to begin with examples that are not too simple. In simple cases, the essential features are so nearly obliterated that they can only be discerned when one knows what to look for. But beginning with suitable examples and thence proceeding to others, one finds that the diagram itself in its individuality is not what the reasoning is concerned with. I will take an example which recommends itself only by its consideration requiring but a moment. A line abuts upon an ordinary point of another line ____/ forming two angles. The sum of these angles is proved by Legendre to be equal to the sum of two right angles by erecting a perpendicular to the second line in the plane of the two and through the point of abuttal. ____/ This perpendicular must lie in the one angle or the other. The pupil is supposed to *see* that. He sees it only in a special case, but he is supposed to perceive that it will be so in any case. The more careful logician may demonstrate that it must fall in one angle or the other; but this demonstration will only consist in substituting a different diagram in place of Legendre's figure. But in any case, either in the new diagram or else and more usually in passing from one diagram to the other, the interpreter of the argumentation will be supposed to *see* something which will present this little difficulty for the theory of vision, that it is of a *general nature*. Mr. Mill's disciples will say that this proves that geometrical reasoning is inductive. I do not wish to speak disparagingly of Mill's treatment of the *Pons Asinorum* because it penetrates further into the logic of the subject than anybody had penetrated before. Only it does not quite touch bottom. As for such general perceptions being inductive, I might treat the question from a technical standpoint and show that the essential characters of induction are wanting. But besides the interminable length, such a way of dealing with the matter would hardly meet the point. It is better to remark that the "uniformity of nature" is not in question, and that there is no way of applying that principle to supporting the mathematical reasoning that will not enable me to give a precisely analogous instance in every essential particular except that it will be a fallacy that no good mathematician could overlook. If you admit the principle that logic stops where self-control stops, you will find yourself obliged to admit that a *perceptual fact*, a logical origin, may involve generality. This can be shown for ordinary generality. But if you have already convinced yourself that continuity is generality, it will be somewhat easier to show that a perceptual fact may involve continuity than that it can involve non-relative generality.

If you object that there can be no immediate consciousness of generality, I grant that. If you add that one can have no direct experience of the general, I grant that as well. Generality, Thirdness, pours in upon us in our very perceptual judgments, and all reasoning, so far as it depends on necessary reasoning, that is to say mathematical reasoning, turns upon the perception of generality and continuity at every step.

LECTURE SIX:
THE NATURE OF MEANING[1]

Ladies and Gentlemen:

I.

I was remarking at the end of my last lecture that perceptual judgments involve generality. What is the general? The Aristotelian definition is good enough. It is *quod aptum natum est praedicari de pluribus*; λέγω δὲ καθόλον μὲν ὃ ἐπὶ πλειόνων πέφυκε κατηγορεῖσθαι (*De Interp.* vii). When logic was studied in a scientific spirit of exactitude it was recognized on all hands that all ordinary judgments contain a predicate and that this predicate is general. There seemed to be some exceptions of which the only noticeable ones were expository judgments such as *Tully is Cicero*. But the Logic of Relations has now reduced logic to order, and it is seen that a proposition may have any number of subjects but can have but one predicate which is invariably general. Such a proposition as *Tully is Cicero* predicates the general relation of identity of Tully and Cicero. Consequently, it is now clear that if there be any perceptual judgment, or proposition directly expressive of and resulting from the quality of a present percept, or sense-image, that judgment must involve generality in its predicate.

That which is not general is singular; and the singular is that which reacts. The being of a singular may consist in the being of other singulars which are its parts. Thus heaven and earth is a singular; and its being consists in the being of heaven and the being of earth, each of which reacts and is therefore a singular forming a part of heaven and earth. If I had denied that every perceptual judgment refers as to its subject to a singular, and that singular actually reacting upon the mind in forming the judgment, actually reacting too upon the mind in interpreting the judgment, I should have uttered an absurdity. For every proposition whatsoever refers as to its subject to a singular actually reacting upon the utterer of it and actually reacting upon the interpreter of it. All propositions relate to the same ever-reacting singular; namely, to the totality of all real objects. It is true that when the Arabian romancer tells us that there was a lady named Scheherazade, he does not mean to be understood as speaking of the world of outward realities and there is a great deal of fiction in what he is talking about. For the *fictive* is that whose characters depend upon what characters somebody attributes to it; and the story is, of course, the mere creation of the poet's thought. Nevertheless, once he has imagined Scheherazade and made her young, beautiful, and endowed with a gift of spinning stories, it becomes a real fact that so he has imagined her, which fact he cannot destroy by pretending or thinking that he imagined her to be otherwise. What he wishes us to understand is what he might have expressed in plain prose by saying, "I have imagined a lady, Scheherazade by name, young, beautiful and a tireless teller of tales, and I am going on to imagine what tales she told." This would have been a plain expression of professed fact relating to the sum total of realities.

As I said before, propositions usually have more subjects than one; and almost every proposition, if not quite every one, has one or more other singular subjects, to which some propositions do not relate. These are the special parts of [the] Universe of all Truth to which the given proposition especially refers. It is a characteristic of perceptual judgments that each of them relates to some singular to which no other proposition relates directly, but, if it relates to it at all, does so by relating to that perceptual judgment. When we express a proposition in words we leave most of its singular subjects unexpressed; for the circumstances of the enunciation sufficiently show what subject is intended and words, owing to their usual generality, are not well-adapted to designating singulars. The pronoun, which may be defined as a part of speech intended to fulfill the function of an index, is never intelligible taken by itself apart from the circumstances of its utterance; and the noun, which may be defined as a part of speech put in place of a pronoun, is always liable to be equivocal.

A subject need not be singular. If it is not so, then when the proposition is expressed in the canonical form used by logicians, this subject will present one or other of two imperfections:

On the one hand, it may be *indesignative*, so that the proposition means that a singular of the universe might replace this subject while the truth was preserved, while failing to designate what singular that is; as when we say "*Some* calf has five legs."

Or on the other hand, the subject may be *hypothetical*, that is may allow any singular to be substituted for it that fulfills certain conditions without guaranteeing that there is any singular which fulfills those conditions; as when we say "Any salamander could live in fire," or "Any man who should be stronger than Sampson could do all that Sampson did."

A subject which has neither of these two imperfections is a *singular* subject referring to an existing singular collection in its entirety.[2]

If a proposition has two or more subjects of which one is *indesigna-tive* and the other *hypothetical*, then it makes a difference in what order the replacement by singulars is asserted to be possible. It is, for example, one thing to assert that "Any catholic there may be adores some woman or other" and quite another thing to assert that "There is some woman whom any catholic adores." If the first general subject is indesignate, the proposition is called particular. If the first general subject is hypothetical, the proposition is called universal.

A particular proposition asserts the existence of something of a given description. A universal proposition merely asserts the nonexistence of anything of a given description. Had I, therefore, asserted that a perceptual judgment could be a universal proposition I should have fallen into rank absurdity. For reaction is existence and the perceptual judgment is the cognitive product of a reaction.

But as from the particular proposition that "There is some woman whom any catholic you can find will adore" we can with certainty infer the universal proposition that "Any catholic you can find will adore some woman or other," so if a perceptual judgment involves any general elements, as it certainly does, the presumption is that a universal proposition can be necessarily deduced from it.

In saying that perceptual judgments involve general elements I certainly never intended to be understood as enunciating any proposition in psychology. For my principles absolutely debar me from making the least use of psychology in logic. I am confined entirely to the unquestionable facts of everyday experience, together with what can be deduced from them. All that I can mean by a perceptual judgment is a judgment absolutely forced upon my acceptance and that by a process which I am utterly unable to control and consequently am unable to criticize. Nor can I pretend to absolute certainty about any matter of fact. If with the closest scrutiny I am able to give, a judgment appears to have the characters I have described, I must reckon it among perceptual judgments until I am better advised. Now consider the judgment that one event C *appears to be* subsequent to another event A. Certainly, I may have inferred this; because I may have remarked that C was subsequent to a third event B which was itself subsequent to A. But then these premisses are judgments of the same description. It does not seem possible that I can have performed an infinite series of acts of criticism each of which must require a distinct effort. The case is quite different from that of Achilles and the tortoise, because Achilles does not require to make an infinite series of distinct efforts. It therefore appears that I must have made some judgment that one event *appeared to be* subsequent to another without that judgment having been inferred from any premiss, without my *controlled and criticized* action of reasoning. If this be so, it is a perceptual judgment in the only sense that the logician can recognize. But from that proposition that one event, Z, is subsequent to another event, Y, I can at once deduce by necessary reasoning a universal proposition. Namely, the definition of the relation of apparent subsequence is well-known, or sufficiently so for our purpose. Z will appear to be subsequent to Y if and only if Z appears to stand in a peculiar relation, R, to Y such that nothing can stand in the relation R to itself and if furthermore whatever event, X, there may be to which Y stands in the relation R to that same X, Z also stands in the relation R. This being implied in the meaning of subsequence, concerning which there is no room for doubt, it easily follows that whatever is subsequent to C is subsequent to anything, A, to which C is subsequent, which is a universal proposition.

Thus my assertion at the end of the last lecture appears to be most amply justified. Thirdness pours in upon us through every avenue of sense.[3]

II.

We may now profitably ask ourselves what logical goodness is. We have seen that any kind of goodness consists in the adaptation of its subject to its *end*. One might set this down as a truism. Verily, it is scarcely more, although circumstances may have prevented it being clearly apprehended.

If you call this utilitarianism, I shall not be ashamed of the title. For I do not know what other system of philosophy has wrought so much good in the world as that same utilitarianism. Bentham may be a shallow logician; but such truths as he saw he saw most nobly. As for the vulgar utilitarian, his fault does not lie in his pressing too much the question of what would be the good of this or that. On the contrary his fault is that he never presses the question half far enough, or rather he never really raises the question at all. He simply rests in his present desires as if desire were beyond all dialectic. He wants, perhaps, to go to heaven. But he forgets to ask what would be the good of his going to heaven. He would be happy, there, he thinks. But that is a mere word. It is no real answer to the question.

Our question is, What is the use of thinking? We have already remarked that it is the argument alone which is the primary and direct subject of logical goodness and badness. We have therefore to ask what the end of argumentation is, what it ultimately leads to.

The Germans, whose tendency is to look at everything subjectively and to exaggerate the element of Firstness, maintain that the object is simply to satisfy one's logical feeling and that the goodness of reasoning consists in that esthetic satisfaction alone. This might do if we were gods and not subject to the force of experience.

Or if the force of experience were mere blind compulsion, and we were utter foreigners in the world, then again we might as well think to please ourselves; because we then never could make our thoughts conform to that mere Secondness.

But the saving truth is that there is a Thirdness in experience, an element of Reasonableness to which we can train our own reason to conform more and more. If this were not the case there could be no such thing as logical goodness or badness; and therefore we need not wait until it is proved that there is a reason operative in experience to which our own can approximate. We should at once hope that it is so, since in that hope lies the only possibility of any knowledge.

Reasoning is of three types, Deduction, Induction, and Abduction. In deduction, or necessary reasoning, we set out from a hypothetical state of things which we define in certain abstracted respects. Among the characters to which we pay no attention in this mode of argument is whether or not the hypothesis of our premises conforms more or less to the state of things in the outward world. We consider this hypothetical state of things and are led to conclude that, however it may be with the universe in other respects, wherever and whenever the hypothesis may be realized, something else not explicitly supposed in that hypothesis will be true invariably. Our inference is valid if and only if there really is such a relation between the state of things supposed in the premises and the state of things stated in the conclusion. Whether this really be so or not is a question of reality, and has nothing at all to do with how we may be inclined to think. If a given person is unable to see the connection, the argument is none the less valid, provided that relation of real facts really subsists. If the entire human race were unable to see the connection, the argument would be none the less sound, although it would not be humanly clear. Let us see precisely how we assure ourselves of the reality of the connection. Here, as everywhere throughout logic, the study of relatives has been of the greatest service. The simple syllogisms which are alone considered by the old inexact logicians are such very rudimentary forms that it is practically impossible to discern in them the essential features of deductive inference until our attention has been called to these features in higher forms of deduction. All necessary reasoning without exception is diagrammatic. That is, we construct an icon of our hypothetical state of things and proceed to observe it. This observation leads us to suspect that something is true, which we may or may not be able to formulate with precision, and we proceed to inquire whether it is true or not. For this purpose it is necessary to form a plan of investigation and this is the most difficult part of the whole operation. We not only have to select the features of the diagram which it will be pertinent to pay attention to, but it is also of great importance to return again and again to certain features. Otherwise, although our conclusions may be correct, they will not be the particular conclusions at which we are aiming. But the greatest point of art consists in the introduction of suitable *abstractions*. By this I mean such a transformation of our diagrams that characters of one diagram may appear in another as things. A familiar example is where in analysis we treat operations as themselves the subject of operations. Let me say that it would make a grand life-study to give an account of this operation of planning a mathematical demonstration. Sundry sporadic maxims are afloat among mathematicians, and several meritorious books have been written upon the subject but nothing broad and masterly. With the modern reformed mathematics and with my own and other logical results as a basis such a theory of the plan of demonstration is no longer a superhuman task. Having thus determined the plan of the reasoning, we proceed to the reasoning itself, and this I have ascertained can be reduced to three kinds of steps. The first consists in copulating separate propositions into one compound proposition. The second consists in omitting something from a proposition without possibility of introducing error. The third consists in inserting something into a proposition without introducing error.

You can see precisely what these elementary steps of inference are in Baldwin's *Dictionary* under Symbolic Logic. As a specimen of what they are like you may take this,

A is a bay horse,
Therefore, A is a horse.

If one asks oneself how one knows that this is certain, one is likely to reply that one imagines a bay horse and on contemplating the image one sees that it is a horse. But that only applies to the single image. How large a horse did this image represent? Would it be the same with a horse of very different size? How old was the horse represented to be, was he tail socked? Would it be so if he had the blind-staggers, and if so are you sure it would be so whatever of the numerous diseases of the horse afflicted him? We are perfectly certain that none of these circumstances could affect the question in the least. It is easy enough to formulate reasons by the dozen; but the difficulty is that they are one and all far less evident than the original inference. I do not see that the logician can do better than to say that he *perceives* that when a copulative proposition is given, such as

A is a horse and A has a bay color,

any member of the copulation may be omitted without changing the proposition from true to false. In a psychological sense I am willing to take the word of the psychologist if he says that such a general truth cannot be *perceived*. But what better can we do in logic?

Somebody may answer that the copulative proposition contains the conjunction "and" or something equivalent, and that the very *meaning* of this "and" is that the entire copulation is true if and only if each of the members is singly true; so that it is involved in the very *meaning* of the copulative proposition that any member may be dropped.

To this I assent with all my heart. But after all, what does it amount to? It is another way of saying that what we call the *meaning* of a proposition embraces every obvious necessary deduction from it. Considered as the beginning of an analysis of what the meaning of the word "meaning" is, it is a valuable remark. But I ask how it helps us to understand our passing from an accepted judgment A to another judgment C of which we not only feel equally confident but in point of *fact are* equally sure, barring a possible blunder which would be corrected as soon as attention was called to it, barring another equivalent blunder?

To this the advocate of the explanation by the conception of "meaning" may reply that is *meant* which is intended or purposed; that a judgment is a voluntary act, and our intention is not to employ the form of the judgment A except to the interpretation of images to which judgments corresponding in form to C can be applied.

Perhaps it may reconcile the psychologist to the admission of perceptual judgments involving generality to be told that they are perceptual judgments concerning our own purposes. I certainly think that the certainty of pure mathematics and of all necessary reasoning is due to the circumstance that it relates to objects which are the creations of our own minds, and that mathematical knowledge is to be classed along with knowledge of our own purposes. When we meet with a surprising result in pure mathematics, as we so often do, because a loose reasoning had led us to suppose it impossible, this is essentially the same sort of phenomenon as when in pursuing a purpose we are led to do something that we are quite surprised to find ourselves doing, as being contrary, or apparently contrary, to some weaker purpose.

But if it is supposed that any such considerations afford any logical justification of primary logical principles I must say that, on the contrary, at the very best they *beg the question* by assuming premises far less certain than the conclusion to be established.

A generation and a half of evolutionary fashions in philosophy has not sufficed entirely to extinguish the fire of admiration for John Stuart Mill,—that very strong but a philistine philosopher whose inconsistencies fitted him so well to be the leader of a popular school,—and consequently there will still be those who propose to explain the general principles of formal logic, which are now fully shown to be mathematical principles, by means of induction. Anybody who holds to that view today may be assumed to have a very loose notion of induction; so that all he really means is that the general principles in question are derived from images of the imagination by a process which is, roughly speaking, analogous to induction. Understanding him in that way, I heartily agree with him. But he must not expect me in 1903 to have anything more than a historical admiration for conceptions of induction which shed a brilliant light upon the subject in 1843. Induction is so manifestly inadequate to account for the certainty of these principles that it would be a waste of time to discuss such a theory.

However, it is now time for me to pass to the consideration of Inductive Reasoning.[4] When I say that by inductive reasoning I mean a course of experimental investigation, I do not understand experiment in the narrow sense of an operation by which one varies the conditions of a phenomenon almost as one pleases. We often hear students of sciences which are not in this narrow sense experimental lamenting that in their departments they are debarred from this aid. No doubt there is much justice in this lament; and yet those persons are by no means debarred from pursuing the same logical method precisely although not with the same freedom and facility. An experiment, says Stöckhardt, in his excellent "School of Chemistry," is a question put to nature. Like any interrogatory it is based on a supposition. If that supposition be correct a certain sensible result is to be expected under certain circumstances which can be created or at any rate are to be met with. The question is, Will this be the result? If Nature replies "No!" the experimenter has gained an important piece of knowledge. If Nature says "Yes," the experimenter's ideas remain just as they were, only somewhat more deeply engrained. If Nature says "Yes" to the first twenty questions although they were so devised as to render that answer as surprising as possible, the experimenter will be confident that he is on the right track, since 2 to the 20th power exceeds a million. Laplace was of the opinion that the affirmative experiments impart a definite probability to the theory; and that doctrine is taught in most books on probability to this day, although it leads to the most ridiculous results, and is inherently self-contradictory. It rests on a very confused notion of what probability is. Probability applies to the question whether a specified kind of event will occur when certain predetermined conditions are fulfilled; and it is the ratio of the number of times in the long run in which that specified result would follow upon the fulfillment of those conditions to the total number of times on which those conditions were fulfilled in the course of experience. It essentially refers to a course of experience or at least of real events; because mere possibilities are not capable of being counted. You can, for example, ask what the probability is that a given kind of object will be red, provided you define red sufficiently. It is simply the ratio of the number of objects of that kind that are red to the total number of objects of that kind. But to ask in the abstract what the probability is that a shade of color will be red is nonsense, because shades of color are not individuals capable of being counted. You can ask what the probability is that the next chemical element to be discovered will have an atomic weight exceeding a hundred. But you cannot ask what the probability is that the law of universal attraction should be that of the inverse square until you can attach some meaning to statistics of the characters of possible universes. When Leibniz said that this world is the best that was possible he may have had some glimmer of meaning, but when Quetelet says that if a phenomenon has been observed on m occasions the probability that it will occur on the $(m + 1)^a$ occasion is $(m+1)/(m+2)$ he is talking down-right nonsense. Mr. F. Y. Edgeworth asserts that of all theories that are started one half are correct. That is not nonsense, but it is ridiculously false. For of theories that have enough to recommend them to be seriously discussed, there are more than two on the average to each general phenomenon to be explained. Poincaré, on the other hand, seems to think that all theories are wrong, and that it is only a question of how wrong they are.

Induction consists in starting from a theory, deducing from it predictions of phenomena and observing those phenomena in order to see *how nearly* they agree with the theory. The justification for believing that an experiential theory which has been subjected to a number of experimental tests will be in the near future sustained about as well by further such tests as it has hitherto been, is that by steadily pursuing that method we must in the long run find out how the matter really stands. The reason that we must do so is that our theory, if it be admissible even as a theory, simply consists in supposing that such experiments will in the long run have results of a certain character. But I must not be understood as meaning that experience can be exhausted, or that any approach to exhaustion can be made. What I mean is that if there be a series of objects, say crosses and circles, this series having a beginning but no end, then whatever may be the arrangement or want of arrangement of these crosses and circles in the entire endless series must be discoverable to an indefinite degree of approximation by examining a sufficient finite number of successive ones beginning at the beginning of the series. This is a theorem capable of strict demonstration. The principle of the demonstration is that whatever has no end can have no mode of being other than that of a law, and therefore whatever general character it may have must be describable, but the only way of describing an endless series is by stating explicitly or implicitly the law of the succession of one term upon another. But every such term has a finite ordinal place from the beginning and therefore if it presents any regularity for all finite successions from the beginning it presents the same regularity throughout. Thus the validity of induction depends upon the necessary relation between the general and the singular. It is precisely this which is the support of Pragmatism.

Concerning the validity of Abductive inference, there is little to be said, although that little is pertinent to the problem we have in hand.

Abduction is the process of forming an explanatory hypothesis. It is the only logical operation which introduces any new idea; for induction does nothing but determine a value and deduction merely evolves the necessary consequences of a pure hypothesis.

Deduction proves that something *must* be, Induction shows that something *actually is* operative, Abduction merely suggests that something *may be*.

Its only justification is that from its suggestion deduction can draw a prediction which can be tested by induction and that if we are ever to learn anything or to understand phenomena at all it must be by abduction that this is to be brought about.

No reason whatsoever can be given for it, as far as I can discover; and it needs no reason, since it merely offers suggestions.

A man must be downright crazy to deny that science has made many true discoveries. But every single item of scientific theory which stands established today has been due to Abduction.

But how is it that all this truth has ever been lit up by a process in which there is no compulsiveness nor tendency toward compulsiveness? Is it by chance? Consider the multitude of theories that might have been suggested. A physicist comes across some new phenomenon in his laboratory. How does he know but the conjunctions of the planets have something to do with it or that it is not perhaps because the dowager empress of China has at some time a year ago chanced to pronounce some word of mystical power or some invisible Jinni may be present. Think of what trillions of trillions of hypotheses might be made of which one only is true; and yet after two or three or at the very most a dozen guesses, the physicist hits pretty nearly on the correct hypothesis. By chance he would not have been likely to do so in the whole time that has elapsed since the earth was solidified. You may tell me that astrological and magical hypotheses were resorted to at first and that it is only by degrees that we have learned certain general laws of nature in consequence of which the physicist seeks for the explanation of his phenomenon within the four walls of his laboratory. But when you look at the matter more narrowly, the matter is not to be accounted for in any considerable measure in that way. Take a broad view of the matter. Man has not been engaged upon scientific problems for over twenty thousand years or so. But put it at ten times that if you like. But that is not a hundred thousandth part of the time that he might have been expected to have been searching for his first scientific theory.

You may produce this or that excellent psychological account of the matter. But let me tell you that all the psychology in the world will leave the logical problem just where it was. I might occupy hours in developing that point. I must pass it by.

You may say that evolution accounts for the thing. I don't doubt it is evolution. But as for explaining evolution by chance, there has not been time enough.

However man may have acquired his faculty of divining the ways of Nature, it has certainly not been by a self-controlled and critical logic. Even now he cannot give any exact reason for his best guesses. It appears to me that the cleanest statement we can make of the logical situation,— the freest from all questionable admixture,—is to say that man has a certain Insight, not strong enough to be oftener right than wrong, but strong enough not to be overwhelmingly more often wrong than right, into the Thirdnesses, the general elements, of Nature. An Insight, I call it, because it is to be referred to the same general class of operations to which Perceptive Judgments belong. This Faculty is at the same time of the general nature of Instinct, resembling the instincts of the animals in its so far surpassing the general powers of our reason and for its directing us as if we were in possession of facts that are entirely beyond the reach of our senses. It resembles instinct too in its small liability to error; for though it does wrong oftener than right, yet the relative frequency with which it is right is on the whole the most wonderful thing in our constitution.

One little remark and I will drop this topic. If you ask an investigator why he does not try this or that wild theory, he will say, "It does not seem *reasonable*." It is curious that we seldom use this word where the strict logic of our procedure is clearly seen. We do say that a mathematical error is not reasonable. We call that opinion reasonable whose only support is instinct.

III.

Let us now come to the question of the maxim of Pragmatism. This maxim runs as follows: "Consider what effects that might conceivably have practical bearings we conceive the object of our conception to have. Then, our conception of these effects is the whole of our conception of the object."

We have already seen some reason to hold that the idea of *meaning* is such as to involve some reference to a *purpose*. But Meaning is attributed to representamens alone, and the only kind of representamen which has a definite professed purpose is an "argument." The professed purpose of an argument is to determine an acceptance of its conclusion, and it quite accords with general usage to call the conclusion of an argument its meaning. But I may remark that the word meaning has not hitherto been recognized as a technical term of logic, and in proposing it as such, which I have a right to do since I have a new conception to express, that of the conclusion of an argument as its intended interpretant, I should have a recognized right slightly to warp the acceptation of the word "meaning," so as to fit it for the expression of a scientific conception. It seems natural to use the word *meaning* to denote the intended interpretant of a symbol.

I may presume that you are all familiar with Kant's reiterated insistence that necessary reasoning does nothing but explicate the *meaning* of its premises. Now Kant's conception of the nature of necessary reasoning is clearly shown by the logic of relations to be utterly mistaken, and his distinction between analytic and synthetic judgments, which he otherwise and better terms *explicatory* (*erlaüerende*) and *ampliative* (*erweitendende*) judgments, which is based on that conception is so utterly confused that it is difficult or impossible to do anything with it. But, nevertheless, I think we shall do very well to accept Kant's dictum that necessary reasoning is merely explicatory of the meaning of the terms of the premises, only reversing the use to be made of it. Namely instead of adopting the conception of meaning from the Wolfian logicians, as he does, and making use of this dictum to express what necessary reasoning can do, about which he was utterly mistaken, we shall do well to understand necessary reasoning as mathematics and the logic of relations compels us to understand it and to use the dictum that necessary reasoning only explicates the meanings of the terms of the premises to fix our ideas as to what we shall understand by the *meaning* of a term.

Kant and the logicians with whose writings he was alone acquainted,—he was far from being a thorough student of logic, notwithstanding his great natural power as a logician,—consistently neglected the logic of relations; and the consequence was that the only account they were in condition to give of the meaning of a term, its "signification" as they called it, was that it was composed of all the terms which could be essentially predicated of that term. Consequently, either the analysis of the signification must be capable of [being] pushed on further and further, without limit,—an opinion which Kant expresses in a well-known passage but which he did not develop,—or, what was more usual, one ultimately reached certain absolutely simple conceptions such as Being, Quality, Relation, Agency, Freedom, etc., which were regarded as absolutely incapable of definition and of being in the highest degree luminous and clear. It is marvelous what a following this opinion that those excessively abstracted conceptions were in themselves in the highest degree simple and facile obtained, notwithstanding its repugnancy to good sense. One of the many important services which the logic of relations has rendered has been that of showing that these so-called simple conceptions, notwithstanding their being unaffected by the particular kind of combination recognized in non-relative logic, are nevertheless capable of analysis in consequence of their implying various modes of relationship. For example, no conceptions are simpler than those of Firstness, Secondness, and Thirdness; but this has not prevented my defining them and that in a most effective manner since all the assertions I have made concerning them have been deduced from those definitions.

Another effect of the neglect of the logic of relations was that Kant imagined that all necessary reasoning was of the type of a syllogism in *Barbara*. Nothing could be more ridiculously in conflict with well-known facts. For had that been the case, any person with a good logical head would be able instantly to see whether a given conclusion followed from given premises or not, and moreover the number of conclusions from a small number of premises would be very moderate. Now it is true that when Kant wrote, Legendre and Gauss had not shown what a countless multitude of theorems are deducible from the very few premises of arithmetic. I suppose we must excuse him, therefore, for not knowing this. But it is difficult to understand what the state of mind on this point could have been of logicians who were at the same time mathematicians, such as Euler, Lambert, and Ploucquet could have been on such subjects. Euler invented the logical diagrams which go under his name; for the claims that have been made in favor of predecessors may be set down as baseless; and Lambert used an equivalent system. Now I need not say that both of these men were mathematicians of great power. One is simply astounded that they should seem to say that all the reasonings of mathematics could be represented in any such ways. One may suppose that Euler never paid much attention to logic. But Lambert wrote a large book in two volumes on the subject, and a pretty superficial affair it is. One has a difficulty in realizing that the author of it was the same man who came so near to the discovery of the non-Euclidean geometry. The logic of relatives is now able to exhibit in strict logical form the reasoning of mathematics. You will find an example of it,—although too simple a one to put all the features into prominence,—in that chapter of Schröder's logic in which he remodels the reasoning of Dedekind in his brochure *Was sind und was sollen die Zahlen*; and if it be objected that this analysis was chiefly the work of Dedekind who did not employ the machinery of the logic of relations, I reply that Dedekind's whole book is nothing but an elaboration of a paper published by me several years previously in the *American Journal of Math-*

ematics which paper was the direct result of my logical studies. These analyses show that although most of the steps of the reasoning have considerable resemblance to *Barbara*, yet the difference of effect is very great indeed.

On the whole, then, if by the *meaning* of a term, proposition, or argument, we understand the entire general intended interpretant, then the meaning of an argument is explicit. It is its conclusion, while the meaning of a proposition or term is all that that proposition or term could contribute to the conclusion of a demonstrative argument. But while this analysis will be found useful, it is by no means sufficient to cut off all nonsense or to enable us to judge of the maxim of pragmatism. What we need is an account of the *ultimate* meaning of a term. To this problem we have to address ourselves.

IV.[5]

Let us ask then what the *end* of a term is. It is plain that no use can be made of it until it is introduced into a proposition; and when it is introduced into the proposition it must form the predicate or some predicative constituent of the predicate. For the subjects of a proposition merely fulfill the function of indices and involve no general conception whatever, while a term is essentially general, although it may involve indexical constituents.

In order to make this matter clear, which is more important than it seems at first blush, I had better explain what I mean by a term. And here I suppose I shall have to devote a minute or two to a most insignificant distinction between a *term* and a *rhema*. Whenever I speak of a *term* I always mean a *rhema*. The difference is that a term is the equivalent of a common noun and cannot form the predicate of a proposition unless a verb is inserted, while a rhema contains a verb within itself. Thus, 'butcher' is a term; 'is a butcher' is a rhema, and so is 'slaughters'. In primitive languages there is strictly no such thing as a common noun. Old Egyptian and Arabic are instances. What proves this is that if in those languages one wishes to say 'Smith is a butcher' and one feels the need of inserting something between Smith and butcher, instead of feeling that a verb is needed, it will be a *pronoun* that will be inserted. In Arabic one will say 'Smith *he* butcher'. No verb is ever introduced unless a definite meaning is attached to it, as in 'Became Smith butcher' or 'Remains Smith butcher' or 'Continues Smith butcher', and in Egyptian the word *pu* which is often translated "is" is unquestionably a relative or originally a demonstrative pronoun. Indeed even in Greek a verb is not necessary in a sentence, and though Aristotle sometimes makes the verb a separate part of the proposition in accordance with one mode of expression in the Greek language, he does not usually do so; so that what modern and medieval logicians called the *copula* of a proposition never received a name until the time of Abelard. Nothing can be more preposterous than to base that *grammatica speculativa* which forms the first part of logic upon the usages of language. But it is a fault which seems so ineradicable among most writers, especially in English, that I think it worth while to point out that the common noun, instead of being a necessary part of speech, is nothing but a late development chiefly restricted to that small and extremely peculiar family of languages which happen to be the most familiar to us.

Imagine that certain parts of a proposition are erased, so that it is no longer a proposition but a *blank form* of a proposition containing one or more *blanks*, all which blanks are such that if they are all filled with demonstrative pronouns or proper names, the result will be a proposition. Then such a blank form of proposition is a *rhema*, or as I am accustomed to call it, a *term*. For I regard the distinction between a *rhema* and a *term* as too insignificant for notice. For example

> Every man loves _____
> _____ prefers some woman to_____

are *rhemata* or *terms*. A rhema containing one blank I call a *monad*, that containing two a *dyad*, etc. An entire proposition I term a *medad*, from μηδέν.

Since nothing is essential to a term except its containing at least one blank, it is plain that this blank form may contain demonstrative pronouns or proper names, that is, indicative words. Thus

> _____ prefers some woman to Victoria

is a term or rhema.

Indeed the question arises whether it is possible to have a term which does *not* implicitly involve an index. If the logic of relatives is neglected, this question cannot arise; because in non-relative logic a term can only be analyzed into terms more abstracted and general than itself, while an index always denotes a reacting singular. The only logical terms which are in perfect strictness singular are the subjects of perceptual judgments and of what I may call volitional judgments which immediately precede action. It is convenient to regard such names as Theodore Roosevelt and Rudyard Kipling as singulars. They denote persons who we may roughly say are equally known to you and to me. However, my knowledge of Theodore Roosevelt or of Rudyard Kipling is a little different from yours. I have rather hazy recollections of having perceived a very young man at the club, in which perceptions there was a direct consciousness of a reaction, and I remember we used to say, "That young Theodore Roosevelt is going to be an important personage." I recollect to have perceived that name many times in the newspapers and to have talked about the person referred to with his neighbors and relatives; and I recollect later perceiving in the White House a person who seemed to be the President, and who talked as if he were acquainted with me. These circumstances have led me semi-instinctively to suppose that one person preserving an identity through the continuity of space, time, character, memory, etc., has been one singular connected with all these phenomena; and though I have not made any formal induction to test this theory, yet my impression is that I am in possession of abundance of facts that would support such an induction quite irresistibly. In a similar way I have no doubt that the phenomena which may have presented themselves to you together with many more that persons whom I know well must recollect all unite to support the hypothesis that there is one singular Theodore Roosevelt quite unmistakable for a phantom or for any other man than himself. In each of my own perceptions, if my memory does not deceive me, there was a decided double consciousness or direct consciousness of reaction, and I have abundance of reason to think it was so with your perceptions and with those of all his acquaintances whom I know or have heard of. The notion that all those reacting singulars were in the relation of personal identity to one another, and that their separate singularities consist in a connection to one singular, the collection of them all, this notion is an element of Thirdness abductively connected with them. We may express the matter by saying that all these singular percepts were aspects or parts of one collective singular which may include non-perceptual parts for aught we are now prepared to say.

It is plain that our knowledge of the majority of general conceptions comes about in a manner altogether analogous to our knowledge of an individual person. Take, for example, the general idea of *dog*. I have had many perceptual experiences with which this word *dog* is associated and have ample reason to believe that others have had such experiences. These are all experiences of a singular,—the singular collection of all dogs, the race of dogs, which, according to the doctrine of germ-plasm, is just as much one thing as a single dog is one thing. I do not mean to say that the theory of germ-plasm has any logical connection with the matter; but only that it aids those whose logical training has been neglected,—as it seems to me it is neglected in this university,—to perceive that a class is an individual. In how many books, even recent books, have I seen Claude Bernard praised for having enunciated a great doctrine of physiology in saying, "Disease is not an entity; it is nothing but an assemblage of symptoms." Now this is not a physiological doctrine at all. It is nothing but a logical doctrine and a doctrine of false logic. But in the light of the positive discoveries of Pasteur and Koch, considered in connection with the theories of Weissmann, we see that, as far as zymotic diseases are concerned, they are just as much a thing as the ocean is a thing. And indeed if Claude Bernard had not had his mind filled with bad metaphysics, he would have seen that an assemblage of symptoms was not only an entity but necessarily a concrete thing; whereupon he might have set himself to work very usefully to obtain some further acquaintance with that thing.

To return to the dog. My perceptual judgments of percepts of dogs have contained sundry general elements and these I have generalized by abductions chiefly, with small doses of induction, and have thus acquired some general ideas of dogs' ways, of the laws of caninity, some of them invariable so far as I have observed, such as his frequent napping, others merely usual, such as his way of circling when he is preparing to take a nap. These are laws of perceptual judgments, and so beyond all doubt are the great majority of our general notions. It is not evident that this is not the case with all general notions. If, therefore, anybody maintains that there are any general notions which are not given in the perceptual judgments, it is fair to demand that he should prove it by close reasoning and not expect us to accept unsupported assertions to that effect nor to assent to it without something better than vague remarks to convince us that it is so. Yet this is what the nominalistic reasoner is continually doing. He would persuade us that the mind,—that is to say our opinions,—are filled with notions wholly unlike anything in the real world. Now the real world is the world of percepts, concerning which perceptual judgments are our only witnesses. When I ask him how he proves this, he produces an argument which according to my logic is manifestly fallacious. He insists that it is sound, because it excites in him a certain feeling, although in me it excites no such feeling. The curious thing is that he frequently will betray by his conduct that he does not believe in the conclusion to which his reasoning should lead, or even frankly confesses this. So that our two systems of logic differ in that the one recommends certain forms of argument which lead from true premises to false conclusions, because they produce a feeling of satisfaction in one man's breast though not in another's, while the other system does not judge of arguments by the feelings they produce but by whether or not they could lead to contradictory conclusions. If a color blind man were to endeavor to persuade me that I had no such sensation as that of redness, I could readily understand how he might imagine that he could bring me round to his opinion, but I, being able to put myself in his shoes, should never imagine that I could convince him of his mistake as long as his only standard was his own feelings.

I do not think it is possible fully to comprehend the problem of the merits of pragmatism without recognizing these three truths:

1st, that there are no conceptions which are not given to us, in perceptual judgments; so that we may say that all our ideas are perceptual ideas. This sounds like sensationalism. But in order to maintain this position, it is necessary to recognize,

2nd, that perceptual judgments contain elements of generality; so that Thirdness is directly perceived; and finally, I think it of great importance to recognize,

3rd, that the Abductive faculty, whereby we divine the secrets of nature is, as we may say, a shading off, a gradation of that which in its highest perfection we call perception.

But while, to my apprehension, it is only in the light of those three doctrines that the true characteristics of pragmatism are fully displayed, yet even without them we shall be brought although less clearly and forcibly to nearly the same opinion.

Granting that there may be some general concepts which are not perceptual, that is, not elements of perceptual judgments, these may make a kind of music in the soul, or they may in some mysterious way subserve some end; but in order to be of any *cognitive* service, it is plain that they must enter into propositions. For cognition proper is true, or at any rate is either true or false, and it is propositions alone that are either true or false. The only form in which a general can enter into a proposition is either as predicate or predicative constituent of the predicate or as subject. But a general subject is either an indesignate individual or a quodlibetical individual of the universe to which no descriptive character is attached. It is therefore not what we mean by a concept. It involves merely directions as to what one is to do to find an individual such as is intended, without at all describing that individual. The general concept therefore must be the predicate or an element of the predicate of the nature of a predicate.

Now there are two questions to be asked concerning such a proposition. The first is, What ground can there be for assenting to it; and the second is, What knowledge does it convey supposing it to be accepted.

As to the first question, What ground can there be for assenting to the proposition, it is obvious that a proposition not assented to has no cognitive value whatever. But nobody will or can assent to a proposition without supposing himself to have sufficient logical reason for doing so, unless a blind force compels him to believe it. But this last cannot be the case with such a proposition as we are considering whose predicate is not wholly perceptual; for the reason that, however the psychologist might class such a compulsory judgment, for the logician it would be perceptual, perception being for the logician simply what experience, that is, the succession of what happens to him, forces him to admit immediately and without any reason. This judgment, then, must be inferred. How can it be inferred?

Plainly only by abduction, because abduction is the only process by which a new element can be introduced into thought and it is expressly supposed that we have to do here with that judgment in which the conception in question first makes its appearance. You now see what I meant when in speaking of Abduction I said that the little that was to be said of the logic of it was highly pertinent to our problem; for we now see that the true doctrine concerning Pragmatism whatever it may be is nothing else than the true Logic of Abduction.

It is now generally admitted, and it is the result of my own logical analysis, that the true maxim of abduction is that which Auguste Comte endeavored to formulate when he said that any hypothesis might be admissible if and only if it was verifiable. Whatever Comte himself meant by verifiable, which is not very clear, it certainly ought not to be understood to mean verifiable by direct observation, since that would cut off all history as an inadmissible hypothesis. But what must and should be meant is, that the hypothesis must be capable of verification by induction. Now induction, or experimental inquiry, consists in comparing perceptual predictions deduced from a theory with the facts of perception predicted and in taking the measure of agreement observed as the provisional and approximative, or probimetric, measure of the general agreement of the theory with fact.

It thus appears that a conception can only be admitted into a hypothesis in so far as its possible consequences would be of a perceptual nature; which agrees with my original maxim of pragmatism as far as it goes.

LECTURE SEVEN: THREE COTARY
PROPOSITIONS OF PRAGMATISM

Ladies and Gentlemen:

I.

I am impelled to express my sense of gratitude at your kind interest in coming to listen to an extra lecture at this busy season of the year. I shall feel myself under an obligation to make a special endeavor to say something germinative.

At the end of my last lecture I had just enunciated three propositions which seem to me to give to pragmatism its peculiar character. In order to be able to refer to them briefly this evening, I will call them for the nonce my cotary propositions.[1] *Cos, cotis,* is a whetstone. They appear to me to put the edge on the maxim of pragmatism.

These *cotary* propositions are as follows:

1st, *Nihil est in intellectu quin prius fuerat in sensu.* I take this in a sense somewhat different from that which Aristotle intended. By *intellectus* I understand the *meaning* of any representation in any kind of cognition, virtual, symbolic, or whatever it may be. Berkeley and nominalists of his stripe deny that we have any idea at all of a triangle in general, which is neither equilateral, isosceles, nor scalene. But he cannot deny that there are propositions about triangles in general which propositions are either true or false; and as long as that is the case, whether we have an *idea* of a triangle in some psychological sense or not, I do not, as a logician, care. We have an *intellectus,* a meaning, of which the triangle in general is an element. As for the other term, *in sensu,* that I take in the sense of in a *perceptual judgment,* the starting point or first premiss of all critical and controlled thinking. I will state presently what I conceive to be the evidence of the truth of this first cotary proposition. But I prefer to begin by recalling to you what all three of them are.

The second is that perceptual judgments contain general elements, so that universal propositions are deducible from them in the manner in which the logic of relations shows that particular propositions usually, not to say invariably, allow universal propositions to be necessarily inferred from them. This I sufficiently argued in my last lecture. This evening I shall take the truth of it for granted.

The third cotary proposition is that abductive inference shades into perceptual judgment without any sharp line of demarcation between them; or in other words our first premisses, the perceptual judgments, are to be regarded as an extreme case of abductive inferences, from which they differ in being absolutely beyond criticism. The abductive suggestion comes to us like a flash. It is an act of *insight*, although of extremely fallible insight. It is true that the different elements of the hypothesis were in our minds before; but it is the idea of putting together what we had never before dreamed of putting together which flashes the new suggestion before our contemplation.

On its side, the perceptive judgment is the result of a process, although of a process not sufficiently conscious to be controlled, or to state it more truly not controllable and therefore not fully conscious. If we were to subject this subconscious process to logical analysis we should find that it terminated in what that analysis would represent as an abductive inference resting on the result of a similar process which a similar logical analysis would represent to be terminated by a similar abductive inference, and so on *ad infinitum*. This analysis would be precisely analogous to that which the sophism of Achilles and the tortoise applies to the chase of the tortoise by Achilles, and it would fail to represent the real process for the same reason. Namely just as Achilles does not have to make the series of distinct endeavors which he is represented as making, so this process of forming the perceptual judgment because it is subconscious and so not amenable to logical criticism does not have to make separate acts of inference but performs its act in one continuous process.

II.

I have already put in my brief in favor of my second cotary proposition, and in what I am about to say I shall treat that as already sufficiently proved. In arguing it I avoided all resort to anything like special phenomena, upon which I do not think that philosophy ought to rest, at all. Still, there is no harm in using special observations merely in an abductive way to throw a light upon doctrines otherwise established, and to aid the mind in grasping them; and there are some phenomena which, I think, do aid us to see what is meant by asserting that perceptual judgments contain general elements and which will also naturally lead up to a consideration of the third cossal [cotary] proposition.

I will show you a figure which I remember my father's drawing in one of his lectures. I do not remember what it was supposed to show; but I cannot imagine what else it could have been but my cotary proposition, No. 2. If so, in maintaining that proposition, I am substantially treading in his foot-prints, though he would doubtless have put the proposition into a shape very different from mine. Here is the figure (though I cannot draw it as skillfully as he did). It consists of a serpentine line.

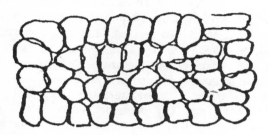

But when it is completely drawn, it appears to be a stone wall. The point is that there are two ways of conceiving the matter. Both I beg you to remark are *general ways of classing the line*, general classes under which the line is subsumed. But the very decided preference of our perception for one mode of classing the percept shows that this classification is contained in the perceptual judgment. So it is with that well-known unshaded outline figure of a pair of steps seen in perspective. We seem at first to be looking at the steps from above; but some unconscious part of the mind seems to tire of putting that construction upon it and suddenly we seem to see the steps from below, and so the perceptive judgment and the percept itself seem to keep shifting from one general aspect to the other and back again.

In all such visual illusions of which two or three dozen are well known, the most striking thing is that a certain theory of interpretation of the figure has all the appearance of being given in perception. The first time it is shown to us, it seems as completely beyond the control of rational criticism as any percept is; but after many repetitions of the now familiar experiment, the illusion wears off, becoming first less decided, and ultimately ceasing completely. This shows that these phenomena are true connecting links between abductions and perceptions.

If the percept or perceptual judgment were of a nature entirely unrelated to abduction, one would expect that the percept would be entirely free from any characters that are proper to *interpretations*, while it can hardly fail to have such characters if it be merely a continuous series of what discretely and consciously performed would be abductions. We have here then almost a crucial test of my third cotary proposition. Now, then, how is the fact? The fact is that it is not necessary to go beyond ordinary observations of common life to find a variety of widely different ways in which perception is interpretative.

The whole series of hypnotic phenomena, of which so many fall within the realm of ordinary everyday observation,—such as our waking up at the hour we wish to wake much nearer than our waking selves could guess it,—involve the fact that we perceive what we are adjusted for interpreting though it be far less perceptible than any express effort could enable us to perceive; while that to the interpretation of which our adjustments are not fitted, we fail to perceive although it exceed in intensity what we should perceive with the utmost ease if we cared at all for its interpretation. It is a marvel to me that the clock in my study strikes every half hour in the most audible manner, and yet I never hear it. I should not know at all whether the striking part were going, unless it is out of order and strikes the wrong hour. If it does that, I am pretty sure to hear it. Another familiar fact is that we perceive, or seem to perceive, objects differently from how they really are, accommodating them to their manifest intention.[2] Proof-readers get high salaries because ordinary people miss seeing misprints, their eyes correcting them. We can repeat the *sense* of a conversation but we are often quite mistaken as to what words were uttered. Some politicians think it a clever thing to convey an idea which they carefully abstain from stating in words. The result is that a reporter is ready to swear quite sincerely that a politician said something to him which the politician was most careful not to say.

I should tire you if I dwelt further on anything so familiar, especially to every psychological student, as the interpretativeness of the perceptive judgment. It is plainly nothing but the extremest case of Abductive Judgment.

If this third cotary proposition be admitted, the second, that the perceptual judgment contains general elements must be admitted; and as for the first, that all general elements are given in perception, that loses most of its significance. For if a general element were given otherwise than in the perceptual judgment, it could only first appear in an abductive suggestion, and that is now seen to amount substantially to the same thing. I not only opine, however, that every general element of every hypothesis, however wild or sophisticated it may be, [is] given somewhere in perception, but I will venture so far as to assert that every general *form* of putting concepts together is, in its elements, given in perception. In order to decide whether this be so or not, it is necessary to form a clear notion of the precise difference between abductive judgment and the perceptual judgment which is its limiting case. The only symptom by which the two can be distinguished is that we cannot form the least conception of what it would be to deny the perceptual judgment. If I judge a perceptual image to be red, I can conceive of another man's not having that same percept. I can also conceive of his having this percept but never having thought whether it was red or not. I can conceive that while colors are among his sensations he shall never have had his attention directed to them. Or I can conceive that instead of redness a somewhat different conception should arise in his mind, that he should, for example, judge that this percept has a warmth of color. I can imagine that the redness of my percept is excessively faint and dim so that one can hardly make sure of whether it is red or not. But that any man should have a percept similar to mine and should ask himself the question whether this percept be *red*, which would imply that he had already judged *some* percept to be red, and that he should, upon careful attention to this percept, pronounce it to be decidedly and clearly *not* red, when I judge it to be prominently red, *that* I cannot comprehend at all. An abductive suggestion, however, is something whose truth *can* be questioned or even denied.

We thus come to the *test of inconceivability* as the only means of distinguishing between an abduction and a perceptual judgment. Now I fully assent to all that Stuart Mill so forcibly said in his "examination of Hamilton" as to the utter untrustworthiness of the test of inconceivability. That which is inconceivable to us today, may prove tomorrow to be conceivable and even probable; so that we never can be absolutely sure that a judgment is perceptual and not abductive; and this may seem to constitute a difficulty in the way of satisfying ourselves that this first cotary proposition is true.[3] I should easily show you that this difficulty, however formidable theoretically, amounts practically to little or nothing for a person skilled in shaping such inquiries. But this is unnecessary, since the objection founded upon it has no logical force whatever.

No doubt in regard to the first cotary proposition follows as a necessary consequence of the possibility that what are really abductions have been mistaken for perceptions. For the question is whether that which really is an abductive result can contain elements foreign to its premises. It must be remembered that abduction, although it is very little hampered by logical rules, nevertheless is logical inference, asserting its conclusion only problematically or conjecturally it is true, but nevertheless having a perfectly definite logical form.

Long before I first classed abduction as an inference it was recognized by logicians that the operation of adopting an explanatory hypothesis,—which is just what abduction is,—was subject to certain conditions. Namely, the hypothesis cannot be admitted, even as a hypothesis, unless it be supposed that it would account for the facts or some of them. The form of inference therefore is this:

The surprising fact, C, is observed;

But if A were true, C would be a matter of course.

Hence, there is reason to suspect that A is true.

Thus, A cannot be abductively inferred or, if you prefer the expression, cannot be abductively conjectured, until its entire content is already present in the premiss, "If A were true, C would be a matter of course."

Whether this be a correct account of the matter or not, the mere suggestion of it as a possibility shows that the bare fact that abductions may be mistaken for perceptions does not necessarily affect the force of an argument to show quite new conceptions cannot be obtained from abduction.

But when the account just given of abduction [is] proposed as a proof that all conceptions must be given substantially in perception, three objections will be [stated]. Namely, in the first place, it may be said that even if this be the normative form of abduction, the form to which abduction *ought* to conform, yet it may be that new conceptions arise in a manner which puts the rules of logic at defiance. In the second place, waiving this objection, it may be said that the argument would prove too much; for if it were valid, it would follow that no hypothesis could be so fantastic as not to have presented itself entire in experience. In the third place, it may be said that granting that the abductive conclusion "A is true" rests upon the premiss "If A is true, C is true," still it would be contrary to common knowledge to assert that the antecedents of all conditional judgments are given in perception, and thus it remains almost certain that some conceptions have a different origin.

In answer to the first of these objections, it is to be remarked that it is only in Deduction that there is no difference between a *valid* argument and a *strong* one. An argument is valid if it possesses the sort of strength that it professes and tends toward the establishment of the conclusion in the way in which it pretends to do this. But the question of its strength does not concern the comparison of the due effect of the argument with its pretensions but simply upon how great its due effect is. An argument is none the less logical for being weak, provided it does not pretend to a strength that it does not possess. It is, I suppose, in view of this that the best modern logicians outside the English school never say a word about fallacies. They assume that there is no such thing as an argument illogical in itself. An argument is fallacious only so far as it is mistakenly, though not illogically, inferred to have professed what it did not perform. Perhaps it may be said that if all our reasonings conform to the laws of logic, this is, at any rate, nothing but a proposition in psychology which my principles ought to forbid my recognizing. But I do not offer it as a principle of psychology only. For a principle of psychology is a contingent truth, while this, as I contend, is a necessary truth. Namely, if a fallacy involves nothing in its conclusion which was not in its premisses, that is nothing that was not in any previous knowledge that aided in suggesting it, then the forms of logic will invariably and necessarily enable us logically to account for it as due to a mistake arising from the use of a logical but weak argumentation. In most cases it is due to an abduction. The conclusion of an abduction is problematic, or conjectural, but is not necessarily at the weakest grade of surmise, and what we call assertoric judgments are, accurately, problematic judgments of a high grade of hopefulness. There is therefore no difficulty in maintaining that fallacies are merely due to mistakes which are logically valid, though weak argumentations. If, however, a fallacy contains something in the conclusion which was not in the premisses at all, that is, was in no previous knowledge or none that influenced the result, then again a mistake due as before to weak inference, has been committed; only in this case the mistake consists in taking that to be an inference which, in respect to this new element, is not an inference, at all. That part of the conclusion which inserts the wholly new element can be separated from the rest with which it has no logical connection nor appearance of logical connection. The first emergence of this new element into consciousness must be regarded as a perceptive judgment. We are irresistibly led to judge that we are conscious of it. But the connection of this perception with other elements must be an ordinary logical inference, subject to error like all inference.

As for the second objection that, according to my account of abduction, every hypothesis, however fantastic, must have presented itself entire in perception, I have only to say that this could only arise in a mind entirely unpracticed in the logic of relations, and apparently quite oblivious of any other mode of inference than abduction. Deduction accomplishes first the simple colligation of different perceptive judgments into a copulative whole, and then, with or without the aid of other modes of inference, is quite capable of so transforming this copulative proposition so as to bring certain of its parts into more intimate connection.

But the third objection is the really serious one; in it lies the whole nodus of the question and its full refutation would be quite a treatise. If the antecedent is not given in a perceptive judgment, then it must first emerge in the conclusion of an inference. At this point we are obliged to draw the distinction between the matter and the logical form. With the aid of the logic of relations it would be easy to show that the entire logical matter of a conclusion must in any mode of inference be contained, piecemeal, in the premisses. Ultimately therefore it must come from the uncontrolled part of the mind, because a series of controlled acts must have a first. But as to the logical *form*, it would be, at any rate, extremely difficult to dispose of it in the same way. An induction, for example, concludes a ratio of frequency; but there is nothing about any such ratio in the single instances on which it is based. Where do the conceptions of deductive necessity, of inductive probability, of abductive expectability come from? Where does the conception of inference itself come from? That is the only difficulty. But self-control is the character which distinguishes reasoning from the processes by which perceptual judgments are formed and self-control of any kind is purely *inhibitory*. It originates nothing.

Therefore it cannot be in the act of adoption of an inference, in the pronouncing of it to be reasonable, that the formal conceptions in question can first emerge. It must be in the first perceiving that so one might conceivably reason. And what is the nature of that? I see that I have instinctively described the phenomenon as a "perceiving." I do not wish to argue from words; but a word may furnish a valuable suggestion. What can our first acquaintance with an inference, when it is not yet adopted, be but a perception, a perception <of mental relations>—a perception of the world of ideas? In the first suggestion of it the inference must be thought of as an inference, because when it is adopted there is always the thought that so one might reason in a whole class of cases. But the mere act of inhibition cannot introduce this conception. The inference must, then, be thought of as an inference in the first suggestion of it. Now when an inference is thought of *as* an inference, the conception of inference becomes a part of the *matter* of thought. Therefore, the same argument which we used in regard to matter in general applies to the conception of inference. But I am prepared to show in detail, and indeed virtually have shown, that all the forms of logic can be reduced to combinations of the conception of inference, the conception of otherness, and the conception of a character. These are obviously simply forms of Thirdness, Secondness, and Firstness of which the last two are unquestionably given in perception. Consequently the whole logical form of thought is so given in its elements.

III.[4]

It appears to me, then, that my three cotary propositions are satisfactorily grounded. Nevertheless, since others may not regard them as so certain as I myself do, I propose in the first instance to disregard them, and to show that, even if they are put aside as doubtful, a maxim practically little differing in most of its applications from that of pragmatism ought to be acknowledged and followed; and after this has been done, I will show how the recognition of the cotary propositions will affect the matter.

I have argued in several of my early papers that there are but three essentially different modes of reasoning: Deduction, Induction, and Abduction. I may mention in particular papers in the *Proceedings of the American Academy of Arts and Sciences* for April and May 1867. I must say, however, that it would be very easy to misunderstand those arguments. I did not at first fully comprehend them myself. I cannot restate the matter tonight, although I am very desirous of doing so, for I could now put it in a much clearer light. I have already explained to you briefly what these three modes of inference, Deduction, Induction, and Abduction are. I ought to say that when I described induction as the experimental testing of a hypothesis, I was not thinking of experimentation in the narrow sense in which it is confined to cases in which we ourselves deliberately create the peculiar conditions under which we desire to study a phenomenon. I mean to extend it to every case in which, having ascertained by deduction that a theory would lead us to anticipate under certain circumstances phenomena contrary to what we should expect if the theory were *not* true, we examine the cases of that sort to see how far those predictions are borne out.

If you carefully consider the question of pragmatism you will see that it is nothing else than the question of the logic of abduction. That is, pragmatism proposes a certain maxim which, if sound, must render needless any further rule as to the admissibility of hypotheses to rank as hypotheses, that is to say, as explanations of phenomena held as hopeful suggestions; and furthermore, this is *all* that the maxim of pragmatism really pretends to do, at least so far as it is confined to logic, and is not understood as a proposition in psychology. For the maxim of pragmatism is that a conception can have no logical effect or import differing from that of a second conception except so far as, taken in connection with other conceptions and intentions, it might conceivably modify our practical conduct differently from that second conception. Now it is indisputable that no rule of abduction would be admitted by any philosopher which should prohibit on any formalistic grounds any inquiry as to how we ought in consistency to shape our practical conduct. Therefore, a maxim which looks only to possibly practical considerations will not need any supplement in order to exclude any hypotheses as inadmissible. What hypothesis it admits all philosophers would agree ought to be admitted. On the other hand, if it be true that nothing but such considerations has any logical effect or import whatever, it is plain that the maxim of pragmatism cannot cut off any kind of hypothesis which ought to be admitted. Thus, the maxim of pragmatism, if true, fully *covers* the entire logic of abduction. It remains to inquire whether this maxim may not have some *further* logical effect. If so, it must in some way affect inductive or deductive inference. But that pragmatism cannot interfere with induction is evident; because induction simply teaches us what we have to expect as a result of experimentation, and it is plain that any such expectation may conceivably concern practical conduct. In a certain sense it must affect deduction. Anything which gives a rule to abduction and so puts a limit upon admissible hypotheses will cut down *the premisses* of deduction, and thereby will render a *reductio ad absurdum* and other equivalent forms of deduction possible which would not otherwise have been possible. But here three remarks may be made. First, to affect the premisses of deduction is not to affect the logic of deduction. For in the process of deduction itself no conception is introduced to which pragmatism could be supposed to object except the act of abstraction. Concerning that I have only time to say that pragmatism ought not to object to it. Secondly, no effect of pragmatism which *is consequent upon its effect on abduction* can go to show that pragmatism is anything more than a doctrine concerning the logic of abduction. Thirdly, if pragmatism is the doctrine that every conception is a conception of conceivable practical effects, it makes conception reach far beyond the practical. It allows any flight of imagination, provided this imagination ultimately alights upon a possible practical effect; and thus many hypotheses may seem at first glance to be excluded by the pragmatical maxim that are not really so excluded.

IV.

Admitting, then, that the question of Pragmatism is the Question of Abduction, let us consider it under that form. What is good abduction? What should an explanatory hypothesis be to be worthy to rank as a hypothesis? Of course, it must explain the facts. But what other conditions ought it to fulfill to be good? The question of the goodness of anything is whether that thing fulfills its end. What, then, is the end of an explanatory hypothesis? Its end is, through subjection to the test of experiment, to lead to the avoidance of all surprise and to the establishment of a habit of positive expectation that shall not be disappointed. Any hypothesis, therefore, may be admissible, in the absence of any special reasons to the contrary, provided it be capable of experimental verification and only in so far as it is capable of such verification. This is approximately the doctrine of pragmatism. But just here a broad question opens out before us. What are we to understand by experimental verification? The answer to that involves the whole logic of induction. Let me point out to you the different opinions which we actually find men holding today, perhaps not consistently, but thinking that they hold them, upon this subject.

In the first place, we find men who maintain that no hypothesis ought to be admitted, even as a hypothesis, any further than its truth or its falsity is *capable* of being directly perceived. This, as well as I can make out, is what was in the mind of Auguste Comte, who is generally assumed to have first formulated this maxim. Of course, this maxim of abduction supposes that, as people say, we "are to believe only what we actually see"; and there are well-known writers, and writers of no little intellectual force, who maintain that it is unscientific to make predictions,—unscientific, therefore, to expect anything. One ought to restrict one's opinions to what one actually perceives. I need hardly say that that position cannot be consistently maintained. It refutes itself; for it is *itself* an opinion relating to more than is actually in the field of momentary perception.

In the second place, there are those who hold that a theory which has sustained a number of experimental tests may be expected to sustain a number of other similar tests, and to have a general approximate truth, the justification of this being that this kind of inference must prove correct in the long run, as I explained in a previous lecture. But these logicians refuse to admit that we can ever have a right to conclude definitely that a hypothesis is *exactly* true, that is, that it should be able to sustain experimental tests in endless series; for, they urge, no hypothesis can be subjected to an endless series of tests. They are willing we should say that a theory is true, because, all our ideas being more or less vague and approximate, what we mean by saying that a theory is true can only be that it is very near true. But they will not allow us to say that anything put forth as an anticipation of experience should assert exactitude, because exactitude in experience would imply experiences in endless series, which is impossible.

In the third place, the great body of scientific men hold that it is too much to say that induction must be restricted to that for which there can be *positive* experimental evidence. They urge that the rationale of induction as it is understood by logicians of the second group, themselves, entitles us to hold a theory provided it be such that if it involve any falsity experiment must some day detect that falsity. We, therefore, have a right, they will say, to infer that something *never* will happen, provided it be of such a nature that it could not occur without being detected.

I wish to avoid in the present lecture *arguing* any such points, because the substance of all sound argumentation about pragmatism, has, as I conceive it, been already given in previous lectures, and there is no end to the forms in which it might be stated. I must, however, except from this statement the logical principles which I intend to state in tomorrow evening's lecture on multitude and continuity; and for the sake of making the relation clear between this third position and the fourth and fifth, I must anticipate a little what I shall further explain tomorrow.

What ought persons who hold this third position to say to the Achilles sophism? Or rather this is not precisely what I wish to inquire, but rather what would they be obliged to say to this, as to Achilles overtaking the tortoise, Achilles and the tortoise being geometrical points, supposing that our only knowledge was derived inductively from observations of the relative positions of Achilles and the tortoise [in] those stages of the progress that the sophism supposes, and supposing that Achilles really moves twice as fast as the tortoise. They ought to say that *if* it could not happen that Achilles in one of those stages of his progress should at length reach a certain finite distance behind the tortoise which he would be unable to

halve, *without our learning that fact*, then we should have a right to conclude that he could halve *every* distance and consequently that he could
make his distance behind the tortoise less than *all* fractions having a
power of two for the denominator. Therefore unless those logicians were to
suppose a distance less that any measurable distance, which would be contrary to their principles, they would be obliged to say that Achilles could
reduce his distance behind the tortoise to *zero*.

The reason why it would be contrary to their principles to admit any
distance less than a measurable distance, is that their way of supporting
induction implies that they differ from the logicians of the second class, in
that [this] third class [of] logicians admits that we can infer a proposition
implying an infinite multitude and therefore implying the reality of the
infinite multitude itself, while their mode of justifying induction would
exclude every infinite multitude except the lowest grade, that of the multitude of all integer numbers. Because with reference to a greater multitude
than that, it would not be true that what did not occur in a finite ordinal
place in a series could not occur anywhere within the infinite series,—
which is the only reason they admit for the inductive conclusion.

But now let us look at something else that those logicians would be
obliged to admit. Namely, suppose any regular polygon to have all its ver-
tices joined by straight radii to its centre. Then if there were any particular

finite number of sides for a regular polygon with radii so drawn, which had
the singular property that it should be impossible to bisect all the angles
by new radii equal to the others and by connecting the extremities of each
new radius to those of the two adjacent old radii to make a new polygon of
double the number of angles, if I say there were any *finite number* of sides
for which this could not be done, it may be admitted that we should be
able to find it out. The question I am asking supposes arbitrarily that they
admit that. Therefore these logicians of the third class would have to admit
that all such polygons could so have their sides doubled and that consequently there would be a polygon of an infinite multitude of sides which
could be, on their principle, nothing else than the circle. But it is easily
proved that the perimeter of that polygon, that is, the circumference of the
circle, would be incommensurable, so that an incommensurable measure

is real, and thence it easily follows that all such lengths are real or possible. But these exceed in multitude the only multitude those logicians admit. Without any geometry, the same result could be reached, supposing only that we have an indefinitely bisectable quantity. <I will mention tomorrow a way in which these logicians might conceivably be able to escape this difficulty.>

We are thus led to a fourth opinion very common among mathematicians, who generally hold that any one irrational real quantity, say of length, for example, whether algebraical or transcendental in its general expression, is just as possible and admissible as any rational quantity, but who generally reason that if the distance between two points is less than any assignable quantity, that is, less than any finite quantity, then it is nothing, at all. If that be the case, it is possible for us to conceive, with mathematical precision, a state of things in favor of whose actual reality there would seem to be no possible sound argument, however weak. For example, we can conceive that the diagonal of a square is incommensurable with its side. That is to say, if you first name any length commensurable with the side, the diagonal will differ from that by a finite quantity (and a commensurable quantity), yet however accurately we may measure the diagonal of an apparent square, there will always be a limit to our accuracy and the measure will always be commensurable. So we never could have any reason to think it otherwise. Moreover if there be, as they seem to hold, no other points on a line than such as are at distances assignable to an indefinite approximation, it will follow that if a line has an extremity, that extreme point may be conceived to be taken away, so as to leave the line without any extremity while leaving all the other points just as they were. In that case, all the points stand discrete and separate; and the line might be torn apart at any number of places without disturbing the relations of the points to one another. Each point has, on that view, its own independent existence, and there can be no merging of one into another. There is no continuity of points in the sense in which continuity implies generality.

In the fifth place it may be held that we can be justified in inferring true generality, true continuity. But I do not see in what way we ever can be justified in doing so unless we admit the cotary propositions, and in particular that such continuity is given in perception, that is, that whatever the underlying psychical process may be we seem to perceive a genuine flow of time, such that instants melt into one another without separate individuality.

It would not be necessary for me to deny a psychical theory which should make this to be illusory in such sense as there can be in saying that anything beyond all logical criticism is illusory, but I confess I should strongly suspect that such a psychological theory involved a logical inconsistency; and at best it could do nothing at all toward solving the logical question.

V.

There are two functions which we may properly require that Pragmatism should perform. Or, if not Pragmatism, whatever the true doctrine of the Logic of Abduction may be ought to do these two services.

Namely, it ought, in the first place, to give us an expeditious riddance of all ideas essentially unclear. In the second place, it ought to lend support [to], and help to render distinct, ideas essentially clear but more or less difficult of apprehension; and, in particular, it ought to take a satisfactory attitude toward the element of Thirdness.

Of these two offices of Pragmatism, there is at the present day not so crying a need of the first as there was a quarter of a century ago when I enunciated the maxim. The state of logical thought is very much improved. Thirty years ago when in consequence of my study of the logic of relations, I told philosophers that all conceptions ought to be defined, with the sole exception of the familiar concrete conceptions of everyday life, my opinion was considered in every school to be utterly incomprehensible. The doctrine then was, as it remains in nineteen out of every score of logical treatises that are appearing in these days, that there is no way of defining a term except by enumerating all its universal predicates, each of which is more abstracted and general than the term defined. So unless this process can go on endlessly, which was a doctrine little followed, the explication of a concept must stop at such ideas as Pure Being, Agency, Substance and the like which were held to be ideas so perfectly simple that no explanation whatever could be given of them. This grotesque doctrine was shattered by the logic of relations, which showed that the simplest conceptions, such as Quality, Relation, Self-consciousness could be defined and that such definitions would be of the greatest service in dealing with them. By this time although few really study the logic of relations, one seldom meets with a philosopher who continues to think the most general relations are particularly simple in any except a technical sense; and, of course, the only alternative is to regard as the simplest the practically applied notions of familiar life. We should hardly find today a man of Kirchhoff's rank in science saying that we know exactly what energy *does* but what energy *is* we do not know in the least. For the answer would be that energy being a term in a dynamical equation, if we know how to apply that equation, we thereby know what energy is, although we may suspect that there is some more fundamental law underlying the laws of motion.

In the present situation of philosophy, it is far more important that Thirdness should be adequately dealt with by our logical maxim of abduction. The urgent pertinence of the question of Thirdness, at this moment of the break up of agnostic calm, when we see that the chief difference between philosophers is in regard to the extent to which they allow elements of Thirdness a place in their theories, is too plain to be insisted upon.

I shall take it for granted that as far as *thought* goes, I have sufficiently shown that Thirdness is an element not reducible to Secondness and Firstness. But even if so much be granted, three attitudes may be taken:

1st, that Thirdness, though an element of the mental phenomenon, ought not to be admitted into a theory of the real, because it is not experimentally verifiable;

2nd, that Thirdness is experimentally verifiable, that is, is inferable by induction, although it cannot be directly perceived;

3rd, that it is directly perceived, from which the other cotary propositions can hardly be separated.

The man who takes the first position ought to admit no general law as really operative. Above all therefore he ought not to admit the law of laws, the law of the uniformity of nature. He ought to abstain from all prediction however qualified by a confession of fallibility. But that position can practically not be maintained.

The man who takes the second position will hold Thirdness to be an addition which the operation of abduction introduces over and above what its premises in any way contain, and further that this element, though not perceived in experiment, is justified *by* experiment. Then his conception of reality must be such as completely to sunder the real from perception; and the puzzle for him will be why perception should be allowed such authority in regard to what is real.

I do not think that man can consistently hold that there is room in time for an event between any two events separate in time. But even if he could he would (if he could grasp the reasoning) be forced to acknowledge that the contents of time consists of separate, independent, unchanging states, and nothing else. There would not be even a determinate order of sequence among these states. He might insist that one order of sequence was more readily grasped by us; but nothing more. Every man is fully satisfied that there is such a thing as truth, or he would not ask any question. *That* truth consists in a conformity to something *independent of his thinking it to be so*, or of any man's opinion on that subject. But for the man who holds this second opinion the only reality there could be would be conformity to the ultimate result of inquiry. But there would not be any course of inquiry possible except in the sense that it would be easier for him to interpret the phenomenon; and ultimately he would be forced to say that there was no reality at all except that he now at this instant finds a certain way of thinking easier than any other. But that violates the very idea of reality and of truth.

The man who takes the third position and accepts the cotary propositions will hold with firmest of grasps to the recognition that logical criticism is limited to what we can control. In the future we may be able to control more but we must consider what we can now control. Some elements we can control in some limited measure. But the contents of the perceptual judgment cannot be sensibly controlled now nor is there any rational hope that it ever can be. Concerning that quite uncontrolled part of the mind logical maxims have as little to do as with the growth of hair and nails. We may be dimly able to see that in part it depends on the accidents of the moment, in part to what is personal or racial, in part is common to all nicely adjusted organisms whose equilibrium has [narrow ranges] of stability, in part to whatever is composed of vast [collections] of independently variable elements, in part to whatever reacts and in part to whatever has any mode of being.[5] But the sum of it all is that our logically controlled thoughts compose a small part of the mind, the mere blossom of a vast complexus which we may call the instinctive mind, in which this man will not say that he has *faith* because that implies the conceivability of distrust, but upon which he builds as the very fact to which it is the whole business of his logic to be true.

That he will have no difficulty with Thirdness is clear enough, because he will hold that the conformity of action to general intentions is as much given in perception as is the element of action itself which cannot really be mentally torn away from such general purposiveness. There can be no doubt that he will allow hypotheses fully all the range they ought to be allowed. The only question will be whether he succeeds in excluding from hypotheses everything unclear and nonsensical. It will be asked whether he will not have a shocking leaning toward anthropomorphic conceptions. I fear I must confess that he will be inclined to see an anthropomorphic, or even a zoomorphic, if not a physiomorphic element in all our conceptions. But against unclear and nonsensical hypotheses whatever aegis there may be in pragmatism will be more essentially significant for him than for any other logician for the reason that it is in action that logical energy returns to the uncontrolled and uncriticizable parts of the mind. His maxim will be this:

The elements of every concept enter into logical thought at the gate of perception and make their exit at the gate of purposive action; and whatever cannot show its passports at both those two gates is to be arrested as unauthorized by reason.

The digestion of such thought is slow, ladies and gentlemen; but when you come in the future to reflect upon all that I have said, I am confident you will find the seven hours you have spent in listening to these ideas have not been altogether wasted.

Notes

Lecture One: Introduction

1. At this point in MS 301, Peirce substituted the following matter:

I shouldn't wonder if they were ashamed of me. What could be more humiliating than to confess that one has learned anything of a logician? But for my part I am delighted to find myself sharing the opinions of so brilliant a company. The new pragmatists seem to be distinguished for their terse, vivid and concrete style of expression together with a certain buoyancy of tone as if they were conscious of carrying about them the master key to all the secrets of metaphysics.

Every metaphysician is supposed to have some radical fault to find with every other, and I cannot find any direr fault to find with the new pragmatists than that they are *lively*. In order to be deep it is requisite to be dull.

On their side, one of the faults that I think they might find with me is that I make pragmatism to be a mere maxim of logic instead of a sublime principle of speculative philosophy.

2. *Apodosis* is, in the most conventional, contemporary sense, according to Webster, the clause expressing the conclusion or result in a conditional sentence, as distinguished from *protasis*, the clause that expresses the condition in a conditional sentence. The *Oxford English Dictionary* defines apodosis as "the concluding clause of a sentence, as contrasted with the introductory clause, or *protasis*; now usually restricted to the consequent clause in a conditional sentence as 'If thine enemy hunger, *feed him*'." It is important to remember that the "clause" which has evolved in modern definitions as the grammatical form of apodosis was understood initially as a "term" which was itself an entire proposition. Richard Whateley, whom Peirce professed to have read in one sitting at the age of twelve, discussed conditional propositions in his *Elements of Logic*, saying, "we must consider every Conditional Proposition a universal affirmative categorical Proposition, of which the Terms are entire Propositions, *viz.*, the antecedent answering to the *Subject*, and the consequent to the *Predicate*, e.g., to say "if Louis is a good king, France is likely to prosper," is equivalent to saying, "the case of Louis being a good king, is a case of France being likely to prosper." It is more useful to think of "apodosis" in this way, as a categorical proposition of a universal kind, as in Whateley. And it is more consonant with the meaning of pragmatism which Peirce engenders insofar as pragmatism is a device of logic. Peirce concluded this lecture with the claim that Logic and the other normative sciences are "positive sciences since it is by asserting positive, categorical truth that they are able to show that what they call good really is so: and the right reason, right effort, and right being of which they treat derive that character from positive categorical fact," having previously lectured that a positive science is "an inquiry which seeks for positive knowledge, that is for such

knowledge as may conveniently be expressed in a *categorical proposition*" (MS 301).

Lecture Two: Phenomenology or the Doctrine of Categories
Part A: Mathematics as a Basis of Logic
(Draft One)

1. Peirce acknowledged the insight and notational system of George Boole (1815–1864), English mathematician and logician. "Boolean algebra of logic" takes note of Boole's insight that logic and algebra are able to share their basic operations as a result of their accord with higher laws of thought. In *A History of Mathematics*, second edition (New York: John Wiley, 1991), Carl V. Boyer attributes the origin of an "algebra of logic" to Boole's 1847 work, *Mathematical Analysis of Logic*, and his 1854 work, *Investigation of the Laws of Thought*, about which Bertrand Russell, in his assertion that the greatest discovery of the nineteenth century was the nature of pure mathematics, said "pure Mathematics was discovered by Boole in a work which he called *The Laws of Thought*" (p. 579). Boyer adds:

> Boole's *Investigation of the Laws of Thought* of 1854 is a classic in the history of mathematics, for it amplified and clarified the ideas presented in 1847, establishing both formal logic and a new algebra, known as Boolean algebra, the algebra of sets, or the algebra of logic. Boole used the letters $x, y, z, \ldots$ to represent objects of a subset of things—numbers, points, ideas, or other entities—selected from a universal set or universe of discourse, the totality of which he designated by the symbol or "number" 1. . . . The symbol or number 0 Boole took to indicate the empty set, containing no element of the universal set, what now is known as the null set. The sign $+$ between two letters or symbols, as $x + y$, he took to be the union of the subsets x and y, that is, the set made up of all the elements in x or y (or both). The multiplication sign X represented the intersection of sets, so that x X y means the elements or objects that are in the subset x and also in the subset y. . . . The sign $=$ represents the relationship of identity. . . . Boole showed that his algebra provided an easy algorithm for syllogistic reasoning (pp. 579–80).

In addition, Peirce's "dichotomic" elements, *bonum* and *malum*, roughly correspond to Boole's notion of a class (represented by a variable) and its complement (represented by the negation of that variable).

2. Leonhard Euler (1707–1783) was a Swiss mathematician and physicist.

3. Peirce wrote a note to himself on the MS:

> I value Schröder's work highly and he was a highly sympathetic man whom it was impossible to know and not to like even more than the great merit of his work justified. But he was too mathematical, not enough of the logician in him. The most shocking thing in his first volume is a fallacy. His mode of presentation rests on a mistake and his second vol-

ume which defends it and is largely retracted in his third is one big blunder. There are very fine things in his third volume and his posthumous volume I hope will contain still better. He was a growing man.

Ernst Schröder (1841–1902) was a German mathematician and logician. Peirce was probably referring to *Operationskreis des Logikkalkuls* (Leipzig, 1877) as the first volume, *Vorlesungen über die Algebra der Logic* (Leipzig, 1890–1905) as the second volume and part of the "posthumous volume." A third volume was published entirely posthumously, *Abriss der Algebra der Logik* (Berlin, 1909–1910).

4. Arthur Cayley (1821–1895) was a British mathematician who developed a theory of invariants and covariants; worked on matrices and analytical geometry. In 1881, while Peirce was also at the Johns Hopkins University, Cayley was invited to give a set of lectures on Abelian and theta functions.

5. James Joseph Sylvester was a British mathematician. It was probably at Johns Hopkins University that Peirce met Sylvester, who taught there from 1876. Peirce was there when Sylvester gave his lectures in 1881. For an account of the algebra of matrices developed by Sylvester and Cayley, see Boyer, *A History of Mathematics*, second edition, pp. 587–91.

6. T. Muir, *The Theory of Determinants in the Historical Order of Development*, New York: Dover, 1960 (4 vols. in 2; paperback edition of London, 1906–1930 editions). Peirce had a still earlier edition.

7. Augustus DeMorgan (1806–1871) was a British mathematician. Later works which Peirce would have been familiar with are *Arithmetical Books* (London, 1847), *Cambridge Philosophical Transactions* (vols. 8–10, 1847–1863) and *Syllabus of a Proposed System of Logic* (London, 1860). The "exaggerated" importance Peirce claims to have attributed to DeMorgan in the development of the logic of relatives is due to a complex of reasons. First, DeMorgan held that the symbols of algebraic operation were empty of actual referents but that their value as symbols and their laws of combination were significant. This discovery was a result of finding that the rules of operation of the real number system were identical to those of the complex number system and the inference that rules of operation apply equally to any system whatsoever. As a matter of fact, he could only derive two, the "single algebra" and the "double algebra" described in his 1830 work, *Trigonometry and Double Algebra*. Peirce was able to prepare the work for over a hundred algebras by 1881, which was published in a posthumous article by Benjamin Peirce, with Charles Peirce's notes and supplementary text. It is probably this article to which Peirce referred in the preceding text of the lecture MS. The tag "exaggeration" may be due to Peirce giving more significance to relations or functions in DeMorgan's logic of algebra than did DeMorgan himself. It was Peirce, not DeMorgan, who initially worked out specific mathematical applications of what is only logically implied in DeMorgan.

8. Peirce paraphrases the proposition of G. W. F. Hegel, that *"pure being* and *pure nothingness* are, therefore, the same." See *Hegel's Science of Logic*, translated by A. V. Miller, foreword by J. N. Findlay (New York: Humanities Press, 1969), p. 82.

Lecture Two: Phenomenology or the Doctrine of Categories
Part A: Mathematics as a Basis of Logic
(Draft Two)

1. Peirce wrote on this draft:

Rejected. No time for this. And it would need two if not three lectures.

2. Augustin Louis Cauchy (1789–1857) was a French mathematician and physicist. Cauchy helped establish the wave theory of light. Works Peirce would have been familiar with are: *Oeuvres Complètes*, 1 ser., 12 vols.; 2 ser., 10 vols. (Paris, 1882–1903), *Histoire des Sciences Mathématiques et Physiques* (Paris, 1883–1888).

3. John Stuart Mill (1806–1873), *System of Logic*, 2 vols. (1843; 8th ed. 1872).

4. Richard Dedekind (1831–1916) was a German mathematician. Peirce refers to *Essays on the Theory of Numbers*, which may be found in two parts: I. *Continuity and irrational numbers*; II. *The nature and meaning of numbers*, translated by Wooster Woodruff Beman (New York: Dover Publications, 1963).

5. An instance of an "auditory diagram" is an old-fashioned radio play, with sound effects. The voices, of course, formally express a variety of concepts in the semantics of whatever language the play was written. However, the sounds, for example, of a "gong," a "rushing stream," or a "crackling fire" might very well express an informal background or foreground which would considerably modify the meaning of the more formally semanticized expressions. The excellence of the genre of radio plays as instances of "auditory diagrams" may be further illustrated by the evolution of the semantics of sound effects. Like the well-known "body English" for lying (averted eyes) or embarrassment (blushing), sound effects became formalized in radio plays, so that a stock sound would inevitably be used to express a stock idea or effect; for example, the "creaking door" in *Suspense Theater* meant "mystery," "ghosts," "crime," or some combination thereof. Peirce's metaphor allows philosophers to be precise (diagrammatic) in their representations, without having to be entirely literal. Further examples may be derived from speech in general, and particularly philosophical speech. Socratic dialectic in *Republic* or arguments put forward in *Federalist Papers* are of the nature of "auditory" diagrams, the "deductions" contained therein contextualized by a loose kind of agreement as to what the terms mean and forever afterward subject to interpretation. The fact that this "speech" is written down causes it to be "visual" but not a visual *diagram* since the transformation which occurs with the change in medium does nothing to elucidate additionally any of the relations contained in the speech. (I am grateful to Kenneth L. Ketner, who originated the general idea that radio plays are auditory diagrams.)—An illustration of a visual diagram, in contrast, is the solution to the problem, "Given that triangle ABC has sides a = 6 feet and b = 4 feet and c = 5.5 feet, find the area of ABC using Heron's Formula, $K = \sqrt{s(s-a)(s-b)(s-c)}$ where s = ½(a + b + c)."—The primary difference between "visual" and "auditory" diagrams is that, while visual diagrams of arguments are exhaustive representations of the in-

ferences possible from a premiss set, "auditory" diagrams are not exhaustive representations and stand in need of further diagrammatic representations to achieve their full effect. The philosopher's preference for auditory diagrams is underscored by Peirce's distinction between "philosophers" who make use of auditory diagrams for their "deductions" and those who perform "necessary reasoning." His distinction rests on a further distinction between nonmathematical reasoning and mathematical reasoning, a distinction later developed in these lectures as being between abduction, induction and deduction. More specifically, both abductive and inductive inferences contain *more* in their conclusions than in their premisses, insofar as their conclusions are synthetic. Both abductive and inductive inferences may be said to contain *less* in their conclusions than in their premisses, insofar as the premisses of an abduction or induction may lead to several equally viable conclusions, only one of which will be identified in any given abductive or inductive inference. Contrarily, correctly performed deductive inferences contain exactly equivalent premisses and analytic conclusions, a situation that adequately can be diagrammed visually by several means such as Venn diagrams, natural deduction, or Peirce's own more than adequate graphing systems.

6. See Charles S. Peirce, "Description of a Notation for the Logic of Relatives, Resulting from an Amplification of the Conceptions of Boole's Calculus of Logic," *Memoirs of the American Academy of Arts and Sciences*, new series 9, 317–78 (reprinted by Welch, Bigelow, and Company, Cambridge, Mass., 1870), in the microfiche edition, *Charles Sanders Peirce: Complete Published Works, including Selected Secondary Materials*, Johnson Associates, 1977, as catalogued in *Peirce, A Comprehensive Bibliography*, second edition, revised, edited by Kenneth Laine Ketner (Philosophy Documentation Center, Bowling Green State University, Bowling Green, Ohio, 1986) P00052: fiches 7, 8.

Lecture Two: Phenomenology or the Doctrine of Categories
Part B: On Phenomenology
(Draft One)

1. Peirce added the note to the draft, MS 304, "*To be rewritten and compressed.*"

2. Peirce deleted this passage from MS 304:

If by direct perception, does he perceive that it is he himself who springs a surprise upon himself? The fact that this sounds absurd to us is sufficient to show that that is not what is perceived. But if it is an inference, how could the theory of surprise ever originate? What materials were there for building such a conception, no instance of any surprise being known?

3. Peirce deleted this passage from MS 304:

Owing to the necessity of bringing my treatment of pragmatism into six lectures, I shall not stop to prove that there is a third category, quite irreducible to the first two, which when I designate it by its most genuine form I call the category of *representation* or *thought* and when I designate it by the lowest form in which it appears I call it the category of *Thirdness* or *mediation*.

Lecture Two: Phenomenology or the Doctrine of Categories
Part B: On Phenomenology
(Draft Two)

1. Peirce inserted this note on his title page of MS 305:

This won't do it will have to be *rewritten*.

2. Peirce put a blank in the manuscript here.

3. Peirce deleted this passage from this location in the manuscript:

I will only say that in order to refute that first objection it is by no means necessary to oppose any psychological theory that the adversaries of the category may find reason to entertain. Let it be true, if you will, that the sense of effort and resistance is a sort of instinctive hypothesis which arises within us in the attempt to comprehend certain feelings connected with contractions of the muscles.

4. Peirce crossed out these sentences from this location in the manuscript:

You may depend upon it that I am not in the habit of adopting logical doctrines without the most searching and impartial criticism. I would not have anybody accept any doctrine of logic because I hold to it. But I do say that when I have given my very closest examination to a logical question and have become entirely confident as to what the true answer to it is, a mere pooh-poohing of my opinion on the part of a person who has never studied the question in a minute and thorough manner, ought not to be sufficient.

Lecture Two: Phenomenology or the Doctrine of Categories
Part B: On Phenomenology, or the Categories
(Draft Three)

1. Section III follows what would have been the compression of the previous draft(s) concerning section I, on the category of Firstness, and section II, on the category of Secondness. Lectures three and four, given in the two succeeding weeks, may be thought of as products of this compression, at least in part, since their topic is the categories. Peirce noted on the cover page of the notebook on which this draft was written:

I begin by making a first draught of what I intend to say about the third category; and what I say of the first two will have to be compressed into so much of the hour as this leaves unoccupied.

'Tis true 'tis pity
And pity 'tis 'tis true.

2. Peirce left the citation from Matthew 13:51 incomplete.

Lecture Three: The Categories Defended

1. Peirce's earlier draft of lecture three, MS 307, includes these sentences:

Whether or not this goes on *ad infinitum* is one of an infinite multitude of questions about the categories that I am not yet prepared to answer. There is ample field for fresh workers here.

2. Peirce's earlier draft, MS 307, gives an alternate formulation for the passage above:

Category the Third evidently must have two degenerate forms, from which the category is not absent but is shaded. For to begin with, the Thirdness in the phenomenon may be such that it can be regarded as arising from a combination of Secondnesses. We have just had an example of this, where one member of a dichotomy is itself bisected, giving therefore a threefold division. In pure Secondness, the reacting objects are Singulars and, as such, are Individuals, not capable of subdivision. Consequently, the idea of *subdivision* is an idea involving Thirdness. But this Thirdness is of a degenerate kind because it can be conceived as a mere complication of Secondnesses.

3. An alternate draft of the above passage, in MS 307, states:

But obviously there is a still lower degree of degeneracy in which the Thirdness may be regarded as a mere way of considering a Quality of Feeling. Thus, some of the philosophers of the past were fond of discoursing upon a *pure* self-consciousness, which was supposed to present no content but self and of course exclusively to that same self. It obviously could be nothing but a Quality of Feeling. A Feeling that somehow involves a dark instinct of being the germ of a thought. A feeling that is three persons in one.

4. The following sentence is included in the earlier draft, MS 307:

This gives an idea of the second degree of degenerate Thirdness.

5. Peirce makes explicit this difference in his earlier draft, MS 307:

> Those of you who have read Prof. Royce's *Supplementary Essay* will have remarked that he avoids this result, which does not suit his philosophy, by not allowing his map to be continuous. But to exclude continuity is to exclude what is best and most living in Hegel.

Peirce's insistence upon the continuity of the points in the map is in distinction from Royce, who states in his "Supplementary Essay," "We should now, indeed, have to suppose the space occupied by our perfect map to be infinitely divisible, even if not a *continuum*." Royce clarifies his comment in a note, stating:

> In the older discussions of continuity, this concept was very generally confounded with that of infinite divisibility. The confusion is no longer made by mathematicians. Continuity implies infinite divisibility. The converse does not hold true. (p. 504, *The World and the Individual*, Dover Publications, New York, 1959)

The continuity of the point on the map which is analogous to pure self-consciousness to the rest of the points which, in each successive mapping, is gained by interpreting the map to the map, rests upon the continuous relationship of each self-representation to the next in a smooth unbroken line. In the mapping illustration, each subset is necessarily continuous with the set from which it is derived, unlike infinite sets in which the subsets derived from the set are not *necessarily* continuous with the infinite set. The illustration of the mapping of a country is not merely made in order to show how a system can be infinite, but to express the manner in which *self-representational* systems are infinite. Royce's error lies in neglecting the *aspect* under which maps of maps are in a one-to-one correspondence while focusing *exclusively* upon the definition of an "infinite" set or system, that an infinite set is one which can be put in a one-to-one correspondence with a proper subset of itself. If Royce (or Peirce) had confined himself to a discussion of the set of natural numbers only, Royce's disclaimer of its continuity would hold. However, the set of natural numbers is not purported to be self-representational, as maps are and as self-consciousness is. And so an infinite set such as the natural numbers can be infinitely divisible without the subsets being continuous with the set. Maps of the kind described by Royce and Peirce, and by analogy, a "map" of self-consciousness are continuous *while* infinitely divisible.

6. The text below, whose content was omitted from the final draft of lecture three, appeared in the earlier draft, MS 307:

> There would be no question that Category the Second is an irreducible conception were it not for the deplorable condition of the science of logic. This is illustrated by the fact that so flippant and wildly theorizing [a]

work as Prantl's *Geschichte der Logik* should be accepted, as it generally
is, even among learned men, as a marvel of patient research. It is true
that one or two chapters of it are relatively well done. The account of
Aristotle's logic, though not good upon any high standard of completeness or of thorough comprehension, is nevertheless the best account of
its subject that we have. But Prantl, to begin with, does not himself understand logic, meaning by logic the science of which he . . . professes to
give an account; and yet with the shallowest ideas, he is so puffed up with
his own views that he disdains to take the trouble to penetrate their
meaning. The crude expressions of contempt in which he continually in-
dulges toward great thinkers ought to put readers on their guard against
him. In the next place he belongs to that too well-known class of German
critics who get bitten with theories deduced from general conceptions,
and who fall in love with these theories because they are their own off-
spring and treat them as absolute certainties although the complete refutation of them is near at hand. You will understand, of course, that I do
not say these things without having read all the chief contributions to the
questions on both sides and without having subjected them to careful
study and criticism. Prantl's opinions about the Megarian philosophers,
about what he calls the Byzantine logic, about the Latin medieval logic,
about the *Parva Logicalia*, are wild theories, utterly untenable, and in
several cases easily refuted by an easy examination of the manuscripts.
Moreover, it is not a history of logic but mostly of the most trivial parts of
logic. But I shall be asked whether I do not think his reading marvelously
extensive. No, I do not. He had the Munich library at his hand. He had
only to look into the books, and for the most part he has done little more
than merely to look into them. He really often has no idea of what the
real substance of the books is; and nothing is more common than to find
in his notes passages copied out of one book which are nothing but tex-
tual copies of celebrated passages in much older works. I do not deny that
the book is useful, because the rest of us haven't access to such a library;
but I do not consider it a work of respectable erudition. There is no need
of mincing words because he himself not only refers most disrespectfully
to such solid students of medieval writings as Charles Thurnot, Hauréau
and others, but frequently descends to what in English we should call the
language of Billingsgate in characterizing ancient opinions which he may
or may not be aware are identical with those held today by analysts of
logical forms whose studies [are] so much more exact than his that they
are not to be named in the same day.

Nevertheless, bad as Prantl's history is, it is the best we have, and
any person who reads it critically, as every book ought to be read, will
easily be able to see that the ancient students of logic [viz.] Democritus,
Plato, Aristotle, Epicurus, Philoponus, even Chrysippus, were thinkers of
the highest order, and that St. Augustine, Abelard, Aquinas, Duns Scotus,
Ockham, Paulus Venetus, even Laurentius Valla were logicians of the
most painstaking and subtle types. But when the revival of learning came,

the finest minds had their attention turned in quite another direction, and modern mathematics and modern physics drew away still more. The result of all this has been that during the centuries that have elapsed since the appearance of the *De Revolutionibus*, and remember, if you please, that the work of Copernicus was the fruit of the scientific nourishment that he had imbibed in Italy in his youth,—throughout these ages, the chairs of Logic in the Universities have been turned over to a class of men, of whom we should be speaking far too euphemistically if we were to say that they in no wise represented the Intellectual Level of their age. No, no; let us speak the plain truth. Modern logicians as a class have been distinctly puerile minds, the kind of minds that never mature, and yet never have the *élan* and originality of youth. Just cast your eyes over the pages of a dozen average treatises, dismissing all preconceived estimates of their authors, and see if that is not the impression you derive from them. Why, in the majority of them, the greatest contribution to reasoning that has been generally applied during these centuries,—the Calculus of Probabilities—is almost entirely ignored. Lambert was so accurate a reasoner that he all but understood the outline of the Non-Euclidean Geometry; and yet what a wretched disappointment his *Genus Organon* is!

Another effect has been that when great ideas have been born into the world they have not been properly cared for and developed. I should have no hesitation in saying that, excluding the mathematicians, Herbart was the greatest logical genius that nineteenth–century Germany produced. But the state of science and of thought of his time forbade the proper development of his ideas, and look at what mountains of platitude his followers have inflicted upon the world! If it were only the common run of logics that were affected by this state of things, it would not much matter; for if only one *per cent* of works on the subject were what they should be, we should still be in possession of a splendid and extensive literature. But unfortunately the general standard has been so terribly lowered that even the treatises written by men of real ability have been but half thought out things. *Arnauld*, for example, was a thinker of considerable force; and yet *L'art de penser*, or the Port Royal Logic, is a shameful exhibit of what the two and a half centuries of man's greatest achievements could consider as a good account of how to think. You may retort that the past three centuries seem to have got on nicely without the aid of logic. Yes, I reply, they have, because there is one thing even more vital to science than intelligent methods; and that is, the sincere desire to find out the truth, whatever it may be; and *that* those centuries have been blessed with. But according to such estimate,—not exactly mere guess-work, although rough enough, no doubt,—as I have been able to form, if logic during those centuries had been studied with half the *zeal* and *genius* that has been bestowed upon mathematics, the twentieth century might have opened with the special sciences generally,— particularly such vitally important sciences as molecular physics, chemistry, physiology, psychology, linguistics, and ancient historical criticism,—in a decidedly more advanced condition than there is much promise that they will have reached at the [?] of 1950. I shouldn't say that human lives were the most precious things in the world; but after all they have their value; and only think how many lives might thus have been saved. We can mention individuals who might probably have done more work; say Abel, Steiner, Gaulois, Sadi Carnot. Think of the labor of a generation of Germany being allowed to flow off into Hegelianism! Think of the extravagant admiration that half of a generation of English,—decidedly the best average reasoners of any modern people,—bestowed on that silly thing, Hamilton's *New Analytic*. Look through Vaihinger's commentary to see what an army of students have been entrapped by Kant's view of the relations between his Analytic and Synthetic Judgments,—a view that a study of the logic of relatives would at once have exploded.

Had logic not been sunk since the time of Copernicus into a condition of semi-idiocy, the Logic of Relatives would by this time have been pursued for three centuries by hundreds of students among whom there would have been no small number who in this direction or in that would have surpassed in ability any of the poor handful of students who have been at work upon it for the last generation or so. And let me tell you that this study would have completely revolutionized men's most general notions about logic,—the very ideas that are today current in the marketplace and on the boulevards. One of the early results of such wide study of the logic of relatives must have been to cause the idea of *reaction* to be solidly fixed in the minds of all men as an irreducible category of *Thought*,—whatever place might have been accorded to it in metaphysics as a cosmical category. This I venture to say, notwithstanding that the lamented Schröder did not seem to see it so. Schröder followed Sigwart in his most fundamental ideas of logic.

7. Christoph Sigwart (1830–1904) was a German philosopher and logician, whose *Logik* was published in two volumes in 1873 and 1878, with a biography by Heinrich Maier (5th ed., Tübingen, 1924).

8. Peirce deleted this sentence:

But I could not sincerely go so far as to say that his accuracy of thought is sufficient to prevent his going wrong upon almost every question of logic.

9. Alfred Bray Kempe, "A Memoir on the Theory of Mathematical Forms," *Philosophical Transactions of the Royal Society*, vol. 177, pp. 1–70 (1886).

Lecture Four: The Seven Systems of Metaphysics

1. The line marks in the diagram indicate which of the categories each system fully admits: one vertical line for Firstness, two for Secondness, and three for Thirdness.

2. Peirce deleted this: Sensualism, and the like.

3. Two versions of a note on multitudes were included in this draft (MS 309) but not delivered in the lecture. It is likely that Peirce was interested in expanding these texts. He wrote these lines in a draft of a letter to William James, dated several days after the date this lecture was delivered:

> In my Lowell lectures [given November 23–December 17, 1903] I want to deal with the supposed paradox of Achilles and the Tortoise. But the difficulty I meet with is that I cannot, for the life of me, see where the paradox, or difficulty, or contradiction, is supposed to lie. I think you could help me . . . .

Both versions of the note in MS 309 follow:

> Version 1: We now recognize that there is no particular difficulty in reasoning with mathematical accuracy about infinity. It is merely that a certain awkwardness has to be conquered in doing so. We all admit that there is no logical impossibility in the idea of a collection of discrete objects, say three. A collection is said to be enumerable if and only if every object of it is in any relation, r, to some object of it to which no other object of it is in this same relation, r, then to every object of the collection some one object of the collection (and only one) stands in the relation, r.

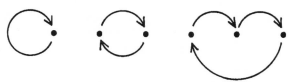

Now to any enumerable collection, it is logically possible that an object should be added. This will make it a *larger* collection, or a collection of *greater multitude* than before, by which we mean that, calling the original collection the collection of As, and the collection of As with one additional singular the collection of Bs, then it is impossible that there should be any relation, ζ, such that every B stands in the relation ζ to an A to which no other B stands in that relation.

That is capable of very easy demonstration:

$$
\begin{array}{cccccccc}
B & B & B & B & B & B & B & B \\
\bullet \leftarrow & \bullet \leftarrow & \bullet \leftarrow & \bullet \leftarrow & \bullet \leftarrow & \bullet \leftarrow & \bullet \leftarrow & \bullet \\
A & A & A & A & A & A & A &
\end{array}
$$

Thus, for every enumerable multitude there is an enumerable multitude greater than it by one. But to admit this is to admit that there is an endless series of multitudes, which is a collection of the grade of multitude called denumeral.

It is easily demonstrated that a collection of denumeral multitude is not rendered larger by the addition to it of a collection of any multitude not larger than itself.

Let us define the *product* of two multitudes as the multitude of that collection whose units are all the possible pairs of units of the two collections. Thus, 2×3 is the multitude of this collection:

The product of the denumeral multitude by any multitude not greater than itself is easily shown to be that same denumeral multitude.

Let us define M^N where M and N are multitudes as the multitude of relations in which every unit of a collection of multitude N can be related to one and one only unit of a collection of multitude M, all these relations being different in respect to the multitude M. Thus 3^2 is the multitude of this collection:

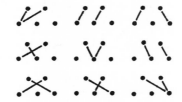

while 2^3 is the multitude of this collection:

A great variety of theorems can now be proved; but the only one which particularly concerns us is one I demonstrated in Vol. VII of the *Monist*.

It is that, whatever multitude x may be, $2^x > x$. To prove this, I have to prove, first, that there will be a collection of which the multitude is 2^x and, second, that there is no relation ζ such that if the Ys be a collection of multitude 2^x and the Xs be a collection of multitude x, then every Y is in the relation ζ to some X to which no other Y is in that relation.

First, since x is a multitude there is a collection of which the multitude is x. Call it the collection of Xs. Then there will be a collection of all possible collections of Xs.

Let *inclusion* and *exclusion* be taken as two objects forming a pair.

Then the different possible ways in which every X can be related either to inclusion or to exclusion but not to both are the different possible collections of Xs that might include some Xs and exclude all the rest. The multitude of that collection of all possible collections of Xs will by the definition be 2^x. Call these possible collections of Xs the Ys.

It only remains then to prove that whatever relation ζ may be, some Y does not stand in the relation ζ to any X to which no other Y stands in this relation. In order to prove that ζ being supposed to be determined, I will describe a Y which does not stand in the relation ζ to any X to which no other Y stands in that relation. For the purposes of that description, I will divide the Xs into four classes, one or more of which may be non-existent.

Class 1 consists of all Xs to which no Y stands in relation ζ.

Class 2 consists of all Xs to each of which more than one Y stand in relation ζ.

Classes 3 and 4 embrace all the Xs to each of which a single Y stands in the relation ζ, Class 3 containing every X that is not a member of that sole Y (or collection of Xs) which is in the relation ζ to it.

Class 4 containing every X that is a member of the sole Y which stands in the relation ζ to it.

Now the Y (or collection of Xs) which I am to describe and of which I say that it does not stand in the relation ζ to any X to which no other Y stands in that relation may contain or exclude any Xs of the first two classes. That will be a matter of indifference. But it will include every X of the third class and will exclude every X of the fourth class. This describes a possible collection of Xs, which is therefore one of the Ys. Call it Y. But this Y stands in the relation ζ to no X to which no other Y stands in this relation. For if it does let that X (or one of them if there be more than one) be called Ξ. Then Ξ cannot be an X of Class 1; for Y is ζ to Ξ while no Y is ζ to any X of Class 1.

Nor can Ξ belong to Class 2; for to Ξ only one Y, namely Y, stands in the relation ζ, while to every X of Class 2 two or more Ys stand in that relation.

Nor can Ξ belong to Class 3, for no X of Class 3 is a member of that Y, or collection of Xs, which is in the relation ζ to it. Therefore if Ξ were a member of Class 3, Y, which is supposed to be ζ to it, could not include it as a member, while by definition Y does include every X of Class 3.

Nor can Ξ belong to Class 4, for every X of Class 4 is included as a member in that Y which stands in the relation ζ to it, so that Ξ would be a member of Class 4 included in Y, while on the contrary Y by the definition of it excludes every X that is a member of Class 4.

There is therefore no kind of X to which Y can be the only Y standing in the relation ζ.

Version 2: All philosophers must in future study the mathematico-logical doctrine of multitude. We now have no difficulty in reasoning with mathematical accuracy about infinity. I regret that I cannot include it in these lectures, but I should be happy, if any of you could find time for them, to give two or three lectures on that subject. However, what I have now to say will require no more understanding of the subject than is requisite to solve the little *quibble* of Achilles and the tortoise. That I may presume you see through clearly.

Let us consider for example the spiral whose equation is

$$\theta = 1/\{\log (P-r) - \log (r-Q)\}.$$

It is obvious that the real values of θ will be those for which the value of r is less than P and greater than Q. Suppose we write $r = \rho P + (1-\rho)Q$ (where ρ varies from 0 to 1)

$$P-r = (1-\rho) (P-Q) \quad \log (P-r) = \log (1-\rho) + \log (P-Q)$$
$$r-Q = \rho (P-Q) \qquad \log (r-Q) = \log \rho \ [+] \log (P-Q)$$
$$\log (P-r) - \log (r-Q) = \log (1-\rho) - \log \rho = \log (1/\rho - 1)$$

The spiral will start outwards and wind round an endless series of times asymptotic to a circle of radius $(P+Q)/2$ which it is within and then leaving the circle will depart from [it] still winding outwards and finally stop again.

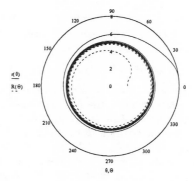

Surely nobody who has ever considered Achilles and the tortoise can imagine any difficulty in supposing that after having made an endless succession of turns inside the circle it goes on outside the circle.

Now let the increasing value of r represent the variable of time.

Let each revolution round the origin represent some kind of operation, those within the circle $r = (P+Q)/2$ to be operations of thought following logically upon one another, those exterior to the circle representing operations of matter under mechanical laws.

The only difficulty is to imagine an endless series of operations taking place in a finite time. But that is no more than happens to Achilles and the tortoise.

Here then *thought* directly influences nothing but thought and *mat-*

ter is directly acted upon only by matter and yet mind is represented as acting upon matter without any *tertium quid* or if we had supposed that the flow of time was in the direction of the shortening radius vector, it would be matter that acted on mind.

This shows that the supposition that thought acts directly only on thought and matter directly only on matter does not in the least interfere with the mutual action of matter and thought. Only it is requisite to suppose that in speaking of matter acting on matter and mind on mind we have adopted a mode of analysis of the phenomenon which requires us to suppose an infinite series, just as in Achilles and the Tortoise.

Perhaps, I shall not confuse the subject too much if I suggest that if the atoms of ordinary matter are vortices in a medium, and if that medium is composed of atoms each of which is a vortex in another medium and so on *ad infinitum*, then if energy is transformed from one to another and the increasing velocity is such as the relative velocities of sound and light would suggest the whole infinite series might well be run through in a fraction of a second.

That no doubt is a wild hypothesis enough. But perhaps it may help to show that there is no contradiction in the idea of symbols influencing *blind reactions* and the reverse.

While Peirce intended to illustrate that the paradox of Achilles and the tortoise is solved through a mathematical analogy of the spiral which crosses over the perimeter of the circle, his equation:

$$\theta = 1/\{\log (P-r) - \log (r-Q)\}$$

does not, in fact, describe such a spiral. Cast in terms of r, as: $r = (P + Qe^{1/\theta}) / (1 + e^{1/\theta})$, where θ is the angle formed by the counter-clockwise motion of the spiral from a distance P to the center of the asymptotic circle, the above equation describes a spiral whose radius *never exceeds* the radius of the asymptotic circle, and which never crosses over the perimeter of the circle. Reversing the values of P and Q in the same equation yields the graph of a spiral asymptotic to a circle outside of which it begins, but which correspondingly has a radius which is *never less than* the radius of this circle. Neither equation describes a spiral which crosses over the circle. I am grateful to my colleague, Dr. Gabriel Lugo, for his help in illuminating this problem.

4. Peirce indicated that he intended to omit this section from his lecture:

The Physicist prides himself on being a Specialist. He would not have it supposed that he busies himself with a *Weltanschauung*, not even a general conception of the physical universe. He is experimenting upon a certain phenomenon and confines himself to making out the relation of that phenomenon to phenomena that are well known. The consequence of this is that when time comes to enunciate any very general principle,—such as that of the Conservation of Energy,—you find there are a dozen physicists who have been long convinced of it, but probably thought it derogatory to say so,—or their Academy or Poggendorf refused to publish their memoir,—and very likely it will turn out that the earliest discoverable enunciation of it belonged to some obscure person outside the ranks of the professional physicists. That is probably less true today than it was fifty years ago. At any rate, it certainly ought to be the duty of some class of physicists to study the general question.

What has led me to this remark is the phenomenon of right and left. It is only when a third dimension enters into the phenomenon,—as in the case of a screw,—that there is any difference of right and left.

As for Hertz's hypothesis of Mechanics, coming from such a man it is certainly my duty to examine it thoroughly. But I have to confess that hitherto I have not found the energy to do more than glance at it. He wishes to get rid of *accelerations* by supposing that in some occult way particles are subject to *absolute constraints*,—as if they slid along through rigid tubes. I can see no reason for that hypothesis except a desire to suppress Thirdness, which appears to me to be evidently impossible. He will only suppress it in one place to find it emerging at another place.

I have looked more closely into Poincaré's views of the logic of physics and in my opinion Boltzmann has the best of the argument. Only Boltzmann is not a logician and the question is a question of logic. Poincaré would have us write down the equations of hydrodynamics and stop there. This I declare to be contrary to demonstrated principles of logic. It is an error analogous to that of *agnosticism*. It is a species of agnosticism,—a recommendation that a certain line of inquiry be entirely abandoned. If reason could be proved to be at war with itself, it would no doubt be well enough to give up reasoning altogether, and simply accept what opinions suit our fancy or convenience, or seem likely to advance our interests,—a method which may be said to be the prevalent one in regard to philosophy, the world over. But it is absolutely impossible that reason ever should be proved to be at war with itself. Such a thing cannot be imagined, for a distinction would very shortly [be] drawn. The argument would be an attempt to dam up an unceasing flow. The flood would be arrested for a time, but the head of water behind it would rise higher and higher—and finally the right distinction would allow it to flow on at first in a mighty burst and ultimately with its former quiet. Let me recommend this Logical Maxim to you: *Never allow yourself to think that any definite problem is incapable of being solved to any assignable degree of perfection.*

The likelihood is that it will be solved long before you could have dreamed it possible. Think of Auguste Comte who when asked to name any thing that could never be found out instanced the chemical composition of the fixed stars; and almost before his book became known to the world at large, the first steps had been taken in spectral analysis. But you must not suppose that the maxim has no more solid basis than historical induction. It rests on the consideration of the nature of reasoning. When I speak of reasoning I conceive experimentation to be a part of it. But it is sufficient to say that my maxim is a special case of the general maxim, *Never say die*—which is an ethical principle of the most fundamental character.

5. Peirce intended to omit these lines from his spoken presentation:

. . . just as this distinction of Righteousness and Wickedness amounts, in the last analysis, to nothing but a particular application of the most general distinction of Esthetic Goodness and Badness. To say this is not to pronounce for hedonism; for the hedonist, on the contrary, instead of admitting that Goodness and Badness is founded on Qualities of Feeling in their multitudinous variety, admits only one—discomfort and its absence; and to admit but one quality of feeling is at bottom not to admit any Quality at all. The Hedonist makes the mistake of supposing Gratification to be a mere Quality of Feeling; but the truth is that gratification is at bottom an affair of reaction having a quality of feeling dependent on it just as all sorts of conscious operations have their indescribable feelings. Since therefore the Hedonist bases Morality on Gratification alone, he bases it on that which is really and principally Reaction and not on Quality of Feeling, the inseparable nature of which it is to be multitudinous.

6. Peirce deleted the following passage here:

There was a certain great painter who happens to be out of fashion today, especially in this longitude,—so I will not mention his name, which is sacred to me, to be exposed to your ribaldry. But I will only say that a man more absolutely free from all affectation, charlatanry, or *réclame* never walked this earth. I was on intimate terms with him. His easel was in front of a great curtain. One day he had begun a new picture and I observed that he had let down another curtain of a different color from the one I was familiar with. I asked him why; and he explained to me that he always saw the picture he was about to paint on the curtain by the side of the easel and for the picture now in hand the new background suited him better. I myself am so utterly destitute of any such hallucinatory imagination that I was astonished. But I know very well that he was entertaining no idea of selling any pictures at that time; and it would have been wildly absurd to suppose that he was talking to me for effect.

For years I used to frequent artists a good deal; and his is not the only case.

7. Peirce deleted the following passage here:

I think I have been present at such a *séance*, but my companion was requested to retire as a sceptic and I chose to accompany him although I seemed to be decidedly a *persona grata* until I confessed myself to be at least as sceptical as he.

8. Peirce indicated that he planned to omit this section from his lecture:

I answer that slight differences there may be, but the books tell of a man blind from birth who remarked that he imagined that *red* was something like the *blare* of a trumpet. He had collected that notion from hearing ordinary people converse together about colors and, since I was not born to be one of those whom he had heard converse, the fact that I can see a certain analogy shows me not only that my feeling of redness is something like the feelings of the persons whom he had heard talk, but also that his feeling of a trumpet's blare was very much like mine. I am confident that a bull and I feel much alike at the sight of a red rag. As for the senses of my dog, I must confess that they seem very unlike my own, but when I reflect to how small a degree he thinks of visual images, and of how *smells* play a part in his thoughts and imaginations analogous to the part played by *sights* in mine, I cease to be surprised that the perfume of roses or of orange flowers does not attract his attention at all and that the effluvia that interest him so much, when at all perceptible to me, are simply unpleasant. He does not think of smells as sources of pleasure and disgust but as sources of information, just as I do not think of blue as a nauseating color, nor of red as a maddening one. I know very well that my dog's musical feelings are quite similar to mine though they agitate him more than they do me. He has the same emotions of affection as I, though they are far more moving in his case. You would never persuade me that my horse and I do not sympathize, or that the canary bird that takes such delight in joking with me does not feel with me and I with him; and this instinctive confidence of mine that it is so, is to my mind evidence that it really is so. My metaphysical friend who asks whether we can ever enter into one another's feelings,—and one particular sceptic whom I have in mind is a most exceptionally sympathetic person, whose doubts are born of her intense interest in her friends,—might just as well ask me whether I am sure that red looked to me yesterday as it does today and that memory is not playing me false. I know experimentally that sensations do vary slightly even from hour to hour; but in the main the evidence is ample that they are common to all beings whose senses are sufficiently developed.

I hear you say: "All that is not *fact*; it is poetry." Nonsense! Bad poetry is false, I grant; but nothing is truer than true poetry. And let me tell the scientific men that the artists are much finer and more accurate observers than they are, except of the special minutiae that the scientific man is looking for.

I hear you say: "This smacks too much of an anthropomorphic conception." I reply that every scientific explanation of a natural phenomenon is a hypothesis that there is something in nature to which the human reason is analogous; and that it really is so all the successes of science in its applications to human convenience are witnesses. They proclaim that truth over the length and breadth of the modern world. In the light of the success of science to my mind there is a degree of baseness in denying our birthright as children of god and in shamefacedly slinking away from anthropomorphic conceptions of the Universe <*God and Nature*>.

Lecture Five: The Normative Sciences

1. The text of this lecture is from Peirce's third draft, MS 312.

2. Peirce indicated 'skip' section I.

3. Peirce deleted the following passage:

At the time I first published this division of inference in 1867, though I had given it in lectures before, I had been for five years immersed in the most intense study of the categories, and certainly handled them with more skill than I do now. Of course, this division of inference was connected in my statement with the three categories. But if I were asked today which of the two propositions, that the three categories are Quality, Relation, and Representation (to use my terminology of that time) or that the three forms of inference are Hypothesis, Induction, and Deduction, which of those two seemed today to be most fully supported by evidence, I should say the latter. And as to the connection between the three categories and the three modes of inference, I am forced to confess that it is obscure. In 1867, as now, I recognized three kinds of representamens (the same three which Mr. Stout misunderstands because of endeavoring to make them applications of psychology). A representamen is either an Icon whose representative character lies in its resemblance or analogy with its object, that is, in its Firstness, or an Index whose representative character lies in its real reaction with its object, that is, in its Secondness, or a Symbol whose representative character lies in the fact that it will be understood as a sign, that is in its Thirdness. Now, I said, Abduction, or the suggestion of an explanatory theory, is inference through an Icon, and is thus connected with Firstness; Induction, or trying how things will act, is inference through an Index, and is thus connected with Secondness; Deduction, or recognition of the relations of general ideas, is inference through a Symbol, and is thus connected with Thirdness. Moreover, I had observed, or thought I had observed,—and I remain of the same opinion still,—that where Thirdness is predominant essential Trichotomies are found, where Secondness is predominant essential Dichotomies are found, while where Firstness is predominant there is an absence of essential subdivision. It is rather a misty doctrine, I must confess. But my connection of Abduction with Firstness, Induction with Secondness, and Deduction with Thirdness was confirmed by my finding no essential subdivision of Abductions, that Induction split, at once, into the Sampling of Collections, and the Sampling of Qualities, while in the logic of relatives the three figures of syllogism gain a reality which is not so easily perceived in non-relative syllogism but really exists there also. The fourth figure merely mixes the characters of the second and third.

But as years rolled on I began to waver from this position. And here I beg you to permit a personal explanation. From the number of times in which I have changed my opinions upon matters of detail it might be supposed that I have the habit of expressing myself inconsiderately. But barring communications in newspapers, the fact is that I have never printed anything about philosophy which was not based on at least half a dozen independent written attempts made at long intervals to analyze the subject far more minutely than I have ever done in print, these statements being themselves preceded by at least two elaborate briefs of the state of the question drawn up in writing and independently of one another at an interval of a year or more, and afterward critically compared.

Very well, in the book called *Studies in Logic by Members of the Johns Hopkins University*, while I stated the rationale of induction pretty well, I confused Abduction with the Second Kind of Induction, that is the induction of qualities. Subsequently, writing in the seventh volume of the *Monist*, sensible of the error of that book but not quite understanding in what it consisted I stated the rationale of Induction in a manner more suitable to Abduction, and still later in lectures here in Cambridge I represented Induction to be connected with the third category and Deduction with the Second. It is needless to say that I had reasons for this which seemed strong to me then and which seem strong to me now. At present, I am somewhat disposed to revert to my original opinion; but I will leave the question undecided.

Whatever incompetence you may infer from these variations, one merit I believe I may claim that they prove. It is that I am unusually free from the tendency to be prejudiced in favor of opinions because they are mine. And perhaps this may add a slight weight to those opinions which I have continued to reaffirm. One of these is that although Abductive and Inductive reasoning are distinctly not reducible to Deductive reasoning, nor either to the other, nor Deductive reasoning to either, yet the *rationale* of Abduction and of Induction must itself be Deductive. All my reflections and self-criticisms have only served to strengthen me in this opinion. But if this be so, to state wherein the validity of mathematical reasoning consists is to state the ultimate ground on which any reasoning must rest.

Lecture Six: The Nature of Meaning

1. Peirce wrote, on the cover of the notebook in which he wrote Lecture Six (MS 314), "(first 35 pages as delivered)." His pagination 1–35 covers sections I and II as follows here.

2. The point that an object can be singular—that is, have an individual and distinct identity—but can also involve elements of generality, is made with another example in the previous draft (MS 313):

> A perceptual judgment certainly refers to a singular object, but so does any proposition and would have no meaning whatever if it did not. Suppose I were to remark that a flying-machine, however successful, could be of no advantage to commerce. This would enunciate a general rule, without asserting that there ever will be any such thing as a flying-machine. But it could convey no meaning to your mind if it did not refer to certain single objects well-known both to you and to me. Commerce, for example, is such an object. It is not merely a general sort of activity. It is an individual although highly complicated event, just as much as the Battle of Waterloo, or the Reformation. The word *machine* is a common noun, it is true; but still it would convey no definite idea if you and I had not had, you your experience and I mine, of the history of the nineteenth century. So it is with the word "flying." You and I would be puzzled to say exactly what we mean by flying, except that it is an action very similar to phenomena familiar to us in experience which collectively make up parts of an individual collection of events. So, then, to say that a perceptual judgment relates to single reacting objects not only is perfectly consistent with its involving elements of generality but does not even preclude its enunciating a general rule.

3. The section below followed the discussion of previousness in the first draft (MS 313). It is a discussion of the generality of perceptual judgment concluding that the sense of continuity and infinity is, in fact, a matter of perceptual judgment.

> Be it noted that mere previousness does not involve continuity nor even infinity. But it is quite clear to my mind that it is undeniable that there is a true flow of time, that such, I mean, is the perceptual judgment, in the sense of our not being able to avoid confessing that there is an appearance of true flow, so that between any two events one of which ceases before the other begins there is room for any multitude of dates. I have often heard a contrary theory stated,—namely that time appears to be a succession of fixed states; and if I saw any sufficient evidence for this, I should be glad, in the interest of my own opinion, to acknowledge that, as a psychological fact, there is such a succession of fixed states of feeling. Because, if that be the case, it puts in the strongest possible light the truth of what I am saying. Because if such be the nature of immediate consciousness, then in any one of these fixed states we have a consciousness of nothing but a series of fixed states, and never any consciousness, or appearance, of change. Now it [is] undeniable that somehow we have an idea of continuous change which we can so little rid ourselves of, that these very theorists introduce it. So if it is not in immediate conscious-

ness, there must be some other consciousness that introduces it without anything in immediate consciousness to justify or even to suggest it; and this other consciousness would be the only one which presents the universe in an intelligible form. Nothing would be gained by supposing these fixed states to be related to one another like the series of rational fractions so that between any two there is an infinite series of others, nor even by supposing they were related like the series of real analytic quantities so that there was such a state at the limit of every endless succession of such states, for they would still remain absolutely fixed states utterly without any intelligible connection with one another; and the law which we perceive in them in perceiving them to be successive would be an absolutely brute affair from which we should be absolutely and forever debarred from comprehending; while on the contrary, as time presents itself to our apprehension, although it requires a good logician to analyze it and scientifically understand the relationship, yet it is presented as continuous, time melting into time without break, so that the connection is entirely comprehensible.

Is there any such thing as true continuity in the real world or not? If there is, what is gained by the unnatural, if not absurd, hypothesis which denies it to the apprehension of time? If there is no true continuity in the real world, how is it that the mind has been able to create the fiction of something the like of which does not exist? And how is it that this utter fiction should enable us to understand the real world and to make predictions that [are] verified? What a marvellous fiction that can generate truth inexhaustibly! But perhaps the doctrine is that there is no such idea, that it is mere words! Then it is still more surprising that complete nonsense or absurdity should be so useful. I grant that there are people who have a difficulty in grasping the idea not merely of continuity but even that of infinite divisibility, which is a far easier conception to analyze. There are people who even fancy they see contradiction in the notion of infinity. These are the persons who lack the patience and power of concentration required to deal with complicated systems of relationship. They are not the class of minds whose mastery of intricacies has advanced our understanding of difficult problems requiring exact thought. They may make great jurists or show great penetration in dealing with human affairs, or with zoology, or linguistics. Many of the men I have admired and loved the most have been unable to master the first book of Euclid. But when the question is whether a formal conception, a mathematical conception, does or does not involve contradiction, it is reasonable to ask that it should be treated by the algebra of logic, or by some of the methods which have proved themselves effective for that purpose. The mere fact that Bishop Berkeley or Hobbes does not understand a conception cannot be taken as having any weight at all.

4. The previous draft (MS 313) contains a much briefer set of definitions of the three types of argument. The present draft includes the previous draft's texts of

these definitions within it, with the exception of an explanation of a term, "probametric," referring to a character of inductive arguments:

> If, however, in place of a deductive argument we are dealing with an inductive argument, by which I mean a course of experimentation and reflection designed to put a theory to the test, the case is different because we have a different end in view. We are now no longer considering hypothetical states of things. We want to know how nearly a given theory represents the facts, and the answer to this question, from the nature of things, must have the well-known character which I have hitherto expressed by calling it "probable and approximate." This, however, is a clumsy and inexact expression. A single word is wanted. Suppose we call it *"probametric,"* meaning that the answer will be a quantity whose value has been so chosen that the probability of its having an error not exceeding a variable magnitude will vary, according to the doctrine of chances, in a convenient manner. The inductive procedure will be sound or otherwise according as it is or is not calculated according to the principles of probability, to reduce the probable error indefinitely as the experimentation is carried further and further.

5. Section IV is MS 316.

Lecture Seven: Three Cotary Propositions of Pragmatism

1. The adjective "cotary" is a neologism adapted by Peirce from the genitive form, *cotis*. He appears to have initially used the nominative form to derive the term "cossal" before changing this term to "cotary" throughout the text. Even on its final page, Peirce edited his text thus, from which we may infer that he not only thought with pen in hand, but fulfilled the requirements of the method of writing which he describes in these lectures.

2. An especially apt discussion of the emergence of breakthroughs in scientific reasoning is given in Thomas Kuhn's *The Structure of Scientific Revolutions*. Kuhn notes in a remarkable passage that the characteristic features of three landmark discoveries in science, of oxygen, of X-rays and of the Leyden jar, are similar insofar as, in each field, there was:

> the previous awareness of anomaly, the gradual and simultaneous emergence of both observational and conceptual recognition, and the consequent change of paradigm categories and procedures often accompanied by resistance. There is even evidence that these same characteristics are built into the nature of the perceptual process itself.

In demonstration of this process, Kuhn uses the Bruner and Postman experiment in which experimental subjects were asked to identify a series of playing cards, some of which were normal and some "anomalous," e.g., "a red six of spades and a black four of hearts." Subjects reported features of their experience like those Kuhn ascribes to scientific discoveries. The experiment rates as one which would serve Peirce's point well. Kuhn's comment that the features are inherent in the perceptual process is worth attention. See Thomas Kuhn, "Anomaly and the Emergence of Scientific Discoveries" in *International Encyclopedia of Unified Science*, vol. 2, no. 2, *The Structure of Scientific Discoveries*, second edition, enlarged (Chicago: University of Chicago Press, 1970), pp. 52–65; esp. pp. 62–63.

3. Initially, Peirce intended to address the objection that it is difficult to determine that a judgment is perceptual and not abductive, by means of these deleted sentences:

> At the same time, this difficulty will appear less serious when we remark that in regard to the vast majority of propositions of which men are in the habit of saying that their falsity is inconceivable, when we put the question in this form "Is this directly perceived?" it will readily be proved that it is not perceived. For example, a man might say, "If I were to face precisely east and walk straight forward sixty steps and were then to turn to the right precisely through a right angle and were to walk straight forward fifty steps and then were to turn to the right precisely through a right angle and were to walk straight forward fifty steps and then were to turn to the right precisely through a right angle and were to walk straight forward until I was on the point of crossing my first path, I directly perceive that I should have to turn precisely through a right angle in order to walk over my previous path." A man, I say, might say that. But I should say to him, You have, no doubt, been supposing that you would be walking on a level surface, although you did not explicitly say so. But it has probably not occurred to you that a level surface may have any shape whatever, according to the distribution of attracting masses. If you were facing due east on the earth's surface and were to walk straight forward along the path of minimum length, when you had walked sixty paces you would no longer be facing due east but a little to the south of east, so that what you have been saying you perceived would not be the fact. Now then you wish to suppose you were walking on a plane surface. But what do you mean by a plane surface? If you mean one upon which what you are saying would be true, then, of course, it is an identical proposition to say that it would be as you say. But if by a plane you mean a surface which turned upside down could be brought into exact coincidence with its former position throughout, then you must acknowledge that you do not evidently perceive any connection between this particular property of a plane surface and the property of a surface on which four right angles should make the quadrilateral close precisely.

In ways more or less like this, the class of cases in which abductions may be mistaken for perceptions can be considerably narrowed. Nevertheless, it must be acknowledged that this class of cases, however it may be restricted, cannot thus be eliminated. It may therefore very likely be objected that doubt must perforce on this account hang over my first cossal [cotary] proposition that every general element of thought is given in perceptive judgment. This objection, however, involves a logical fallacy.

4. Peirce deleted this alternate draft of part III:

You will not expect me to interpolate into this short course of lectures any discussion of the general principles of logic; and at the same time if logic has any value it cannot easily be believed that such a question as that of Pragmatism can be fundamentally and scientifically considered otherwise than in the light of the principles of logic.

In the *Proceedings of the American Academy of Arts and Sciences* for 1867 April 9, followed by another paper of May 14, in a paper "On the Validity of the Laws of Logic" in the *Journal of Speculative Philosophy* for 1869, Vol. II and in a paper in *The Popular Science Monthly* for August 1878, I have set forth my reasons for holding that there are but three modes of inference, Deduction, Induction, and Abduction. A fourth, Analogy, merely combines the principles of the other three. I do not mention my paper on probable inference in the book called *Studies in Logic by Members of the Johns Hopkins University* because in that paper I almost altogether neglect Abduction which I was led temporarily to confuse in some measure with a variety of Induction.

But my views have naturally developed and matured very much indeed during the twenty-three years that have elapsed since I printed the last of the pages I have mentioned, and I am happy to say that I shall have an opportunity of presenting the matter afresh next winter in some lectures I am going to give at the Lowell Institute.

The maxim of Pragmatism, if it is sound, or whatever ought to replace it, if it is not sound, is nothing else than the logic of abduction.

A mass of facts is before us. We go through them. We examine them. We find them a confused snarl, an impenetrable jungle. We are unable to hold them in our minds. We endeavor to set them down upon paper; but they seem so multiplex intricate that we can neither satisfy ourselves that what we have set down represents the facts, nor can we get any clear idea of what it is that we have set down. But suddenly, while we are poring over our digest of the facts and are endeavoring to set them into order, it occurs to us that if we were to assume something to be true that we do not know to be true, these facts would arrange themselves luminously. That is *abduction*.

The best example of it in its fullness is that of Mendeleev's Table of the Chemical Elements. Mendeleev came upon this in an attempt to write a clear book upon inorganic chemistry. To get an idea of what he was aiming at one must read the book which he produced and which no doubt falls short of his ideal. Still even as it stands, it is amazing what a vast variety of facts it comprises and still more astonishing to what an extent he has presented those facts so that the reader can carry them away with [him]. In endeavoring to put the facts into some comprehensible order, he no doubt noted a considerable number of fragmentary relationships, of which one can get some idea from Venable's *History of the Periodic Law*, although Mendeleev's own remarks no doubt went far beyond what had hitherto been published. At length, he perceived that if a good number [of] atomic weights were halved or doubled, concerning which no decisive evidence existed at that time, and if a few other atomic weights were supposed to be ill-determined, if certain elements existed that had never been discovered, and a considerable number of facts about other elements were other than they had been found to be, but not incredibly so, then the elements would all constitute that system with which I suppose you are familiar.

The anticipation that such might be the truth, not amounting to positive assertion yet by no means sinking to a recognition of a bare possibility, was the Abductive conclusion.

Now the question is what is requisite to justify such an expectation?

We need not at first undertake to say how strong an expectation is warranted. We may suppose it to be very slight, so long as it is distinctly something more than the mere recognition of a bare mathematical possibility. What can warrant anything more than that, however little the excess may be?

Now, as I remarked in a former lecture, anything is good in so far, and only in so far, as it conforms to its *end*.

The question is, then, what can come of an abductive theory? Someone may say that it is a grand and adorable idea just as it is. That may be. Its contemplation may fill the soul with a sort of music. But that is esthetic goodness. Our inquiry relates, however, to cognitive goodness. What can the theory teach us? I should make the same reply if anybody said that there was some sort of mysterious result to be expected from certain theories. It is not necessary to deny that there are mysterious agencies in ideas. It is sufficient to say that it is not rational cognitive goodness. To have that goodness the theory must lead to some further knowledge. It must be the basis of some advance in reasoning. If it embody clear and definite ideas of relationship, it may be the foundation of a lofty edifice of mathematical developments, which may be good in various ways, esthetically (for the esthetic element in mathematics is intense), educationally in training the mind to deal with analogous ideas, and cognitively in teaching us its lesson of the world of ideas.

But those modes of goodness of the theory it would possess just the same if there were no anticipation of its proving actually true of the real world, and therefore independently of its having the character of an abduction. If it is to be good as an abduction it must subserve the end of abduction. Now the end of abduction is that the deductive consequences of it may be tested by induction. So alone is any application made of its essential anticipatory character. Consequently the good of abduction, as such, that is, its adaptation to its end, will consist of its being of such a character that its deductive consequences may be experimentally tested.

Thus, the logic of abduction will be expressed by Auguste Comte's maxim that no hypothesis ought to be entertained which is not verifiable, that is, supposing that by a verifiable hypothesis is meant one whose consequences are capable of comparison with experience. Comte does not make it clear to his reader, and apparently did not make it clear to himself, what he meant by a verifiable hypothesis. His general aim appears to be to exclude every element from his hypotheses except that of such physical events as can present themselves to direct perception. But I do not wish to be led aside from the general discussion by the consideration of the accidents of Comte's inconsistencies. Let us consider what positions a man could consistently hold with reference to the maxim of admissible hypotheses.

Comte does not make it clear what he means by a verifiable hypothesis. It was not clear to his own mind. It is plain that the doctrine which he aimed to establish so far as a man can be said to have an aim which is not distinctly defined in his mind, as may very properly be said, I think. For we never thoroughly comprehend an unrealized purpose. Comte's aim, translated into the terms which I have endeavored to render clear to you, was to show that there is no idea of Thirdness distinct from a complication of the idea of Secondness. But that complication he and his followers seem to have thought never presents itself in direct experience and therefore, although the mind swarms with such theological and metaphysical ideas, ideas of ideas being operative in the real world, he held that all such elements ought to be excluded from our scientific theories. Strictly physical hypotheses were alone to be admitted. That it seems to me is what Pragmatism must logically come to if one maintains that there is no element of Thirdness in the phenomenon radically distinct from any complication of Secondness. At the same time, Comte dearly felt the utter insufficiency of this doctrine in human society and therefore tried with all his might to persuade himself of a huge fiction utterly at variance with his own principles, the Religion of Humanity, which should hold society together. The French have since Bartholomew's day been firmly persuaded of the advantages of certain wholesome lies upheld by all the forces of society. It is a variety of pragmatism which holds that a doctrine that ought never to be entertained as a scientific conception, because not verifiable, ought nevertheless to be embraced as a faith because it is wholesome.

It is plain that a man cannot consistently engage in this discussion or in any discussion unless he admits that there is a distinction between truth and falsity. It is also plain that to admit this distinction is to admit that there is something whose characters are what they are independently of what he may think that they are; and further the words truth and falsity are not appropriate unless he wishes to make his opinions conform to that object and thinks that in some measure he can do so. Neither is it what we mean to wish to satisfy some man, or body of men, or other being or beings, with his opinions. We must mean by the real that which has such characters as it has independently of what any particular mind or minds may think those characters may be. At the same time, these characters of the real must be of the nature of thoughts or sufficiently so to impart some sense to our talking of thoughts conforming to those characters. But this thought or quasi-thought in which the characters of the real consist cannot be any existential happening or being. Thus suppose we were to say that the real is what men will ultimately come to think. Then the real fact that they will so come to think would have to consist in their coming to think that they would come so to think and this again would consist in their coming to think that they would come to think that so they would come to think, and so on *ad infinitum*, and it is plain that this would not be making the reality consist in the existential coming to pass of anything. I am forced to say that that which thought conforms to has a representational mode of being that does not consist in any reactional existence. At the same time, it will be too manifestly false for me to say that the redness of a red thing consists in anything but the immediate positive quality itself. Neither can I deny that when I make an effort it is then and there that the event takes place, however it is represented. I must thus acknowledge the distinctness of the three categories, and at the same time that Thirdness is continuous up to the other two as limits before I can have any clear notion of truth and falsity; and without such clear notion I have no basis for any discussion of the maxim of abduction.

5. While the manuscript page on which this sentence is written is now damaged so that several words are missing from Peirce's text, the *Collected Papers of Charles Sanders Peirce* contains the observations made some fifty years ago by Charles Hartshorne and Paul Weiss that the (missing) words are "narrow ranges" and "collections" (CP 5.212).

INDEX

abduction
  Aristotle on, 217
  and chance, 230–31
  conclusion of
    as plausible not merely possible, 283n. 4
    as problematic or conjectural, 245–47
    in relation to its premisses, 94–95, 242, 245–48, 255, 261n. 5
  deductive validity as rationale of, 219, 277n. 3
  definition of, 85, 94–95, 97–98, 218, 230, 239, 242, 245–46, 249–50, 276n. 3, 282n. 4
  and the distinction of truth and falsity, 285n. 4
  faculty of
    as a gradation of perception, 93, 238, 242–46, 281n. 3
    as insight, 231, 242
    as instinct, 231
  goodness of, 250, 283–84n. 4
  and hypothesis, 94–95, 97, 189, 230, 239, 245–47, 249–50
  irreducibility of, 218–19, 277n. 3
  logical form of, 245–46
  and nominalism, 163, 188
  and the origination of true ideas, 144, 159, 230
  and perceptual judgment, 93–95, 231, 242–47
  and the pragmatic maxim, 97, 239, 249–50, 282n. 4
  pragmatism as the logic of, 93, 97, 239, 249–50, 254, 282n. 4
  and psychology, 94
  and really existent generality, 95, 231
  as suggestion, 85, 95, 97, 230–31, 242, 244–45, 248–49, 276n.3
  validity of, 230

abductive judgment
  criticism of, as rationally possible, 245
Abelard, Peter
  and the copula, 105n. 3, 234–35
abstract and concrete, 132, 140, 154–55
abstraction
  definition of, 84, 134–36, 140–41, 155, 226
  in diagrams of deductive inference, 84, 226, 250
abstractions
  as relations, 137–38
Achilles and the tortoise
  sophism of, 79, 97, 223, 242, 251–52, 268n. 3, 271–72n. 3
action and intention
  conformity of, as available in perception, 256
agent and patient
  distinction of
    in the mode of representation, 179
    in ordinary language and philosophy, 178–79
    in struggle, 155–56
aggregation
  definition of, 124, 138
agnosticism, 164, 273–74n. 4
analogy
  as a mode of inference, 282n. 4
analytic system
  of logical representation, 184–85
anthropomorphism
  element of, in every conception, 256
  and the reality of Firstness, 63
  and science, 156–58, 275–76n. 8
apodosis, 110, 257n. 2
architectonic
  and philosophy, 27
  and the proof of pragmatism, 26–28, 31–33, 35–36
  of sciences, 35, 98n. 5

argument
    classification of, as a qualitative approval, 212
    conclusion of, as its intended interpretant, 83, 85–86, 171, 232, 234
    definition of, 216
    logical truth of, 75, 216
    meaning of, 85–86, 88, 104–5n. 3, 232, 234
    moral goodness of, as veracity, 216
    quantitative goodness of, 217
    soundness of, 75, 79–80, 82–84, 217, 225
    strength of, 246–47
    as a subdivision of the symbol, 171
    three radically different kinds of, 217
    universe as, with qualities as premisses and realities as conclusions, 63, 201
    validity of, 246–47
arguments
    classification of, 52, 68–69, 210, 212
argumentation
    ultimate end of, 81
Aristotelian metaphysics
    and the three categories, 190
Aristotle
    on abduction, 217
    and the copula, 105n. 3, 235
    his definition of generality, 221
    on the definition of a proposition, 175
    on logic, 265n. 6
    on normative science as the basis of metaphysics, 151
    on potentiality and actuality, 190
    on the priority of the senses, 24
    on two orders of categories, 153
Arnauld, Antoine, 266n. 6
assertion
    definition of, 116–17
    sheet of, as the univeral universe of truth, 184–85
associationism
    as the metaphysics of the qualities of feeling, 171

beauty
    and normative science, 208, 213
    reductive concept of, as relative exclusively to human taste, 211
    as self-evident, 69

belief
    and the apprehension of a concept, 30–31
    definition of, 116–17
    and psychology, 29–31, 90–92, 116
    and philosophy, 162
Bentham, Jeremy, 151, 224
Berkeley, George, 78, 143, 279n. 3
    his nominalism and general ideas, 241
Berkeleyan metaphysics
    and the unreality of Secondness, 143, 172, 190
Bernard, Claude, 236–37
Boltzmann, Ludwig, 273n. 4
Boole, George, 125, 137, 258n. 1, 261n. 6
Boolean logic, 35, 124, 137–38, 258n. 1
Boyle, Robert
    his corpuscular philosophy, 163

Cantor, Georg, 89, 161
Cartesian metaphysics
    and the three categories, 172, 190
Cartesianism
    and dualism, 161
    and the human mind as correlative to reality, 211
    and mechanistic reductionism, 163
categorical imperative
    criticism of Kant's doctrine, 73, 214
categories
    application of
      in the analysis of a proposition, 176
      in a system of mathematical representation, 186
    definition of, 49, 65–66, 87, 120, 153, 208, 232–33
    and forms of logic, 248
    genuine and degenerative forms of, 50, 54–57, 167–71
    as independent constituents of thought, 188
    irreducibility of, 49–50, 154, 172, 177, 182–87, 218–19, 277n. 3, 285n. 4
    Kant's concept of, as indefinable, 87, 232–33, 254
    as metaphysico-cosmical elements, 171
    and metaphysics, 49, 59, 154, 171–72, 189–90
    and modeling, 53–57
    and the pragmatic maxim, 92
    and pragmatism, 28, 65, 68, 154

psychological aspect of, 34, 68
as realities of nature, 188–89
reality of, 59, 64, 189–90
shapes and aspects of, in the phenomenon, 154
and the truth of nature, 189
two orders of, 120, 153
unintelligibility of first and second, 143, 159
categories, particular
as a series, 120, 153
categories, universal
definition of, 65–66, 120, 153
category
predominance of one, in a phenomenon, 56, 153, 169, 194, 198, 276n. 3
proof of its reality, 64
category, first
as immediate, 139–40, 155
as presentness, 139–41, 154–55
as quality, 141, 155, 188–89, 195, 200–201, 208–9
See also Firstness
category, fourth
as impossible, 154
category, second
as reaction, 143, 147–48, 158, 167, 172, 177, 189, 195
as struggle, 141, 147, 149, 155–59
as twoness, includes degenerate forms, 149
See also Secondness
category, third
definition of, 149
genuine and degenerate forms of, 149–50, 261–62n. 3
as representation, 53–56, 167–69, 179, 187, 194, 261–62n. 3
its universal presence in the phenomenon, 163–64
See also Thirdness
Cauchy, A. L., 130, 260n. 2
Cayley, Arthur, 125, 259nn. 4–5
certainty
of logical principles, as not from intention or induction, 227–28
as perception of the general truth of an inference, 226–27
chance
hypothesis of, 60, 192–93, 230–31
and radical novelty, 64

change, continuous
idea of, as an intelligible form of the universe, 278–79n. 3
class
as an individual, 236–37
classification
as inherent in perceptual judgment, 93–94, 243
collection
definition of, 136
collection, individual or singular, 235–36, 278n. 2
commotion
sense of, as vividness of feeling, 141
Comte, Auguste, 239, 250, 273n. 4, 284n. 4
concept
and belief versus apprehension, 31
explication of, as the enumeration of its universal predicates, 87, 232, 254
concept, general
as a collective singular, 236
conceptual reasoning
of philosophers, 219, 265n. 6
conclusion
as the interpretant of an argument, 83, 85–86, 171, 232, 234
logical matter of, as available in the premisses of any inference, 247–48
conclusion, particular
as the aim of a deduction, 84, 226
Condillac, Étienne, 171
conditional judgment
antecedents of, as available in perception, 246–48
consciousness
definition of, as a degenerate form of third category, 55, 150, 168, 263n. 3
consciousness, immediate
of a series of fixed states, 278–79n. 3
continuity
as generality, 220, 253
and infinite divisibility, 264n. 5, 279n. 3
of motion or change, 135, 278–79n. 3
perception of, 220, 253, 278n. 3
of points, 253
continuity, true
reality of, and prediction, 279n. 3
Thirdness as, in relation to any multitude of correlates, 167

copula
  in diverse languages, 105n. 3
  of inclusion, 124, 138
corpuscularism
  as the metaphysics of mechanism, 163–
    65, 172
correspondence
  truth as, of theory with reality, 191, 218,
    225, 229, 239, 255, 284–85n. 4
cotary propositions
  and the inference of generality and conti-
    nuity, 253
  and the perceptibility of Thirdness, 255–
    56
  and the pragmatic maxim, 92–93, 241–48
criticism
  and self-control, 146, 161, 196–97, 199,
    212, 214, 223, 256

Darwin, Charles
  The Origin of Species, 164
Dedekind, Richard, 132, 136, 219, 233,
    260n. 4
deduction
  conclusion of, in relation to its premises,
    261n. 5
  and the copulative colligation of percep-
    tual judgments, 247
  definition of, 83–84, 97–98, 217–18, 225,
    230, 276n. 3
  irreducibility of, 218–19, 277n. 3
  as necessary reasoning, 83, 217–19, 225
  and observation, 83–85, 225–26
  and the pragmatic maxim, 249–50
  and prediction, 82, 97, 229–30, 239, 249
  as the reasoning of mathematics, 84, 210,
    217–19, 226, 277n. 3
  subdivision of, as three figures of syllo-
    gism, 277n. 3
  validity of, 82–83, 225, 246
    as the rationale of abduction and in-
      duction, 219, 277n. 3
definition
  and the logic of relations, 87–88, 232–33,
    254
  and terminology, 24–25
DeMorgan, Augustus, 125–26, 219, 259n. 7
Descartes, René
  criticism of, 105n. 3
  *Discourse on the Method of Rightly Con-
    ducting the Reason*, 96

his method of enumeration, 96
  on normative science as the basis of
    metaphysics, 151
  Rules for the Direction of the Mind, 40
desire
  self-satisfaction of, as a fallacy of circu-
    larity, 173–74, 176
diagrammatic reasoning
  features of, 84, 219, 225–26
diagrams
  of deductive inference, 84, 225–26,
    261n. 5
  of mathematical relations, 52–53, 83–84,
    124, 130–31, 136, 219, 261n. 5
  and modeling, 53
  and necessary reasoning, 84, 136, 219,
    225, 261n. 5
diagrams, auditory, 136, 260–61n. 5
diagrams, visual, 137, 219, 260–61n. 5
dialectic, 53, 260n. 5
discovery
  and surprise, 144–45, 159–60
discrimination
  and phenomenology, 152
doubt
  and belief, 30, 90
  and logic, 31–32, 90–91
dualism
  and immediate perception, 161
duality
  category of, 182–83
  of expectation and unexpected in surprise,
    147, 202–3
  genuine and degenerate forms of, 149
dyad
  as a rhema with two blanks, 235
dyadic relation
  definition of, 138, 148
  two types of, as genuine and degenerate,
    148–49

Edgeworth, F. Y., 229
enumeration
  in mathematics, 96–97
  and the pragmatic maxim, 97
esse in futuro, 142–43, 158, 190
esthetic consciousness
  as a representation of a quality of feeling
    (a Thirdness of a Firstness), 199
esthetic goodness, 283n. 4
  of an admirable ideal, 72, 213

definition of, 69–70, 213–14
moral goodness as a species of, 213
esthetic enjoyment
as a cognition of the totality of a reasonable quality of feeling, 198–99
esthetic ideal
deliberate adoption of, 73–74, 213
esthetic judgment
its abstraction from attraction and repugnance, 69, 211
and a naive state of mind, 197
as opposed to hedonism, 197
esthetics
as the basis of ethics, 27, 34, 68, 70–73, 119, 197, 199, 213
definition of, 71, 119, 212
Peirce's study of, 67–68, 211
and pragmatism, 68
qualitative differences in, 70, 210–11, 213–14
esthetica utens
Peirce's, 68
ethical goodness
definition of, 73
ethics
and admirable action, 72, 214
as the basis of logic, 27, 33, 68, 71, 118–19, 196–97, 212–13
definition of, 71, 74, 118–19, 212
esthetics as the basis of, 27, 34, 68, 70–73, 119, 197, 199, 213
and possible ends, 73–74, 214–15
and qualities of good, 210
and voluntary action, 212–13
Euclid, 131, 279n. 3
Euler, Léonhard, 233, 258
Eulerian diagrams, 35, 124, 233
evolution
and chance, 231
Peirce's idea of, 64
evolutionism
and the death of nominalism and mechanism, 164
excluded middle
principle of, and the definition of individuality, 175
expectation, 249, 283n. 4
and chance, 60, 192–93
and surprise, 64, 144–47, 160, 202–3, 250
experience
definition of, 238

and the elimination of false ideas, 144, 159
explanation of, 98
and reaction, 143, 147, 191, 200
Secondness and Thirdness in, 225
and surprise, 144–45, 147, 159–60, 202
and the prediction of facts, 82–83, 191
experiment
definition of, 228, 239, 249, 280n. 4
and falsifiability, 60–61, 192
and hypothesis, 148, 162, 249–50, 284n. 4
and mathematics, 130–31
as mental manipulation of a hypothesis, 141–42
and the role of surprise in discovery, 144–45, 159–60
and prediction, 190–93, 229, 239, 249
and theory, 218, 228–29, 239, 249, 251, 280n. 4, 283–84n. 4
and verification, 239, 250–53, 255, 284n. 4
explanation
and abstraction, 133

faith
and pragmatism, 284n. 4
fallacy
definition of, 246–47
fallibilism
and science, 102n. 6
falsifiability
and science, 60–61, 192, 251
Faraday, Michael, 165
feeling
quality of, and its attribution to a non-ego, 146, 202
and esthetics, 71, 198–99, 212
as the first category, 141, 155, 167
and pain and pleasure, 198
and perceptual judgment, 200
as positive and simple, 140–41
and self-consciousness, 55, 168, 263n. 3
and the soundness of reasoning, 173, 177
and surprise, 63–64, 146–47, 202
as unintelligible, 143
a succession of fixed states of, as a psychological fact, 278n. 3
vividness of, as a state of mind, 141
See also logical feeling
feelings
laws of the succession of, 201–2

fiction
  definition of, 222
Firstness
  definition of, 167
  and esthetic feeling, 197
  independence of, 187
  no degenerate form of, 167
  reality of, 59, 62–63, 190, 201
  of Thirdness, 55, 168–69
Fisch, Max ·
  on the proof of pragmatism, 26
form, logical
  as logical matter, 248
formal fallacies
  in ordinary logic and the logic of rela-
    tions, 181
formal logic
  general principles of, as mathematical,
    227–28
formal-logical analysis
  and Secondness, 177
  and Thirdness, 177–78
formula
  of a law of nature as a representation,
    191–94
  as a reality, 191–94
free will
  and necessitarianism, 142

Gauss, Carl, 233
general
  Aristotle's definition of, 221
  definition of, 193
  as predicate of judgment, 78, 221
  no direct experience of, 220
general concept, nonperceptual
  as the predicate of a proposition, 238
general concepts
  as abductive generalizations of perceptual
    judgments, 237
general notions
  as laws of perceptual judgments, 237
general principle
  as really operative in nature, 59–60, 191–
    94, 255
general signs
  and predication, 149
generality
  a degenerate form of, and multitude, 193
  no immediate consciousness of, 220

and perceptual judgment, 78–79, 93–95,
    149, 220–21, 238, 241–44, 278nn.
    2–3
  as a premiss of abduction, 94–95
  and Thirdness, 95, 184, 193, 220, 231,
    238
generality, non-relative
  perception of, in a perceptual fact, 220,
    253
generalization
  and abduction, 237
  and esthetic pleasure, 198
  and mathematics, 131, 152
  and phenomenology, 152–53
geometry
  abstractions of, 135–36, 253
God
  and anthropomorphism, 158
  and nominalism, 163
  and the reality of Firstness, 63
goodness
  definition of, 80, 199, 224, 250, 283n. 4
  as either negative or quantitative, 211,
    213–14
goodness, cognitive
  as the furtherance of knowledge, 283n. 4
grammatica speculativa
  first part of logic as, and the usages of
    language, 235
graphs, existential and entitative, 124
Gray, Asa, 164

Haekel, Ernst, 162
hallucination
  and reality, 200
Hamilton, William, 164, 245, 267n. 6
hedonism
  and morality as a matter of feeling, 173–
    74, 197, 274n. 5
Hegel, G. W. F.
  and the absolute, 181, 187
  on abstract and concrete, 132, 139–40,
    154–55
  on actuality and possibility, 120, 190
  and the category of struggle, 144
  and continuity, 264n. 5
  and esthetics, 67
  on immediacy, 139, 154
  and the metaphysics of Thirdness, 172,
    190

nominalism of, 120, 163
phenomenology of, 35, 65–66, 119–21, 140
and philosophy as a practical science, 162
on presentness as abstract, 139–40, 154–55, 259n. 8
his refutation of phrenology, 60
on Thirdness as the only category, 161, 187–88
on two orders of categories, 120, 153
Helmholtz, Hermann, 172
Herbart, Johann, 266n. 6
Hertz, Heinrich, 273n. 4
history
    as an admissible hypothesis, 239
Hobbes, Thomas, 78, 279n. 3
Hume, David, 78, 157
hypothesis
    and abduction, 94–95, 97, 189, 230, 239, 245–47, 249–50
    and anthropomorphism, 157–58, 256
    and the category of reaction, 148
    and deduction, 83–84, 218, 225, 230
    and experiment, 148, 162, 249–50, 284n. 4
    general elements and forms of, as available in perception, 244–48
    and guesses, 230–31
    and mathematics, 34–35, 121, 124, 130, 151, 181, 210, 218
    mental experiment on, 141–42
    and necessary reasoning, 137
    and the normative sciences, 210
    and Ockham's razor, 115–16, 162
    as ready to hand, 91–92
    verifiability of, and direct perception, 239, 250–51, 284n. 4
hypothesis, abductive
    admissibility of, as its inductive verifiability, 239, 245, 249–50, 284n. 4
hypothesis, verifiable
    definition of, 284n. 4

icon
    definition of, 54, 170, 179, 276n. 3
    subdivision of, 170
icon, diagrammatic
    of the hypothetical premises in a deduction, 84, 225
idealism
    and the self-perception of perception, as a fallacy of circularity, 174

ideas
    world of, 248, 283n. 4
identity
    general relation of, in a singular proposition, 221
    as the self-relation of a primary substance, 138
illusion
    quality of feeling as, 195–96, 200
illusion, visual
    as perceptual interpretation, 93, 243
imagination
    and the concept of conceivable practical effects, 250
    and reaction, 147, 156
immediate
    definition of, 140, 145, 147, 155
inclusion
    copula of, as a dyadic relation, 124, 138
index
    definition of, 54–55, 170, 176, 235, 276n. 3
    as propositional subject, 105n. 3, 176, 234
    subdivision of, 170–71
index, degenerate (monstrative)
    definition of, 180
index, genuine (informational)
    definition of, 179–80
index, monstrative, 180–81
individuation
    principle of, 195
induction
    conclusion of, in relation to its premises, 261n. 5
    as a ratio of frequency, 85, 97–98, 218, 228–30, 239, 247
    deductive validity as rationale of, 219, 277n. 3
    definition of, 85, 97–98, 218, 228–30, 239, 249, 276n. 3, 280n. 4
    and experimental verification, 239, 250–53, 255, 284n. 4
    and general perception, 219–20
    and an infinite series, 251–52
    irreducibility of, 218–19, 277n. 3
    and mathematics, 131, 227–28
    and observation, 82–83, 85, 130–31, 229, 239, 251–52
    and the pragmatic maxim, 249–50

induction (*cont.*)
  rationale of, as experimental falsification, 251–53
  soundness of, 280n. 4
  subdivision of, as sampling of collections and qualities, 277n. 3
  validity of, 230
inference
  act of, as voluntary, 212
  class of logically analogous inferences as the basis of, 196, 212, 248
  conception of, as available in perception, 247–48
  three elementary steps of, as copulation, omission and insertion, 84, 226–27
  three modes of, in relation to the categories, 218, 276–77n. 3 (*see also* reasoning, three kinds of)
infinity
  idea of, as a contradiction, 279n. 3
inquiry
  and intellectual intuition, 105n. 3
  and logic, 91–92
  method of, 27
  and the pragmatic maxim, 97
  and psychology, 90–91
  and reality, 255
intellect
  and the senses, 93, 95
intellectual intuition
  and inquiry, 105n. 3
intelligibility
  as a category, 143, 159
interpretant
  of a representamen as another representamen it determines, 216
interpretant, intended
  meaning as, of a symbol, 53–54, 85–86, 88, 232
  as the meaning of a term, proposition or argument, 234
interpretation
  and perception, 93, 146–47, 161, 203, 243–45

James, William, 24–25, 28–29, 33, 36–37, 39, 68, 98–99n. 6, 268n. 3
Jouffroy, Théodore, 197
judgment
  and assertion, 116–17
  definition of, 199
  meaning of, as its intended use, 227
  predicate of, as general, 78, 221
  self-verification of, as a fallacy of circularity, 174–76
judgment, analytic and synthetic, 232, 267n. 6
judgment, nonperceptual
  as an abductive inference, 238–39

Kant, Immanuel
  on analytic and synthetic judgments, 232, 267n. 6
  on architectonic, 26–27
  categorical imperative of, 73, 214
  on categories as indefinable, 87, 232–33, 254
  Critic of the Pure Reason, 35, 67, 126, 211
  Critique of Judgment, 69
  and ethics, 197
  and immediate perception, 145, 161, 203
  and the meaning of a term, 87–88, 91, 232–33
  his metaphysics and the three categories, 172, 190
  on necessary reasoning as the explication of premisses, 232
  on normative science as the basis of metaphysics, 151
  his refutation of idealism, 145
  on space and time as forms of intuition, 195
  on two orders of categories, 153
Kempe, Alfred, 177, 182–86, 267n. 9
Kirchhoff, Gustav, 254
knowledge
  as apprehension of reality, 191
  possibility of, 225
Kuhn, Thomas, 280–81n. 2

Lambert, Johann, 233, 266n. 6
language
  use of, implies concepts of logic, 79
Laplace, Pierre, 228
law
  and reaction, 142, 157–59
  of the succession of feelings, 201–2
  of succession as the mode of being of an endless series, 229

law, active
  as efficient (reasonable) reasonableness,
    208
law of nature, 230, 255
  enforcement of, and the second category,
    142, 158
  reality of, an as *esse in futuro*, 142–43,
    158–59, 190–92
  as a hypothesis, 59–61, 190–93
  and an existent reaction, 195
  as a general formula or symbol, 194–95
  as an idea in the mind of a deity, 195
Legendre, Adrien-Marie, 219, 233
Leibniz, Gottfried, 125, 161
  on the best possible world, 229
  on method, 40
  his nominalism as the definitive modern
    case, 163
  on space and time as relations, 195
Leibnizian metaphysics
  and the three categories, 190
logic
  approval of certain voluntary acts by, 212
  and architectonic, 32, 35, 98n. 5
  as the classification of arguments, 52,
    68–69, 210, 212
  as critic and methodeutic, 52
  as the criticism of arguments, 196, 212
  as a criticism of common sense, 175, 177
  definition of, 52, 71, 118–19, 196, 212
  ethics as the basis of, 27, 33, 68, 71, 118–
    19, 196–97, 212–13
  forms of, as reducible to forms of the
    three categories, 248
  general principles of, and pragmatism,
    282n. 4
  and inquiry, 91–92
  and the instinctive mind, 256
  and kinds of truth in the classification of
    arguments, 210
  and mathematics, 28, 136, 210, 217–20,
    233–34
  and necessary reasoning, 136–37, 173,
    217, 219
  in the normative sciences, 33, 92
  as a positive science, 121, 257n. 2
  and psychology, 31, 40, 52, 116, 197,
    207, 223, 246
  on abduction, 230–31
  on belief and doubt, 30–32, 90–92, 116

  on deductive inference, 83–84, 225–27
  idea of generality in, 241
  on logical soundness, 80
  necessary and contingent truth in, 246
  and the perception of continuity, 253–
    54
  on perceptual (compulsory) judgment,
    223, 238
  and the pragmatic maxim, 249
  in Sigwart's doctrine, 81–82, 173, 176–
    77
  and reasoning, 32, 84, 136–37, 173, 196,
    212, 217–19, 225–26
  reductive concept of, as relative exclu-
    sively to human reasoning, 211
  and the special sciences, 266–67n. 6
logic of relations, 35–36, 99n. 7, 125–26,
    137–38, 173, 247, 259n. 7, 267n. 6,
    277n. 3
  and the analysis of deduction, 84, 225
  and the deducibility of universal from
    particular propositions, 242
  and the definition of categories, 87, 232–
    33, 254
  and generality in a singular proposition,
    78–79, 221
  and the irreducibility of Thirdness, 177
  and Kant's concept of necessary reason-
    ing, 232
  and the predicate of a proposition, 221
  and reaction as an irreducible element of
    thought, 172–73, 267n. 6
  and the reasoning of mathematics, 233–34
  and the subjects of a proposition, 175–76,
    221
  and the three logical subjects of a triadic
    fact, 178
  and traditional logic, 126
logica docens
  definition of, 52, 69, 72
logica utens
  definition of, 52, 69, 72
  and doubt, 90–91
  and reasoning, 212
  and science, 61
  as self-control, 199
  as a species of morality, 196
logical analysis
  of the subject and predicate of a proposi-
    tion, 181

logical correctness
  as one line of argument, 217
logical feeling
  and logical goodness, 81–82, 173, 176–
    77, 224–25, 237
logical form
  elements of, as available in the perceptual
    premisses of any mode of inference,
    247–48
logical goodness
  and cognitive self-control, 199, 212
  deductive validity as the foundation of,
    219
  definition of, 75, 79–80, 82, 196, 215–17
  and esthetic satisfaction, 81–82, 224, 237
  as the goodness of representation, 215
  possibility of, and the approximate confor-
    mity of human reasonableness with
    the reasonableness operative in expe-
    rience, 225
  of possible inferences, 196
  possible sources of, 52, 81–82, 173, 176–
    77, 196, 212, 224, 237
  as a species of moral goodness, 196, 212–
    13
  as truth, 216
logical matter
  elements of, as available in the perceptual
    premisses of any mode of inference,
    247–48
logical principles
  certainty of, as not from intention or in-
    duction, 227–28
logical representation
  analytic system of, 184–85
logical soundness
  definition of, 75, 79–80, 82, 173, 176–77
  and the quality of feeling, 173
  and self-control, 196–97
logical truth
  of arguments, 75, 216–17

Marshall, Henry, 119
material truth
  as all possible lines of argument in sup-
    port of a certain proposition as a
    conclusion, 217
  of propositions, 75, 216–17
matter
  abstractions of, 135–36

its interaction with mind, 163, 194, 271–
    72n. 3
mathematical arrangements, 126–29, 229–
    30
mathematical calculus
  as enumeration, 96–97
mathematical demonstration
  plan of, 84, 225–26
mathematical diagrams
  and abstractions, 84, 226
  and observation, 52–53, 83–84, 130–31,
    219–20
mathematical enumeration
  and modeling, 97
mathematical infinity, 268–72n. 3
mathematical knowledge
  as knowledge of purposes, 227
mathematical reasoning
  abstraction in, 133, 136–38
  analysis of, into logical steps, 84, 131–36,
    226, 233–34
  as diagrammatic, 52–53, 83–84, 130, 136,
    219
  and necessary reasoning, 136–37, 217–
    20, 233
  validity of, as the ultimate ground of any
    reasoning, 28, 277n. 3
mathematical theory
  goodness of, as esthetic, pedagogic and
    cognitive, 283n. 4
mathematics
  and architectonic, 35
  as the basis of phenomenology, 28, 34–
    35, 67, 121
  certainty of, 227
  collection in, 136, 268–70n. 3
  as deductive, 84, 210, 217–19, 226, 277n. 3
  definition of, 124, 130
  different branches of, 137–38
  experimentation and induction in, 130–
    31
  and extreme cases, 131
  and generalization, 131, 152
  and the Greeks, 130
  and hypothesis, 34–35, 121, 124, 130,
    151, 181, 210, 218
  and logic, 28, 136, 210, 217–20, 233–34
  matrices in, 125, 259nn. 4–5
  multitude and continuity in, 89, 96–97,
    251–53, 271–72n. 3

and normative science, 210–11
and phenomenology, 28, 34–35, 67, 121
and the positive sciences, 151
and quantity, 130
and relations, 129
and self-evident truth, 128–29
as the study of relations between sets of
    hypothetical singulars, 181–82
mathematics, dichotomic, 35, 124–26, 129,
    137–38
mathematics, trichotomic, 35, 126–28
maxim, pragmatic, 32, 36, 86, 97, 116, 213,
    234, 254
and abduction, 97, 239, 249–50, 282n. 4
and the admissibility of a hypothesis, 239,
    249–50, 245, 284n. 4
application of, 112, 117–18, 248–49
and belief versus apprehension, 30–31
and concrete reasonableness, 25–26, 29
and the cotary propositions, 92–93, 241–
    48
and deduction, 249–50
definition of, 24–25, 29–30, 92, 110–11,
    150, 214, 231, 249–50
and enumeration, 97
and induction, 249–50
on reality and truth, 134
and a *reductio ad absurdum*, 249–50
McCarthy, Jeremiah
on the proof of pragmatism, 26, 32, 35,
    98n. 3
meaning
of any conception, 150
definition of 85–86, 88, 227, 231–32
and logic, 85–86, 227, 232
and modeling, 83
and purpose, 88, 227, 231–32
of a representation and the element of
    generality, 241
mechanism
and the three laws of motion, 165
mechanistic reductionism
and the reality of the third category, 163–
    64, 273n. 4
medad
definition of, 181, 235
mediation
Thirdness as, between Firstness and Sec-
    ondness, 193–94, 208, 261–62n. 3
Mendeleev, Dmitri, 282–83n. 4

metaphysics
as the basis of special science, 151, 208
definition of, 66, 208–9
and logic, 189
normative science as the basis of, 151
systems of, and the three categories, 49,
    59, 154, 171–72, 189–90
method
of inquiry, 91–92, 105n. 3, 228–29
method, pragmatic, 38, 46
Mill, John Stuart, 29, 98–99n. 6, 130–31,
    216, 219–20, 227, 245, 260n. 3
his associationism and nominalism as
    metaphysics, 164
mind
its interaction with matter, 163, 194,
    271–72n. 3, 284n. 4
model
adequacy of, 55
of self-consciousness, 55–56
of a category, 64
of thought, 51
model, mathematical, 51–53, 97
and meaning, 83
modeling
and pragmatism, 53, 55
as representation not duplication, 56
monad
as a rhema with one blank, 235
moral evil
as want of an ultimate end, 214
moral goodness
logical goodness as a species of, 196,
    212–13
as a species of esthetic goodness, 213
Muir, T., 125, 259n. 6
multitude
and a degenerate form of generality
    (Thirdness), 193, 195
multitude and continuity, 67, 89, 96–97,
    251–53, 167, 271–72n. 3
multitudes, denumeral and enumerable,
    268–69n. 3

nature
premisses of, as qualities, 201
naturalism
fallacy of, and the normative sciences,
    73–74, 209–10
and the validity of reasoning, 81–82

necessary reasoning, 83–84, 173
  certainty of, 227
  as deduction, 83, 217–19, 225
  as diagrammatic, 84, 136, 219, 225
  Kant on, as syllogism in *Barbara*, 233
  Kant's concept of, as the explication of
    premisses, 232
  and mathematical reasoning, 136–37,
    217–20, 233
  and the perception of generality and con-
    tinuity, 220
necessitarianism
  and the premisses of nature, 201
  and the second category, 142
Newcomb, Simon, 117
Newton, Isaac, 165
  and mechanistic reductionism, 163
  on space and time as substance, 195
nominalism
  and the difference between being real and
    being represented, 191–92
  and general ideas, 241
  and Hegel, 120, 163
  and Ockham's razor, 162–63
  and the reality of struggle, 142, 158
  and the reality of the third category, 163,
    172, 191–92, 208
  and the source of general concepts, 237
  and thought, 68, 172
  and the three categories, 172, 190
normative science, 28, 33–34, 39, 65, 119–21
  analysis in, as not principally deductive
    but induced by the facts (categories)
    of phenomenology, 210
  its appreciation of the conformity of phe-
    nomena to non-immanent ends, 210
  as the basis of metaphysics, 151
  as categorical and positive, 34–35, 121,
    151, 257n. 2
  definition of, 66–67, 71–73, 119, 151–52,
    208–9, 212
  and the degree of goodness of a phenom-
    enon, 210–11
  division of, and the three categories, 68,
    71, 211–12
  and mathematics, 210–11
  phenomenology as the basis of, 28, 33–
    34, 119–20
  reductive concept of, as relative exclu-
    sively to the human mind, 211

  and the special sciences, 209
  as theoretical not practical, 72–73, 151,
    209
noun
  definition of, 222

object
  genuine and degenerate forms of, 54–57
  of the subject of a proposition, 176
observation
  of an icon of the premisses in a deduc-
    tion, 84, 225
  and logic, 82–85, 225–26
  of a mathematical diagram, 52–53, 83–
    84, 130–31, 219–20
  of a model, 53
  of natural events, 61, 82–83, 229
  and phenomenology, 145, 152, 160
Ockham's razor
  as the basis of modern nominalism, 162–
    63
  as a logical maxim of scientific procedure,
    40, 115–16, 162–63

pain
  as a struggle not a quality of feeling,
    198
parsimony
  maxim of, 171–72, 195
Peano, Giuseppe, 219
Pearson, Karl, 118–19
Peirce, Benjamin, 93, 100–101n. 2, 259n. 7
Peirce, Charles Sanders
  his analytic system of logical representa-
    tion, 184–85
  his metaphysics as scholastic Aristote-
    lianism, 190
  his method of philosophy, 40–46, 95, 97,
    105n. 3, 139, 205–7, 218, 277n. 3
  his phenomenology of his own feelings,
    198
  his philosophy of education, 47, 99n. 8,
    100n. 4, 123, 139, 207
percept, 62–63, 93, 145, 160, 199, 221, 236,
    244–45
  and abductive interpretation, 243
  definition of, 199
  and perceptual judgment, 93, 216–17,
    237, 243
  and self-control, 93, 199–200, 243

perception
  definition of, 238
  as a direct consciousness of reaction,
    145–47, 156, 235–36
  as a double consciousness of ego and
    non-ego, 145–47, 160, 236
  of a general truth, 226–27
  of generality and continuity, 220, 253,
    278n. 3
  as an inference from an existent quality,
    62–63, 94–95
  and interpretation, 93, 146, 161, 203,
    243–45
  and reality, 255
perception, direct
  of externality and the cognizance of a re-
    lation, 145–46, 161, 203
perceptual fact
  and certainty, 223
  continuity and generality in, 220
perceptual facts, 145, 147, 160, 203, 239
perceptual ideas
  all ideas as, 238
perceptual judgment
  and abductive inference, 93–95, 231, 242–47
  as an abductive result of a subconscious
    process, 242–43
  classification inherent in, 93–94, 243
  as the cognitive effect of a reactive exis-
    tence, 223, 278n. 2
  criticism of, as rationally impossible, 62,
    93, 145–47, 160–61, 199–200, 223,
    242, 244–45
  definition of, 146, 149, 160, 199, 238
  every general element or concept available
    in, 238, 241, 244–47, 256, 282n. 3
  as the first premiss of any inference, 200–
    1, 241–42
  and generality, 78–79, 93–95, 149, 220–
    21, 238, 241–44, 278nn. 2–3
  generality in the predicate of, as expres-
    sive of the quality of a percept, 221
  as an inference, 62–63, 94, 242–43
  predicate of, as an icon of a quality, 201
  and psychology, 94, 160, 227
  of the quality of a feeling, 200
  of a reaction in a suprise, 146–47, 161,
    202–3
  and self-control, 62, 93–94, 145–47, 160–
    1, 199–200, 223, 242, 248, 256

  subject of, as a singular, 221–22, 235,
    278n. 2
  and a theory of the facts, 216
  of time, 79, 253, 272n. 3, 278–79n. 3
  universal proposition deducible from, 93,
    241
  veracity of, 75, 216–17
personal identity
  hypothesis of, as a collective singular,
    235–36
phenomena
  definition of, 34, 50, 119–120
phenomenology
  application of three mental faculties in,
    152
  as the basis of the normative sciences, 28,
    33–34, 119–20
  definition of, 34, 65–66, 71, 119–20, 139,
    152–53, 208–9
  and mathematics, 28, 34–35, 67, 121
  as the primal positive science, 120–21
  of thought, 51
phenomenon
  as perceptual fact, 145
philosophers
  and auditory diagrams, 136–37, 260–61n. 5
philosophical concept
  ultimate meaning of, 77
philosophy
  as analytical, 151
  and belief, 162
  as a positive theoretical science, 65, 151,
    162, 207–8
  and the special sciences, 151
  three divisions of, and the three catego-
    ries, 65–66, 151–52, 208–9
  and pragmatism, 33, 110, 257n. 1
philosophy, idealist
  and the cognizance of relations, 146,
    161
philosophy, modern
  as nominalistic, 162–63
  its reductive concept of normative sci-
    ence, 211
physicists
  general concepts and, 61, 272–73n. 4
  on the reality of Thirdness and Second-
    ness, 195
  on the unreality of Firstness (quality),
    195–96, 200

300   *Index*

Platonic metaphysics
  and the three categories, 190
pleasure
  as a cognition not a quality of feeling,
    198
Ploucquet, Gottfried, 233
plurality
  as Thirdness, 183
plurality, irrational
  as a degenerate form of Thirdness, 168
Poincaré, Jules Henri, 229, 273n. 4
positive science
  definition of, 34, 120–21, 257–58n. 2
  and mathematics, 151
  normative science as, 34–35, 121, 257n. 2
  phenomenology as, 120–21
  philosophy as, 65, 151, 162, 207–8
pragmatic maxim. *See* maxim, pragmatic
pragmatism
  basis of, as the necessary relation between
    the general and the singular, 230
  and the categories, 28, 65, 68, 154
  definition of, 23–25, 65, 97, 109–11, 150,
    164, 214, 249–50
  and the difference between logical and
    material truth, 217
  and the end of action, 68, 214
  and esthetics, 68
  and a false species of practicality, 117–18,
    150
  foundations of, and Boolean logic, 137
  function of, as the definition of clear and
    the elimination of unclear ideas, 254,
    256
  as a hypothesis, 29, 36
  as an instinctive attraction for living
    facts, 164
  as the logic of abduction, 93, 97, 239,
    249–50, 254, 282n. 4
  and mathematics, 137, 139
  as a maxim of logic, 24, 26, 28–29, 31–
    33, 92, 95, 97, 109–10, 189, 257nn.
    1–2
  and the meaning of a symbol as a de-
    scription of the ultimate end of ac-
    tion, 214
  as methodeutic, 98n. 3
  origin of, 99–100n. 9
  and personality, 110
  and phenomenology, 152

and philosophy, 33, 110, 257n. 1
proof of, 23–24, 28–29, 31–33, 35–36,
  77, 95–96, 98n. 3, 116, 129–30
  and architectonic, 26–28, 31–33, 35–
    36
  and logical goodness, 213
  and mathematics, 35, 96, 130
  and philosophy 95–96
  and psychology, 28, 30–32
  quasi-Berkeleyan, and the unintelligibility
    of the second category, 143
  and the reality of an abstraction, 134,
    136
  and reasoning, 32
  revision of, 24–25, 91, 109
  and Secondness, 173, 284n. 4
  and Thirdness, 284n. 4
  truth of, 26, 29, 32–33, 35, 115, 118, 134,
    150
  utility of, 29, 36, 109, 111, 115
pragmatist, practical
  and the vulgar utilitarian, 81
Prantl, Karl, 265n. 6
precept
  as a subject of a proposition, 176
predicate
  definition of, 180
  generality of, 78, 193, 221, 234
  term as, of a proposition, 234
predicate, monadic, dyadic and polyadic,
  180–81
prediction
  and deduction, 82, 97, 229–30, 239, 249
  and direct perception, 250–51
  and experiment, 190–93, 229, 239, 249
  general proposition as the basis of, 60,
    191–93, 255, 279n. 3
premiss
  any phenomenon as, 63
premisses
  hypothesis of, in deduction, 83, 225
  inspection of, 83
presentness
  definition of, 139–41, 154–55
  positivity of, 140, 155
primary substance
  definition of, 135
primary substances
  more and less, 135–36
  universe of only two, 137

probability, 111–15, 173, 248, 266n. 6,
    280n. 4
  definition of, 228–29
probametric
  definition of, 280n. 4
pronoun
  definition of, 222
proper names
  as singulars, 235–36
proposition
  blank form of, as a rhema or term, 234
  definition of, 174–76, 180, 216, 238
  about general idea, as true or false, 241
  material truth of, 75, 216
  meaning of, 86, 104–5n. 3, 116–17, 227,
    234, 278n. 2
  moral goodness of, as veracity, 216
  self-reference of, as pragmatically impos-
    sible, 176
  as a subdivision of the symbol, 171
  subject of, and the principle of excluded
    middle, 175
    as a singular, 221–23, 278n. 2
  subject of every, as the totality of real-
    ities, 221–22
  subjects of, as indices, not generalities,
    105n. 3, 176, 234
proposition, copulative
  and the rule of omission, 226–27
proposition, general
  as a representation, 191–92
proposition, particular
  definition of, 78, 223
  universal proposition deducible from,
    223, 242
proposition, singular
  general proposition deducible from, 78–
    79
proposition, universal
  definition of, 78, 223
  as inferable from a particular proposition
    or a perceptual judgment, 223–24,
    241–42
psychological reaction
  and Secondness, 167
psychology
  of belief and doubt, 31–32, 90–92
  and the fallacy of naturalism, 73–74,
    209–10
  and logic (see under logic)

and perceptual judgment, 94, 160, 227
  as a special science, 31, 151, 209
  of struggle, 155–57, 262n. 3
psychophysical parallelism
  and mechanistic reductionism, 163
purposive action
  as available in perception, 256

qualities
  as dots on Kempe's graphs, 182–85
  as premisses of nature, 201
quality
  as in consciousness but not in nature,
    195–96, 200
  as delusion or illusion, 62
  as first category, 141, 155, 188–189, 195,
    200–201, 208–9, 276n. 3
  independence of, 188
quantity
  three elements of, as cases of Secondness
    and Thirdness, 195–96
Quetelet, L., 229

radical novelty
  from chance and surprise, 64
radicle
  in mathematics and chemistry, 125
reaction
  definition of, 147–48
  distinctive general characters of the two
    objects in, 178
  genuine and degenerate forms of, 148–49
  and imagination, 147, 156
  independence of, 188
  as an irreducible element of thought,
    172, 267n. 6
  and mechanistic reductionism, 163–65
  object of, as *ipso facto* real, 191
  and perception, 145–47, 160, 235–36
  reduction of, to quality of feeling, 187
  as second category, 143, 147–48, 158,
    167, 172, 177, 189, 195
  and the soundness of reasoning, 173
  unintelligibility of, 143, 147, 159
  use of the category, in a hypothesis, 148
  and volition, 147–48
reaction, psychological
  as a degenerate form of Secondness, 167
reactions
  as lines on Kempe's graphs, 182–85

realism
and the reality of struggle, 142–43, 158–59
realism, scholastic
and the reality of generality, 158–59, 190, 193
reality
of abstractions, 134–36
of the categories, 18–19, 59, 64, 189–90
definition of, 284–85n. 4
and the force of experience, 192
of a formula (uniformity), 191–95
of the laws of nature, 142–43, 158–59, 190–95, 255
and perception, 255
a pragmatic definition of, 134
as regularity, 208
reasoning
and logic, 32, 84, 136–37, 173, 196, 212, 217–19, 225–26
obstacles to, 102n. 6
perceptual judgment as the first premiss in any, 200
and self-control, 196, 223, 248
self-validation of, as a fallacy of circularity, 173–74, 176–77
soundness of, as a matter of fact, 173
three kinds of, as abduction, induction and deduction, 217–19, 225, 248–49, 276n. 3, 282n. 4
ultimate end of, 82, 90–91, 97
regularity
as active law, 208, 229–30
as a formula not a substance, 142
of nature, 59–60, 82, 192
regularity, past
and expectation of the future, 192, 229–30
Reid, Thomas
and immediate perception, 145, 161, 203
his metaphysics and the three categories, 190
relation
as second category, 276n. 3
relations
as abstractions, 137–38
cognizance of, and the direct perception of externality, 145–46, 161
relations, possible
analytic system of, 185

relativism
and the normative sciences, 211
representamen
definition of, 215–16
esthetic goodness of, as expressiveness, 215–16
generality as, 193
genuine and degenerate forms of, 53–57, 170–71
as icon, index or symbol in relation to the object of a representation, 179, 276n. 3
and meaning, 231–32
and modeling, 53
and psychology, 276n. 3
as rhema, proposition or argument, 216
representation
as not all-sufficient, 56, 169
distinction of represented object, representamen and interpretant in, 179
formula as, 191–94
genuine and degenerate forms of, 54–56
goodness of, as logical, 215
meaning of, and the element of generality, 241
moral goodness of, as veracity, 215–16
object of, as not *ipso facto* real, 191
reduction of, to reaction and quality of feeling, 187
and self-consciousness, 55–56, 150, 168
as third category, 53–56, 167–69, 179, 187, 194, 276n. 3
rhema
definition of, 105n. 3, 216, 234–35
right
definition of, 212
and normative science, 208
reductive concept of, as relative exclusively to human conduct, 211
Royce, Josiah, 56, 103–4n. 7, 169, 264n. 5
Russell, Bertrand, 219, 258n. 1

Schelling, Friedrich, 190
Schiller, Friedrich, 25, 67, 69, 73
Schröder, Ernst, 124, 126, 132, 173, 219, 233, 258–59n. 3, 267n. 6
science
and anthropomorphism, 156–58, 275–76n. 8
and belief, 162

condition of the possibility of, 62
and falsifiability, 60–61, 192, 251
science, abstract and concrete, 32
Scotism
  metaphysics of, and the three categories, 190
Secondness
  definition of, 167
  a degenerate form of, 167
  and the distinction of good and bad, 197
  in formal-logical analysis, 177
  independence of, 187
  irreducibility of, 64, 172, 264n. 5
  melded to a Third, 60
  reality of, 59, 63–64, 190, 201
    and the feeling of surprise, 63–64
  of Thirdness, 168–69
  unreality of, 143, 157, 159, 172, 190, 201
Secondness, genuine
  individuals as correlates in, 168, 263n. 2
self-consciousness
  as analogous with a map, 55–56, 103–4n. 7, 168–69, 264n. 5
  as a Firstness of Thirdness, 55, 168, 263n. 3
  as infinite self-representation, 56, 103n. 7, 264n. 5
self-control
  and the approval of an act of inference, 212
  and criticism, 146, 161, 196–97, 199, 212, 214, 223, 256
  as inhibition not origination, 248
  and logic, 220, 256
  and perceptual judgment, 62, 93–94, 145–47, 160–61, 199–200, 223, 242, 248, 256
senses
  veracity of, 200, 275n. 8
sign
  as an example of the third category, 149
signification
  of a representamen as an inherent quality, 216
  of a term, 232
Sigwart, Christoph, 52, 81–82, 173, 176–77, 267nn. 6–7
singular
  definition of, 176, 221
singulars
  as a universe of discourse, 175

space and time
  as phenomenally real, 195
special science
  definition of, 151, 209
  metaphysics as the basis of, 151, 208
  physical and psychical divisions of, 151
  of psychology, 31, 151, 209
  and the ultimate end of action, 214
Spencer, Herbert, 165
Spinoza, Benedict, 172, 190
Stöckhardt, A., 228
struggle
  agent and patient in, 155–56
  definition of, 142, 158–59
  psychology of 155–57, 262n. 3
  reduction of, to a law or uniformity, 157–59
    to a quality of feeling, 143, 157, 159
  as second category, 141, 147, 149, 155–59
  two types of, between ego and non-ego, 147
  unintelligibility of, 159
subdivision
  of representamen, 170–71, 276n. 3
  of Secondness, 167–68, 263n. 2, 276n. 3
  as a Secondness of Thirdness, 168, 263n. 2, 284n. 4
  of Thirdness, 169–71, 263n. 2, 276n. 3
subject
  of a proposition, 104–5n. 3, 175–76, 178–81, 221–23, 234, 278n. 2
subject, propositional
  non-singular, as indesignative or hypo-thetical, 222–23, 238
subjects, logical
  of a proposition, 178–81
substance
  modes of, 134–36
surprise
  cognizance of, by perception or inference, 146–47, 202, 261n. 2
  experience of, and discovery, 144–45, 159–60
  feeling of, and the reality of Secondness, 63–64, 146–47
  as an interaction of ego and non-ego, 145, 147, 160, 202–3
  and radical novelty, 64

syllogism
 analysis of, into inferential steps, 184, 219
 as a rudimentary form, 84, 225
 as a symbol of a phenomenal argument, 63
Sylvester, James, 125, 259n. 5
symbol
 definition of, 53–54, 63, 170, 276n. 3
 law of nature as, 194–95
 subdivision of, 171
 universe as, with indices of reactions and
  icons of qualities, 201

term
 analysis of, in non-relative logic, 235
 definition of, 234–35, 257n. 2
 meaning of, 85–88, 104–5n. 3, 234–35,
  257n. 2
 as a subdivision of the symbol, 171
 ultimate meaning of, 86–87, 234
theoretical judgment
 perceptual judgment as the test of, 200
theory
 abductive invention of, 85, 218, 230–31,
  276n. 3
 definition of, 229
 and inductive experiment, 218, 228–29,
  239, 249, 251, 280n. 4, 283n. 4
theory, abductive
 cognitive goodness of, as the furtherance
  of knowledge, 283n. 4
Third
 as law of action, 142
Thirdness
 as both complex and simple, 186
 as continuous with Firstness and Secondness as its limits, 285n. 4
 definition of, 167, 193–94
 degenerate, and multitude, 193, 195
 Firstness of, 55, 168–69
 and formal-logical analysis, 177–78
 and generality, 95, 184, 193, 220, 231, 238
 genuine and degenerate forms of, 54–55.
  169–71, 186–87, 193, 195, 263–
  4nn. 2–4
 and the independence of Firstness and
  Secondness, 187–88
 and infinite collections of individuals, 184
 irreducibility of, 177, 182–87, 255, 261–
  62n. 3
  and the idea of representation, 186

 as mediation between Firstness and Secondness, 193–94, 208, 261–2n. 3
 as the only category, 187–88
 as operative in nature, 190–95, 231
 perceptibility of, and the continuity and
  order of time, 79, 223–24, 253,
  255
 in perceptual judgments (via the senses),
  220, 224, 238, 255
 and personal identity, 236
 as plurality, 183
 qualitatively and reactionally degenerate
  forms of, 168–71
 reality of, 59–62, 95, 190, 201, 255
 as a law of force in space and time, 195
 as representation, 53–56, 167–69, 179,
  187, 194
 Secondness of, 168–69
 subdivision as a degenerate form of, 168,
  263n. 2, 284n. 4
 three attitudes to, as (1) not verifiable,
  (2) verifiable but not perceptible, and
  (3) perceptible, 255–56
 as true continuity in relation to any multitude of correlates, 167
thought
 end of, 80–81
 and general signs, 149
 as genuine form of third category, 261–
  62n. 3
 Peirce's concept of, 68
time
 antecedence and subsequence in, 79,
  223–24, 278–79n. 3
 flow of, in perceptual judgment, 79, 253,
  272n. 3, 278–79n. 3
 multitude, continuity and order in, 79,
  223–24, 253, 255, 271–72n. 3, 278–
  79n. 3
 as a succession of fixed states, 79, 255,
  278–79n. 3
triadic fact
 distinctive general characters of the three
  objects in, 178–79
 as an intellectual fact, 179
triadic relation
 between dyadic relations, 138
truth
 and an anthropomorphic hypothesis,
  157–58

as correspondence of theory with reality, 191, 218, 225, 229, 239, 255, 284–85n. 4

distinction between, and falsity, 196, 284–85n. 4

in future, 142–43, 147, 158, 190–93, 203

of a general proposition by chance, 192

of a hypothesis, 148, 251

kinds of, in the classification of arguments, 210

as logical goodness, 216

as moral goodness in logic, 196

of nature and the categories, 189

and normative science, 208

preservation of, in a deductive inference, 225–27

and psychology, 80, 116

as a subject of every proposition, 181, 221–22

as the universal universe or aggregate of all singulars (realities), 175, 181, 221–22

universal universe of, and the sheet of assertion, 184–85

truth, approximate or exact

and experimental verification, 251

truth, logical and material, 75, 216–17

tychism

and the premisses of nature, 201

ultimate end

of action as an admirable ideal, 213–15

definition of, 71–74, 214–15

of reasoning, 82, 90–91, 97

uniformity

as a formula not a substance, 142, 191

uniformity of nature, 220, 255

from chance or really operative principle, 59–62, 192–93

unity

category of, 183

universe

as an argument with qualities as premisses and realities as conclusions, 63, 201

economy of, and qualities, 201

the growth of its reasonableness, 64

as a symbol with indices of reactions and icons of qualities, 201

as a work of art, 201

universe of discourse

as a subject of every proposition, 175, 181

utilitarianism, 224

and ultimate ends, 81

utilitarians, vulgar

and ultimate ends, 81, 224

veracity

as material truth, 216

as moral goodness of representations, 215–16

volition

and reaction, 147–48

volitional judgment

subject of, as singular, 235

Voltaire, François-Marie

and mechanistic reductionism, 163

voluntary act

moral approval of, 212

Whateley, Richard, 257n. 2

Whewell, William, 197

willing

and Secondness, 167

words

production by, as symbols, of physical effects, 194

Wright, Chauncey, 164